Henry Hartwright

The story of the House of Lancaster

Henry Hartwright

The story of the House of Lancaster

ISBN/EAN: 9783744715324

Printed in Europe, USA, Canada, Australia, Japan

Cover: Foto ©ninafisch / pixelio.de

More available books at **www.hansebooks.com**

PREFACE.

THE fourteenth and fifteenth centuries are full of interest to English people. This story of the times is put together in a series of sketches drawn from various sources, and does not lay claim to being a history, properly so called. An endeavour has been made to render it more life-like by giving an accurate account, as far as possible, of the family of each of the principal characters introduced, instead of merely a string of names.

The book was originally commenced and intended only for young people, but it is hoped that it may also be received with favour by their elders.

CONTENTS

SKETCH	PAGE
I. FLUCTUATING FORTUNES	1
II. A STEP FORWARD	14
III. FOREIGN KINGDOMS GAINED	30
IV. UNCLE AND NEPHEW	42
V. THE PRISONER OF CALAIS	60
VI. A COURT OF CHIVALRY	73
VII. ROYALTY ACHIEVED	78
VIII. THE LAST OF A LINE	96
IX. SOME FRUITS OF USURPATION	108
X. THE RIGHTFUL HEIR	124
XI. 'THIS SMILING FRANCE OF OURS'	134
XII. THE REGENT AND HEIR OF FRANCE	147
XIII. THE KING OF FRANCE AND ENGLAND	160
XIV. FRANCE AND SCOTLAND	171
XV. THE MAID OF ORLEANS	181
XVI. THE BROKEN ALLIANCE	195
XVII. PEACE OR WAR?	206
XVIII. DUKE AND CARDINAL	218
XIX. NORMANDY AND GUIENNE	227
XX. TROUBLOUS TIMES	237
XXI. UNITY, PEACE, AND CONCORD	250
XXII. DEPOSED	260
XXIII. IMPRISONED	275
XXIV. 'MARRYING AND GIVING IN MARRIAGE'	285
XXV. 'COMING EVENTS CAST THEIR SHADOWS BEFORE'	294
XXVI. CHANGING SIDES	303
NOTES	321

AUTHORITIES CONSULTED.

Matthew Paris's Chronicle (Bohn's edition).
Florence of Worcester's Chronicle (Bohn's edition).
Matthew of Westminster's Chronicle (Bohn's edition).
Froissart's Chronicles (translated by Johnes).
Monstrelet's Chronicles (translated by Johnes.)
Philip de Commines' Memoirs. Bohn's edition.
Jean de Troye's 'Scandalous Chronicle' (Bohn's edition).
Ingulph's 'Chronicle of Croyland,' with Continuation by Peter of Blois and others (Bohn's edition).
The Paston Letters.
Creton's 'Deposition of Richard II.' (translated by the Rev. John Webb).
Hardyng's Metrical Chronicle.
Wyntown's 'Cronykil of Scotland.'
Hall's Chronicle.
Holinshed's Chronicle.
Stow's Chronicle.
Grafton's Chronicle.
Warkworth's Chronicle.
Fabyan's Chronicle.
Polydore Vergil's History.
Fleetwood's 'Historie of the Arrivall.'
Rymer's 'Fœdera.'
Sandford's History.
Anderson's 'Royal Genealogies.'
Dean Hook's 'Archbishops of Canterbury.'
Collins's Peerage.
Hume.
Lingard.
Knight.
'Pictorial History of England.'
Tytler's 'History of Scotland.'
Miss Strickland's 'Queens of England.'
Miss Yonge's 'Cameos.'
Gairdner's 'Houses of Lancaster and York.'
Church's 'Life of Henry V.'
Green's 'Short History.'
Doyle's 'Chronicle of England.'
Doyle's 'Official Baronage.'
Hepworth Dixon's 'Royal Windsor.'
And others mentioned in the text.

ERRATA.

Page 30, line 4, *for* 'inquire' *read* 'enquire.'
Page 36, line 34, *for* 'inquired' *read* 'enquired.'
Page 56, line 28, *for* 'inquiries' *read* 'enquiries.'
Page 103, line 41, *for* 'Spencer' *read* 'Spenser.'
Page 148, line 12, *for* 'entrusted' *read* 'intrusted.'
Page 175, line 34, *for* 'partizans' *read* 'partisans.'
Page 172, line 38,
Page 173, line 18, } *for* 'Montague' *read* 'Montagu.'
Page 185, line 3,
Page 222, line 16, *for* 'Portchester' *read* 'Porchester.'
Page 264, line 44, *put* ';' *after* 'Warwick.'
Page 281, line 10, *for* 'Augus' *read* 'Angus.'
Page 281, line 43, *for* 'Hillyard' *read* 'Hilyard.'

dazzling but insecure position. Queen Eleanor was of one mind with her husband in this act for the advancement of the interests of their son. Towards the close of the year the boy was formally invested with the kingdom by the legate of the new Pope, Alexander IV. But the country had yet to be won from the representatives of Frederick, and money was therefore required. The boy was dressed in the full costume of a Sicilian prince, and, as such, presented to the barons assembled in Parliament, who were asked to find the necessary means. Even this little theatrical display did not loosen the purse-strings. As Henry had come under heavy obligations to the Pope, who had raised money in his name from the Lombard merchants, he had to fall back on the clergy.

While oppressing the clergy, the disputes between Henry and his

THE STORY OF THE HOUSE OF LANCASTER.

SKETCH I.

FLUCTUATING FORTUNES.

FREDERICK II., Emperor of Germany, who had married Isabella, the sister of King Henry III. of England, was likewise King of Naples and Sicily. He had been an object of dread, if not hatred, to more than one Pope.

Innocent IV. went so far as to call a council at Lyons, and 1245. pronounce sentence of deposition upon him, when an opposition King was elected by the prelates, but was slain in battle two years later.

On December 13, 1250, Frederick died. The Pope claimed Sicily as a fief of the Church. After vainly tendering it, as such, to Richard, Earl of Cornwall, it was offered to King Henry for his younger son EDMUND, then five years old.

At first it was refused, because the Emperor had left a son Henry, 1254 who was the King's nephew. But he died, and, the offer being renewed, in one of his many weak moments Henry accepted the dazzling but insecure position. Queen Eleanor was of one mind with her husband in this act for the advancement of the interests of their son. Towards the close of the year the boy was formally invested with the kingdom by the legate of the new Pope, Alexander IV.

But the country had yet to be won from the representatives of Frederick, and money was therefore required. The boy was dressed in the full costume of a Sicilian prince, and, as such, presented to the barons assembled in Parliament, who were asked to find the necessary means. Even this little theatrical display did not loosen the purse-strings. As Henry had come under heavy obligations to the Pope, who had raised money in his name from the Lombard merchants, he had to fall back on the clergy.

While oppressing the clergy, the disputes between Henry and his barons increased. Instead of winning a foreign crown for his son, he had to do battle for his own.

Manfred, an illegitimate son of the late Emperor, was triumphing in Naples and Sicily, either for himself or Conrad his young nephew.

1263. The farce of any English rule in Sicily was ended by Pope Urban IV. offering the crown to Charles of Anjou, the brother of St. Louis, and brother-in-law of Henry's Queen Eleanor, whose sister Beatrice was his wife. The offer was accepted, and in

1266. January, 1266, Charles was crowned at Rome by Clement IV. He had, however, to fight for his kingdom. He was opposed by Manfred, who, being forsaken by many of his followers, was routed and slain at Benevento, February 26. Conrad, or, as he is usually called, Conradin, the grandson of Frederick, endeavoured to drive out the robber, as he considered him, from his patrimony. Many Italians joined him, Rome opened its gates to him, but, being defeated by the overwhelming force of the enemy at Tagliacozzo,

1268. August 23, 1268, he fled. He was, however, captured and brought before Charles of Anjou, who, after cruelly, falsely and unblushingly upbraiding him, the rightful heir, with being a rebel to his King, ordered his beheadal in the market-place at Naples. 'Oh, deed of deathless shame!'

Thus in a youth of sixteen ended the once mighty house of Hohenstaufen. Conradin's last thoughts were of home, and his last words, 'Oh, my mother!'

One direct consequence of this murder was the rising known as the Sicilian Vespers.

1265. After the battle of Evesham, EDMUND received the forfeited estates and honours of Simon de Montfort, Earl of Leicester and Baron of

1267. Hinckley. Two years later he was created EARL OF LANCASTER; he was also lord of the honours of Derby and Monmouth. Thus was the foundation laid of that enormous power which enabled his descendant, Henry of Bolingbroke, to wrest the sceptre from the hands of his cousin Richard II.

The termination *caster*, in place-names, is, like that of *chester*, derived from the Latin *castra*. The name of the river Lune, on which the county town of Lancaster stands, as the Rev. Isaac Taylor says in his 'Words and Places,' is derived from the Gaelic *all*, white, whence we obtain *al-aon*, 'white afon,' Latinized by the Romans into Alauna. Lancaster is, therefore, the 'castra on the Lune,' in the same way that Doncaster is the 'castra on the Don.' It is not explained why, from Alauna, the river should be called Lune and the county *Lan*caster. Lunecaster would appear to be the proper name, particularly if it was, as is believed, Lunecastre in Saxon times.

It is somewhat uncertain whether the Saxons had a castle here, but in the time of the first William, who recognised the capabilities of the place as an assembly-ground for men to guard against either Scots or Saxons, one was certainly built, eight hundred years ago, by Roger of Poitou, who for some eight years held the lordship of the place, but he was then banished and deprived. Some old Roman foundations are pointed out in one of the towers, and Roger's Keep still dominates over all. Roger is also credited with the erection of the church of St. Mary near by, which, partly rebuilt and with a tower added, still exists.

Edmund took the cross, and, in token of a vow which he had made, 1268. wore a cross on his back, hence he obtained the name of 'Crouchback'; not, as Henry of Bolingbroke or some of his partisans in after years asserted, because he was humpbacked, and therefore, although the eldest son of Henry III., set aside in favour of his brother Edward.

He went with his brother to the Holy Land. When Edward received 1271. the assassin's stroke at Acre, Edmund ran to his assistance, and finding Eleanora in a frantic state, he carried her away, telling her that · it was better she should scream and cry than that all England should lament.' Eleanora was probably as much alarmed at her husband's treatment by the surgeon as at anything else. We know that she made a capital nurse afterwards. It must not be supposed from this that Edmund was a rough and brutal kind of man. He was the exact reverse. Taking somewhat after his father, he was gentle and genial in all his ways, with a great sense of religion about him. But he had great love for his brother, looked up to him as a younger brother so frequently does to an elder one, and probably feared that Eleanora's cries might unnerve him. Some writers say, indeed, that it was at Edward's request his wife was removed from the tent.

Edmund lost his young wife, Aveline, on November 4, 1273, not long after his return from the Holy Land. She was a daughter of William de Forts III., Earl of Albemarle, and widow of Ingelram de Percy. She was buried in the Abbey of Westminster, and a monument to her memory may still be seen in the chapel of St. John the Baptist.

His first wife not having left him any children, the Earl, three years later, married again. His second choice was another widow, Blanche of Artois, whose first husband, Henry 'the fat' King of Navarre, died July 22, 1274, leaving one daughter. This daughter, Jeanne, subsequently married Philippe IV., commonly called 'le bel,' grandson of St. Louis, and so brought the kingdom of Navarre to the crown of France. The daughter of Philippe and Jeanne was that Isabel who, unfortunately for him, was afterwards married to Edward II., King of England.

Blanche was a daughter of Robert Comte d'Artois, a brother of St. Louis, but of a very different character. He was a rash young man, proud, passionate, and headstrong. It was he who was the cause of dissensions in the crusading army, and he entertained particular animosity against William Longespée II., Earl of Salisbury, whom he more than once openly insulted. Both fell fighting bravely, it is hoped in charity and peace with one another, on that black Shrove Tuesday, 1250, at Mansourah. Three generations following Robert fell in battle. His son Robert was slain at Courtrai in 1302; and his grandson Philippe at Furnæ, in 1296. His great-grandson Robert, who had been deprived of his inheritance by his aunt Mahaut, with the approval of Philippe V., 'le long,' King of France, unfortunately for this country, came over here and was one of the principal instigators of Edward III. to put forward his claim to the crown of France, which was carried on at the cost of so much blood and treasure. Robert was slain at Vannes in 1342, fighting in support of the famous Jeanne of Flanders, Countess of Bretagne, and her infant son.

We shall see later on that the temper of the d'Artois family was continued in the house of Lancaster.

When Edmund returned to England with his bride, he brought from Provence some of the roses which flourished there abundantly. They were planted in the garden of the Savoy, and became in after years the badges of two rival houses.

By his marriage with Blanche he obtained the Castle of Beaufort on the Loire, which in the next century gave a name to some members of the House of Lancaster.

'Great events from little causes spring.'

1293. In a Norman seaport an English sailor had a quarrel with a native of the place. They fought, and the Norman was killed. The Englishman escaped to his ship. In revenge the Normans boarded the first English vessel they met with, and took out an innocent passenger, whom they hanged from the mast-head, tying a dog to his heels as a further mark of indignity. Retaliation followed. Cruelty begat cruelty. Men of all countries became engaged on either side. England had assistance from Ireland, Gascony, and Holland; the Normans from France, Genoa, and Flanders. At length, by mutual consent, the combatants assembled at a given spot in the Channel. After a stubborn fight the English were completely victorious. They captured, every ship to the number of two hundred and forty, with immense booty, and the greater portion of the crews perished, either by the sword or by drowning.

Philippe, the wily King of France, took advantage of the opportunity to summon King Edward, as Duke of Aquitaine, to answer for the misconduct of his subjects in Gascony who had taken part in the affray. Edward made offers for mutual compensation, which were not accepted, and therefore sent over his brother Edmund, who, as husband to the mother of the Queen of France, he hoped might prove an acceptable and successful negotiator. But Edmund's simplicity was no match for Philippe's guile. Under the specious pretence that Philippe only wanted to guard his honour, he persuaded Edmund to cede Guienne to him, on a promise that it should be returned to Edward at the end of forty days. King Edward agreed to the proposal. The period fixed upon arrived. Then Philippe declared his intention of keeping not only Guienne, but all

Aquitaine, because Edward had not answered the original summons in person.

Edward was on the point of sailing for France, when a rising in Wales called him there, and Edmund accompanied him. Having quelled that, he again made preparations to start, when, hearing of an alliance, offensive and defensive, being concluded between France and Scotland, he marched into Scotland, with the result that Baliol was dethroned. He, however, sent a small force into Guienne under the command of his brother Edmund, who gained some advantages at Bordeaux; but, being seized with a distemper, the command devolved on Henry de Lacy, Earl of Lincoln. Edmund died at Bayonne, June 5, 1296, at the age of fifty-one. His body was brought home and buried in the chapel of St. John the Baptist in Westminster Abbey, where a monument to him is still in existence.

1294.

1295.

Edmund and his second wife founded a convent for Franciscan nuns, or *sorores minores*, in London, and the place where it was erected hence acquired the name of 'The Minories.' The church of the Holy Trinity was built upon a portion of the site.

1293.

The foundation of a priory for Franciscans at Preston, in Lancashire, is also attributed to Earl Edmund. It was turned into a prison, and so remained until about a hundred years ago.

The Queen-Countess Blanche survived her husband nearly six years. She died May 2, 1302. Her body was buried at Paris, and her heart at Nogent l'Artault.

They had three sons—THOMAS, HENRY, and JOHN—and a daughter, Mary. The eldest son, Thomas, who was born about 1278, succeeded to his father's titles and possessions, and to these were added the earldoms of Lincoln and Salisbury on the death of his father-in-law, Henry de Lacy, in 1311.

Henry de Lacy had married Margaret Longespée, the last of a family of gallant warriors and Crusaders who sprang from the loves of Henry of Anjou and the fair Rosamond Clifford. Margaret was second-great-grand-daughter of Henry and Rosamond. She died in 1309, leaving only one daughter, Alice, a great heiress.

This daughter Alice was married, when a child not more than eleven years of age, to Thomas of Lancaster, and the union does not appear to have been for the happiness of either party. Many years afterwards she claimed her freedom on account of a prior contract, and apparently allowed herself to be carried off by a knight or retainer of the Earl of Warenne. The King told Earl Thomas, as he then was, to proceed against Warenne by law, but this he declined to do, for fear of losing her estates; and so the ill-assorted couple had to bear their bonds as best they could.

1294.

As the Countess Alice will not appear again, it may be added that, after her first husband's death, she was twice married: first, to Eubulo Lord l'Estrange, who died 1335; and, secondly, five months afterwards, to Hugh Lord de Freyne, who died in December, 1336. The Countess died childless, October 2, 1348.

During the reign of King Edward I. the Earl appears to have taken some part in the wars in Scotland.

At the coronation of Edward II. he was the bearer of 'curtana,' the sword of mercy—most inappropriately, as will afterwards appear—and two years later was appointed one of the ordainers of reform.

Thomas was a fine-looking man, of great ambition, but assuming a gracious demeanour when posing as the people's friend, with a glib tongue. In that respect he was in advance of the times. Then, as now, the people were caught by clap-trap. It would be hard to tell what good he achieved, or tried to achieve, for them. Although apparently devout, his private life seems to have been anything but immaculate. He was the richest and most powerful, and at the same time the most factious and most turbulent man in the kingdom; but he was not brave withal.

Though born an Englishman, his sympathies were altogether French. He was the head of all opposition to his cousin, King Edward II., and the encourager of his niece Isabella in her treachery towards her husband and King. He was the first to spread reports that Edward I. was not the elder son of Henry III., and that Edward of Caernarvon was not the true son of the former. The story, as told, was that the child of Edward I. and Eleanora of Castile, having been put out to nurse, was mangled in the face by a sow, which, by some unexplained means, got into the room where the child was lying in his cradle, and the nurse in her alarm, snatching up the boy, substituted for him the son of a carter. A few years later—1318—a man appeared, with marks on his face said to have been made by a sow, who claimed to be the veritable Edward of Caernarvon. He was proved to be one John Poydra, son of a tanner at Exeter, and was hanged as an impostor.

As shown elsewhere, Thomas relentlessly pursued Piers Gaveston till he had the satisfaction of seeing him done to death; and later on it will be seen how he commenced the persecution of another favourite, although he did not live to see the consummation of the tragedy. To sum up: in the words of Dr. Lingard, 'he was the fomenter and patron of every faction in the kingdom.'

The Earl of Lancaster had been present at the capture of Kildrummie Castle in 1306, where Nigel Bruce was slain. But when Edward II., seven years afterwards, put forth his call to arms for a march on Scotland, he, with the Earls of Surrey, Warwick, and Arundel, deserted him, and must be considered in a great measure responsible for the defeat at Bannockburn.

'Oh, give their hapless prince his due!'

1314. At Bannockburn Edward showed gallantry equal to either his father or son, but was forced from the field by the Earl of Pembroke when all was lost, and fled to Dunbar, and thence in a fishing-boat to Bamborough.

Two years later, in the Parliament at Lincoln, the Earl of Lancaster was at the head of the Government, and thought it certain he could have the celebrated 'ordinances' carried into effect, but there was always a hitch. It would appear that he had not capability sufficient to carry on a Government himself, and yet that he invariably opposed any measures brought in and supported by anybody else. Even so early as this it was bruited about that he was in alliance with the King of Scotland, and he thought it necessary to offer wager of battle to anyone daring to renew the accusation.

King Robert, in the meantime, had been able to seize the castle 1318. of Berwick and many other places, in consequence of the dissensions between King Edward and his nobles. Therefore, by order of the King, the Chancellor visited the Earl of Lancaster, and a reconciliation was arrived at.

Lancaster and his friends met their opponents in a Parliament at 1319. York, when it was determined to retake Berwick. Bruce, failing in an attempt to raise the siege, made a diversion by sending a large army under Randolph and Douglas to York with the intention of capturing Queen Isabella, who was in residence there, and then dictating terms of peace. But the plan had been betrayed, and their prey escaped. They then commenced ravaging the country, and as the military were all before Berwick, it fell to the lot of the Archbishop of York, with the Bishop of Ely, to head a motley force against them. Needless to say that such troops could not stand against the hardened Scotsmen. Three hundred clergy and ten times as many laymen are said to have lost their lives. This event occurred at Myton-on-Swale, September 20, 1319, and is known as the Battle of the Chapter, or the Chapter of Myton, from the number of clerics who fought and fell there. When the news of the disaster reached Berwick, the Earl of Lancaster and his friends left King Edward to his fate, and returned home. A truce for two years was concluded between England and Scotland.

Men said and believed that the departure of Lancaster was paid for by King Robert Bruce making him a gift of forty thousand pounds. It says little for his honour or his bravery that on the King's return this same Earl had the audacity, the cruelty, the meanness, to stand at his castle of Pontefract with all his men and jeer at his unfortunate monarch as he passed by for an event which he himself had brought about.

A year or two before the time when the above narrated events occurred, the Earl of Lancaster introduced to the notice of the King a young man named HUGH LE DESPENSER, who had until then formed one of his own household. No doubt this was done with the idea that, being thus indebted to him for his advancement, Hugh would be a willing tool in his hands. Never was he more mistaken.

Hugh was accomplished, with a good address and a fine figure. He devoted himself to the service of the King, and manifested so much ability that he soon won Edward's favour, and obtained almost as much ascendancy over him as Gaveston had formerly possessed.

He was married to the King's niece, Eleanor, a daughter of Gilbert de Clare, Earl of Gloucester, and Lady Joan of Acre, and received as marriage portion a large part of Glamorgan.

The family of Le Despenser probably took the name from the office of Steward, which was filled by their ancestors in the households of our first three Norman Kings. Thurstan, in the reign of Henry I., is usually considered to have been the founder. His second-great-grandsons were Hugh and Geoffrey. The latter was the ancestor of the Dukes of Marlborough. The former was one of the twelve barons chosen under the Provisions of Oxford, in the reign of Henry III. He was appointed Chief Justiciary of the kingdom, and was slain at the battle of Evesham, August 5, 1265, fighting on the side of the Earl of Leicester and the barons. His son, another Hugh, born 1260, was the father of the young man mentioned above.

The rapid advancement of Hugh le Despenser roused the ire and jealousy of Earl Thomas, who accused him of being haughty, covetous, and ambitious, or, in short, such another as himself.

1321. Events occurring in the West soon added fuel to the flame. A knight of Gower, named William de Breos, or Braose, had two daughters, Aliva and Jane, married respectively to John de Mowbray and James de Bohun, one of the Hereford connection, and on them he settled his estates. Notwithstanding that, he sold them three times over: firstly to Hugh le Despenser the younger, secondly to Roger Mortimer, and thirdly to Humphrey de Bohun, Earl of Hereford.

Mowbray took possession in right of his wife, but Despenser came down upon him, and drove him out of what he naturally considered his own property. Mowbray then allied himself with Mortimer and the Earl of Hereford, and James de Bohun sided with his relative. Roger Mortimer's uncle, another Roger, made an onslaught on the lands of Lady Eleanor Despenser, and did damage to the amount of several thousands of pounds. The King summoned the Earl of Hereford to appear before the Council; but he required that the favourite should first be committed to the custody of the Earl of Lancaster. This the King at once refused. The Earl then, at the head of his marchers, over ten thousand strong, harried the property of the two Despensers, father and son, destroying or carrying off all live or dead stock, and any other property upon which they could lay their hands. After that they marched into Yorkshire, and obtained the protection of the Earl of Lancaster. The two Earls bound themselves to prosecute the Despensers until they should either fall into their hands or be driven into exile.

Lancaster now led the confederate forces towards London, allowing the men to live at free quarters, and to plunder any estate belonging to either of the Despensers. From St. Albans he had the coolness to send a message to his King requiring the banishment of both father and son, and an Act of Indemnity for the barons.

Edward replied promptly and spiritedly that the elder Despenser was on his service beyond sea, and the son with the fleet; that he would not punish men without hearing their defence; and that it would be contrary to his coronation oath to pardon men in arms who were disturbing the public peace.

The barons, with Lancaster at their head, marched into the capital, and quartered their followers in Holborn and Clerkenwell. After a fortnight's deliberation they proceeded to Westminster, where Parliament was then sitting. They filled the hall with their men, well armed, and wearing a white band to distinguish them. In the presence of the King they brought forward an accusation in eleven counts against the Despensers, and concluded by banishing them, and pardoning themselves for rising in arms, as also for any trespasses committed during the past six months.

The prelates protested in writing against such a sentence, but the King and his party were powerless in the presence of so large an armed force. The sentence was therefore entered on the rolls.

Two months later, on October 13, Queen Isabella, when on her way to the shrine of St. Thomas at Canterbury, desired to rest for a night at Leeds Castle, in Kent, now one of the finest seats in that county, which then belonged to her, as it had formerly formed part of the dower of Queen Eleanora of Castile. To her great surprise, she was refused admission to her own castle by Lady Badlesmere, the wife of the castellane. Not only that, but several of her attendants, who had been sent forward to make preparations, were killed by a volley of arrows from the walls. Isabella, as may be supposed, was indignant, and rightly so, at such conduct; but Lord Badlesmere, to whom she complained, in an impudent letter expressed his full approval of it. As Isabella had always taken the side of the barons, she, of course, expected her uncle of Lancaster to come to her assistance. But Earl Thomas cannot even be credited with being faithful to his most ardent supporter, the niece he was thought to love so well. It may be that he felt himself in a quandary. Bartholomew, Lord Badlesmere, was a man who, having betrayed the secrets of his master the King, had joined the party of the barons; and Lancaster did not like, or rather could not afford, to act in opposition to him, lest he might change his side again in a similar manner. The Earl therefore remained neutral, and took neither side.

It was, however, a fine opportunity for King Edward, and he availed himself of it by promptly summoning to his aid a body of Londoners, with whom the Queen was always popular, to go and avenge this insult to her.

On the last day of the month the castle was forced to surrender. The seneschal and eleven of the garrison were hanged before the castle gates, whilst the Lady Margaret, one of the fiery family of De Clare, was sent to the Tower, where she suffered a long and rigorous imprisonment. Her husband, Lord Badlesmere, took part in the rising of the barons in the following year. He escaped at the time, but was subsequently captured at Stowe Park—the seat of a connection of his by marriage, Henry Burghersh, Bishop of Lincoln—and hanged at Canterbury.

This energetic action on the part of King Edward infused new life into his friends.

The two Le Despensers returned to England. The younger one surrendered himself a prisoner until the judgment against him should be reversed. His petition to that effect was referred to the prelates, then in convocation, who replied that they had always protested against the judgment as contrary to law, and therefore now prayed that it might be repealed. Edmund, Earl of Kent, the King's brother; Aymer de Valence, Earl of Pembroke; John de Dreux, Earl of Richmond, and Edmund Fitz-Alan, Earl of Arundel, joined them, declaring that they had formerly assented through fear. Thus supported, the King took both father and son under his protection until Parliament could be assembled.

The Earl of Lancaster's influence was shaken. His popularity began to wane; his abrupt departure from Berwick was brought to mind, and it was again bruited about that he had been handsomely paid by King Robert Bruce for making that move. Subsequent events confirmed the idea. He and the Earl of Hereford entered into a treaty of alliance with the King of Scotland, who was himself to head an invasion of England, and join his forces to those of the Earls.

1322. Lancaster was in the north, and Hereford marched with three thousand men to join him. King Edward, having heard of their proceedings, collected his forces and marched in person to attack them. The insurgents had possession of Burton-on-Trent, and for three days defended the bridge across the river against the Loyalists. At the end of that time the Royal army discovered a ford by which they could cross over the river. Lancaster immediately set fire to the town and retreated into Yorkshire. On arriving at Pontefract he wrote to the King of Scotland, and then continued his retreat northwards. His further progress was stopped at Boroughbridge, about eight miles north of Knaresborough, by Sir Andrew Harcla and Sir Simon Ward, governors of Carlisle and York.

In attempting a charge on foot on March 16, across the bridge over the river Ure, Humphrey de Bohun, Earl of Hereford, the King's brother-in-law, was slain by a Welshman standing below, who thrust a lance into his body.

Lancaster, after trying and failing to bribe Sir Andrew, begged a truce for one night in the hope, which proved vain, that the Scots might yet arrive. He went into a chapel, and, looking on the crucifix, said: 'Good Lord, I render myself to Thee, and put me into Thy mercy.' Next morning he was taken to York, and thence to his own castle of Pontefract. He was brought to trial before the King, six earls, and a number of barons, and, his guilt being manifest from papers found on the body of Hereford, was sentenced to death as a traitor. In consideration of his royal descent, Edward remitted the ignominious part of the sentence, which included disembowelling. As he was led up the hill, now known as St. Thomas's, on a grey pony without a bridle, the mob pelted him with mud, calling him in derision 'King Arthur,' which was the name he had assumed. 'King of Heaven,' he cried, 'grant me mercy, for the King of earth hath forsaken me.' He knelt down by the block with his face towards the east, but was told to turn to the north, that he might look towards his friends the Scots, and in that position he was beheaded on March 22.

'Nothing in his life
Became him like the leaving it.'

His body was buried in the church of a Cluniac Priory, which had been founded by Robert de Lacy in the eleventh century. A stone coffin was found, some seventy years ago, at Water Fryston, near Pontefract, which was supposed to contain the bones of the Earl, the head being between the thighs.

Earl Thomas built Dunstanborough Castle in Northumberland, which was destroyed by the Yorkists during the Wars of the Roses. There are some ruins of it still standing on a precipitous cliff overlooking the sea.

Within a very few years the fickle multitude, forgetting his crimes and his treason, and remembering only his liberality, called him the 'good earl,' and declared that miracles were wrought at his tomb, which entailed the appointment of a guard of men-at-arms to prevent all access to the place. The Commons in Parliament were even induced to write to the Pope to ask for his canonization. But the request was not noticed.

Two months later a Parliament was held at York. The indemnity granted to the pursuers of the Despensers was annulled, ' by reason of assent having been given to it in dread of the great force brought by the Earl of Hereford and others into the House at Westminster.' At the same time the petitions of the Despensers themselves were heard and granted, and the award against them was ordered to be struck out of the rolls. The elder was created Earl of Winchester on May 10, and received several forfeited estates as compensation for his great losses. He was, by inheritance, eighth Baron le Despenser. As such he sat in Parliament, and was also a member of the Privy Council in the reign of King Edward I. He was a man respected for his wisdom, valour, and integrity. So much were his talents and experience valued by the late King that he was employed in many capacities. He was one of those engaged in examining into the merits of the various claims put forth for the Scottish throne at the time of the death of the Maid of Norway, after which the crown was awarded to John Baliol. He was several times ambassador to France, Germany, and Flanders, and on two separate occasions to the See of Rome. When Edward of Caernarvon came to the throne,

Baron le Despenser assisted at the coronation, and his services were enlisted on several occasions and in many capacities.

The younger Hugh was at once reinstated in his former office, and soon regained his influence with the King. Unfortunately, prudence and moderation appear to have been cast aside when he began to feel his position of strength, although he did not exhibit the folly and extravagance in which Gaveston had indulged. But a more powerful enemy than Lancaster had ever been rose against him. He had deemed it advisable to curtail the Queen's revenue, and to reduce the royal establishment. This was probably done because Isabella, by her loose conduct, had already forfeited her husband's confidence; but she made this act an excuse for waging war against him. Every charge she had formerly made against Gaveston she now launched against Despenser, and she wrote her complaints to her brother, Charles le Bel, King of France. Despenser retorted by advising King Edward to deprive her of the income from the earldom of Cornwall, which had been granted to her, and this he at once did. The King and Queen became totally estranged, and forsook one another's company. This also was laid by Isabella to the charge of Despenser. The amiable Canon Froissart was quite the champion of Isabella, whom he would fain persuade people to look upon as a modest and virtuous though much maligned wife, whilst Despenser is portrayed in the darkest colours and as the fomenter of differences between her and her husband. His remarks must be taken *cum grano salis.*

1325. Then came the mission of the Queen to France, and a reconciliation was apparently effected with the Despensers, who were both delighted at the prospect of her departure.

When the demand was made by Charles of France that Edward should go over to do homage personally for Guienne, Hugh did not like him to go alone. Still less did he care to accompany him, as he was in fear of Isabella, who, having accused him of an intention of putting her to death, might effectually and for ever bring such a scheme, if he had it, to an end. He therefore felt relieved when it was proposed that Prince Edward should go in place of his father. He did not know the arts and wiles of the woman he had to deal with, and thus fell into the snare she had carefully prepared.

1326. Isabella landed with her foreign mercenaries September 24, 1326. The Earl of Winchester, who was Governor of Bristol Castle, was betrayed by the garrison, who delivered him into the hands of his enemies. Without any form of trial, accusation, witness, or defence, he was condemned to death. He was hanged on October 27. His body was cut to pieces and thrown to the dogs. His head was sent to the city whence he derived his title, and was set up on a pole at the top of the castle gate to be the mark of the insults of the populace. It might be taken as a warning against too great loyalty to a king.

The dignity of the earldom was not restored to his family; but the barony of Le Despenser, one of the oldest, if not the oldest, in the kingdom, was continued, and is at this time held by the Earl of Falmouth as twenty-fourth baron.

A month later Hugh le Despenser the younger was taken by Henry of Lancaster in the woods of Lantressan. He was charged with being the cause of every calamity which had happened in the kingdom, and therefore, as a robber, traitor, and outlaw, was condemned to be drawn, hanged, embowelled, beheaded, and quartered. Dressed in a black gown, with the arms of his family reversed, and a wreath of nettles on his head, he was hanged on a gallows fifty feet high on November 24, at Hereford. Some portions of his body were buried at Tewkesbury Abbey, of which he was patron in right of his wife. He left two sons and a daughter. The former will be heard of again later on.

HENRY OF LANCASTER, commonly called Wryneck, was created Earl of Lancaster and Leicester in 1324. Following in the footsteps of his brother Thomas, he joined the party of his niece Isabella, and went to meet her soon after her landing. After he had obtained possession by bribery of the Chancellor Baldock and Hugh le Despenser, King Edward voluntarily surrendered to him, and was taken to Kenilworth Castle.

There is something very mysterious about the whole revolution against Edward II. True, he was weak in character, indolent, and easily led by favourites, though he could be obstinate at times. He was not deficient in courage, but was never guilty of an act of oppression. Why, then, did he now and later on give in so tamely without a struggle, or even, so far as we know, without a remonstrance of any kind? 'Time unveils truth,' and perhaps some day an unravelment may be made.

Henry's treatment of his captive was too lenient, and his endeavours to alleviate the sufferings of the poor King too pronounced, to meet the views of Isabella and Mortimer. He was therefore relieved of his charge, who was handed over to Sir John Maltravers and taken to Berkeley Castle, where the end soon came.

1327. The judgments given against the late Earl were reversed, and his heirs restored to their estates. Earl Henry was appointed chief of the Council of Regency, which consisted of four bishops, four earls, and six barons. Mortimer, however, superseded them all, and took the whole authority into his own hands.

1328. Henry's eyes were opened to the truth. He must have repented his dereliction from the path of duty and loyalty, to follow in the wake of an infamous woman and her lover. He advanced in arms with his followers against Mortimer, who had plundered his domains near Leicester, and was joined by Thomas of Brotherton, Earl of Norfolk, and Edmund of Woodstock, Earl of Kent, brothers of the late Edward of Caernarvon. But, being deserted by these colleagues, he had to submit to ask pardon, and to swell the fortunes of Isabella and Mortimer by a fine equal to half the value of his estates.

1330. After Edward III. assumed his proper station as King, we hear little more of Earl Henry, but a good deal of his more able son—of whom hereafter.

1340. 1345. He was appointed Councillor to the Duke of Cornwall (the Black Prince), and on July 1, 1345, Councillor of Regency, when the war for the Succession in France was about to commence. He died on September 22, leaving by his wife Maud, daughter and heir of Sir Patrick Chaworth, one son, HENRY OF GROSMONT, and six daughters: BLANCHE, who married Thomas, Lord de Wake, and died without issue; MAUD, who married William de Burgh, Earl of Ulster, whose daughter Elizabeth married Lionel, son of King Edward III.; JOAN, married to John, eighth Lord Mowbray; ELEANORA, first married to John de Beaumont, Earl of Buchan, and secondly to Richard Fitz Alan, fifth Earl of Arundel; MARY, married to Henry de Percy IV., whose grandson was the celebrated Hotspur; and ISABEL, a nun, afterwards Abbess of Ambresbury.

By his marriage with Maud Chaworth the Earl of Lancaster added to his other possessions the Castle of Kidwelly in Caermarthenshire, one of the strongest and best preserved in Wales.

SKETCH II.

A STEP FORWARD.

HENRY OF GROSMONT was a man of character the very opposite to his uncle Thomas. He, from his first entrance into public life, obtained, and to the last kept, the esteem and confidence, not only of his King, but of men of all ranks, who knew him to be good, brave and chivalrous, if he was not always fortunate.

He was born about 1299 in the Castle of Grosmont, whence he derived his name, situated about ten miles from Monmouth, of which some ruins are still standing. This castle, when besieged by Llywelyn, the last Prince of Wales of the old line, was relieved by King Henry III., who granted it to his second son, Edmund.

Henry's first employment was as a crusader, along with the Knights of the Teutonic orders, against the infidels of Prussia—that same Prussia which, in conjunction with Brandenburg, was to become so powerful in after years, and, in our own time, to dominate over almost entire Germany.

1337. At the time when Edward III. was meditating his war against France, he made a friend of Jacob von Arteveld, and by his intervention obtained the permission of the Flemings for the English army to march through the country on their way. The Earl of Flanders, not being willing to have his land thus disposed of to the enemies of his ally, threw strong garrisons into the Isle of Cadsand, with instructions to do as much damage to the English as they could, and then made his own escape to France. King Edward, hearing of this, sent over forces under the command of Henry of Grosmont, who was created Earl of Derby on March 16, and Sir Walter de Manny, to reduce the place. A very fierce and severe battle was fought, in the course of which the Earl was at one time struck to the ground, but valiantly rescued by Sir Walter. The result was a complete victory for the English, the enemy having lost more than three thousand men. On October 7, King Edward made his claim to the crown of France.

In consequence of this French scheme the wars in Scotland, which had been intermittingly carried on, grew languid. Sir Andrew Moray was chosen Regent. The country generally was cleared of its enemies, and the English, for the most part, shut up in their castles.

But in the midst of a state of warfare pacific encounters occasionally took place. That perfect knight, the Earl of Derby, with great courtesy sent to request that Sir William Douglas, the Knight of Liddesdale, would try three courses at the jousts with him. In the first course Douglas was wounded in the hand by a splinter from his own lance, and had to retire. The Earl then sent an invitation to Sir Alexander Ramsay, of Dalhousie to hold a joust at Berwick for three days, twenty against twenty, which was accepted. Two English knights were slain, and one of the Scots mortally wounded. Sir William Ramsay had a lance run so deeply through the visor of his helmet into his head that it seemed certain he must die if it were pulled out. He therefore made his confession whilst he lay on the ground with all the other knights surrounding him. 1338.

'So help me, Heaven!' said the Earl of Derby, 'I would desire to see no fairer sight than this brave Baron thus shrived with his helmet on; happy man should I be could I ensure such an ending.' Sir Alexander Ramsay now came forward, and, placing his foot on his brother's helmet, by sheer force dragged the iron out. The wounded man at once sprang up, declaring that he should soon do well enough, and the Earl could not but exclaim, 'What stout hearts these men have!' William, however, died almost immediately afterwards.

Such were the fierce pastimes in those days. Earl Henry received and entertained his guests most nobly, and was liberal in the distribution of gifts and prizes. The prizes for the Scots were fixed by the English, and those for the English in like manner by the Scots.

In the meantime, affairs abroad had not prospered with King Edward. His treasures were exhausted, his allies refused to fight without money, and he had to submit to an armistice for some months, negotiated by Jeanne, Countess of Hainault, the mother of Queen Philippa. The King was in such sore straits for money, having mortgaged all his own property, in addition to the jewels of the Queen, that he was compelled to leave the Earl of Derby, his third-cousin, in pledge with his creditors. Henry was therefore 1340.

detained by some merchants in Flanders until the following year, when fresh supplies were voted by Parliament.

1343. The quarrel with France might, perhaps, have been adjusted but for disputes as to the succession in the duchy of Bretagne, in which Edward espoused one side, and Philippe the other. However, Clement VI. charged two of his cardinals to mediate a peace. The Earl of Derby was empowered to treat on behalf of England, and a truce for three years and some odd months was concluded. But it did not last so long. Philippe interfered in the affairs of Bretagne and Normandy. Gascony sent at the same time to beg for aid against the French, and the English Parliament recommended the renewal of hostilities.

1344. In May the Earl of Derby proceeded at the head of an army to Guienne. They landed at Bayonne, and then marched to Bordeaux. About a fortnight later, on a sudden impulse of Sir Walter de Manny, who was again with him, the Earl and he, with several knights, but not any considerable number of men, started off for Bergerac, on the river Dordogne. On arriving there, they had a slight skirmish with a part of the garrison, who soon retreated to that part of the town which lay across the river. Next morning the Earl and his followers went up the river by boats, and there ensued a fight in the streets which lasted the whole day, but when night came the garrison escaped. On the following morning the inhabitants surrendered, and swore fealty to the King of England. In consequence of this achievement the Earl of Derby was two years later created Lord of Bergerac.

The Earl had another success in the relief of Auberoche. The place was invested by the Count of Lisle, with 12,000 men under his command, who with their engines threw such continued showers of stones against the walls that the garrison felt compelled to hide themselves. The Earl, with 300 men-at-arms and 600 archers, was on his way to their assistance. By indirect paths they arrived at the French camp, and burst upon it when all were at supper. There was not time even to sound an alarm. The principal officers were killed or taken prisoners, either sitting at table or preparing to take their seats. If any body of men assembled together, they were quickly dispersed by showers of arrows from the archers. Another body of the French, who were attacking the place from a different quarter, came to the succour of their friends, and a severe contest ensued, which was turned into a still more complete victory for the English by the garrison of the castle issuing forth and charging on the rear of the French. It is said that each Englishman had at least two or three prisoners for his share of the spoils. The

Aug. 9. battle was fought on the eve of St. Laurence's Day.

A long time was consumed ere La Reole could be won. Henry lay before it for nine weeks, until the townspeople were so much
1345. reduced by famine that they agreed to surrender. The defender of
May. the castle, however, determined to hold out, having contrived to lay

in a store of wines and provisions. The place was too strongly built
to suffer from any engines which the Earl could bring to bear against
it, and therefore he proceeded to undermine it. On discovering this, Sept.
the governor offered to surrender, on condition that the lives and
fortunes of the whole should be spared. The Earl would only accept
an unconditional surrender. To this the governor at last agreed,
trusting, as he said, to the honour of the English. In this he acted
wisely. The whole force was allowed to retreat, and La Reole
passed into English possession, as did many other castles and places
of importance, where the Earl's treatment of the inhabitants was
always so considerate that their attachment to English rule became
sincere. 'His army gained so much riches that it was marvellous to
think on.'

On Christmas Day Philippe of France sent orders to his son Jean,
Duke of Normandy, to assemble all his vassals at Orleans on
February 3 ensuing. The army was so numerous that the Earl 1346.
of Lancaster—such he had now become by his father's death—saw
he could not keep the field without reinforcements, and therefore remained at Bordeaux. Sir Walter Manny, in the meantime, with forty
knights and 900 men, was defending Aiguillon against the assaults of
Duke Jean. King Edward intended sending supports, but diverted
them to Normandy, where he landed at La Hogue. The siege of
Aiguillon was raised after the lapse of four months, as the forces were
required at Créci. No sooner were the French gone than the Earl Aug.
of Lancaster issued from Bordeaux, crossed the Garonne, and, in
revenge for depredations which the enemy had committed in Guienne,
laid waste the country he passed through until he arrived at Poitiers,
which he stormed and captured. Then he led his troops, laden with Oct.
the spoils of victory, back to Bordeaux to pass the winter.

The Earl left Guienne early in the spring, and was present at the 1347.
investment of Calais, where he had charge of the bridge of Neuillet,
and the subsequent surrender. It was while here that, on June 1, he
received his new title as Lord of Bergerac. In a sea-fight off Win-
chilsea, against a fleet of Spaniards, he decided the victory, and at the
same time saved the Prince of Wales by grappling with, and conquering, one of the largest of the enemy's ships.

For the next few years there is not anything very interesting or
exciting to record of him. He acted in various characters, both military and pacific. It was probably in recognition of the latter services
that, on August 20, 1349, he was created Earl of Lincoln, and on
March 6, 1352, he was advanced from the dignity of Earl to that of
Duke of Lancaster, the only other Duke in the kingdom at that time
being the King's eldest son, Edward, Prince of Wales, and Duke of
Cornwall.

The Duke's next employment was to support the claims of JEAN V. 1355.
DE MONTFORT to the dukedom of BRETAGNE, or BRITTANY.

Bretagne had been intimately connected with England ever since
the Conquest, and her counts and dukes had, in many instances,

borne the title Earl of Richmond. All will remember Arthur of Brittany, the undoubted heir to the English throne, according to our present ideas, who was murdered by his uncle, the craven King John. His mother, Constance, took for her third husband Sir Guy de Thouars. Their daughter, Alix, Duchess of Bretagne and Countess of Richmond, married Pierre de Dreux, or Mauclerc, as he was called, that is to say, bad scholar, though in fact he was a poet and a man of talent. They were the founders of a new race of Breton dukes, who ruled until the middle of the fifteenth century.

Their grandson, Jean de Dreux II., Duke of Bretagne and Earl of Richmond, married Beatrice, second daughter of Henry III., King of England. Their son, Arthur, fourth Duke of Bretagne, died in 1312, leaving three sons, Jean de Dreux III., his successor, Guy and Pierre, by his first wife; and another son, Jean, called de Montfort, by a second wife.

Jean de Dreux III. died without issue in 1341, both his own brothers having preceded him to the tomb. Some time before his death he bequeathed the duchy to his niece, Jeanne de Penthièvres, the only child of his late brother Guy. Jean IV. de Montfort objected to this, and after his brother's death seized the treasures at Nantes, possessed himself of most of the strong places, then crossed over to England, where he did homage to Edward III., and was created Earl of Richmond.

Jeanne de Penthièvres was married to Charles de Blois, a nephew of King Philippe VI. of France, whose sympathies were naturally in their favour.

Hostilities were soon commenced. Jean IV. de Montfort was taken prisoner in 1342, and died September 26, 1345, leaving by his wife Jeanne, daughter of Louis de Nevers, Count of Flanders, one son, Jean V., to succeed to the disputed inheritance. The brave Jeanne of Flanders, the heroine of the age, who, Froissart writes, possessed the courage of a man and the heart of a lion, had, with extraordinary ability and courage, carried on the contest for many years until now, when Edward III. thought it right that her son, Jean V. de Montfort, who had lived the greater part of his life in England, should go over to fight his own battles.

1357. Siege was at once laid to Rennes, the capital of the duchy, which
May. was at that time held in the name of Charles of Blois. The garrison were at length reduced to very nearly a point of starvation, when a stratagem saved them. One of the citizens was, by a plot of his own, taken prisoner and carried before the Duke of Lancaster, to whom, with apparent dread, he conveyed the information that the people were dying of hunger, but that a large convoy of provisions was on the way, which might, however, easily be cut off. Duke Henry fell into the snare thus artfully laid, and marched off with his men to intercept the supplies. In the meantime, the man had escaped and warned Du Guesclin, who was not far off. Bertrand, with his troop, at once fell on the almost deserted English camp and

despoiled it of all Lancaster's stores, which were carted off to the beleaguered city.*

Du Guesclin held the city until the news that a truce for two years had been agreed to at Bordeaux, after the battle of Poitiers, put an end to the siege in June, 1357.

The struggle in Bretagne continued with varying fortune until 1364, when, on Michaelmas Day, at the battle of Auray, Charles de Blois was slain. Jean V. de Montfort was acknowledged as Duke, and did homage to Charles V., King of France, as his suzerain. Jean had two wives of English blood, who both died childless, viz., Mary, daughter of King Edward III., and Joan, daughter of Thomas Holland, Earl of Kent, and the fair Countess. For his third wife Jean took Juana, daughter of Charles 'the Bad,' King of Navarre, who brought him a large family of sons and daughters, and after his death, in 1399, married Henry IV., King of England.

When the truce expired, and King Edward was preparing for a new invasion of France, he sent the Duke of Lancaster in advance with 400 men-at-arms and 2,000 archers, in order that incursions might be made into the surrounding districts. They returned to Calais, on the arrival there of the King with his army. After the ineffectual siege of Rheims, and an abortive march to Paris. Duke Henry was greatly instrumental in bringing about the peace of Bretigni, which was concluded on May 8. His race was nearly run, and it was a good act with which to bring a stirring life to a close. 1359. Nov. 1360.

Henry, Duke of Lancaster, was generally acknowledged as a man of piety and valour, a liberal benefactor to the religious, and known as the 'good Duke.' He had endowed a hermitage near the abbey of Whalley, in Lancashire, which had been founded by his ancestor, Henry de Lacy, for the benefit of recluses. But, in course of time, the privileges were abused, and it was dissolved by letters patent, two chaplains being appointed to say Mass daily for the soul of Duke Henry. The hermitage does not now exist. He died of the plague on March 13, 1361, much lamented by the King and all his barons, leaving by his wife Isabel, daughter of Henry, first Lord Beaumont, two daughters, MAUD and BLANCHE.

Maud married, in 1339, William V., Count of Holland. In 1358 he went mad, and the two factions which had been disturbing the country for many years, and continued to do so for more than a century, had a struggle for the mastery. The Kabelljaus, or the burghers, chose Maud as Regent; but the Hoecks, or the nobles, chose William's brother, Albert of Bavaria, and their side prevailed. Maud died, without issue, about a year after her father.

BLANCHE married, May 19, 1359, in the abbey at Reading, JOHN OF GHENT, fourth son of King Edward III., who succeeded in her 1361.

* With the kind permission of the gifted authoress, this account is taken from Miss Yonge's 'Cameos,' second series, p. 73, where also may be read an interesting description of a combat between the Breton hero, Du Guesclin, and an Englishman named William Bamborough.

2—2

right as fifth Earl of Lancaster, was admitted to the vacant stall of
1362. the Order of the Garter, and was next year advanced to the Dukedom. At or about the same time Lancaster was created a County Palatine, in the same degree and with the same privileges as Chester. John's son Henry, when he came to the throne, passed an Act declaring that the inheritance and titles of the duchy should remain with him and his heirs for ever, as distinct from the possessions of the crown. The sovereigns of England since then have borne the title of Duke or Duchess of Lancaster.

John of Ghent restored and added to the castle of Lancaster, and one of the towers is known by his name. An effigy in a niche over the principal gateway is said to represent him, but it certainly does not date from his time. Since the wars of the Commonwealth the castle has been degraded to a county gaol.

By the death of his sister-in-law, the Countess of Holland, John of Ghent came into possession of many castles and manors belonging to the Duchy of Lancaster. Among these was Tutbury Castle, in Staffordshire, which had formerly belonged to the Ferrars family as Earls of Derby, but fell to the House of Lancaster in the time of King Henry III. The ruins now existing are supposed to be those of the castle erected by John of Ghent, who frequently resided here in royal state. As great hospitality was exercised, numerous bodies of minstrels from various quarters always assembled here, and a curious custom arose for the delectation of those of them who attended at service in the church on the festival of the Assumption, August 15. After a dinner in the hall of the castle, a bull was turned loose with its horns and tail cut off, its body closely shorn and well greased, and its nostrils stuffed with pepper. It became the property of whichever of them could catch it before sunset without its crossing the river Dove into Derbyshire. Often the sport would end in the animal being taken to the market cross, first baited and then eaten; but generally it escaped, and still remained the lord's property. Hence arose the rustic game of bull-running, which lasted till towards the close of last century; but it degenerated into such a scene of disturbances and outrages that it had to be stopped.

As part of his wife's dower, the Earl received the palace of the Savoy, which had been rebuilt by her father, and it was the most magnificent building of its kind in England. He also received Kenilworth Castle, to which he made many important additions, more especially what are known as the Lancaster Buildings, including the Great Hall, which was finished only two years before his death, and also, perhaps, the Strong Tower.* Halton Castle, near Runcorn, one of the strongholds of the De Lacys, another of his possessions, was a favourite hunting-seat with him.

1369. In the month of August, 1369, John lost his first wife, Blanche, whom Geoffrey Chaucer, the father of English poetry, thus commemorated in his 'Boke of the Duchesse; or, Deeth of Blaunche the Duchesse.'

* Beattie's 'Castles and Abbeys.'

> 'Goode faire white she hete,
> That was my lady name ryghte.
> She was bothe faire and bryghte,
> She hadde not hir name wronge.'

The description of Queen Alcyone may also be taken as applying to the Duchess:
> 'My lady swete,
> That was so faire, so fresh, so fre,
> So goode that men may wel se
> Of al goodenesse sche hadde no mete.'

Blanche left three children—Henry, Philippa, and Elizabeth.

When the Prince of Wales was summoned by King Charles V. of France to appear at Paris and give an account of himself, the Duke of Lancaster was despatched with a body of men to Calais. He marched through Guisnes, crossed the river Dostre, overran the country and plundered the Abbey of Liques. He also made an excursion to Boulogne, doing considerable damage. Philippe, Duke of Burgundy, was sent to oppose him, and the two armies drew up opposite one another at Tournehem.

It was whilst here that Duke John received the announcement of the death of his mother, Queen Philippa, on August 14, the vigil of the Assumption. He was particularly moved at the news, but public affairs displace private griefs.

The only noticeable incident at this time was a projected encounter between some French knights and squires and one wing of the English army under the command of Sir Robert de Namur. But it came to nothing, for, as soon as the French saw their opponents were prepared for battle, they retreated. The same may be said of the whole body of men. The two armies lay for some weeks opposite one another without striking a blow, until Philippe received orders from his brother, King Charles, to break up his camp and return to Paris, when John of Lancaster went back to his quarters at Calais. It was part of King Charles's policy to harass the enemy without coming to blows.

After the lamentable death of the gallant old hero, Sir John Chandos, the conduct of the war in a great measure rested with the Duke of Lancaster, who was not fitted for the post, as even his most ardent admirers cannot claim that he made a good general. It has been surmised that he was jealous of the superior talents of his elder brother, the Prince of Wales, and not averse to taking advantage of his enfeebled state of health. Anyway, he was sent to Aquitaine with full power to act independently if necessary. 1370.

In the following year he went to England and busied himself in the government of the country. By his great influence he induced the Parliament to petition against any great offices of the State being entrusted to ecclesiastics, who, up till that time, had been the only persons competent to fill them. The bill was aimed more especially against that honest and good man, William of Wykeham, Bishop of Winchester, whom the duke disliked, who had filled the post of 1371.

Chancellor for four years, and he was now forced to retire. The experiment only lasted two or three years, when the Duke of Lancaster found himself compelled to appoint a clerical Chancellor. The office continued to be filled by ecclesiastics until the sixteenth century, with one exception. The Duke's party was very powerful, but gradually became most unpopular. The opposition, as it may be called, was led by the Bishop of Winchester.

1372. The Duke of Lancaster was in Aquitaine when he heard of the arrival at Bayonne of the two daughters of the late PEDRO, King of Castile. He gave them a hearty welcome, and in June married the elder, CONSTANÇA, or Costança, in a village near Bordeaux. The wedding was numerously attended by both lords and ladies, for whom a splendid feast was provided. John, at the same time, assumed the title of King of Castile and Leon. The first result of this was a closer union between Enrique, King of Castile, and Charles, King of France. A junction of the fleets of the two nations was effected at Rochelle, when the action took place in which the Earl of Pembroke was made prisoner, shortly after his marriage, leaving the Captal de Buch as governor in Guienne. The Duke of Lancaster returned to England with his newly-made wife and her sister ISABEL, who was soon afterwards married to his brother EDMUND, Earl of Cambridge, and great festivities took place at Windsor in honour of the brides.

1373. Nominally at the request of the Duke of Bretagne, who had been expelled from France, another splendid force left England, under the command of the Duke of Lancaster, which was joined at Calais by many mercenaries from Hainault and elsewhere. What the special object of the expedition may have been it is difficult to determine. That its result was disastrous is very certain. Soon after crossing the river Somme, an advance party of eighty men was attacked and defeated by a force of like number under the Lord de Boursiers. Near Soissons a portion of the army was surprised by a body of French and Burgundians, and defeated with great loss. King Charles's tactics were to let the enemy severely alone. No general engagement was to be hazarded. The Duke therefore continued his march, burning and wasting as he went. Winter was coming on, and supplies for men and horses were becoming scarce. Occasionally food and forage were furnished by the terrified peasantry, but oftener the men were reduced to bread and the horses to nothing. They suffered, in fact, an actual famine; men and horses died daily, and, of the proud array which left Calais, very, very few arrived, weary and worn, after traversing Picardy, Champagne, Berri and Limousin, at Bordeaux about Christmas.

1375. The Duke went in February to a congress at Bruges as joint plenipotentiary with William de Montagu VI., Earl of Salisbury, and Simon of Sudbury, Bishop of London, to treat for a truce with France, which was continued until the death of King Edward III. The result of the negotiations was not, however, satisfactory to the nation, as some concessions had been made at the same time to

Pope Gregory XI., in order that the Duke might triumph over prelates and clergy. As a consequence, the Duke's party was dismissed from office.

The Duke was rendered more unpopular by reports, both at home and abroad, that he had designs on the crown. If he really ever entertained the idea, he did not find himself strong enough to try and carry it into effect.

On the death of the Prince of Wales, his brother, the Duke of 1376. Lancaster, made a proposition that the succession to the crown should be settled on the heirs male of the King, to the exclusion of females. It had an ugly look with it. After Richard of Bordeaux, the direct heir was Philippa, the daughter of the late Lionel of Clarence, John's elder brother, and she would thus have been passed over, should Richard die childless, in favour of Lancaster and his son. The Commons refused their consent, and Richard, then a boy in the tenth year of his age, was at once presented as heir-apparent to both houses, who received him with every demonstration of joy. Whether this proposal was the cause of it or not, it is singular that John, Duke of Lancaster, was never afterwards in favour with the people.

Duke John had constituted himself the supporter and defender 1377. of Wycliffe, for whom he had obtained the living of Lutterworth, Leicestershire. The learned Doctor had been summoned by the Bishop of London, William Courtenay, to appear before the Archbishop, Simon of Sudbury, on February 19, on a charge of heresy.

The trial was to take place in the Lady Chapel of St. Paul's Cathedral. On the appointed day the place was thronged with prelates, earls, barons, and gentry. The accused arrived, attended by the Duke and Henry, Lord Percy, afterwards first Earl of Northumberland, whom Lancaster had recently created Marshal of England. There was a perfect crowd of people in the church, who were prepared to protect their Bishop against the men whom the Marshal had appointed to act as police, which they considered an insult to their chief magistrate. The ducal party had great difficulty in making their way to the chapel, and Percy ordered his men to force a passage. Bishop Courtenay mildly remonstrated with him, saying that, 'could he have foreseen such conduct, he would have prohibited his entrance into the church.'

The Duke hereupon called out in a loud voice that 'notwithstanding the Bishop, the Lord Marshal should be master there.'

In time they arrived at the Lady Chapel, where the Duke and Percy were accommodated with seats, but Wycliffe was left standing. The Marshal then took on himself to order that a seat should be brought, remarking that 'he would need a soft one to bear all the questions that would be put to him.'

The Bishop directed that no seat should be brought, and quietly observed that 'it would be contrary to law and reason for a clerk to be seated during his trial.'

The Duke, in a great rage, vowed he would bring down all the prelacy of England, and, pointing to the Bishop, said: 'As for thee, thou bearest thyself so brag upon thy parentage, but they shall not be able to help thee: I will take care they shall have enough to do to help themselves.'

'My confidence,' replied the Bishop, 'is not in my parents, nor in man, but in God only. By His assistance I shall be bold enough to speak as I ought to speak, and to maintain the truth.'

The Duke muttered to himself, but so that he could be heard, 'Rather than tolerate such words from the Bishop, he would drag him out of the church by the hair of his head.' Perhaps he would have done so, had his followers been of sufficient number. But his speech so exasperated the people, with whom he was never at any time popular, that he deemed it safest for himself to retreat, and the meeting was dissolved. He and Percy, by their intemperate conduct, had defeated their own purpose. Wycliffe had received a hint not to concern himself in party politics, while at the same time the charges against him had not been proved.

The Duke had not yet done with the people. As soon as the Council was broken up, at nine in the morning, he went with Percy to Parliament, and there proposed to disfranchise the City of London, abolish the office of Mayor, and invest the Lord Marshal with the duty of preserving order.

This soon became known, and further roused the people. Next day the Marshal inaugurated his new office by imprisoning a citizen of London. The populace attacked his house, released the man, making a bonfire of the stocks wherein he was fastened, and vowed death to Percy if they could find him.

He and the Duke had gone to a feast given by one of the principal citizens, named John Yper. The mob went there, broke through the gates, and just as the Duke was in the act of taking an appetizer before going to dinner, he had to flee for his life. In doing so he was in such a hurry that he scarred his knees in clambering over the benches. He and Percy escaped by boat, and made their way to Kennington, there to seek protection from the very people to whom they were opposed, Prince Richard and his mother the Princess of Wales.

The Londoners, supposing they had gone to the Savoy, at once proceeded there with the full intention of destroying it. Fortunately, Bishop COURTENAY arrived on the scene just in the nick of time. He was a great favourite with them, and was heartily cheered. He waved his hands for silence, and entreated them not to desecrate the sacred season of Lent by such an act as they were meditating. At length they were pacified, but they reversed the ducal arms in the chapel, and wherever they could be found in the City, which gave great offence to the Duke, who looked upon it as a personal insult.

With reference to John of Ghent's sneer at the Bishop of London, it may be remarked that they were third-cousins. Each was great-grandson of King Edward I., William Courtenay being a son of Hugh, second Earl of Devonshire, and Margaret de Bohun, grand-daughter of Edward I. His family dates back to the time of Robert II., King of France, 996-1031. Rainaud de Courtenay came to England in the reign of King Henry II., and by a second marriage was the founder here of the house of Courtenay, which is now represented by Henry Hugh, thirteenth Earl of Devon.

The Duke of Lancaster's protection of Wycliffe was not an enduring one. He had taken him up more for party and political purposes than on account of his theological ideas. He had even tried to persuade him to retract some of his opinions, but failed. When, therefore, some of the reformer's party at Oxford appealed to him for protection in 1382 he would not have anything to do with them; he had other objects in view.

Wycliffe himself died quietly in his parsonage at Lutterworth in December, 1384.

It is noticeable also that the Duke and Courtenay, who became Archbishop of Canterbury in 1381, were on more friendly terms than they had been.

The good which had been effected by the Prince of Wales was immediately undone when the Duke of Lancaster regained his influence in Parliament. Sir Peter de la Mere, the Speaker, was arrested and imprisoned under false pretences; the celebrated William of Wykeham, Bishop of Winchester, was banished from the King's presence, and condemned to forfeit his temporalities; whilst Alice Perrers was brought back and had the poor King abandoned to her tender mercies by his loving son John. King Edward at the time was living at Eltham, but she removed him to Shene and kept him secluded from all except her own creatures. She did not even enlighten his ignorance as to the condition of his health. She had taken good care to enrich herself; yet, even when the King lay dying, she snatched the jewelled ring from his finger and left him alone — absolutely alone! for all the other servants, following her example, were busy plundering the palace and picking up any unconsidered trifles for their own use and benefit. It will be remembered that another mighty man of battles, our first Norman King, was in like manner plundered and deserted by all his attendants. Fortunately for King Edward, a friar who was passing by looked in, and, seeing that his monarch was dying, reminded him of the need he had of preparation to appear before his Maker. Edward had but just strength enough left to express his thanks. Then he took the crucifix in his hands, kissed it, wept, and drew his last breath, on June 21, 1377. He was utterly worn out, both in mind and body, and perhaps it was as well that he was so; otherwise he could not but have mourned over his fruitless endeavours to win for himself the crowns of France and Scotland. For all the lives and money expended there was nothing as a set-off but the possession of Calais, Bordeaux, Bayonne, and a few other places. The King was buried in St. Edward's Chapel in Westminster Abbey, in the same grave with his Queen, Philippa of Hainault, but there is a separate monument for each of them.

The day after his grandfather died RICHARD OF BORDEAUX made his entry into London, where all that the short space of time allowed for preparation would admit was done to show the loyalty of the people.

The coronation took place on July 16, in Westminster Abbey, which the royal boy entered under a canopy of blue silk, borne on spears of silver by barons of the Cinque Ports, and with his uncle, the Duke of Lancaster, bearing the sword curtana. While the Litany was chanted Richard lay prostrate before the altar, whence he was conducted by the Dukes of Lancaster and Bretagne to a throne erected in the nave on a high platform. As soon as he had taken the usual oath, and the people, by their loud acclamations, had signified their willingness to have him for their King, he was anointed and crowned by Simon, Archbishop of Canterbury. A solemn mass followed. After receiving the homage of his uncles and other nobles the young King created his youngest uncle, Thomas of Woodstock, Earl of Buckingham; Henry de Percy, Earl of Northumberland; and Sir Guichard d'Angle, companion in arms of the Prince of Wales, who had appointed him governor of his son, Prince Richard, he made Earl of Huntingdon. The usual banquet, ball, and festivities concluded the day.

Next morning the Government was appointed, in which the Duke of Lancaster was not included, though he took care that some of his partisans had places in the Council, and then retired to his castle of Kenilworth.

Oct. In Richard's first Parliament the Commons consisted principally of those men who had always opposed the Duke, and Sir Peter de la Mere was again the Speaker. However, when asked for their advice how to oppose the enemies of the realm, they requested the assistance of 'my lord of Spain' and other peers.

The Duke rose, bent his knee to the King, and said that the commons had no claim on him for advice. They had charged him with what amounted to treason. As the son of a king, and one of the first lords in the realm, he would not apply to any business until his character had been cleared. There had never been a traitor, he said, among his ancestors of either line—thus ignoring Earl Thomas —and he would not be the first to sully their fame. He avowed himself ready to meet any one in single combat, or in any way that the King might award.

After entreaties by the prelates and lords, and assurances on the part of the Commons of their belief in his innocence, he allowed himself to be persuaded and to forget all that was past. Business then proceeded.

The Duke abandoned his former tool, Alice Perrers, who was tried by a committee of the house, consisting of himself and four earls. She was found guilty of various crimes and misdemeanours, and condemned to banishment, with forfeiture of all her goods, tenements, and chattels. It appeared subsequently that she was, at the time, the wife of Sir William Windsor, and he obtained the restoration of her lands, except four manors, on the ground that she had been impeached as a *feme sole*. Six years later the judgment was entirely revoked.

The Duke took an army to Bretagne, besieged St. Malo, lay before it several weeks, then had to retire with great loss and return home, having spent all the money raised for war expenditure which he had cajoled Parliament into placing in his hands. It really reads very much like the old nursery rhyme of 'The King of France, and twice ten thousand men.' 1378.

The Duke was connected with an affair which made a great noise at the time. As claimant to the crown of Castile, he desired to obtain possession of the son of a certain Count Denia, a relation of the then reigning family. The Count himself had been taken prisoner by two esquires, Schakel and Haule, and left his son in their custody until he should be able to pay his ransom. The Duke offered to pay the ransom, on condition that the youth should be handed over to him. This was very properly refused. He made several attempts to secure the prisoner, and, failing in that, obtained an Act of Parliament for the committal of Schakel and Haule to the Tower unless he was produced on a day named. The two threatened men escaped from the Tower, and were pursued by retainers of the Duke. Schakel was captured in the precincts of Westminster, and carried back to prison. Haule entered the Abbey, was followed by Lancaster's men, penned into a corner close to the altar, and, whilst calling on them not to violate the sanctuary, had his skull cleft in twain. The Londoners were greatly excited at the outrage, and demanded the excommunication of the offenders. The Archbishop, Simon of Sudbury, was a partisan of the Duke, and was slow to act; but at length he issued the sentence, excepting therefrom the King and his mother, *and* the Duke of Lancaster, but not one other person. In Parliament, which was held at Gloucester, be it noted, in order to be away from the Londoners, the supporters of Lancaster, when the case came on, made a counterclaim to the effect that the privilege of sanctuary could not be extended to debtors, in which character they insinuated that Haule had sought shelter. The matter was allowed to drop.*

In the autumn of this year the Duke of Lancaster went to the borders of Scotland, ostensibly to renew the truce, which was nearing its end. Objections being, however, raised to the presence of the army which he had brought with him, it was disbanded, and a truce for three years was soon afterwards concluded between the two countries. On seeking admission to Berwick, the Duke was both surprised and angered to find the gates closed against him. The Scottish lords, with the Earl of Douglas and Sir Archibald Douglas at their head, therefore courteously conducted him to Haddington 1380.

* Abridged from Dr. Hook's 'Archbishops of Canterbury,' vol. iv., pp. 280, 282.

and thence to Edinburgh, where the Abbey of Holyrood was fitted up for his reception, and many valuable gifts were presented to him. There the Duke remained until recalled by his nephew, King Richard. On his return he was escorted to the borders by a body of eight hundred Scottish spears. Now, all these circumstances, taken together, had given rise to the opinion that he was inclined to turn traitor, and take the part of the King of Scots.

1381. During his absence the insurrection of Wat Tyler had occurred, wherein the King had evinced so much courage and resolution. Tyler's supporters showed their animus towards the Duke on his return by inducing his officers at Pontefract to refuse him admission to the Duchess; and the Earl of Northumberland to exclude him from the castle of Bamborough. They ransacked and burnt his magnificent palace of the Savoy, with all its costly plate and fittings, and blew up the Great Hall. The keeper of the Duke's wardrobe afterwards declared on oath that the plate destroyed would have loaded five carts. To show that theft was not their object, one fellow, who was detected in appropriating some article of value, was thrown, together with his booty, into the flames. Every man was made to swear not to accept a king of the name of John, thus certainly making evident how little confidence they had in his honour or honesty.

1383. The most eminent man in England as a leader of armies at this time was HENRY LE DESPENSER, generally styled Henry Spenser, the grandson of Hugh, the unfortunate favourite of King Edward II. Pope Urban VI., in reward for various services rendered by him, had consecrated Henry Bishop of Norwich. He was now about to undertake a crusade against the anti-Pope, Clement VII., who was acknowledged in France. Everyone concurred in wishing him success, and looked for a return of the days of Créci and Poitiers. He and his army landed at Calais on April 23, it being understood that the expedition was to march into France. The Bishop would appear to have persuaded himself and his followers, contrary to the advice of Sir Hugh Calverley, that, as Flanders had been conquered by France, and was now subservient to her, it would be fully carrying out their object if they reconquered the former country, although the inhabitants were, like themselves, Urbanists. He took Gravelines, Dunkerque, and became master of the coast as far as Sluys. The town of Ypres was next besieged; but, hearing of the advance of the French King with an overwhelming force of 80,000 men, the English were at length obliged to retire, and to return to their own country, as they had been deprived of the assistance of a body of men assembled at Dover ready to embark, who were purposely kept back by the Duke of Lancaster. The Bishop was impeached for misconduct, and the temporalities of his see were confiscated, but restored in 1385 on the application of Thomas of Arundel, Bishop of Ely. The warlike Bishop continued as popular as ever, and the ill-success of the expedition was openly attributed to the selfishness of John of Ghent, who, to say the least, did not regret the failure. A short armistice was concluded with France.

When the truce with Scotland expired, the Duke of Lancaster 1384. again invaded the country, but the expedition was unfortunate. He burnt the huts of many towns, and, it being a bitterly cold March, he cut down forests to make fires to keep some warmth in his men, who were exposed to many privations. In the meantime a party of French knights, under Sir John de Vienne, arrived in Scotland, who were very desirous of having a brush with the English, but King Robert II. desired peace to be kept. On the Duke's return, reports of disloyalty were again revived. When he appeared at the Council, he was accompanied by a number of armed men, saying he had been warned of a plot against him. There is little doubt that King Richard both feared and distrusted him, feelings which his mother vainly tried to subdue.

King Richard took the field in person against the Scots and their 1385. French allies, who had been ravaging the northern counties, but retreated as he advanced. He had with him his three uncles; his two half-brothers, Sir Thomas and Sir John Holland; the Earl of Northumberland; Thomas de Mowbray, Earl of Nottingham, and many others. The force consisted of fully 50,000 archers and as many lances, and 300,000 horses, it has been computed, were employed. The Scots, following their usual policy, retreated before this mighty host, which went on its way, plundering and destroying. The beautiful abbeys of Melrose and Dryburgh were given to the flames; Edinburgh was sacked and burnt, only Holyrood being spared at the request of John of Ghent, who had not forgotten his kind entertainment there. But the army, through their own action, suffered great troubles, provisions became scarce, and multitudes perished for want of food. The Duke of Lancaster advised crossing the Firth and passing into Fife. King Richard said to him next morning, after taking further advice: 'You, sir, may go with your men wherever you think best, but I, with mine, shall return to England.'

'Then I shall follow you,' said the Duke, 'for there is not a man in your company who loves you so well as I and my brothers. If anyone but yourself dare say to the contrary, I am ready to throw him my glove.'

The King, whether acting for himself or at the prompting of others, was wise in his decision. The army was consequently disbanded.

An embassy arrived from Portugal, craving assistance against the reigning King of Castile from the Duke of Lancaster. King Richard was overjoyed when his uncle agreed to go, and half of the supply voted for the year was appropriated to defray his expenses.

The expedition, consisting of 4,000 men, in two hundred vessels, 1386. sailed in May, from Plymouth, under convoy of seven galleys and eighteen ships from Portugal, with the High Admiral in command.

SKETCH III.

FOREIGN KINGDOMS GAINED.

LEAVING John of Ghent and his army to speed over the waves towards the country of which he claimed to be king, in right of his wife Constance, let us look back a little on the events which have passed in the Peninsular, and inquire why Joao I., the reigning King of Portugal, should ask his assistance against Castile.

Alfonso IV., called 'the Brave,' was King of Portugal 1324-1357, and by his wife Beatrix, daughter of Sancho IV., King of Castile, had a son, PEDRO, who succeeded him, and, like his two contemporaries of the same name, Kings of Castile and Aragon, bore the name of 'the Severe.'

The great interest, the romance of Pedro's life, centres in his second wife. He first married Constance Manuel, a daughter of the Lord of Villena, who, when she came to Lisbon, brought with her Inez de Castro, her cousin, and close companion, whose superior charms soon won the heart of Pedro, who entertained an overpowering and most unfortunate passion for her.

1345. When Constance died in childbed, in 1345, Pedro might have married his mistress, and ought to have done so. But, though brave and impetuous, he was irresolute. It is possible that he shared the doubts of many as to the legitimacy of Inez herself, which would
1354. have been a bar to her ascending the throne. Nine years later he did marry her, in the presence of the Bishop of Guarda and many other persons.

King Alfonso had in vain urged Pedro to marry again after the death of his wife, who had only left him one son, Fernando, and he was very suspicious about the constant visits of his heir to Coimbra, where Doña Inez was living in the convent of Santa Clara. Stirred up by three enemies of the house of de Castro, who represented to him the possible danger to Fernando through that family, the King weakly consented to the removal of Inez. The three base knights accordingly went to Coimbra during the absence of the Prince, murdered the unhappy lady, and then fled into Castile. Inez left two sons, Joao and Diniz, and a daughter, Beatrix, who married Sancho, a brother of Enrique of Trastamare.

Pedro never thoroughly recovered from the effects of this awful tragedy. He raised a revolt against his father, which was only stayed by the prayers of his mother, and the profession by Alfonso of great grief for the desolation he had brought upon his son.

After a time Pedro attached himself to another lady, Teresa Lorenzo, by whom he was the father of a son, also named Joao, of whom more will be heard as Master of Avis.

1357. When Pedro ascended the throne he made a solemn declaration before the states of the kingdom that he had been lawfully married to

Doña Inez in the presence of witnesses. Then he caused the ghastly ceremony of her coronation to be performed, of which a most interesting description may be read in Miss Yonge's 'Cameos,' second series.

Pedro, like his ancestor Diniz, of happy memory, was on intimate terms with England, and valued the friendship of King Edward III. He was a stern yet just man, meting out punishment to men of all ranks with equal severity, whence he derived his name. He died on January 8, 1368. Legend says that after death, when his body was cold, he revived, sent for his father confessor, to whom he acknowledged several sins which he had before forgotten, and then quietly laid down again. 1368.

Fernando, who succeeded to the throne of Portugal, was a weak, dissolute, yet ambitious man. The year following his accession, on the death of Pedro 'the Cruel,' he claimed the crown of Castile in right of his grandmother, Queen Beatrix. In truth he was justified in so doing, for his title to it was better than that of the daughters of Pedro, or of that King's brother, Enrique of Trastamare ; but, though he was well thought of in some few places, the country generally remained faithful to Enrique. He then offered to marry Enrique's daughter Leonor, having previously been affianced to another Leonor, and ended by carrying off a married woman, also named Leonor, the wife of Dom Joao da Cunha. According to a report given in Froissart, as delivered to the Duke of Lancaster, the lady protested that, being a wife already, she could not become Queen of Portugal, to which the King replied that he would have her divorced from her husband, and then marry her. He acted up to his word ; obtained by some means the sanction of the Bishop of Coimbra, and afterwards had her crowned as Queen.

Enrique, King of Castile, entered Portugal and laid siege to Lisbon, when Fernando threw over his young daughter Leonor. Fernando applied to the Duke of Lancaster for assistance, and offered his infant daughter Beatrix, or Brites, to one of the Duke's younger sons so as to unite their claims to Castile. The Duke was unable to go over at that time, and after some reverses Portugal had to make peace with Castile in 1374. 1374.

Juan I. succeeded his father, Enrique, on the throne of Castile in 1379, when Fernando, espousing the cause of the two daughters of the late King Pedro, declared war against him, and sent to England to entreat for help. It was granted. Edmund, Earl of Cambridge, who had married Isabel, the younger daughter, arrived with a considerable force at Lisbon, where they were received with great joy, and it was understood that the Duke of Lancaster would follow as soon as the disturbances in England were quelled. 1379. 1381.

King Fernando and Queen Leonor lavished great hospitality upon the Earl, and offered their daughter Brites to his son Edward, who accompanied him. The children, not either of them more than eight years of age, were married, and laid together in the same bed, and great festivals were held in honour of the event.

The English and Gascons had been many months in the country without any movement being made against the enemy, except expeditions against some castles on their own responsibility. Their greatest exploit was the capture of the town of Jaffre, about ten miles from Seville, which they burnt, pillaging a monastery close by, and driving off a considerable number of cattle, sheep and pigs.

1382.

At length King Juan of Castile sent to King Fernando to enquire when and where it would suit him for the two armies to meet and decide their differences. The latter fixed upon a spot between Elvas, in Portugal, and Badajoz, in Spain. Fernando knew his forces to be inferior in point of numbers to his opponent, therefore, after they had remained for fifteen days opposite to each other, vainly expecting the Duke of Lancaster with additional troops, he sent negotiators to treat of a peace. Juan consented, on condition that the English were dismissed, and that Brites was affianced to his second son, Fernando, who was then two years old.

The Earl of Cambridge and his followers were naturally indignant at this tame termination to their enterprise, and only regretted not being strong enough to enter upon a war against Castile on their own account. The Earl went back to England shortly after, with his forces and his son—but not that son's bride.

At the end of the year the Queen of Castile died. King Juan then proposed himself as a fitter husband for Brites than was his baby boy, with the understanding that any child they might have should inherit Portugal. In May, 1383, the marriage was solemnized, but Brites only had two children, who died infants.

1383.

King Fernando died on October 20. Unfortunately for his peace of mind, he discovered that the woman he had loved only too well had been for the past ten years notoriously unfaithful to him. He therefore exacted a solemn promise from his half-brother Joao, Master of Avis, that her lover, Dom Joao Fernando Andeyro, whom she had persuaded him to create Count of Ourem, should, as soon as possible, be put to death.

King Juan of Castile was advised to come and assume the government of Portugal in right of his wife, but he only caused her and himself to be proclaimed in several of the chief cities. The nobility were willing to acknowledge Brites as their Queen, but the burghers objected, as they detested Leonor, who was to be Regent, and raised the cry of 'Dom Joao, the lawful son of Dom Pedro and Doña Inez de Castro.' The only effect of this was to ensure the imprisonment of both Joao and his brother, who were at the time in Castile.

Leonor and her lover took possession of the palace at Lisbon, but the Master of Avis, mindful of his late brother's dying request, stabbed Andeyro to the heart on December 6, and his mistress fled to her son-in-law. Joao, Master of Avis, was thereupon declared Regent, and defender of the realm.

King Juan laid siege to Lisbon, but the defence of Joao was so well conducted that he had to retire in a few months' time. One of the defenders who was slain was Dom Joao da Cunha, Leonor's lawful husband, who had returned to Portugal from Castile when she entered the latter country. In order to show of what wickedness a really bad woman is capable, let us finish her story. She had refused—certainly not from religious scruples—a proposition which had been made by some of her friends, that she should marry Dom Joao, but she now allowed her hand to be offered to a certain Count of Trastamare, on condition that he should murder her son-in-law, King Juan, and be proclaimed King of Portugal in his place. The plot was discovered, and the King sent her as a captive to the convent of Tordesilla, where she ended her miserable life in 1386.

After the successful defence of Lisbon the Cortes met at Coimbra, and on April 6 declared that Brites had no real right; that the crown was elective; and, the Infantas Joao and Diniz being out of reach, that the Regent Joao, Master of Avis, should be King. The proclamation was received with almost universal joy. 1385.

The King's first duty was to rid the country of the Castilian invaders. For this purpose he gladly accepted the services of a small body of English adventurers, who, under the command of a squire named Northberry and two others, had recently arrived. He left Lisbon for Santarem, where King Juan of Castile was posted with an army three or four times the strength of his own, which did not comprise more than 10,000 men, all told.

King Joao took up his position round a monastery, in the village of Aljubarota. The battle was commenced by the Castilians about the hour of vespers, on Saturday, August 14. At first they had some success, but before nightfall they were completely vanquished, with the loss of more nobles and other men than at the fatal battle of Navaretta, eighteen years previously.

King Juan was at the time very ill, and so weak that he could not stand without support. His standard and sceptre were lost, and his gorgeous helmet, rich in gold and jewels, and valued at £10,000 of our present money, nearly shared the same fate. It had been given in charge to one of the knights of the household prior to the battle, and he, not being able to find the King, put it on his own head when the fighting was over, and carried it off for safe-keeping to Ville Arpent. It was three days before the costly head covering could be restored to its royal owner, who was at Santarem.

King Joao's throne was now firmly established, and those who had formerly held back took the oaths and paid their homage to him. In the Parliament held at Lisbon, soon afterwards, it was decided to send a message to the Duke of Lancaster that if he wished not to surrender his right to the crown of Castile, he should now hasten to Portugal with a strong body of men-at-arms and archers.

The fleet with the Duke of Lancaster had fine weather for the passage. After coasting the Isles of Wight and Guernsey they made for Brest, in Brittany, which was being blockaded by the French, and having raised the siege, continued the voyage until Coruña in Galicia was reached.

1386.
July.
The army lay for a month before Coruña without being able to obtain admission for the King and Queen of Castile, as John and his Duchess Costança now styled themselves, but the town agreed to act in the same manner as Santiago di Compostella might do. Santiago eventually capitulated, and there the King and Queen, with their three daughters, Philippa, Elizabeth and Catherine, set up their Court, after having offered up their prayers at the shrine of the saint and placed rich gifts upon the altar. The barons and knights, with the men-at-arms and archers, had to find lodgings for themselves outside the town, for the most part in rudely constructed huts, as there were not houses sufficient to accommodate all. Meat and drink were there in plenty—in too great plenty for the health of the men, who indulged so freely in new wine that they were laid up with fevers. In order to give the men something to do, and at the same time to find means of support, Sir Thomas Moreaux and other knights led a body of men to the attack of Rouelles. The town was defended most gallantly by all the inhabitants, men and women, and the English had to retreat when night came on. But when the assault was renewed next day the place was forced to surrender. In like manner Villeclope submitted.

Meantime, an active correspondence had been going on, and an interchange of presents taking place between the crowned King of Portugal and the titular King of Castile. The latter had sent to the former two pilgrim falcons and six well-trained English greyhounds, in return for which he had received two handsome white mules. At length, by the advice of the English councillors, steps were taken to bring about a conference, and the King of Portugal was well pleased to have one. There was as much rigid ceremony in fixing time and place as if, instead of being friends and allies, the two interested parties had been the direst foes.

King Joao was to go to the town of Moncao in Portugal, whilst the Duke of Lancaster, as it is more convenient and more natural to call him, was to proceed to Melgaço, in Galicia, and the interview was to take place on the bridge called Pont de More, which spans the river running between the two towns. The King appeared in the dress which he had worn at his coronation—white satin with crimson lining, and the red cross of St. George, which was the costume of the order of Avis, and on the first day, which was Thursday, entertained the Duke at dinner in a bower covered with leaves.

In the conference next day it was decided that the desultory attacks on Castilian towns should be continued during the winter, and that, in the spring, their united forces should march against King Juan. The King's council then introduced the subject of his marriage, about which they were very anxious.

'Sir King,' said the Duke with a smile, 'I have two girls at Santiago, and I will give you your choice; you may take which of them shall please you best. Send your council thither, and I will return her with them.'

'Many thanks,' said the King, 'you offer me even more than I ask. I will leave my cousin Catherine;* but I demand your daughter Philippa in marriage, and will make her my queen.'

The King again provided a banquet for the Duke and his company. Next day, Saturday, the Duke entertained the King and his attendants at dinner. The apartment was decorated with the richest tapestry, emblazoned with his arms, and was as splendidly ornamented as if he had been at Hertford or any of his other castles in England. When this festival was over, King Joao returned to Oporto, and Duke John to Santiago.

The Duchess Constance was very eager for the return of her husband, and for a full account of the conference. In reply to her questions as to King Joao, the Duke said that he was a young man of thirty,† very agreeable in manner, strong and well made, and, according to all accounts, a valiant man, much beloved by his subjects, who considered themselves very fortunate in having such a king to reign over them. 'I have promised him one of my daughters,' continued the Duke.

'Which one?' queried the Duchess.

'I gave him his choice of Philippa or Catherine, and he fixed upon Philippa.'

'He is in the right,' said the Duchess. 'Catherine is much too young for him.'

During the winter, which in Galicia is never severe, various expeditions were undertaken by the commanders in the Duke's army. Pontevedra submitted to Sir Thomas Moreaux, who took up his quarters with his troops in the town, and was supplied by the inhabitants with wine, bread, and poultry in abundance. Soon afterwards they marched against Vigo, Bayona, and several other places, which all yielded, saying they might as well have the Duke of Lancaster, who had married a daughter of Don Pedro, for King, as the son of Don Enrique of Trastamare.

The Duke and Duchess in the meantime remained at Santiago, whilst King Juan of Castile was at Valladolid, expecting to hear of an invasion of England by his allies the French.

The Archbishop of Braganza and Sir Joao Rodriguez de Sâ, 1387. arrived at Santiago, in accordance with the engagement of the King of Portugal, to receive the hand of the Lady Philippa. The ceremony of marriage was accordingly performed, the Archbishop, by the King's procuration, personally espousing her, in the name of Dom Joao, and

---

* They were, in fact, distant cousins, each of them being seventh in descent from Henry II., King of England. Joao was descended from Henry's daughter Eleanora, who married Alfonso VIII., King of Castile; and Catherine from Eleanora's brother, King John.

† Froissart says twenty-six. Anderson's 'Royal Genealogies' gives April 11, 1350, as the date of his birth.

then they were laid beside each other on a bed in accordance with the usual custom.

On the morrow the Lady Philippa, after a tearful parting from her father and the Duchess, mounted her palfrey. Accompanied by her sister Elizabeth, and that sister's husband, Sir John Holland, Sir Thomas Percy, Sir John d'Amberticourt, and a bevy of fair damsels, she started for Portugal, escorted by a force of one hundred spears and two hundred archers.

Near the city of Oporto they were met by the King and his Court and conducted to the palace. On dismounting, King Joao kissed his bride and all her ladies, and then led her to her apartment.

On the following morning, Tuesday, February 11, the marriage took place in the Cathedral of St. Mary, after which great and solemn feastings were held in the palace. There were tournaments and joustings by day, singing, dancing, and various sports at night, as long as the English remained there. Prizes were distributed after the tilting matches, and Sir John Holland gained the one appointed for strangers.

In the course of a month the King and Queen of Portugal were visited at Oporto by Duchess Constance and her daughter Catherine, and not long afterwards the whole Court went to Entença, which had surrendered to the Duke, in order to be present at a tournament between Sir John Holland and Sir Reginald de Roye, one of the French knights in the service of King Juan at Valladolid.

This Sir John Holland was the second son of Joan, the 'Fair Maid of Kent,' and was now about twenty-eight years of age. He was a hard, rough, and reckless soldier, who, according to his own account, loved nothing better than fighting.

Five or six years after the accession of his half-brother, Richard II., to the throne, a Carmelite friar gave into the hands of the King, at Salisbury, a paper purporting to contain the full account of a conspiracy against his life by the Duke of Lancaster. Of course the Duke swore that the whole was a tissue of falsehoods. In order that the matter might be further inquired into, the friar was placed in charge of Sir John Holland, to be safely kept until the following morning. But when morning came the friar was dead. Sir John admitted that he had strangled him with his own hands, and then caused the body to be dragged through the streets of Salisbury as that of a traitor. It seems possible that, under the impression there might be some truth in the allegation, he thought he would be doing his prospective father-in-law good service by putting such an accuser out of the way, and human life was not much considered in those days. The affair was altogether mysterious, and neither the King nor the Duke was satisfied with this ending. The murderer was arrested, and John of Ghent, not thinking himself safe, shut himself up in his castle of Pontefract. Lord Zouch, who had been mentioned as the author of the paper, denied all knowledge of it. Thomas of Woodstock burst into the council chamber, declaring he would murder any man who should dare to charge his brother, the Duke of Lancaster, with treason. The Princess of Wales by frequent journeyings effected a reconciliation between the King and his uncle. She also obtained pardon for her elder son, on condition of his making a pilgrimage to the Holy Land; but instead of that he went soldiering into Italy.

Two years later he was back again and marching with the army 1385. which King Richard led towards Scotland. Two of his squires had a quarrel with a knight of Bohemia, an attendant on Queen Anne, respecting some lodgings at York. At that moment two archers belonging to Sir Ralph Stafford came up and interposed on behalf of the stranger and guest. During the scuffle which ensued one of the squires was shot. When he heard of the affray Sir John was like a madman, and swore a great oath he would have his revenge. He started at once, with his followers, for the knight's lodgings, but on his way met Sir Ralph Stafford. It was night, and dark; they therefore did not recognise each other until after mutual question and reply. Then Sir John, saying: 'One of your servants has murdered my favourite squire,' drew his sword, struck Sir Ralph to the ground, and went on his way. Sir Ralph's servant called after him that his master was dead. 'Be it so,' replied Sir John, 'better he than a meaner man; thus I am well avenged for the loss of my squire.' He hastened, however, to take sanctuary in the church of St. John at Beverley.

Sir Ralph was a young, handsome, and accomplished knight, not twenty years of age, the eldest son of his father the Earl, and was buried in the church of the village near which he was murdered. Earl Hugh reported the occurrence to King Richard, who declared that full justice should be done, although the culprit was his brother. But the march into Scotland was continued, and for a time the matter had to rest. The Earl submitted to a reconciliation with his son's murderer. In the following year he went as a pilgrim to the Holy Land, and there he died.

The Princess of Wales wept and prayed for four days that her son, the King, would pardon her other—perhaps better-loved—son, and, failing in this, she died of a broken heart at her castle of Wallingford. By her own desire she was laid to rest at Stamford, by the side of her first love, Sir Thomas Holland, in preference to sharing the tomb in Canterbury Cathedral of her more renowned husband, the Black Prince. The King then relented, and pardoned his brother, who soon after married Elizabeth of Lancaster, and accompanied his father-in-law to Castile.

The Duke of Lancaster having made full preparation for the 1387. reception and entertainment of his son-in-law, the King of Portugal, and all his party at Entença, went on the way with a numerous company to receive them, and escort them into the town. Three days after their arrival came Sir Reginald de Roye, with knights and squires to the number of six score in attendance, who were all suitably lodged, in accordance with the Duke's instructions.

The friendly combat was fixed to take place on the following day, and scaffoldings were erected for the accommodation of the royal party, and others desirous of witnessing the prowess of two such noted knights. The agreement was to tilt three courses with the lance, three with the sword, three with the battle-axe, and three with the dagger. In the first course Sir Reginald's lance was shivered to pieces by the force with which he had struck Sir John's visor. Sir John's blow had been equally well-aimed and equally hard, but the effect was different. There was not the same resistance, as Sir Reginald's helmet was so slightly laced that it came off and left him bareheaded. In the second course they again came on at full gallop, and struck sparks from each helmet, but again that of Sir Reginald came off on to the crupper of his horse. The English hereupon called out: 'He does not fight fair; why is his helmet not buckled on as firmly as Sir John Holland's?' The Duke of Lancaster, however, contended that 'in arms everyone takes what advantage he can, and that Sir John might follow the example of his adversary in the matter of the helmet, if he chose to do so.' It certainly would appear to be of great assistance to an inexpert horseman to break the force of a blow by loosening the object of attack. In the third course both lances were broken, neither of the knights was unseated, but again Sir Reginald was unhelmed. The ladies all expressed their admiration of the skill shown by both, the King also praised them very much, as did the Duke, but the English still blamed Sir Reginald. It is not necessary to follow the other courses, in which both combatants bore themselves gallantly, and both, happily, came off unwounded.

The Duke entertained the French knights and squires at dinner, and the Duchess particularly distinguished Sir Reginald de Roye by her conversation. She could not forbear asking 'how he and the other French knights could think of supporting the claims of the son of a bastard to the crown of Castile, when she and her sister were the legal daughters of the late King Pedro.' 'Madam,' replied Sir Reginald, 'we may believe what you say to be true, but, as subjects of the King of France, we are bound to obey him, and he holds different opinions.'

The day after the tournament the French returned to Valladolid, and the King and Duke settled their plan of action. An invasion of Leon was resolved upon. The Duke and his army first took the town and castle of Orense, and there waited the arrival of their allies. The weather was becoming warm, as it was now April. Water and forage were becoming scarce, and journeys of twelve to twenty miles had to be taken to find food for the men and horses. The wine was too hot and fiery for consumption undiluted by persons not accustomed to the use of it, but, in default of water, they were obliged to take it as it was.

The English and Portuguese forces crossed the river Douro by a ford and entered Leon. A slight skirmish occurred with the garrison of Vilapando without loss on either side. But the Duke was dispirited. He saw his troops continuing to suffer from famine and want of water. Fevers and other ailments attacked them; numbers died, and most part of the remainder were confined to their beds. It was a repetition of the experience of his brother, Prince Edward, after Navaretta, twenty years before. The Duke himself was so ill that King Joao recommended his returning to Galicia, as did also Sir John Holland. The latter saw that by the continued sickness they were losing more men than they would have done in any battle, and therefore advised a general disbandment of the army. The King of Castile was approached on the subject, and permission was obtained from him for all the sick to pass in safety through Castile at once, or to remain until their health was re-established, and then to depart.

Thus the expedition ended, and a bitter disappointment it must have been to the Duke of Lancaster. All his hopes, his ambitions, his expectations, annihilated at one blow. And yet, could he but have

'Dipt into the future far as human eye could see,
Seen the vision of the world, and all the wonder that would be,'

he might have been satisfied. He had seen his daughter established on the throne of Portugal, and her direct descendants ruled there until Dom Sebastiao fell on the field of Alcazar, on August 4, 1578.

Miss Yonge, in her Cameo XIV., second series, says rightly: 'Philippa of Lancaster was a Queen who was an honour to the country that gave her birth, and a blessing to her new home. Tokens of her influence and the affection of her people may be seen to this day in the Plantagenet arms in some of the windows of the churches, and perhaps especially in the grand foundation set on foot by her husband in 1404, on conclusion of peace with Castile, of another Battle Abbey—Batalha, as the Portuguese call it—as a thank-offering on the decisive field of Aljubarota.'

Queen Philippa died June 9, 1415, and from her deathbed sent her blessing to her sons, bidding them ever to fight in the cause of God and His Church. She left five sons: Duarte, or Edward—so-called after his great-grandfather—the gallant successor to his father Joao; Pedro, the upright guardian of his young nephew Alfonso; Enrique, the famous maritime discoverer; Joao, the grandmaster of St. James; and Fernão, 'the Constant Prince,' who preferred death in captivity rather than gain release by giving up a Christian city to the Moors. There was one daughter, Isabel, who married Philippe le Bon, Duke of Burgundy.

On the death of King Sebastiao in 1578, Catherine, the daughter of Edward, Duke of Guimarãens, brother of King Joao III., was the next heiress to the throne. She married Joao, Duke of Braganza, who was the descendant of Alfonso, an illegitimate son of King Joao I. The grandson of the Duke of Braganza and his Duchess Catherine was crowned King of Portugal as Joao IV. on December 13, 1640, and his daughter Catherine married Charles II., King of Great Britain.

1387. The Duke and Duchess of Lancaster returned to Santiago for a short time, where he was very low-spirited and so ill that at one period it was reported he was dead. He, however, recovered, went to Coimbra and Oporto, and after a stay of two months in Portugal, sailed for Bayonne, having been appointed by his nephew, King Richard, Lieutenant of the Duchy of Guienne.

Sir John Holland, or, as he must now be styled, Earl of Huntingdon, having been so created June 2, 1387, and the Lady Elizabeth, left Santiago at the same time as the Duke and Duchess, and after residing for a few weeks at Bordeaux, went back to England.

The Duke of Lancaster was highly gratified by a proposal from Jean, Duke of Berri, then a widower, uncle of King Charles VI. of France, for the hand of his daughter Catherine. It was so agreeable to him that he published it far and wide, excepting in England, where he did not think it would be well received. It came to the knowledge of King Juan of Castile, as probably was intended. The King's Council warned him that such a marriage might bring about an alliance between France and England, and that he might suffer as much from the French as he had lately gained by them. They advised him, therefore, to tender his son Enrique in place of the Duke of Berri. Special ambassadors were accordingly sent to Guienne with an offer to settle the quarrel between the families by a marriage between the young Castilian Prince, then nine years of age, and the Lady Catherine, who was between fourteen and fifteen. The Duke and Duchess must have been charmed at seeing the object of their desires so nearly attained. Still, they did not betray any great anxiety, and did not give a decided answer to either suitor for some time.

Finally, the following terms were agreed upon. The Duchess Constance was to waive all her claims upon Castile and Leon, in favour of King Juan, with the exception of two or three towns of which she was to have possession for her life only.

The King, Don Juan, was to pay the sum of 600,000 francs to the Duke of Lancaster as the price of the above-named renunciation, and a further annual sum of 40,000 francs to the Duke and Duchess during their respective lives.

Don Enrique and Catherine were to be married within two months of the signature of the treaty; were to receive the titles of Prince and Princess of the Asturias—the first introduction of such titles—to have certain towns assigned to them for the support of their household; and to be acknowledged as successors to the throne of Castile.

Free pardon was to be granted to all who had taken part with the Duke of Lancaster.

Notwithstanding this alliance, Don Juan stipulated for the preservation of his ancient treaties with France. For this very consistent condition he should receive the highest praise.

FOREIGN KINGDOMS GAINED

The marriage accordingly took place at Burgos, and as Don Juan was accidentally killed by a fall from his horse on October 9, 1390, the Duke and Duchess of Lancaster had the satisfaction of knowing their daughter to be Queen of Castile.

Enrique was of a sickly constitution, but he had a wise brother, Fernando, as well as his wife, Queen Catherine, to aid him, and his rule altogether was wise and successful. When he died the same government was carried on in the name of his son Juan II., until death dissolved it, and Juan himself assumed the reins of government. By his second wife, Isabel, a grand-daughter of Joao I., King of Portugal, Juan was the father of the celebrated Isabella the Catholic, who was thus a descendant of John of Ghent, Duke of Lancaster, and, by her marriage with Ferdinand of Aragon, united the whole of Spain under one head. The youngest daughter of the King and Queen of Spain, was the gracious and virtuous, but ill-treated Catalina, or Katharine, the first wife of that very-much-married King, Henry VIII. of England. They were sixth cousins, but Catalina's descent from their mutual ancestor, John of Ghent, was nearer by one degree, and purer than that of Henry, who came of the Beaufort blood.

Catalina's elder sister, Juana, married Philip the Fair, son and heir of the Emperor Maximilian, and their son was the famous Charles V., Emperor of Germany, and, at the same time, King of Spain.

```
John of Ghent, Duke of Lancaster,              Enrique II. of Trastamare, King of
   m. 2ndly, Costança (ob. 1394),                   Castile, ob. 30 May, 1379.
     dau. of Pedro the Cruel,
         King of Castile.                    Juan I., ob. 9 Oct., 1390; m. Leonor
                                                (ob. 1381), dau. of Pedro IV.,
                                                        King of Aragon.

Catalina, m. 1387;    Enrique III., King of     Fernando, King of Aragon 1412;
   ob. 1418.          Castile, b. 4 Oct.,       b. 27 Nov., 1380; ob. 2 April,
                      1379; ob. 25 Dec.,        1416; m. Leonor (ob. 1435),
                            1406.                   niece of Enrique II.

   Juan II., b. 1405; ob. 1454,        Maria,        Juan II. of Aragon,
m. 1stly, his cousin,  m. 2ndly, Isabel   m. Juan II.    b. 1397; ob. 1479;
 Maria of Aragon;      of Portugal;      of Castile.    m. 2ndly, Juana
    ob. 1445.            ob. 1496.                         Henriquez.

  Enrique IV.           Isabel, m. 1474;             Fernando,
   ob. 1474.          b. 22 April, 1451;         b. 10 March, 1453;
                       ob. 26 Nov., 1504.          ob. 23 Jan., 1517.

    Juana, b. 6 Nov., 1479;         Catalina, b. 5 Dec., 1485;
  ob. 11 May, 1555; m., 1497,           ob. 8 Jan., 1536;
     Philip the Fair; ob. 1506.          m. Henry VIII.

   Charles V., b. 24 Feb., 1500;     Mary, b. 18 Feb., 1516;
       ob. 21 Sept., 1558.             ob. 17 Nov., 1558.

         Philip, b. 21 May, 1527.
```

SKETCH IV.

UNCLE AND NEPHEW.

RICHARD OF BORDEAUX was one of the most ill-fated of our kings. Pity, rather than blame, should, however, be accorded to him. He laboured under many and serious disadvantages. He succeeded to the seat of an able, and on the whole successful, monarch. He was the son of a warlike and victorious prince, the idol of the nation. It was therefore expected of him that he should follow in their steps. It had, moreover, not been taken into account that he was equally the son of the Lady Joan, whilom called 'the Fair,' but who was not overwise withal. Perhaps he more nearly resembled his maternal grandfather, Edmund Earl of Kent, who was a fine-looking, affable, and well-liked, yet rather weak-minded man. He must have been a lovely boy, and, as such, was spoiled by a doting mother and his half-brothers and sisters, who indulged him in every way, and instilled into his mind great ideas of his own importance.

The Black Prince intended his father's stanch friend and his own companion-in-arms, Sir Simon Burley, to have the control of the boy's education. But Richard ascended the throne at too early an age to derive as much benefit as he otherwise might have done from the sage counsels of the worthy knight. He came under the power and influence of his uncles, and his utter ruin was the consequence.

John of Ghent's behaviour towards his nephew has been shown elsewhere. He provoked antagonism till it became a kind of duel between them, ending at last in a better understanding. But with Thomas of Woodstock it was different. He was a coarse, brutal, selfish man, who appeared to look upon Richard as an interloper, and hated him accordingly with a most bitter hatred. He bullied and browbeat him at every possible opportunity, and for slight cause or none at all. With a youth of a mild and affectionate, but sensitive, disposition, such as it would seem probable Richard had when young, there is no surer way of inducing and encouraging lying and deceit than a constant course of looking out for small venial faults, and inflicting punishment entirely disproportionate to the offence. Such appears to have been the action of Earl Thomas towards his nephew, as soon as he had any show of authority. It is not too much to say that to him, more than to any other person or cause, must be ascribed all the vacillation and deceit of which Richard was in after-life guilty.

1381. June. That Richard was not wanting in courage is proved by the well-known facts of his behaviour towards the insurgents under Wat the Tyler. Perhaps he had been stimulated thereto by the action of his mother, the Princess of Wales. She was the first to meet with them on Blackheath, as she returned from a pilgrimage to the tomb of her husband at Canterbury. She purchased her immunity from insult by her ready wit and the distribution of a few kisses to the chief leaders. Next day Richard went down the river as far as Rotherhithe; but the cries and shouts of the multitude assembled there so alarmed his attendants that they would not hear of his landing. Two days later the young King, who was only fourteen years old, rode out, with but few attendants, and those unarmed, to Mile-end, where he met a body of some 60,000 men, chiefly from Essex and Hertfordshire. Their demands were simply for the abolition of villeinage, the reduction of the rent of land, free liberty of buying and selling anywhere, and a general pardon for past offences. These were moderate claims, and Richard had no hesitation in agreeing to them. He promised them also that clerks should at once be employed in drawing up charters to give effect to them. The men then retired, bearing the King's banner. Unfortunately, Wat the Tyler was not satisfied with the charter when sent to him next day. With a band of four hundred Kentish followers he rushed to the Tower. They burst into the apartments of the Princess, who had to be carried out in a fainting state and taken across the river. They next seized the Archbishop of Canterbury, Simon of Sudbury, who had just celebrated Mass, and five or six other persons, one of whom was the King's confessor, and led them to instant execution. On the following day the King, after calling to see his mother, went boldly, with only sixty followers, and met Tyler surrounded by 20,000 men at Smithfield. A parley ensued, but Tyler's words became insolent. He played with his dagger, and placed his hand on the King's bridle. The Lord Mayor of London, William Walworth, therefore struck him to the ground, and one of the King's esquires, named John Standish, despatched him with his dagger. The insurgents became infuriated when they saw their leader fall, and bent their bows to avenge him. Richard would doubtless have been slain if he had not manifested unexpected heroism and intrepidity. Riding up to them alone, he called out: 'What are you doing, my men? Tyler was a traitor; come with me, your King. I will be your leader.' Surprised and cowed by his demeanour, the rebels followed him to the fields at Islington. Meanwhile the news of the King's danger had spread. A large force was collected by Sir Robert Knollys, the Lord Mayor, and some of the City magnates, who went to his protection. Thus reinforced, the King ordered the rebels to disperse at once, and return to their homes, which they proceeded to do, after first kneeling to implore his mercy. Lord Mayor Walworth, Standish, and Nicholas Bramber were knighted. 'Thank God, Madam!' said Richard, on rejoining his mother. 'I have recovered the kingdom which I thought I had lost.' By the end of the month the rebellion was quelled. To that end no one contributed more than Henry Spenser, the Bishop of Norwich, who acted in Cambridge, Huntingdon and Norfolk, alternately as commander, judge, and priest. The King was obliged to revoke the charters he had granted, on account of illegality. He tried, however, to secure the abolishment of the state of bondage in which the villeins were held, but his views were thwarted, as neither the Lords nor Commons would give their consent.

A general pardon to all concerned in the late rising, whether as abettors or opponents, was granted on the occasion of Richard's marriage.

Bernabo Visconti, Duke of Milan, had offered one of his daughters, with a large dowry, as the wife for Richard; but the lady decided upon was Anne of Bohemia, daughter of the late Emperor Charles IV., and sister of the reigning Emperor Wenzel. Her grandfather, on the father's side, was John, the blind King of Bohemia, who was slain at Créci; and for great-grandfather, on the mother's side, she had Casimir 'the Great,' King of Poland. Wenzel never did anything without receiving a 'consideration.' It is not, then, a matter of surprise to be told that a loan was made to him of 18,000 marks, half of which was to be forgiven when his sister arrived at Calais. In due time she came, escorted by Sir Simon Burley, one of the foremost gentlemen of the time, a man of great attainments and affability, who conducted her to England.

The first of the royal family to receive the Lady Anne was Thomas, Earl of Buckingham, who met her at Canterbury.

1382. The wedding of Richard II. and Anne of Bohemia took place in the chapel of St. Stephen in Westminster Palace on January 14, 1382, the bride being a few months younger than her husband. From the first she obtained the title of 'the good Queen Anne,' as it was believed she had been instrumental in procuring the pardon of those connected with the late rebellion, and the title ever after remained with her. She has been called the beauteous Queen, but portraits of her do not convey that idea. The bond of love which from the first held the two together was never loosened. Time only appeared to add to its enduring strength, and Anne's influence, which was great, was almost always exerted in a good cause.

At the end of a week the King and Queen went to Windsor, having with them the Princess of Wales and her daughter Joan, Duchess of Bretagne.

Jean V. de Montfort, Duke of Bretagne, had left his wife in England when he returned to his own country after attending Richard's coronation. Things were in a very unsettled state with him. He had surrendered to Richard, in exchange for an estate in England, the fortress of Brest, which was the only one not in posses-

1378. sion of the French. After the Duke of Lancaster's abortive expedition, King Charles V. annexed the duchy to France—a precipitate act on his part, as all the Bretons now joined in requesting assistance from England to expel their neighbours.

1380. The Earl of Buckingham with an army of 6,000 men crossed from
July. Dover to Calais. Froissart gives a detailed account of their progress, including private combats *pour passer le temps*, but nothing of great

interest took place until, on their arrival at Noyon, news was received of the death of Charles V., on September 16.

The army proceeded to Rennes. The Duke was at Vannes and sent ambassadors to the Earl appointing a day on which they should agree to lay siege to Nantes. Jean never put in an appearance. The Earl, after spending two months before the place, during which many men were killed and wounded, thought it wisest to retire to Vannes. Admittance to the town could, however, only be obtained at the special request of the Duke, and on Earl Thomas promising to depart fifteen days after being requested to do so.

Duke Jean's personal feelings were most probably on the side of England, having lived there in his youth. But some of the chief barons were at that time at the Court of France negotiating for a peace. Finding it would be more to the interest of his country, Jean agreed to it, on condition that his English allies should be allowed to march away unharmed.

Buckingham and his army sailed for England on April 7.   1381

King Richard's ministers were not all selected from the higher classes ; they, however, served him well and faithfully. By so doing they gained his esteem and affection, but if they were rewarded the nobles and ancient families deemed it an injury to themselves, and denounced it as a crime. Such ministers were called favourites, and the opposition aroused against them naturally gave great annoyance to the King.

His chief friend and confidant was a fine, handsome young man, about five years his senior in age, named ROBERT DE VERE, ninth Earl of Oxford. His ancestor, Aubrey or Alberic de Vere, came from the district of the Cotentin with Duke William of Normandy. After the battle of Senlac he obtained from the Conqueror the manors of Castle Camps and Shudy Camps, in Cambridgeshire, together with other lands in Essex and Suffolk. He died in 1088, and was succeeded by his son, another Aubrey, who was created Lord Great Chamberlain by King Henry I., and the office was hereditary in the family for many generations. This Lord de Vere took part in the first crusade. It is related of him that one night he saw in the heavens a star with five points, which was shining upon his shield, and that he therefore adopted it as the cognizance of his family. He married one of the De Clares of Essex, but ultimately became a monk at Earl's Colne in that county, and was buried in the chapel there. His son Aubrey III. was created Earl of Oxford in 1155, and the title remained in the family until the commencement of last century. He also was a crusader and a great friend to the Religious, for whom he built two or three houses in Essex.

Another of King Richard's ministers was Sir MICHAEL DE LA POLE, his Chancellor. He was the son of William de la Pole of Hull, one of the merchant princes of the period, who, in the time of need, had advanced immense sums of money to the late King Edward, in order to save the country from pressing dangers. This money had never been repaid, but grants of land and offices had been conferred upon him, and he had received the honour of knighthood. Michael, his son, had also been knighted by King Edward, and summoned to Parliament during his reign as Baron de la Pole. His merits had been acknowledged after Richard's accession by being called to the Privy Council, being sent as ambassador to some foreign potentates, and on his return named as one of the governors to the young King. In 1383 Richard appointed him Chancellor.

1385.
Aug. 6. On the return of the expedition from Scotland, Richard advanced his two uncles to the ducal dignity. Edmund of Langley, Earl of Cambridge, became Duke of York, and Thomas of Woodstock, Earl of Buckingham, was created Duke of Gloucester. Each of them received, at the same time, a grant of land of the yearly value of £1,000 for the support of their new dignity.

Having thus, as he thought, gratified his relations, Richard now, to please himself and reward his friends, raised their rank. He invented for his friend De Vere a new title, and created him Marquis of Dublin—subsequently changed to Duke of Ireland—with a grant for life of the revenue of Ireland, on condition of paying a yearly sum of five thousand marks into the exchequer. De la Pole was created Earl of Suffolk, with the reversion of the estates of the late Earl, William de Ufford, on the death of the Countess and of the Queen. At the same time Roger Mortimer, Earl of March, was declared heir presumptive to the throne as grandson of Lionel, Duke of Clarence.

1386. However much Richard may have dreaded his uncle of Lancaster, he now lamented his absence, as Thomas of Gloucester, who had been held in check by him, now increased in pride and presumption. He assumed the direction of affairs, encouraged the discontent of the nobility, and left to Richard only the title, without the authority, of King.

This was the year of the threatened invasion by France, which never took place. They had collected an immense fleet at Sluys. Richard Fitz-Alan, fifth Earl of Arundel, and Henry Spenser, Bishop of Norwich, with a fleet of about forty ships, captured or destroyed about one hundred and sixty of the enemy's vessels, and landing their troops at Sluys, laid waste the country for ten miles round. Three of the ships which were taken contained the wooden framework of a fortress which Charles VI., King of France, had caused to be constructed for erection when he should land in England. King Richard ordered it to be put together and exhibited at Winchelsea.

In anticipation of the landing of the French, levies had been made, beacons erected, and troops assembled at different points. Orders had at the same time been given to avoid a general engagement, but to lay the country waste before the enemy, according to the tactics of the late King Charles V., of France. The Duke of Gloucester seized the occasion to form a plot for the advancement of his own interests and the overthrow of the government. He pretended that the public revenue was turned to the private use of the King's officers; that the

Commons had been impoverished by inordinate taxation—whereas it is a fact well-known that Richard had voluntarily remitted to the people a tenth and a fifteenth which had been granted by Parliament —that the highest classes could not get their rents, and that the tenants had to give up their farms through distress. In short, he was the demagogue of the period, and, as you will see, succeeded for a time.

It was reported that a tax was to be laid upon every fire ; that each one was to pay a noble, but that the rich were to make up the deficiencies of the poor.

Here was a special opportunity to pose as the friend of the people, of which Gloucester did not fail to take advantage. Then, as now, a glib tongue and a plausible manner could easily delude a crowd of men popularly supposed to be the most gullible on earth. He caused it to be spread abroad in London that the inhabitants would be oppressed, and that an account should be demanded of the immense sum which would accrue to the treasury.

The hint took, as it was intended. A deputation of citizens waited upon the Duke and entreated him to institute an enquiry into the expenditure of the country and find a remedy for existing abuses.

The Duke received them very graciously. ' If you wish,' said he, ' to see your grievances redressed, you should confederate with other towns ; also with some nobles and prelates ; then go to the King, where I and my brother of York will advocate your cause.'

In response to a request as to the form in which they should address King Richard on the occasion, Gloucester said that a speech to the following effect would answer the purpose : ' Your Majesty was crowned young and have had ill advisers to counsel you. Things have gone wrong. We pray therefore that the people who now complain may receive their just rights. We pray that the doings of your counsellors may be looked into by means of your Parliament, that those who have done well may hold their places, but that such as have done ill may be removed, with your assent, that of your uncles and the lords of the kingdom.'

The Duke then continued : ' When you have made your remonstrance, if the King should say, " We will consider of it," cut the matter short—say boldly the country will suffer it no longer. The Archbishop of Canterbury, the Earls of Arundel, Salisbury and Northumberland, besides my brother and myself, will be with the King. Should we not be present, say nothing, for we are the principal personages in England, and will affirm that what you require is only reasonable and just.'

' You have spoken well, my lord,' said the leader of the party, ' but it will be difficult to find the King with so many lords as you have named around him at one time.'

' Not at all,' replied Gloucester, ' St. George's Day will be within ten days and the King will be at Windsor. The Duke of Ireland and Sir Simon Burley will also be there. Do you come, and act according to circumstances.'

The citizens left, well pleased with their reception. As they had been instructed, so did they.

When the day was come, a band of sixty horsemen from London arrived at Windsor, and lodged themselves in the town. Another band of sixty came from York, and a like number from Winchester, Norwich and other towns. There must have been some hundreds who wended their way to the castle gates, and requested an interview with the King. Richard was about to leave the castle, and stayed only at the urgent request—almost equal to a command—of his uncles. The citizens were admitted to the castle and taken to the lower hall, which had been long dismantled and disused, but was the only room large enough to hold the assemblage. Here they found King Richard, attended as the Duke had informed them he probably would be.

Simon of Sudbury—so says Froissart, but it sounds like an assumed name—a citizen of London, was put forward as spokesman. His speech was, as near as may be, a repetition of Gloucester's words.

The King replied: 'Ye Commons of England, your requests are great and important, and cannot be immediately attended to, as we shall not remain long here, and all our council are not with us. Return, therefore, quietly to your homes and remain there until Michaelmas, when Parliament will assemble.'

The men declared that would not satisfy them: they must have an account of the sums collected and expended during the last nine years. The spokesman wound up thus: 'If those who have been your treasurers shall give a just account, or nearly so, we shall be rejoiced and shall leave them in office; but those who cannot produce honest acquittances for their expenditure shall be treated accordingly.' Truly, my lord of Gloucester, you had apt pupils!

The King looked to his uncles for assistance. Gloucester, according to his promise, said: 'I see nothing but what is just and reasonable in the demands made by the people,' and the nobles of his party agreed with him.

A commission to enquire into the accounts was accordingly appointed, and it was in connection with these proceedings that Sir Simon Burley's name was mixed up. Dr. Lingard writes in his history: 'The sequel affords a strong presumption that the royal administration had been foully calumniated. We hear not of any frauds discovered, or of defaulters punished, or of grievances redressed.'

Oct. 1. A Parliament was summoned to meet at Westminster. The session was opened by the Earl of Suffolk, as Chancellor, who informed the House that the King proposed to lead an army into France in support of his claim to the crown, and that, if they approved the design, it would be necessary to supply funds. The Lords and Commons, instead of reply, required the removal of all the ministers, particularly the Chancellor, whom they proposed to impeach as soon as he should be deprived of office.

'At such bidding.' said Richard, with the hasty Plantagenet temper,

'I would not displace the meanest scullion in my kitchen.' He immediately retired to his palace at Eltham, whence he sent orders to the Houses to proceed with the consideration of supply. Here he was waited upon by Thomas Arundel, Bishop of Ely, and the Duke of Gloucester. The latter's bearing and language must have been most domineering, as they forced from Richard the declaration that it would be better for him to acknowledge himself a vassal of the King of France than of a mob. The Commons sending to inform him that, if he stayed away forty days, they should disperse without granting any supply, the King was, at the end of three weeks, compelled to return and dismiss his ministers. The Bishop of Ely was appointed Chancellor, and the Bishop of Hereford Treasurer.

The Earl of Suffolk was at once impeached of high crimes and misdemeanours upon seven different charges. He and his brother-in-law, Sir Richard Scrope, had no difficulty in disproving them. Nevertheless, though he was acquitted on four of the charges, on the other three his answers were declared insufficient. He was adjudged to pay certain fines, and to be imprisoned during the King's pleasure. Gloucester's intention, doubtless, was that he should remain in durance for the rest of his life. The integrity of his career and the honesty of his administration did not suit the Duke's views, who regarded him as an upstart and an enemy to be crushed. The able and trusty Earl was sent to Windsor Castle, which was in charge of the King's good friend, Sir Simon Burley, and, as soon as Parliament rose, he was set at liberty. One of the charges against Suffolk was, that the troops which were levied at the time when the French were expected ate up all the food near London! The three last charges referred principally to grants from the crown, such as when he received his earldom. Now, if he was guilty of anything on this head, so much more so were the Dukes of York and Gloucester.

The new Chancellor, the Bishop of Ely, although called Arundel, was in fact a FITZALAN, and brother of Richard, sixth Earl of Arundel. According to the prevailing opinion at present, we are asked to believe that the noble family of FitzAlan and the royal house of STEWART derive their origin from a Norman soldier named Flataldus. No attempt appears to have been made to show who he was. We must therefore conclude that he was the son of *Nemo*.

Three centuries ago Holinshed wrote, that when Bancho, Thane of Lochaber, reproached the wild women on the heath for appointing everything to his fellow and nothing to him, one of them said: 'We promise greater benefits unto thee than unto him, for he shall reign indeed, but with an unlucky end; neither shall he leave any issue behind him to succeed in his place, where, contrarily, thou indeed shalt not reign at all; but of thee shall be born which shall govern the Scottish Kingdom by long order of continual descent.'

Or, as Shakspere gives it:

'1st Witch. Lesser than Macbeth and greater.
'2nd Witch. Not so happy, yet much happier.
'3rd Witch. Thou shalt get kings, though thou be none.'

Again, Banquo soliloquizes:

> 'It was said
> That myself should be the root, and father
> Of many kings.'

Legend and poetry, it will be said! There is a substratum of truth to most, if not all, legends. The writer's first introduction to the Scottish portion of the subject was 'An Historical Genealogy of the Royal House of Stuarts,' by the Rev. Mark Noble, published in 1795. That to the English portion was 'The Early Genealogical History of the House of Arundel,' by S. Pym Yeatman, Esq., published in 1882. Both works adopt Banquo as the ancestor of the respective families, and as such he will be shown herein.

Bancho, or Banquo, was slain in 1043. His only son, Fleance, fled to Cumberland, and thence to Wales. He gained the love of Gwenta, the daughter of Gruffydd ap Llwyelyn, the King of the country. They had a son named Walter. The King was wroth when he heard of it, believing that no marriage ceremony had passed between the parents, and caused Fleance to be murdered in 1045. Gwenta either shared his fate or was sent to a nunnery.

Where or how Walter was brought up is not known. He is next heard of as slaying the supposed murderer of his father, and then fleeing to England. Having got into some quarrel there with a retainer of Earl Harold, he went over to Bretagne, and put himself under the protection of the Duke, Alain the Red. Now the Duke, it is well known, was one of the commanders in the Norman army at the battle of Senlac, and he took Walter with him as leader of part of his forces.

At this time it seems most probable that Walter may have adopted his father's name of Fleance, either as a substitute for, or as an addition to, his own, such changes of name not being infrequent. The Normans, not knowing anything of such a name, came as near to it as they could in Flaald, and hence Flatellus, or Flataldus.

Ill-luck, however, still clung to him. He was believed to favour the cause of Edgar Etheling, and consequently thought it prudent to go to Scotland. Here he was royally welcomed by Malcolm Canmore and his good Queen, Margaret Etheling. He received a grant of Kyle and Strathgrief; also the Isle of Bute, and the land of Cowal in Argyle. He was further appointed High Steward of Scotland. Walter died between 1093 and 1099, leaving a son Alan, who succeeded him in the stewardship. It may be here suggested that Alan received his name in remembrance of the protection bestowed upon his father by the Duke of Bretagne.

Mr. Yeatman says that 'Alan FitzFlaald was placed in the front rank of the nobility, and was witness at the Great Court of King Henry I. holden at Windsor on the 3rd September, 1101.' Alan appears to have been twice married—to Ameline, daughter of Waryn 'the Bald,' Sheriff of Shropshire, and to Margaret, daughter of Fergus, Lord of Galloway. It is not, however, clear which of the two was the first wife. Neither is it decided whether William or Walter was his eldest son; but Mr. Yeatman shows cause for supposing that Walter was the younger of the two. There was another son, Simon.

William FitzAlan followed his father as Sheriff of Shropshire, and died before 1138. He married Elena, a granddaughter of William Peverel, the illegitimate son of William the Conqueror. Their great-grandson, John, married Isabella de Albini, heiress to her brother Hugh, Earl of Arundel. John FitzAlan, son of John and Isabella, was the first Earl of Arundel of the name. The fourth in descent from him was Richard II., fifth Earl of Arundel, who married Eleanora, daughter of Henry, third Earl of Lancaster, and aunt to Blanche, Duchess of Lancaster. Their eldest and third sons were Richard, sixth Earl of Arundel, and Thomas, Bishop of Ely, who were therefore second cousins of Henry of Bolingbroke, Earl of Derby.

Gloucester's ambition was by no means satisfied. His real wish was to deprive the King of all power. He desiderated a Council, such as had been formed in the reign of Edward II. Richard objected to that, until he was shown the statute by which that King had been deposed. Gloucester then had the meanness to put forward one of his tools to represent to Richard that, if he persisted in his present state of mind, his life would be in danger. Therefore Nov. 19. the King signed a commission appointing a Council, but stipulated that it should only continue in force for twelve months. He also made a public protest, at the close of the session, against anything which had been done contrary to the liberties and prerogatives of his crown.

For twelve months the Duke of Gloucester had the satisfaction of seeing the King's power extinguished.

Richard went into Wales, about Easter, with his friend De Vere, 1387. who was on his way to the seat of his government in Ireland. Thence the King made a journey to York, and one or two to Chester, which was always favourable to him, and ever continued a loyal county. The gentry in the country and the chief citizens in the town were charmed by his gracious demeanour. All gladly mounted his badge, the white hart, and swore to stand in his defence against all enemies. In Shrewsbury and in Nottingham he assembled a Aug. council of judges, and enjoined them to declare whether the acts of the late Parliament were valid; and whether, in face of his protest, he was bound by what had been extorted from him. It is surely to Richard's credit that he considered his oath inviolable without an express judicial declaration to the contrary. The judges, with Sir Robert Tresilian, Lord Chief Justice, at their head, unanimously declared that the commission was subversive of the Constitution; that the introducers were liable to capital punishment; and that all were guilty of treason. Unfortunately, Sir Roger Fulthorpe, Justice of the King's Bench, betrayed the secret to Thomas Holland, Earl of Kent, and he in turn communicated it to the Duke of Gloucester.

It is not easy to understand why Kent should thus take part against his King and brother, unless, indeed, he considered his own interests more nearly connected with those of Gloucester's ally, Richard, Earl of Arundel, whose sister Alice he had married.

Armed with this judicial pronouncement, Richard determined to resume the royal authority, and to indict all opponents for a conspiracy against his prerogative. Sir Nicholas Bramber, the Lord Mayor of London, answered for the support of the citizens, and swore in the different companies to fight, if need were, in defence of the King.

Nov. 10. Nine days before the date of the expiry of the commission King Richard entered London, where he was received with joyful acclamations by the principal citizens, who all bore his colours of white and crimson, and was conducted first to St. Paul's, and afterwards to his palace at Westminster. Here he rested quietly for the night, but, to

Nov. 11. his great surprise, heard next morning that 40,000 men were assembled at Hackney, under the leadership of the DUKE OF GLOUCESTER, with his allies, Richard FitzAlan, EARL OF ARUNDEL,

Nov. 12. and Thomas Mowbray, EARL OF NOTTINGHAM. Next day they were joined by Henry, EARL OF DERBY, the King's cousin, and Thomas de Beauchamp, fourth EARL OF WARWICK. These five noblemen—whose names it may be well to bear in mind—pretended that their only object was to deliver the King from the hands of traitors, who kept him under coercion. They accordingly 'appealed,' as it is called, five of his friends and advisers of treason. Richard, being completely overawed, agreed to hear them on the Sunday following.

Thomas of Gloucester and Henry of Derby were uncle and nephew. But they were also brothers-in-law, as their wives were sisters, daughters and co-heiresses of Humphrey, Earl of Hereford, the last of the great Bohuns. Gloucester had married Eleanor, the elder daughter, and, in his grasping desire of wealth, conceived the idea of devoting the younger, Mary, to a religious life, so that all the Bohun possessions might fall to his children. Without divulging his purpose, he took the advice of his brother, John of Ghent, who had been appointed guardian to the young lady, as to bringing Mary to live with her sister, and the Duke of Lancaster thought it the most natural course to pursue. Little he suspected that Thomas's plan was to surround the young girl with attendants who by every means should endeavour to wean her from the world, and to stimulate a desire for cloistral seclusion. When, however, Henry of Bolingbroke was about eighteen years of age, it occurred to his father that it would be a good thing to have him married, and that Mary de Bohun was just the bride for him. Thomas of Woodstock was at the time away from home, and therefore John suggested to Elizabeth, Countess of Arundel, that she should invite Mary, who was her niece, to visit her, and at the same time Henry went there.

'Happy is the wooing that is not long a-doing.'

Before the Earl of Buckingham returned the young couple were husband and wife.

There was no love or affection between the two men thus closely related, and it can only be surmised that their mutual connection, the Earl of Arundel, kept their ill-feeling towards one another in check.

The Earl of Nottingham was

> 'Of ancient name, and knightly fame,
> And chivalrous degree.'

He was not, however, a descendant of the ancient family of the Mowbrays, the last of whose line was the Earl of Northumberland, so cruelly imprisoned by the second Norman William for over thirty years, and who died about 1130, a monk in St. Alban's Abbey. The Earl's lands, but not his title, had been bestowed some twenty years or more previously by King Henry I. on Nigel de Albini, an uncle of William, Earl of Arundel, who afterwards married the widowed Queen Adelicia.

Nigel's son, Roger, adopted the name of Mowbray. His descendant, John, eighth Lord Mowbray, of Axholme, married, as told in Sketch I., Joan, daughter of Henry, Earl of Lancaster. Their son, another John, married Elizabeth Segrave, daughter of Margaret, Duchess of Norfolk, and granddaughter of King Edward I. This John died in 1368, leaving two sons. The elder one, John, was created Earl of Nottingham in 1377, but, dying in 1383, at the early age of nineteen, was succeeded by his brother Thomas, born in 1367, whom we now find in arms against his King, although doubly related to him, being his seventh cousin on the father's, and fifth cousin on the mother's side.

Now, after this digression, let us proceed with the story.

On the day appointed for hearing the barons, King Richard, in his royal robes, with sceptre in hand, took his seat on the throne in Westminster, where they kept him waiting two hours before they deigned to appear. After most solemn assurances of attachment to the King, they named as traitors Alexander Neville, Archbishop of York, the Duke of Ireland, the Earl of Suffolk, Sir Robert Tresilian, and Sir Nicholas Bramber, and flinging their gauntlets on the floor, offered to prove their words by single combat. Richard decided that a Parliament should be summoned in which the matter might be discussed, and in the meantime took both parties under royal protection. 1387. Nov. 17

The Archbishop was a son of RALPH, LORD NEVILLE, and brother of John Neville, the heroes of the battle of Neville's Cross, October 17, 1346. The family of Neville was, and is, perhaps, the oldest in the kingdom. Saxon and Norman blood is in their veins. They claim descent from Elfgiva, the daughter of Ethelred the Unready, whose third-great-grandson, Robert FitzMaldred, married Isabella, the heiress of the Norman Nevilles, early in the thirteenth century, and their son, Geoffrey, took his mother's name. Their luckless descendant, the Archbishop, fled first to Scotland, but afterwards went abroad and accepted a curacy in Louvain, where he died in 1394.

The Earl of Suffolk fled in disguise to Calais. Seeking entrance to the castle with a basket on his back, as a vendor of fish and poultry, the governor, Sir William Beauchamp, thought it advisable to send him back to England. He was taken to Windsor, but soon afterwards, most probably with royal assistance, made his escape. He died next year at Paris, September 5, 1388—

> 'Unhoused and unfriended,
> An exile from home.'

He had married Catherine, daughter of Sir John de Wingfield, of Suffolk, and converted the ancient residence of the family into a castle, of which some extensive remains still exist. In Hull, his birthplace, he founded a Charterhouse, which was destroyed during the siege of the town, but was rebuilt in 1780.

The Duke of Ireland went, accoutred as an archer, to Chester. He asserted that the Duke of Gloucester's conduct would soon destroy all England, and that the King believed his uncle's ambition aimed at the crown. Armed with the King's authority and assisted by Molyneux, Constable of Chester, he raised a body of 5,000 men in the loyal county and the neighbourhood, and with these he marched southward. Arrived in Oxfordshire, he sent Sir Nicholas Bramber to make enquiries as to the feeling of the Londoners. The Governor of the Tower assured him there was not any prospect of their assisting Richard, unless he consented to be guided by his uncle. When Vere received this disheartening intelligence, he still determined to keep the field.

In the meantime the Duke of Gloucester had a meeting with his associates at Huntingdon. After taking clerical and legal advice on the matter, he proposed to depose Richard and take the crown into his own custody. The Earls of Arundel and Warwick, and Sir Thomas Mortimer, agreed to this. But, to their honour be it said, the Earls of Derby and Nottingham strongly objected, saying that, though they were willing to pursue the favourites, they would not consent to drive their cousin Richard from his throne. The armies were put in motion. Gloucester, with his followers, marched through Brentford and Colnbrook, and took the road to Reading. They found the bridges at Staines and Windsor had been broken down, but contrived by some means to cross the Thames. Bolingbroke aimed for a point higher up the river, and halted not until he arrived at Radcot Bridge, opposite the town of Bampton, in Oxfordshire. Vere found it impossible to cross the bridge as he intended, and, turning the other way, found himself confronted by Gloucester's troops. He was hemmed in. His courage failed him. Waiting for night, he divested himself of his helmet and armour, and plunged on horseback into the river. When morning dawned and these trappings were discovered, it was concluded that the Duke was dead. Short work was made of the royal army. Molyneux the constable was slain, with a few of the men. Many more were drowned, but the majority were taken, stripped to the skin, and left to find their way home as best they could on a cold winter's day—it was the 20th day of December.

The Duke of Ireland fled to the north, and thence embarked for Holland, landing at Dordrecht. The reigning Duke, Albert of Bavaria, ordered him to depart on account of his ill behaviour to his wife. Thus his misdeeds were brought home to him in a foreign country. This treatment of his wife was one of the great causes of offence which Vere had given to all connected with the royal family of England, more especially to his cousin Henry, Earl of Derby. He had married Philippa, the elder daughter of Enguerrand de Coucy, created Earl of Bedford on his marriage with Lady Isabella, the sister of Edward the Black Prince. He had totally neglected his wife, and fallen under the sway of a Landgräfinn of Luxemburg, who had come over to fill some post in the household of the Queen. This lady he desired to marry. Richard favoured his suit, not from any ill-feeling towards his cousin Philippa, but simply because he could never deny anything to the solicitation of his bosom friend. Vere made an application to Pope Urban VI., and, it is sad to say, even Queen Anne committed the one great fault in her life of writing to His Holiness to sanction the divorce and re-marriage. The decree of divorce was obtained, but Miss Strickland says it was not carried into effect. There is certainly no evidence of any second marriage. He had no wife with him when he went abroad.

From Dordrecht the Duke appears to have gone to Utrecht. He was well provided with funds, as the Lombards of Bruges had 60,000 francs in hand for him, part of the ransom of Jean de Blois, and a further sum of like amount was nearly due. This Jean de Blois, with a younger brother, Guy, were sons of that unfortunate Charles de Blois, who, in contending for the rights of his wife, Jeanne de Penthièvre, the true heiress of Bretagne, had been slain by Jean V. de Montfort at the battle of Auray, September 29, 1364. The two boys had been sent to England at the time. Guy died, and when Richard came to the throne, he gave the remaining captive to his favourite De Vere. The Constable of France, Olivier de Clisson, had agreed to ransom Jean on condition that he would marry Marguerite his daughter. Thus it came to pass that, after nearly twenty-five years' captivity, Jean de Blois obtained his freedom, and Robert de Vere had money to support him in exile. The Duke received an invitation from King Charles VI. of France, who wished to obtain some reliable information as to matters in England, to pay him a visit. He accordingly went to Paris, where he was well received, and found a hotel especially prepared for his abode. Here he remained about a year. On the occasion of the public entry of Queen Isabeau into Paris, June 20, 1389, he took part in a tournament, but soon afterwards he received an intimation, at the request of Lord de Coucy, says Froissart, that he had better quit France, which he accordingly did at Michaelmas. The Duke of Ireland disappears from history. We hear no more of him, except that he died at Louvain in 1392, of a wound received in hunting a wild boar. The Duchess was allowed one hundred marks a year for her support.

1387. On the return of the Duke of Gloucester from his expedition
Dec. 26. against the loyal troops under Vere, he caused the issue of a proclamation for the arrest of the 'appealed' lords, three of whom, however, as we have seen, were happily out of his clutches. Eleven of the royal confidants were sent to prison. Ten lords and knights, with three ladies, were dismissed from Court. Even the King's confessor, the Bishop of Chichester, was forbidden by Gloucester to enter Richard's presence.

1388. Now commenced what has been called 'the Wonderful,' and also,
Feb. 3. with far more justice, 'the Merciless Parliament.' As soon as the session was opened, the Duke of Gloucester bent his knee to the King, and complained that he had been accused of aspiring to the crown. Some of the lords well knew how true that was. But Richard at once declared that his confidence in him was unshaken. This answer smacks of the *suppressio veri* on Richard's part. By this time it is to be feared that he was so cowed by his uncle's tyrannical treatment, he absolutely dared not, King though he was, give expression to his true opinion. The five appellees were found guilty of treason. All were condemned to death except the Archbishop, who, being a churchman, could not have such a penalty pronounced against him, but his temporalities were confiscated.

Sir Robert Tresilian was still at large, as was also Sir Nicholas Bramber. One day a travel-stained, poor-looking man, who described himself as a tradesman from Bristol, arrived on a wretched hackney at an inn in Holborn. Here he made all sorts of inquiries as to the condition of public affairs, as also those of the King and his uncles. Next morning he departed. On the same day, but later, a countryman took up his quarters at an ale-house nearly opposite the palace gates at Westminster. Asking if he could have a room, he was shown one where the window looked into the palace-yard. He ordered his mug of ale, and sat at the window narrowly observing all who came to Parliament. He was, in turn, intently scrutinized, and for a long time, by a squire of the Duke of Gloucester. The squire entered the house and asked the landlady who that was in the room above. 'On my truth,' answered she, 'I know not, but he has been here some time.' The squire at these words went upstairs and opened the chamber-door. A closer view convinced him that he had discovered the missing Lord Chief Justice, but he dissembled.

'God preserve you, master!' said he. 'I hope you will not take my coming amiss. I thought you had been one of my farmers from Essex.'

'By no means,' said the countryman; 'I am from Kent, where I hold lands from Sir John Holland, and wish to lay my complaints against the tenants of the Archbishop of Canterbury, who encroach much on my farm.'

'If you will come into the hall,' said the squire, 'I will conduct you before the lords.'

'Many thanks,' replied the man,—'not at this moment; another time I shall be glad of your assistance.'

The squire, after ordering a quart of ale, perhaps to stimulate his courage, took his departure. He hastened to the council chamber and requested instant audience of the Duke of Gloucester on affairs of State.

Coming up to the Duke, he said: 'My lord, I bring you great news.'

'Of what?' inquired the Duke.

'My lord, I will tell it aloud, for it concerns not only you but all the lords here present. I have seen Sir Robert Tresilian, disguised like a peasant, in an ale-house close to the palace gate.'

'Tresilian!' cried the Duke.

'On my faith, my lord, it is true; and you shall have him to dine with you if you please.'

'I should like it much,' said the Duke, 'he will tell us news of his master, the Duke of Ireland. 'Go and secure him, but take power enough to run no risk of failing.'

The squire selected four powerful bailiffs, and bidding them arrest whomsoever he should point out to them, he made his way back to the ale-house. Mounting the staircase and entering the room, he said: 'Tresilian, you are not come here for any good. My lord of Gloucester sends for you.'

'I am not Tresilian, but a tenant of Sir John Holland.'

'That is not true. Your body is Tresilian's though your dress is not.'

The sign was given. The four bailiffs rushed into the house, and soon emerged with the Lord Chief Justice, for it was indeed he, whom they carried through a dense crowd, which had quickly assembled, as far as the palace.

On his being brought into the council chamber, the Duke said to him: 'Tresilian, what has brought you hither?'

'I was sent to learn news.'

'How is this? You do not come dressed like an honest man, but like a spy.'

'If I have done wrong, I hope you will excuse me. I have only done what I was ordered.'

After a pause the Duke said to him: 'Tresilian, Tresilian, your actions are neither fair nor honest; you have committed a great piece of folly in coming to these parts. You and others of your faction have deeply injured my brother and myself. The day of retribution is now come; look to your affairs, for I will neither eat nor drink until you are no more.'

Tresilian was led out and delivered to the hangman, who, after Feb. 19. cutting off his head, hung him by the arms to a gibbet.

Sir Nicholas Bramber had been taken in Wales and lodged in Feb. 20. the Tower. When brought before Parliament he offered wager of battle to his accusers. Such defence was, however, not considered applicable in his case, and he was ordered to immediate execution.

March 6. All the judges connected with the opinion given at Shrewsbury and Nottingham in the preceding year were condemned to death, but their lives were spared at the intercession of the bishops, who begged that a stop might be put to the effusion of so much blood. They were, however, banished to Ireland. Two lawyers, named Blake and Usk, who pleaded that they had merely obeyed the orders of the King, were informed that their defence was but an aggravation of their crime. They were condemned and executed. The King's confessor was also sent as an exile to Ireland, but they graciously permitted him to receive forty marks a year from any friend who would give him so much.

March 12. Gloucester's vindictiveness and his thirst for blood were not half satisfied. Sir Simon Burley, the King's early and staunch friend, together with Sir John Beauchamp, Sir James Berners, and Sir John Salisbury, were impeached as the aiders and abettors of those already condemned. All pleaded not guilty, and offered to prove their innocence in true knightly fashion. The deliberations were interrupted by the Easter holidays.

Surely mercy is the King's prerogative:

> ' 'Tis mightiest in the mightiest ; it becomes
> The throned monarch better than his crown ;
> .   .   .   .
> And earthly power doth then show likest God's
> When mercy seasons justice.'

Richard humbled himself to plead for his valued servant's life. The relentless Gloucester told him that if he wished to retain his position as King he must abandon his old supporter.

Even the Earl of Derby spoke up in favour of the old knight, and was so excessively angry at his intercession meeting only denial and abuse, that uncle and nephew were never again thorough friends.

Good Queen Anne was for three whole hours on her knees before the obdurate Gloucester, beseeching him to spare the life of the first Englishman she had known, the man who had brought about her own happy marriage. All in vain : she could not realize what a sanguinary monster she had to deal with. Gloucester had no mercy. The milk of human kindness was not in his nature. He hated the man, and the man must die.

May 5. After the re-assembling of Parliament, and during a temporary absence of the King, who for three weeks had refused his assent to the proceedings, Sir Simon Burley, Knight of the Garter, Warden of the Cinque Ports, and Constable of Windsor Castle, and three other knights were condemned, on a vague charge of conspiracy against the founders of the late commission of government, and immediately executed. This execution of Burley appeared to affect King Richard more than any of the others. It was indeed one of cruelty, without the slightest plea of justice ; he never forgot or forgave it, and swore it should not be unavenged.

The 'Merciless Parliament,' after a long session of four months, at June 3. last came to an end. It was simply a packed assembly of Gloucester's friends. All the members had taken an oath to stand by the 'lords appellant,' to whom, at the close, they made a grant of £20,000. Their own acts and judgments, they, by special ordinance, declared irreversible. Their very last act was to declare that no judge in future should have power to give judgment of treason by taking the action of the Parliament just ended as a precedent. This was surely tantamount to an admission that they knew all their own acts to be illegal.

For nearly twelve months the Duke of Gloucester was supreme, and King Richard was a cipher.

There is not anything very special to record. The Earl of Arundel had again the good fortune to capture a fleet of French merchantmen on August 9; while, on the 15th of the same month, the English, under Henry Percy, known as Hotspur, were beaten by the Scots under James, Earl of Douglas, at the battle of Otterburn. Ballads under the titles of 'Chevy Chace' and 'Battle of Otterburn,' by both English and Scottish authors, were called forth by the occasion, and are well worth reading.

Richard at length plucked up his courage to confront his tyrant. 1389. At one of the Council meetings, he suddenly enquired what was his May 3. age. 'Your Highness,' answered Gloucester, 'is in your twenty-second year.' As a matter of fact he was in his twenty-third year, and ought to have known it. Gloucester, most probably, was well aware of it, but chose to ignore the fact. 'Then,' returned the King. 'I must be quite capable of managing the affairs of myself and kingdom.' I have been under governors longer than any ward in my dominions. I thank you, my lords, for your past services, but I need them no longer.' The great seal was taken from the Archbishop of York, Thomas Arundel, who had caused himself to be so appointed when Alexander Neville had been attainted, and the keys of the exchequer from the Bishop of Hereford. The remainder of the Council, including the Duke of Gloucester, who retired sullenly to his house in the country, were dismissed.

A new government was formed, with the venerable William of Wykeham, Bishop of Winchester as Chancellor. With him were also Edmund, Duke of York, the King's uncle, and Henry, Earl of Derby, his cousin.

Richard issued a proclamation that he had assumed the government, and that the last subsidy granted would not be collected until he should be certified that it was actually needed.

Holinshed writes that, in July of this year, when Richard was at Shene, flies and gnats swarmed in such multitudes, that they slaughtered one another, and were swept away in great heaps. It was considered a prognostication of evil to fall on the land.

The evil came. Whether the flies and gnats had anything to do with it is another matter.

SKETCH V.

THE PRISONER OF CALAIS.

1390. THE return of the Duke of Lancaster from his Spanish expedition was greeted by the King with the liveliest satisfaction. Richard now looked to his eldest uncle for advice and support against his youngest one. He judged rightly that John of Ghent was not likely to cause him any more trouble. The Duke's ambition was satisfied. If he had not obtained a crown for himself, he had at least the satisfaction of knowing that two of his daughters were queens; and as the price of his, or his wife's, renunciation, he had brought home gold enough to content even a king. But his homecoming was signalized by a bitter quarrel between him and his eldest son, Henry, Earl of Derby, in which the King had to act the part of mediator. Henry thought it best to absent himself for a time, and therefore went as a crusader to Prussia, where he remained about a year.

As a further mark of esteem, the King created his uncle John Duke of Aquitaine, and granted to him and his heirs the whole rights, rents and lordships in such manner as they had been held by his grandfather, King Edward III. Truly a magnificent gift! But the inhabitants of the territory were not willing to submit to this transfer of sovereignty, and Richard had subsequently to recall it.

At the special request of the Duke of Lancaster, the King was so far reconciled to his uncle Thomas of Gloucester as to call him to a seat at the Council. It was a mistake. There could never be any affection between the two. Gloucester could no more alter his malicious nature than a leopard can change its spots. The injuries which Richard had suffered at his uncle's hands were too deep to be easily forgotten.

Under Richard's regal authority there was no resort to extreme measures, such as had characterised the rule of Gloucester and the barons. He more strictly kept himself within his prerogative than his predecessor, Edward III., had done.

1392. There was, however, a difference between the King and the city of London. Richard had asked a loan of £1,000 from the citizens, which they refused. One of the Lombard merchants offered him the sum desired. This becoming known, a riot was raised, during which the unfortunate man was seriously ill-used, if not killed. Richard hereupon revoked the charters of the city, declared the people were not worthy of exercising free election, and that a warden should be appointed to govern them. By the mediation of Queen Anne he consented to receive a deputation of the citizens. On their promising to give £10,000 as security for their future good behaviour, he agreed to restore the right of self-government to the city and to pay them a visit.

The royal pair were welcomed with joyous enthusiasm. The Lord Aug. 29.
Mayor and Council met them with presents of white steeds, perfectly
trained and splendidly caparisoned. The handicraftsmen of the city
appeared with all the symbols of their trade. Men, women and
children crowded the streets, which were hung with cloth of gold and
silver, and beautiful tapestry. Bands of music were heard everywhere;
and the conduits at Cheapside and St. Paul's were running with wine.
Presents were also made to both King and Queen of rich gold circlets,
and of tablets studded with gems. Never had the joy and enthusiasm
been excelled, if equalled, but it must be admitted that the people
had to pay dearly for their Council being so ill-advised as to refuse the
moderate loan for which the King had asked.

Richard now remembered his banished supporters. Those of the
judges who survived in Ireland were recalled to England. His
former confessor was promoted to a bishopric in that island, and,
as the revenue was inadequate, a small annuity was granted to
him. As soon as he heard of the death of his friend De Vere, he
created the Duke's uncle, Aubrey, Earl of Oxford, January 20, 1393.
He had his favourite's body brought home. By his special desire
the coffin was opened, in order that he might look once more upon
the face which he had loved so well. The body was afterwards
interred in the Priory Church at Earl's Colne, in Essex. A monument
was erected to his memory, but it perished, with many others, when
the church was destroyed. There is, however, in the parish church
a monument to the Duke's ill-fated wife, Philippa de Coucy.   1394.

This was a memorable year. The intermittent hostilities with May 27.
France were terminated by a truce for four years.

Queen Anne fell sick of the pestilence, and died after a few hours' June 7.
illness at her favourite residence, the Palace of Shene. Richard was
inconsolable for the loss of his beloved wife. He took it so much
to heart as to curse the place where she died, and cause a large
part of the building to be thrown down. It may be added that
Henry V. rebuilt the Palace, and Henry VII. changed the name to
Richmond.

The Queen was buried with great pomp in the Chapel of St. Edward Aug. 3.
in Westminster Abbey, and 'so great was the illumination on the
day of the ceremony that nothing like to it was ever before seen.'
'In order to make all the flambeaux and torches, it was necessary to
send for wax to Flanders.'

The ladies of England are indebted to Queen Anne for intro-
ducing the custom of riding sideways on a species of bench with a
step to it instead of astride, like men. She is also said to have
brought with her pins, such as are now used.

There was at this time great mortality in the royal family.
Isabel, Duchess of York, had died towards the close of November in
the previous year, and her sister Constance, Duchess of Lancaster,
was carried off in the same month as the Queen, and by the same
fell disease. Perhaps the saddest death of all was that of Mary de

Bohun, the young wife—not more than twenty-one years of age—of Henry, Earl of Derby, who was at the time on a pilgrimage to the Holy Land. She left four boys and two girls, the eldest, Henry of Monmouth, being at the most seven years of age, and the youngest quite a baby, who were taken into the care of their maternal grandmother, Lady Joan FitzAlan, Countess of Hereford, Essex, and Northampton. The Countess of Derby was buried at King's College, Leicester.

Oct. In order to divert his grief, King Richard made an expedition to Ireland, accompanied by his uncle Thomas, Duke of Gloucester; his cousin Edward, Earl of Rutland, son of the Duke of York; his half-brother, Thomas de Holland, Earl of Kent, with his son, another Thomas, and Thomas de Mowbray, Earl of Nottingham; leaving the Duke of York as Regent of the kingdom. The force consisted of 4,000 men-at-arms and 30,000 archers.

The four principal Kings of the island, as they styled themselves, did homage and promised a yearly tribute. They received the honour of knighthood, and were banqueted at the King's table, when Richard, who was at all times fond of show, made a grand parade of all his followers. At the same time he did not neglect the reformation of the government, but gradually reconciled the natives to English supremacy.

1395. March. Richard had often been solicited to marry again. He had no desire to see another occupy the place of his adored Anne. Nevertheless, to please his subjects, he was willing so far to sacrifice his own feelings as to take another consort; but he must be permitted to please himself in the choice of one. Gloucester wished him, pressed him, to take one of his daughters. Apart from the close affinity in blood,—they were cousins-german, to which Richard had, very properly, serious objections—he had no desire to form an additional tie with the man who had before so controlled and ill-treated him.

Although Richard had done all in his power to please his uncle, by calling him to the Council, employing him to negotiate a peace with France, and associating him with himself in the expedition to Ireland, Gloucester was by no means satisfied, and still in his heart nourished great hatred towards his nephew. This refusal to marry his daughter did not tend to allay it. He was jealous of the greater attention paid by the King to his other two uncles of Lancaster and York, and even stooped to make it a matter of complaint that Richard in walking often took his elder uncle's arm. When summoned to the Council, he would go if it suited his pleasure and convenience, but more frequently he stayed at home; when he condescended to obey, he was always the last to appear and the first to depart.

King Richard's wish was, if he must marry, to secure a permanent peace with France by means of an alliance with the royal house. King Charles VI. of France, though nearly two years younger than

Richard, had a daughter Isabelle, then between seven and eight years of age,* and she was the bride selected. Great objections were raised to the match on account of the great disparity in age, to which Richard smilingly replied that every day would remedy her deficiency in age, and that in the meantime she would get accustomed to English manners and customs, whilst he could direct her studies and form her mind after his own, so as to enable her to grace his throne. The truth appears to be that he purposely chose a child in order that some years must necessarily elapse before she could be to him a wife indeed in the place of his lost Anne. He was simply treading in the footsteps of his father, who would rather die unmarried, regardless of the throne, than not have the Lady Joan to wife.

Councils were frequently held to discuss this question of re-marriage, July 12. and about the same time Sir John Froissart, Canon of Chimay, poet and historian, arrived in England on a visit, of which he gives a long account. He brought with him, as he tells us, a book of his poetry on love and morality, written out fairly and illuminated, which he had caused to be bound in crimson velvet, and decorated with silver-gilt clasps and ten studs, all with roses in the middle. After paying his devotions at the shrine of St. Thomas at Canterbury, he went to Ospringe and Leeds Castle in Kent, where he had a short interview with the King, and with the Duke of York, and received a gracious welcome. He followed the King and Council to Eltham, where a meeting was to be held on St. Mary Magdalen's day. On the Sunday July 22. following he was summoned to the King, who desired to see his book. 'I presented it to him in his chamber,' says Froissart, 'and laid it upon his bed. The King asked me what it treated of. I replied, " Of love." He was pleased with the answer, and dipped into several places, reading parts aloud; for he read and spoke French perfectly well; and then gave it to one of his knights to carry to his oratory, and made me many acknowledgments for it.'

An embassy, consisting of the Earl of Rutland, the Earl of Notting- Sept. ham and others, was at length sent over to France, and finally the Lady Isabelle was betrothed to Thomas Mowbray, Earl of Nottingham, Oct. Marshal of England, as proxy for King Richard.

The King's uncles were not all satisfied. Edmund of York, an easy, indolent prince, had never forfeited Richard's friendship and esteem, and never thought of putting any obstacles in the way.

John of Lancaster and Aquitaine had a boon to crave. He meditated marrying again, and taking for his wife the woman who ought to have held that position years before, as she possessed his heart, and was the mother of many of his children. Richard consented to the marriage, and legitimated the children. John therefore approved his nephew's marriage.

The lady whom the Duke took for his third wife was Catherine, daughter of Sir Payan de Rouet, a Knight of Hainault, and widow of Sir Hugh Swynford, of Kettlethorpe, Lincolnshire. After the death

* Born November 9, 1387.

of Duchess Blanche, she had been engaged as governess to the motherless children. She was a charming, well-educated and clever woman. All the children became very much attached to her, and so also did the father. The consequence was the birth of four children, three boys and a girl, at the château of Beaufort, already mentioned, whence they derived their name. They are most important characters in connection with the history of England, and the succession to the crown. The Duchess of Gloucester, and some of the other titled dames at Court, disdained and looked down upon the new Duchess. On the other hand, the young Queen Isabelle found her far more gentle and womanly than those proud ladies, and so grew very fond of her. Catherine, on her part, had dignity enough to hold her own station. She outlived her husband about four years (dying in 1403), and was buried on the south side of the choir in Lincoln Cathedral, but the tomb erected to her memory has been considerably knocked about.

Catherine de Rouet had a younger sister Philippa, who was one of the maids at the Court of Queen Philippa. There she became acquainted with a valet in the household of King Edward III., named Geoffrey Chaucer, the renowned father of English poetry.

> 'Chaucer! our Helicon's first fountain-stream,
> Our morning-star of song, that led the way
> To welcome the long-after coming beam
> Of Spenser's light and Shakespeare's perfect day.
> Old England's fathers live in Chaucer's lay,
> As if they ne'er had died.'

Falling in love, they obtained the consent of the King and Queen, and in 1366 were duly married. After the death of the Queen, the poet and his wife left Windsor for the Savoy, where they entered the service of the Duke of Lancaster and Duchess Constance. Philippa Chaucer died about 1387, before the ennobling of her sister. She had only two sons, Thomas and Louis. The latter died young, but the former lived to become a famous man, and at one time Speaker in the House of Commons. Geoffrey Chaucer was thus brother-in-law to a royal duke, and that duke's son, when King of England, acknowledged the connection. But, one hundred years after the marriage of Geoffrey Chaucer and Philippa de Rouet, not only was the kinship owned, but their granddaughter Alice's grandson was declared heir to the throne by Richard III. We narrowly escaped a dynasty of De la Pole cum Chaucer, with a dash of the White Rose thrown in. The combination might have been a good thing for the country. Knowing what we know, it does not seem that it could possibly have been worse than the Tudor tyranny under which the nation had to groan. But Henry of Richmond barred the way. This Henry was great-great-grandson of John of Ghent and Catherine de Rouet. Now the house of York, against which Henry was contending, had also Beaufort blood in their veins, for Joan, the only daughter of the Duke of Lancaster's third marriage, became the wife of Ralph Neville, first Earl of Westmorland, and their daughter Cicely—the 'Rose of Raby' or 'Proud Cis'—as wife of Richard, Duke of York, was the mother of Kings Edward IV. and Richard III. But, more than all, by the marriage of Joan, the daughter of John Beaufort, first Earl of Somerset, with James I., King of Scotland, the Beaufort blood was mingled with the Stewart for the first time, and to this day runs in the veins of our royal family.

Thomas of Gloucester was, as usual, the stumbling-block in his nephew's way. He did all that lay in his power, by appealing to the prejudices of the nation, to oppose the match. He frequently, but vainly, endeavoured to draw York over to his way of thinking. With Lancaster, however, he never even dared to mention such a matter.

Valeran Count de St. Pol, who had married Maud Holland, Richard's half-sister, and widow of Hugh de Courtenay, came over about this time. To him the King admitted that Gloucester was violently opposed to the match with France, saying: 'He leads Londoners as he will, and may attempt to stir up another rebellion against me; he has also other barons with him of the same mind as himself.' St. Pol's advice was in effect: 'Speak him fair, and grease his palm.'

So said, so done. Richard gave his uncle 50,000 nobles, and promised to his son Humphrey the Earldom of Rochester, with an income of £2,000. When the marriage was solemnized the Duke also received many handsome presents from the French. Filthy lucre caught him.

> 'The jingling of the guinea helps the hurt that honour feels,'

and Gloucester's opposition was then withdrawn.

A treaty was at length signed. It was agreed that 300,000 francs should be paid to Richard in gold, and 500,000 in five yearly instalments; that the issue of the marriage should not have any claim, through the mother, to the crown of France; and that, should the King die before Isabelle reached her twelfth year, she should be sent back with all her personal property, which was considerable, and so much of the 500,000 francs as had been already paid. The truce already existing was prolonged for twenty-eight years and made to include the respective allies. *1396. March 9.*

On All Saints' Day, which this year fell on a Tuesday, Richard, King of England, and Lady Isabelle of France, were married in the church of St. Nicholas at Calais by Thomas Arundel, Archbishop of Canterbury, he having been translated to that See from York on the death of William Courtenay the preceding 31st of July. *Nov. 1.*

Richard of Bordeaux was one of the handsomest of a handsome line. He was above the middle size, well made, and had a ruddy complexion, with the long fair hair of his race. He had most gracious manners and refined taste; a soft and winning voice, with a slight lisp in it. In elegance and attractiveness he was far superior to any of the rough, rude barons of the period. Considering the

5

manner in which his education had been carried on, he was well informed. He was fond of poetry and music, and would occasionally chant a psalm in church. As a companion he was most agreeable, and would enliven the conversation with occasional flashes of wit. Good-natured he certainly was, and devoted to his friends. Perhaps a little too much so, as he invariably believed everything they told him. Had he not been wanting in self-confidence he would not so easily have allowed himself to be led by them. His temper was hasty, but he was irresolute and procrastinating. Above all, he was pure in life, although Hardyng describes his court as being most corrupt. His great taste led him perhaps into too much indulgence in dress, for it is acknowledged that he was the greatest of fops, amidst universal foppery. His household is also said to have been conducted on a most lavish scale, but he never, on that account, called for assistance from his subjects, as many of his predecessors had done.

If his nature changed and he became, as his enemies say, irascible, false, vindictive, and untrue to his word, let it be remembered how he had been, to put it mildly, coerced and constrained in every way, first by his uncle of Lancaster, but, above all, by him of Gloucester. He would have been something more than human if, when he really felt his power, he did not desire to repay in kind all the cruel murders and other punishments inflicted on his friends and those who had stood up for his rights, for truth, and justice.

Isabelle of Valois had all the virtues of her father, without his weakness of mind, and all the great beauty of her mother, Queen Isabeau, without any taint of the dissoluteness for which that queen was, in after years, only too noted. She had raven tresses, and large black, brilliant eyes, traces of the Italian blood which ran in her mother's veins.

There is one little anecdote worth recording as showing the precociousness of the child. When the Embassy first went to Paris they had an audience of the Queen and her children. The Earl of Nottingham, Marshal of England, knelt before Isabelle, saying: ' Madam, if it please God, you shall be our lady and Queen.' Without prompting, she replied at once: ' My lord, if it please God, and my lord and father, that I be Queen of England I shall be well pleased, for I have been told that I shall then be a great lady.' Then, taking the Marshal by the hand, she led him to Queen Isabeau, her mother, who was much pleased at her answer, as were all who heard it.

The King and Queen arrived at Dover on November 4, and went afterwards to Eltham, where they stayed a week. The public entry into London was made on the 13th, when such multitudes flocked to see their new little Queen that, most unfortunately, nine people were crushed to death. The City Council made her several rich presents. The coronation took place on the first Sunday after Epiphany.

Windsor was Isabelle's chief residence, and Richard spent as much time with her as he possibly could; to a certain extent superintending her education. He treated her with the utmost deference as Queen. At the same time he played and sang to her, kissed and fondled her, calling her his little wife. Thus he entirely won her young heart, and she never forgot him.

Those halcyon days were, however, not of long continuance. Gloucester was as much opposed to the King as ever. He inveighed against the peace with France, choosing to ignore the one good act of his life, the negotiation of a truce in 1393. Perhaps he was ashamed of having thus, if only for once, deserted his path of faction, unreason and injustice. He took the occasion of a visit of the Count of St. Pol to England to insinuate that Richard intended to surrender Calais to the French, and stirred up the Londoners to a tumult, which was only put down with considerable difficulty. He affected to lament the King's pusillanimity, stating that he was only fit for the society of ladies and bishops.

It was convenient for him to forget Richard's early display of valour with the insurgents in London, and his march to Scotland. He himself had certainly no deeds of valour whereof to boast. Once, indeed, he had made an inglorious incursion into Brittany. Once, in emulation of his nephew, Henry, Earl of Derby, he embarked to join in the crusade against the Prussians. But his courage failed him: in a very few days he returned, declaring he had been driven back by a storm, and he never tried again.

Not open fighting, but secret plotting was the delight and occupation of Thomas of Gloucester, who was

> 'Luxurious, avaricious, false, deceitful,
> Sudden, malicious, smacking of every sin
> That has a name.'

He stirred up the citizens of London to go to the King at Eltham and demand the abolishment of all taxes, seeing that they could not be needed now that a long peace with France had been settled. The Duke of Lancaster was, happily, present. He, by his reasoning and calm exhortations, managed to satisfy the people that no alteration was then possible.

Gloucester's machinations now reached a climax. At Arundel Castle he had a meeting with the Archbishop of Canterbury, his brother Richard Fitz-Alan, sixth Earl of Arundel; Henry, Earl of Derby; Thomas Mowbray, Earl of Nottingham and Earl Marshal; Thomas Beauchamp, fourth Earl of Warwick; the Abbot of St. Albans and the Prior of Westminster. 'They sware to each other to be assistant in all such matters as they should determine; and therewith received the Sacrament at the hands of the Archbishop, who celebrated Mass before them the following morning, which done they withdrew into a chamber and fell into conversation together. In the end they light upon this point: to take King Richard, the Dukes of York and Lancaster and commit them to prison, and also the lords of the King's Council they determined should be drawn and hanged.

Such was the purpose they meant to have accomplished in the August following. But the Earl Marshal, Arundel his son-in-law, discovered all to the King.'*

Although the Earl of Derby had had a quarrel with his father, he had been fully reconciled to him and the King, with whom he acted in opposition to his uncle of Gloucester. It is not probable that he would now, without apparent cause, turn against both his King and his father. If Mowbray, who had been for some years on the side of the King, was present, it can only have been that he was the most changeable and malleable of men, or that he purposely came as a spy into the enemy's camp.

About this time, Roger Mortimer, Earl of March, was on a visit to England from his Lieutenancy of Ireland. Him Gloucester invited to come to his castle of Pleshy. There the Duke unfolded to his guest the scheme, in which he said he was joined by the Earl of Arundel, Sir John Arundel, the Earl of Warwick, many prelates and barons, of deposing King Richard, who, with his Queen, was to be put into strict confinement for life, and raising Roger himself to the throne. The young Earl—he was only twenty-three—was thunderstruck at such a revelation, as well he might be, but would not have anything to do with the proposal. He would not even listen to any more reasoning on the subject. But, at the Duke's desire, he weakly promised to keep secret all that he had been told, instead of at once divulging the plot as he ought to have done, and so returned to his office in Ireland.

Richard, having received information as to Gloucester's plots, appealed to his other uncles for advice. 'Have a little patience,' they said. 'We know our brother is the most passionate and wrongheaded man in England, but you need not fear him. He talks of things he cannot accomplish. Neither he nor his abettors can break the peace, or confine you in any castle. With patience everything will be well.' Thus for a time they calmed the King, but, recognising that things were not being well managed, they retired each to his own castle.

It will have been seen that Richard was not a bad man at heart, but a weak one. A young man who has been long subject to coercion becomes a moral coward, and is apt to resort to secrecy and trickery if he resolves upon any project of his own mere motion, without taking other advice.

> 'The smallest worm will turn, being trodden on;
> And doves will peck in safeguard of their brood.'

Richard was now in fear for the lives of himself and Queen, as well as for his throne. He felt that he must either destroy or be destroyed, and so he set to work. Requiring help, he bethought him that Mowbray might serve his purpose, and the Earl Marshal, having his own ends to gain, was perfectly willing to act.

* Such is Holinshed's account. Dr. Lingard does not credit the story, and Dr. Hook, in his 'Life of Archbishop Arundel,' rejects it.

Messengers were sent to Gloucester, Arundel, and Warwick, asking July 8. them to come to Westminster. The two former declined. The Earl of Warwick received an invitation to dine with the Lord Chancellor, Edmund de Stafford, Bishop of Exeter, when he would have the honour of meeting the King. The Bishop's house was in the Strand, not far from the spot where Temple Bar once stood, and the gardens went down to the river. The dinner passed off pleasantly and with apparent enjoyment. But when the Earl was leaving, instead of being allowed to enter his own barge, he was hustled into a boat and conveyed to the Tower. His name is still perpetuated in the place where he was lodged. He was afterwards, for greater safety, removed to Tintagel Castle, Cornwall—

> 'Old Arthur's stern and rugged keep.
> There, where proud billows dash and roar,
> His haughty turret guards the deep.'

The Archbishop of Canterbury was now desired to request his brother, the Earl of Arundel, to come up to see the King. The Archbishop was, however, evidently suspicious, for he enquired what security there was for his brother's safety. 'Pledge him your word,' said Mowbray. But Arundel wanted an assurance from the King himself that the Earl should come and go in peace. It is said that the King took an oath to that effect, and then the Archbishop gave way.

The Earl came up to town, and, after spending one night with his brother, the two crossed the river to Westminster. The Earl was at once admitted into the King's cabinet, but, as soon as he appeared, Richard went out of the room, saying to Mowbray, Earl of Nottingham, who was in attendance: 'Take him away, take him away.' The Archbishop waited at the palace all the morning and all the afternoon. When night came he had to return to Lambeth without learning anything of his brother, whom he never saw again. The Earl, in the meantime, had been kept locked up in a closet, without food, water, or attendance, until, in the darkness of night, he was shipped off to the Tower, and thence to Carisbrooke Castle, in the Isle of Wight.

With the Duke of Gloucester it was necessary to adopt different tactics. Richard went to his hunting-box at Havering-atte-Bower in Essex. From there he rode, with but few attendants, to Pleshy, a distance of twenty miles, and at five o'clock in the afternoon entered July 12. the courtyard of his uncle's castle. Gloucester came out to meet him, and was urged to have his horse saddled at once and proceed to London, there to take counsel with the Dukes of Lancaster and York respecting some trouble which the citizens were causing. The Duke having consented they started on their ride, which was continued until they arrived at Stratford, where stood the bridge erected over the River Lea by the good Queen Maude, the Saxon consort of Norman Henry. There an ambuscade had been laid, with the Earl Marshal in command, and John Holland, Earl of Huntingdon. As soon as the Duke appeared, the men surrounded him, and

Mowbray called out, 'I arrest you in the King's name.' Gloucester cried out to his nephew for help, but Richard went on his way. Mowbray put his prisoner into a boat, carried him to a vessel he had in waiting on the Thames and sailed away to Calais, where the Duke was lodged in the castle, of which Mowbray was captain.

When the disappearance of the Duke became known, it was generally believed that he had been murdered, and the story ran that July 15. he had been smothered in bed. Richard, to allay the public ferment, issued a proclamation, stating that the arrests had been made with the consent of his uncles of Lancaster and York, his cousins of Derby and Rutland and other nobles; and that none of his subjects had occasion to be alarmed on account of the part they might have taken in the transactions of the 'Merciless Parliament.' The noblemen who had approved the arrests now 'appealed' Thomas, Duke of Gloucester, Richard, Earl of Arundel, and Thomas, Earl of Warwick of treason, and the trial was fixed to take place in September.

Aug. It was resolved to take the deposition of the Duke of Gloucester in prison, and a commission to that effect was prepared for Sir William Rickhill, one of the judges. No use was made of it for three weeks, then suddenly, in the middle of the night, Sir William was awakened by a King's messenger, who instructed him to go to Dover, where he would find the Earl of Nottingham. By the Earl he was Sept. 5. taken to Calais, and then had the commission handed to him, in which he was required to examine a man whom he had believed to be dead. Rickhill was a wary man. He declined to examine Gloucester except in the presence of two witnesses. He also advised the prisoner to put his answer in writing and to keep a copy. The Duke's confession in writing was to the effect that he had forced the King to appoint a Commission of Regency in 1386; had appeared before him with an armed force; had spoken of him slanderously; had enquired whether he could not give up his homage; and had conspired with others to depose the King, but added that it was only intended to be for a few days. Orally, he admitted to Sir William that he had employed threats to induce the King to condemn Sir Simon Burley, and this was incorporated in the confession. He protested, however, that since he had taken an oath to his nephew at Langley, on his resumption of his authority, he had always been faithful to him. The confession concluded with a most eloquent appeal for mercy. Very, very humbly and earnestly did the man who had never, when in power, shown mercy or compassion, entreat that such might be extended to him in his extremity. 'As he had sowed, he would have to reap.' Rickhill did not see the prisoner again, but, after a few days spent at Calais, returned to England, and gave an account of his proceedings to the King.

Sept. 16. Parliament met next day, and Richard appeared with a formidable bodyguard of Cheshire men, with knights and squires, all wearing his badge of the white hart. One of the first measures was to petition that the Act confirming the Commission of Regency, passed

1386-87, be repealed; that all who had acted in virtue of such commission should suffer the penalties of treason; and that all pardons heretofore granted to the Duke of Gloucester, the Earl of Arundel, and the Earl of Warwick should be revoked, as being wrung from the King by coercion. The unanimous consent of Parliament was given to these petitions.

The first person impeached of high treason was Thomas Arundel, Sept. Archbishop of Canterbury. He was a ready and eloquent man, and rose at once to give his answer to the charge, but the King, at whose right hand he was sitting, advised him to defer his defence to another opportunity, and he consented. He therefore retired to his residence at Lambeth, where, however, he was under surveillance.

The lords appellants next presented their charges against the three Sept. 18. peers. The Earl of Arundel was the only one to appear. He pleaded not guilty, and offered wager of battle to prove his innocence. Bidden to speak to the facts alleged against him, he said that on two separate occasions he had received a pardon. 'Both have been revoked,' replied the Duke of Lancaster, who acted as High Steward. As the Earl had nothing more to say, the usual judgment for treason was pronounced against him. He was led back to the Tower, and there beheaded the same day. The Earl was much esteemed as a noble and valiant man. His victory over the French fleet, ten years before, was the only brilliant action of the reign. He was a perfect gentleman, of courteous manner, but subject to bursts of passion, like most men of the time. He preferred mild measures when such were possible, but, necessity compelling, he could be very stern. On his way to the scaffold he had his hands loosened, in order that he might distribute such money as he had about him among the people, who always admired, and afterwards much lamented, him. To the last he maintained his innocence. He was accompanied by the Earl of Nottingham, his son-in-law, and Thomas Holland, the young Earl of Kent, his sister's son. 'It would have been more seemly of you,' he said to them, 'to have absented yourselves from such a scene. The time will come ere long when as many shall marvel at your misfortunes as do now at mine.' He was a true prophet. The Earl was buried in the church of the Augustine Friars, Bread Street, and the people, regarding him as a martyr, expected miracles to be performed at his tomb. The King, on the other hand, is said to have been glad to hear of the Earl's death, but to have been ever after exceedingly vexed in his dreams concerning him.

The Earl of Nottingham * was ordered to bring over his prisoner, the Duke of Gloucester. He replied that he was unable to do so, the said Duke having died in prison of apoplexy. The confession, Sept. 25. which had been taken by Sir William Rickhill, was therefore read in Parliament, and the lords appellants hereupon demanded judgment, in which they were seconded by the Commons. By the mouth of

* From this it does not seem probable that Nottingham could have been present at Arundel's execution. All transactions in this reign are variously related.

the Duke of Lancaster, Thomas of Woodstock, Duke of Gloucester and Aumerle, Earl of Buckingham, Essex and Northampton, and Lord of Holderness, was declared a traitor, and all his property confiscated to the crown. The body was embalmed, sent over to England, and buried in the church at Pleshy, which the Duke had founded; but there is nothing left to indicate his resting-place, although there are many tombs which are supposed to be those of the family. Holinshed says the body was removed to St. Paul's. He was only forty-two years of age. There is a monument to the Duke in St. Edward's Chapel in Westminster Abbey.

Several years later, when Henry IV. was on the throne, a confession was put forth, said to have been made by one John Hall, a servant of the Earl Marshal. According to this paper, Hall, with a valet of Edward, Earl of Rutland, and two or three other persons, had smothered the Duke of Gloucester between feather beds, some time in September. As soon as the paper had been read, Hall was executed, without having undergone any examination. None of the men named as accomplices were so much as questioned, nor was the master of the principal one. It will be remembered that Henry, Earl of Derby, was one of the appellant lords against the Duke of Gloucester, but now that he was King it suited his purpose to try and blacken the character of the cousin whose throne he had usurped.

When Gloucester had been condemned, judgment was prayed against the Primate. King Richard declared that the Archbishop had confessed that he was mistaken, and had erred in the exercise of the commission, and had thrown himself on the royal mercy. Sentence was therefore given that he should be banished for life, and that his temporalities should be forfeited to the crown.

Thomas Arundel, as Archbishop of York, had had the great seal confided to him on the retirement of the Bishop of Winchester, William of Wykeham, September 27, 1391, and kept it for five years, until he was called to the Primacy of England. Richard, by his present action, made an irreconcilable enemy of a man who subsequently did more than any other, in a quiet way, to overthrow him.

Sept. 28. The Earl of Warwick, when brought to the bar of the House, pleaded guilty. Sentence of death was passed upon him, but it was commuted into exile in the Isle of Man, with deprivation of his estates.

Thus three of those lords who had 'appealed' the favourites ten years before received their punishment.

Sept. 29. Now came a shower of promotions. The King's cousin Henry, Earl of Derby, became Duke of Hereford, and Edward, Earl of Rutland, Duke of Albemarle; John Holland, Earl of Huntingdon, the King's brother, became Duke of Exeter, and Thomas Holland, Earl of Kent, his nephew, Duke of Surrey; Thomas de Mowbray, Earl of Nottingham and Earl Marshal, was created Duke of Norfolk; Thomas le Despenser received the title Earl of Gloucester; John de

Beaufort, son of John of Ghent, who had been created Earl of Somerset in February, was now advanced to the dignity of Marquis, and was also created Marquis of Dorset, by which title he was known. Ralph, Lord Neville of Raby, was created Earl of Westmorland; Thomas de Percy, brother of Henry, Earl of Northumberland, was created Earl of Worcester; and Sir William le Scrope, son of Richard Lord Scrope of Bolton, was created Earl of Wiltshire. Michael de la Pole, son of the banished minister, was restored to the Earldom of Suffolk.

SKETCH VI.

A COURT OF CHIVALRY.

THE next act in the drama was a display of treachery, duplicity and meanness seldom approached, probably never surpassed. The newly-created DUKES OF HEREFORD and NORFOLK were the only two remaining of the five lords appellants of 1387, and they are the principal characters. The latter, as you will have seen, had, as Earl of Nottingham, been long active on the part of the King, with whom he was apparently a favourite.

As Norfolk was returning one day from Windsor, he overtook Hereford at Brentford. Riding on together towards London, they naturally fell into conversation, and affairs of Court occupied a prominent position therein.

'We are like to be undone,' said Norfolk.

'Why so?' asked Hereford.

N. 'On account of the affair at Radcot Bridge.'

H. 'How can that be? The King has pardoned us, and has declared us in Parliament to be good and loyal subjects.'

N. 'Nevertheless, our fate will be like that of others. He will annul that record.'

H. 'It will be marvellous indeed, if the King, having said so before the people, should cause it be annulled.'

N. 'It is a marvellous and false world that we live in; I know well that, but for myself and others, my lord your father of Lancaster and yourself would have been entrapped and put to death the last time you went to Windsor. This project belongs to the Duke of Surrey, the Earls of Salisbury and Wiltshire, who are drawing to themselves the young Earl of Gloucester. They have sworn to undo the Dukes of Lancaster, Hereford, Albemarle, and Exeter, the Marquis of Dorset, and myself. They have also sworn to reverse the attainder of Thomas, Earl of Lancaster, which would disinherit us and many others.'

H. 'God forbid! it will be a wonder if the King should assent to such designs. He has promised to be my good lord; indeed, he has sworn it by St. Edward.'

N. 'So has he sworn to me, but I do not trust him the more for that. He is attempting to draw the Earl of March into the scheme of the four lords to destroy the others.'

H. 'If that be the case we can never trust them.'

N. 'Certainly not. Though they may not accomplish their purpose now, they will contrive to destroy us in our houses ten years hence.'

The gist of these remarks was most probably divulged to King Richard by his cousin, the Duke of Hereford, as he was summoned before the Council and charged to communicate the whole of the conversation. That he did in writing, and was then enjoined to appear before a Parliament to be held at Shrewsbury. To this Parliament, 1398. which was held January 27, 1398, the Earl of March was especially summoned from Ireland as Heir-presumptive to the crown.

The first proceeding was to declare illegal, and to repeal all the judgments, statutes, and ordinances of Gloucester's 'Merciless Parliament.' The next was to enact that any attempt to invalidate their own doings should be considered treason. The King, it is said, enquired if he could bind his successors, and, when told that he could not, said that he would at least apply to the Pope to excommunicate anyone who should attempt to reverse any act of the present Parliament. A liberal aid was voted to the King, and, in addition, a tax on wool and hides was granted to him for the term of his natural life. Having sat for four days, all the powers of Parliament were delegated to a committee of twelve peers and six commoners, to whom, accordingly, the charge against the Duke of Norfolk was referred.

Before the opening of the session the Duke of Hereford had obtained a pardon under the Great Seal for any treasons or other offences he had ever committed. Not satisfied with that he, on the following morning, threw himself on his knees before the King to crave further grace. 'My liege lord,' said he, 'there have been riots, troubles, and evil deeds in your realm to the offence of you and your royal estate, and in them I know that I have taken a part; not, however, for an evil end, or to displease you, as I did not then know that I was doing wrong. But now, sir, I know it, and confess my fault. Wherefore, sir, I cry you mercy, and beg your pardon.' The King assented to his petition, promised to be his good lord, and announced to the several estates that he had granted him a full pardon.*

March. The Duke of Norfolk had not appeared at Shrewsbury, but he obeyed a summons to attend at Oswestry, and loudly maintained his innocence. Bending his knee before the King, he said: 'My dear lord, with your leave, if I may answer your cousin, I say that Henry of Lancaster is a liar; and, in what he has said, and would say of me, lies like a false traitor as he is.' Brave words indeed! but who was to decide between accuser and accused? Witnesses there were none. Either Henry of Lancaster was, what Mowbray called him, a liar, and

* Dr. Lingard, quoted from 'Rot. Parl.'

also a slanderer, or Mowbray a traitor to his King. The matter was therefore referred to a High Court of Chivalry, and meantime both the dukes were ordered into custody.

The Court, composed of all the principal barons and knights in the kingdom, assembled at Windsor about six weeks afterwards, and thither also went the King. Hereford there not only repeated all his former accusations against Norfolk, but charged him in addition with appropriating 8,000 nobles, which had been sent to him to pay the King's soldiers at Calais, and with being the occasion of all the treasons contrived in the realm for eighteen years.

Norfolk instantly gave him the lie. As to the money at Calais, he said that three parts of it had been duly disbursed, and the remainder, with the consent of the King, he had kept in payment of expenses incurred when he went over to France to fetch the Queen. He acknowledged having once laid an ambush to slay the Duke of Lancaster, but said he had confessed the sin and hoped it had been forgiven him.

The King required that they should be asked if they would, even then, agree and make peace together; but both flatly answered that they would not. By award of the court, therefore, it was agreed that wager of battle should decide the matter; the place to be Coventry, the date September 16.

On the appointed day the lists were erected on Gosford Green, outside the city of Coventry. Edward, Duke of Albemarle, the King's cousin, was High Constable on the occasion, and Thomas de Holland, Duke of Surrey, the King's nephew, acted as Marshal in the place of Mowbray, the actual holder of the office. They entered the lists with a great company of men, all apparelled in silk sendal, embroidered with silver, and carrying tipped staves to keep order.

About the hour of prime the Duke of Hereford arrived at the barrier, mounted on a white courser, barded with green and blue velvet, sumptuously embroidered in gold with swans and antelopes. His arms and armour he had specially obtained from Gian Galeazzo, Duke of Milan.

The Constable and Marshal came to the barrier, demanding who he was, to whom he answered that he was Henry of Lancaster, Duke of Hereford, come to do his endeavour against Thomas de Mowbray, Duke of Norfolk, as a traitor, untrue to God, the King, and his realm. He swore upon the holy evangelists that his quarrel was true and just, then sheathed his sword, put down his visor, made the sign of the cross, and, with spear in hand, entered the lists. Having dismounted from his horse, he sat down in a chair of green velvet to abide the coming of his adversary.

Next came King Richard, accompanied by all the peers of the realm and the Count of St. Pol, his brother-in-law. He also had with him a force of ten thousand men-at-arms, to guard against any unforeseen tumult.

The last to appear was the Duke of Norfolk, who had lodged the preceding night at the castle of his relative, Lord de Segrave. He arrived on a horse with crimson velvet trappings, embroidered with lions of silver and mulberry trees. After making oath that his quarrel was just and true, he also entered the field, saying aloud: 'God aid him that hath the right.' He then sat down in a chair of crimson velvet, curtained with white and red damask.

The Lord Marshal then examined the spears, to see if they were of equal length, and, after handing one to the Duke of Hereford, sent the other by a knight to the Duke of Norfolk. The traverses and chairs were then removed, and proclamation was made by the herald that the champions should mount.

Both, accordingly, were quickly horsed, Hereford being the more expeditious of the two; but while the trumpet yet sounded to urge them on, and before they could meet, the King threw down his warder, and the herald called out, 'Halt!' They had to relinquish their spears, to return to their velvet chairs, and there wait patiently until the King and Council should determine what was best to be done in so weighty a matter. Richard declared that he could not permit the continuance of a combat in which either one or the other of two persons who were allied to him in blood and bore his arms must come to disgrace.

After waiting two hours, sentence was at length pronounced. The Duke of Hereford was ordered to quit the kingdom within four months, and to remain in exile for ten years. The Duke of Norfolk was ordered to leave the realm at the same time, to make a pilgrimage to the Holy Land, and to remain for the rest of his life in banishment, either in Germany, Hungary, or Bohemia. A sum of £1,000 a year was reserved for his own use, but all his lands were appropriated for the payment of arrears said to be due from the time of his government of Calais, and other debts. Both were forbidden to hold any communication with Thomas, late Archbishop of Canterbury, or with each other during the time of their exile. Hereafter, we shall see how this order was obeyed.

> 'You never shall (so help you truth and heaven!)
> Embrace each other's love in banishment;
> Nor ever look upon each other's face;
> Nor ever write, regreet, or reconcile
> This lowering tempest of your homebred hate;
> Nor ever by advised purpose meet,
> To plot, contrive, or complot any ill
> 'Gainst us, our state, our subjects, or our land.'

This was the speech put into the mouth of King Richard by the immortal Shakspere. And Norfolk's last words, addressed to Bolingbroke, who advised him to confess his treasons, were:

> 'No, Bolingbroke; if ever I were traitor,
> My name be blotted from the book of life,
> And I from heaven banish'd as from hence!
> But what thou art, heaven, thou and I do know;
> And all too soon, I fear, the King shall rue.'

The Duke of Norfolk appears to have first gone to Germany, and afterwards to the Holy Land, on his return from which he died of a broken heart at Venice, September 27, 1400.

> 'Many a time hath banish'd Norfolk fought
> For Jesu Christ; in glorious Christian field
> Streaming the ensign of the Christian cross
> Against black Pagans, Turks, and Saracens;
> And, toil'd with works of war, retired himself
> To Italy; and there, at Venice, gave
> His body to that pleasant country's earth,
> And his pure soul unto his captain Christ,
> Under whose colours he had fought so long.'

The line of Mowbray ended with John, the fourth Duke, in 1476. But through the marriage of Margaret, the eldest daughter of the banished Duke, with Sir Robert Howard, all the titles and possessions of that ancient family went to, and still continue in, the noble house of Howard.

Henry, Duke of Hereford, fared better than did his rival. The sentence of ten years' exile was abridged by four years, and it was suggested that, as he had already travelled to Prussia and the Holy Land, he might well spend some of the time in visiting his sisters, the Queens of Portugal and Castile. He parted from the King on apparently very friendly terms, and on landing at Calais received from him a present of a thousand marks. He was accompanied a great part of the way by troops of friends, some going even as far as Dover, where he embarked on October 13, the Translation of St. Edward, King and Confessor.

It is far from improbable—judging from after events it is most likely—that from this time forward the Duke of Hereford cherished ill-will against his cousin, King Richard, and began his crafty course of intrigue by making a confidant of their mutual cousin, Edward, Duke of Albemarle, who, instead of returning to Court, retired to his father's seat at Langley.

The following description of the Duke's departure is given by King Richard, and it is historically true, for Henry, even at that time, courted the good opinion of the Londoners.

> 'Ourself and Bushy, Bagot here, and Green,
> Observ'd his courtship to the common people :—
> How he did seem to dive into their hearts,
> With humble and familiar courtesy;
> What reverence he did throw away on slaves;
> Wooing poor craftsmen with the craft of smiles,
> And patient underbearing of his fortune,
> As 'twere to banish their affects with him.
> Off goes his bonnet to an oyster-wench;
> A brace of draymen bid—God speed him well,
> And had the tribute of his supple knee,
> With Thanks, my countrymen, my loving friends,
> As were our England in reversion his,
> And he our subjects' next degree in hope.'

SKETCH VII.

ROYALTY ACHIEVED.

1398. AFTER the banishment of the Dukes of Hereford and Norfolk, King Richard did not feel himself safe from vengeance. He had a force of two thousand Cheshire archers, who were on guard day and night. In order to evince his great love for, and confidence in, Cheshire and its inhabitants, Richard ordained that the shire should be thenceforward known as the Principality of Cheshire, and he took the title 'Prince of Chester.' The Act was revoked in the next reign. The guidance of the State he entrusted to his own pet Council, which consisted of Sir William Scrope, Earl of Wiltshire, treasurer; Sir John Bussy, or Bushy, who had been Speaker in the late Parliament; Sir William Bagot and Sir Henry Green. 'He assumed greater state than any king before him, and expended large sums of money,' says Froissart.

Hardyng says:

> 'Great hoshoulde helde he, as I can understand,
> Far passyng kynges of any other lande;
> For whiche the voyce on hym rose and name
> Through Christendom he bare then furth ye fame.'

So also William Langland, the author of 'William's Vision of Piers Plowman,' a contemporary of King Richard, commences a poem called 'Richard the Redeless,' which he said in the prologue was

> 'to wissen him better,
> And to meuve him of mysserewle.'

He thus begins the fourth part:

> 'For where was euere ony cristen Kynge that ye euere knewe,
> That helde swiche an household be the half-delle
> As Richard in this rewme thoro myserule of other?'

and goes on to complain that the poor could not be repaid for all which the purveyors had taken from them.

Yet Richard's expenditure was no greater than that of his predecessors, and his demands on his subjects had certainly been less. His character, however, now slowly, but surely and distinctly, deteriorated. He apparently desired to bring his subjects into a state of subjection to himself similar to the one under which he had suffered from his uncle Gloucester. Money was raised by means of forced loans from all who had been in any way implicated in Gloucester's doings or the affair of Radcot Bridge. Blank charters were issued, to which wealthy citizens were compelled to set their seal, without even knowing the sum for which they became responsible. Justice was not properly administered. Bands of highwaymen arose, who molested all travellers, whilst petty pilferers robbed the people generally of their goods in house or barn, and their cattle or grain in field. The fickle multitudes now turned against the King who had formerly been so popular with them. One short year sufficed to undo all the good effected in the nine previous years. The merchants were alienated by the exactions to which they were subjected. The clergy had been previously offended by the favour extended to the Lollards, as the followers of Wycliffe were called, and the nobles were estranged by his adherence to a policy of peace, as opposed to their craving for the possible glory and gain of war. The state of affairs was gloomy, but might have improved if Richard, by an act of injustice, had not set a ball rolling which eventually overturned his throne.

'Old John of Gaunt, time-honoured Lancaster,' died on February 3, 1399. He was only fifty-seven years of age, but men were not as long-lived then as they are now. He is said to have died brokenhearted at the loss of his son; but that can scarcely be the case, for he himself had assented to his banishment, and for long before that had not lived on very friendly terms with him—indeed, he rather sided with his nephew, King Richard, to whom he was a great loss. Richard, however, did not apparently feel it much, though he wrote to inform his father-in-law, King Charles, of the Duke's death, without giving any notice of the event to his cousin. Henry, however, received intimation of the fact from some quarter, and had his father's obsequies performed on a grand scale, in the presence of himself and his attendants, all clothed in deep mourning garments. The Duke was laid to his rest in St. Paul's Cathedral, London, where a fine monument was erected to his memory, which perished in the great fire of the seventeenth century. _{1399.} _{Feb.}

Contrary to all right or reason and to his own promises, Richard now revoked all letters patent granted to his cousin, Henry of Hereford, and the King's officers seized all the lands, rent, revenues, and other possessions belonging to him, on the specious plea that a banished man could not inherit property. To say the least, the Act, although supported by the Committee of Parliament, was one of great indiscretion, but the results were beyond anything that could have been anticipated. _{March.}

These iniquitous proceedings raised a spirit of resentment in the whole nation, from the highest to the lowest, and yet Richard chose that very time to leave the kingdom for Ireland, in order to avenge the death of his second cousin, Roger Mortimer, Earl of March. Before leaving, he proclaimed a tournament, to be held at Windsor by forty knights and forty squires, all clad in green and bearing the white falcon, the badge of Queen Isabelle, who was to be present and distribute the prizes. The entertainment was a failure. Not one of the principal barons was present. Distrust appeared to have affected one and all. His widowed niece, Lady Eleanor Mortimer, he appointed lady-in-waiting on the young Queen, instead of Lady de Coucy, who was to be dismissed for extravagance after he had left. _{May.}

The final parting from Isabelle was in the church at Windsor.

Husband and wife together attended the celebration of Mass, at which the King chanted a collect, and made his offering at the shrine. Arrived at the door, they were presented with wine and confections, of which both partook. Then, taking the poor little child Queen up in his arms, Richard kissed her over and over again according to his wont, and saying, 'Adieu, madame, adieu until we meet again,' he put her gently down and mounted his horse.

Unknown to them, it was a final parting. They never saw each other again.

Having appointed his uncle, Edmund, Duke of York, to be Regent during his absence, Richard proceeded to Bristol. At Milford Haven he and his army embarked in a fleet of two hundred sail for Waterford, where they arrived in two days' time. Three weeks were wasted here waiting, but in vain, the arrival of the King's cousin, Edward,

June. Duke of Albemarle, who was to have brought up reinforcements. At length Richard marched to Kilkenny to meet the Irish chief Macmurrough, who defied the power of England. The King was obliged, as a last resort, to order everything to be set on fire, which was accordingly done; but even then Macmurrough held out, and negotiations which had been set on foot with Despenser, Earl of Gloucester, the commander of the rear-guard of the royal army, came to nothing. Want of provisions at last compelled the retreat of the English forces to Dublin, where, in a fortnight's time, the

July. Duke of Albemarle appeared with men and provisions. More time was wasted, and when preparations were being made for continuing the campaign, a barge arrived with news which caused great grief and consternation.

1398. We must now see how it fared with the Duke of Hereford. His first visit was to Paris, where, contrary to all expectation, he was received with great cordiality. The Court believed, or seemed to believe, that Richard had been deceived in his suspicions regarding the Duke. King Charles VI. was, at the time, just recovering from one of his periodical fits of insanity. Perhaps, if he had been quite in his right mind, so much friendship might not have been shown to a man whom his son-in-law had sent into exile. With Louis of Orleans, the King's brother, Henry appears to have made a special alliance for their mutual support.

The Duke found at the Court a magnet who attracted him considerably in the person of Marie, the King's cousin, and daughter of Jean, Duke of Berri. Although already twice a widow, she was only twenty-three years of age, and must have been possessed of many charms to conquer the heart of the disconsolate widower of Mary de

Dec. Bohun. The lady's father and the King both proved favourable to the suit, thinking it might be of great advantage to Queen Isabelle to have so near a relative at the Court of England, and would, at the same time, tend to strengthen the bonds of amity between the two countries. All things were making satisfactory progress, but everyone had forgotten to consider the sentiments of the King of England.

As soon as Richard heard of the proposed match, he sent over John de Montagu, Earl of Salisbury—nephew of Earl William, who had at one time been contracted to Lady Joan of Kent—to entreat his father-in-law to refuse his consent to such an alliance, seeing that Duke Henry was a traitor to his Sovereign. The Earl was by no means pleased with his commission, but had to comply. He accordingly had an audience with the King and Queen, to whom he delivered his credentials and narrated all which had been enjoined him.

1399.

'Earl of Salisbury,' said King Charles, returning to him his letters, 'our son of England bears too great a hatred to our cousin of Derby; we wonder he has continued it so long, for we think his Court would be adorned if the Earl of Derby were near his person.'

'Sire,' replied Salisbury, 'I can only act as I have been ordered.'

'We blame not you,' said the King; 'execute the commission with which you have been charged.'

The Earl then left the presence and waited on the Duke of Berri, to whom he gave the same particulars as to the King. It was afterwards settled in Council that the proposed match with the Countess d'Eu should not be proceeded with, and Salisbury returned home without seeing the Duke of Hereford at all. The young lady was married in the following year to Jean, Duke of Bourbon.

It was not until a month after Salisbury's return home, when Henry resumed the subject of marriage, that he heard of the Earl's mission. Philippe, Duke of Burgundy, another uncle of King Charles, who had been charged with the reply, then said to him: 'Cousin of Derby, we cannot marry our cousin to a traitor.'

Derby instantly changed colour. 'Sir,' he said, 'I am in the presence of my lord the King, and I must interrupt you to say I never was and never thought of being a traitor. If any one dare to charge me with treason, I am ready to answer him now or at any time it may please the King to appoint.'

'Nay, cousin,' said the King, 'I do not believe you will find any man in France to challenge your honour. The expression used by my uncle comes from England.'

'That,' replied Derby, kneeling down, 'I willingly believe. May God preserve all my friends and confound mine enemies.'

The King caused him to rise, and begged him to be appeased, saying: 'This matter will end well, and when you shall be on good terms with everyone, we will again speak of this marriage. But you must first receive the Duchy of Lancaster, for in this France of ours, as in other lands, it is the custom that, when a lord marries, he settles a dower on his wife.'

So ended the conversation, when wines and spices were brought in.

Henry was living at the Hôtel de Clisson. The house had been built during the reign of King John of England by Peter de Rupibus, Bishop of Winchester, and was thence called Hôtel de Winchester. This name was corrupted by the French into Vincestre, and in after years, by an easy transition, it became Bicêtre, when it was used as a lunatic asylum. On his return to his hôtel, Henry was greatly enraged at this interference with his private affairs, and at the departure of the Earl of Salisbury without his having seen him and been able to call him to account for the insulting accusation which he had brought over.

Whilst brooding over these insults, he received a visit from his second-cousin, Thomas Arundel, the deprived and banished Archbishop of Canterbury, now titular Bishop of St. Andrews, which caused a revolution in affairs.

Arundel had, at first, gone to Rome, but soon retired to Florence, where he appears to have enjoyed himself for some time. When he heard the news of the confiscation of the Duke of Lancaster's property by King Richard, he felt that the hour of vengeance had arrived, and he then sought the man. From Florence he went to Cologne, and there received a request that he would go to Paris and communicate to the Earl of Derby the desire of the Londoners that he should at once return to England to take over the management of affairs. It was an awkward situation for the deprived Archbishop to go to Paris, where doubtless he would easily be recognised, to stir up rebellion against the son-in-law of the King of France. But he was equal to the occasion. Divesting himself of all appearance of ecclesiastical rank, he started in the habit of a simple monk on a pilgrimage. From Cologne it appears that he went to Utrecht, and then worked his way south until he arrived at Valenciennes. Here he made a halt of a few days to rest himself, and then hired a guide to conduct him to Paris.

On arrival at the hôtel the Archbishop was at once recognised by the Duke's retinue, who hailed his coming as a sign that they would soon return to their own country. They eagerly poured into his willing ears a full account of all the wrongs and indignities which had been heaped upon their lord, to whom in turn they gladly announced his coming.

A private interview at once took place in which the Duke doubtless recapitulated all his griefs, and the Archbishop then in return unfolded the desire of the citizens of London that Henry should go over to England as the deliverer of the country from oppression. It is remarkable that Arundel, whilst complaining that no reliance could be placed on the word, or even oath, of King Richard, quietly declared that Henry was not bound by any oath which he had at any time taken to the King. This lax morality of the age was to be applied afterwards in a manner not at that time contemplated. The Archbishop appeared ambitious of acting the part once filled by the 1399. Duke of Gloucester, and reducing the King to a puppet; but he had not sufficiently considered the cool, calculating nature of the man with whom he was now treating. The Duke listened attentively to all that Arundel had to urge, but for long made no reply. He was looking out of a window into a garden below, then in full springtide glory. Perhaps he was weighing love against ambition, or pondering if it might be possible to join the two; perhaps meditating another and final visit to the Holy Land, with an ending to his days at Jerusalem. Who can tell? At length he spoke: 'My lord,' he said, 'your speech requires too much consideration to receive an immediate answer, but I hope some means may be found to redress the wrongs of which you speak.' The Archbishop then made the suggestion, to which the Duke agreed, that the subject should be referred to a council consisting of members of the household. The decision at which the council arrived was, that the Duke had as much right to drive robbers from his dukedom, as the King had to drive traitors from his kingdom. On that principle the Duke determined to act.

It now seemed desirable, either to King Charles or to the Duke, it is not very clear which of them, that the latter should leave Paris. He therefore turned his steps towards Bretagne, but halted at Blois, whence he sent forward one of his knights to enquire if he would be well received by his uncle the Duke.

'Why has our nephew stopped on the road?' asked Duke John the Valiant. 'There is no knight whom I would so gladly see as my fair nephew, the Earl of Derby. Let him come, he will find a hearty welcome.'

After receiving this message, Henry proceeded to Nantes, where Duke John met him, and received both him and his company with every symptom of joy and satisfaction. Although the two called each other uncle and nephew, the only relationship between them was, that Duke John's first wife, who died within six months of her marriage and before Henry was born, had been Mary of England, daughter of King Edward III., and consequently aunt to Henry, as well as to King Richard. Now Duke John's connection with the latter was still closer, as for his second wife he had taken Joan de Holland, Richard's half-sister.

Henry explained the position in which he was placed and asked his uncle's advice. 'You are in an awkward position,' said the Duke, 'but the straightforward way is best. My advice is, trust the Londoners. They will compel the King to treat you better. I will lend you ships to convey you to England, and men-at-arms to defend you from any perils on the voyage.' The Duke was as good as his word, and went with his guests to Vannes to see them embark.

The Duke of Bretagne died on November 2 following, not without suspicion of poison having been administered to him by Margaret de Clisson, the wife of Jean de Blois, Count of Penthièvre, so that before he died he would hear the result of the strife between his two nephews. Of the widowed Duchess, Jeanne or Juana of Navarre, there will be more to tell.

On July 4 three ships arrived at Ravenspur, from which landed July 4. Henry of Bolingbroke, Archbishop Thomas de Arundel, his nephew, Thomas FitzAlan, son of the late Earl of Arundel, fifteen men-at-arms, and a few servants, not forty persons in all. Ravenspur was situated at the mouth of the Humber, close to Spurn Head, and was at that time a most important shipping centre, but it disappeared beneath the sea three centuries ago. It is somewhat singular that of Bolingbroke Castle in Lincolnshire, the place of Henry's birth, there is also nothing left; the last remains crumbled away about eighty years ago.

On landing, they were received with joyful acclamations. The first to meet them and give them welcome were the Lords Willoughby and Roos, and the first place for which they made was Pontefract, the ancient possession of the House of Lancaster, where a faithful number of troops was left. Thence the march was continued to Doncaster, and here, in the church of the Carmelite Friars, in the presence of Henry Percy, Earl of Northumberland, and Ralph Neville, Earl of Westmorland, who had come to join him, Henry took a solemn oath upon the Host that he was only come to claim his father's lands, his mother's heritage, and his wife's, and that he had not any views upon the crown. Henceforward the march was like a triumphal progress, and vast numbers, though mostly undisciplined, joined the invaders. The way was taken through Derby, Leicester, Kenilworth, and in all these places, so intimately connected with his family, Bolingbroke was received with unbounded enthusiasm.

The Duke of York, who received early intimation of all these movements, was not the man to cope with his energetic nephew, if Hardyng's picture of him be correct:

> 'Edmonde hyght of Langley, of good chere,
> Glad and mery, and of his owne ay lived,
> Without wronge, as chronicles have breved.
> When all the lordes to councell and parlyament
> Went, he wolde to hunte and also to hawekyng,
> All gentyll disporte as to a lorde appent,
> He used aye, and to the pore supportyng,
> Where ever he was in any place bidyng,
> Without suppryse or any extorcyon
> Of the borayle or any oppressyon.'

However, he summoned the royal forces to meet at St. Albans, and an army of 40,000 men was assembled; but there was no zeal or heartiness manifested in the cause. Rather was there an inclination to join the rebels. The King's trusted ministers—the Earl of Wiltshire, Sir John Bussy, and Sir Henry Green—fled to Bristol, and the Duke of York, with his army, followed, leaving the road to London open to the invaders.

July 12.

By the time that Henry reached St. Albans, he had 60,000 men under him. Messengers and letters had everywhere preceded him, magnifying his own wrongs, as well as the grievances of the people.

In his letters to the nobility he accused Richard of a design to deliver to the King of France all English possessions in that country for a sum of money to be paid in ten years. At London he was met by rejoicing processions of clergy and people. 'Welcome, long-wished-for Earl of Derby and Duke of Lancaster!' was the cry. 'May all joy and prosperity attend you!' So great was the public rejoicing that every shop was shut, and no more work was done than if it had been Easter Day. Only a stay sufficiently long to add the train-bands to the army was made in London, and then Henry marched westwards. He arrived at Evesham on the same day that July 27. his uncle York arrived at Berkeley.

An interview was arranged to take place in the church of the castle of Berkeley between the two leaders, and York then agreed to join Henry. They marched to Bristol, and summoned the castle to surrender, but the loyal governor, Sir Peter Courtenay, refused to open the gates at the order of the Duke of Lancaster. He had, however, to submit when he received instructions from the Regent, the Duke of York, to do so.

Next morning the three fugitives, Wiltshire, Bussy, and Green, July 29. were, in response to an outcry of the people, without going through any form of trial, sentenced by Henry to death, and led to immediate execution. If anything had been needed to show in what direction his thoughts were tending, this act of sovereign authority must have been sufficient. In truth, it was an overt act of treason.

Sir William Bagot, who had been one of the Council with these three ill-starred men, had the good fortune to escape to Ireland. He was, however, subsequently brought back and committed to Newgate, but was acquitted in full Parliament.

The Duke of York remained at Bristol, whilst Bolingbroke took his way through Ross, Hereford, Leominster, Ludlow, and Shrewsbury to Chester, where he arrived August 8. As a warning of what Aug. 8. the inhabitants of the loyal city might expect, he caused Sir Piers Legh, ancestor of the well-known family the Leghs of Lyme, a devoted adherent of King Richard, to be executed, and ordered his head to be placed on one of the highest towers in the city.

Here he assumed the office and title of Steward of England, which, on October 8 following, he bestowed on his second son, Thomas of Lancaster, Thomas de Percy acting as his deputy during the minority of the Prince.

We left King Richard in despair at the news he had just received from England. It must, indeed, have been startling. It included the beheading of Scrope and his fellow ministers, the taking of castles and towns by the invader, and the stirring up of the people in general to insurrection. The King's face turned pale with anger, while he said to his friends: 'Good Lord! this man designs to deprive me of my country! Ah! fair uncle of Lancaster,' he continued, 'heaven reward your soul! Had I believed you, this man would not have injured me. Thrice have I pardoned him: this is his fourth offence.' Then, turning to Henry of Monmouth, who was his godson, and whom he had but recently knighted, along with Humphrey, son of the late Duke of Gloucester, and eight or ten other youths, he said: 'See, Harry, what your father has done to me. He has invaded my land as an enemy, killed and imprisoned my subjects without pity. Indeed, child, I grieve for you, as this proceeding may perchance cost thee thine inheritance.'

'Truly,' answered the boy, 'the news distresses me; but you will see that I am innocent of what my father has done.'

'I know it,' said the King, 'and I hold you guiltless.'

The young Prince was, however, sent with Humphrey of Gloucester to the castle of Trim for security.

When the Council met, on Saturday, it was decided, at the suggestion of the Earl of Salisbury, that the King should embark on the following Monday.

The Duke of Albemarle, however, judging from his subsequent behaviour, wilfully deceived and betrayed his cousin, the King, by persuading him to wait another week, and let the Earl of Salisbury first go over to collect the Welsh under the Royal banner.

The brave and loyal Earl sailed accordingly, and soon raised a force of 40,000 men from Wales and Cheshire at Conway. But Richard did not appear. Reports of Henry of Lancaster being at Chester, and the King being dead, were rife among the troops, who began to be uneasy, and to wish to depart. The Earl wept and entreated that they would remain yet a little longer. A second week, however, having gone by without any sign of the King's coming, the men gradually disbanded, and Salisbury, with not more than a hundred men, took up his quarters in the castle.

At length, on the eighteenth day, Richard landed in Wales—almost all writers say at Milford Haven, but, judging from after movements, that does not seem possible. It is much more probable to have been at Harlech, in Merionethshire, or, as Miss Yonge suggests, at Holyhead; at any rate, somewhere in the North. He had with him three or four noblemen, as many Bishops, and an army of 20,000 men. This force, though inferior in number to those in the Lancastrian camp, might have done the King good service, but whether from fear of superior numbers or through a spirit of disaffection, it dwindled away, and in two days only 6,000 men remained.

A Council was held, when someone suggested —can it have been Albemarle?—that the King should flee to Bordeaux. To this his brother, John Holland, wisely and strongly objected, 'that such a step would be equivalent to abdicating the throne.' He advised his hastening at once to Conway to meet the Earl of Salisbury, leaving the remnant of his troops behind. This plan was adopted. At nightfall Richard, clad in the gray gown of a Franciscan friar, set out, accompanied by his brother the Duke of Exeter, his nephew the Duke of Surrey, Thomas Despenser, Earl of Gloucester, Sir Stephen Scrope, Sir William Feriby, the famous Welsh chieftain Owain Glyndwr, a firm friend and adherent of King Richard, the Bishops of Carlisle, Lincoln, and St. David's, and four others, and rode all night.

As soon as their flight was known, there was a general break-up in the camp. Plunder appeared to be the order of the day. The King's treasures in gold, silver, and jewels, even his robes and his horses, were divided among the men and their leaders. The traitor Duke of Albemarle and Thomas Percy, Earl of Worcester, brother to Northumberland, went off, with some of the men, to their relatives in the train of Bolingbroke. There is some satisfaction in reading that the plunderers were, in their turn, despoiled of their ill-gotten gains by parties of Welshmen who set upon them and put them to flight.

By break of day the Royal party reached Conway, where a woeful meeting took place with the Earl of Salisbury, whose face was pale with watching and anxiety, and who had his sad tale of desertion to relate, ending with 'All is lost!'

The Duke of Exeter and his nephew undertook a mission to Chester, to enquire the intentions of the Duke of Lancaster in appearing in such warlike array without authority. Bending the knee to him on arrival, they delivered the message from the King. Henry took little or no notice of the young Duke of Surrey, but leading his brother-in-law, Exeter, on one side, he endeavoured to persuade him to join his cause, and substitute his badge of the rose for the white hart of Richard. It must have been a severe struggle for John Holland, who, hard and fierce as he was, could not refrain from tears. Harder still was it when Henry refused to let either him or his nephew return, but kept both under watch and ward, and the treacherous Albemarle said: 'Fair cousin, be not angry. If it please Heaven, things shall go well.'

The King continued all sorrowful with his few remaining friends. Whilst waiting the return of his envoys he went to visit the castles of Beaumaris and Caernarvon. But these he found dreary in the extreme. There was no furniture, nothing to lie down upon but straw, and scarcely anything in the way of food. Such rough living would not suit the luxurious nature of Richard. And we are told by an eye-witness that he frequently appealed to the 'douce Vierge Marie' to have pity on him. In four or five days the whole party returned to Conway, and then Richard broke out into passionate lamentations for his little Queen. 'My mistress and my consort; accursed be the man who thus separateth us! I am dying of grief because of it. My fair sister, my lady, and my sole desire. Since I am robbed of the pleasure of beholding thee, such pain and affliction oppresseth my whole heart that I am ofttimes hard on despair. Alas! Isabel, rightful daughter of France, you were wont to be my hope, my joy, my consolation. Now I plainly see that, through the violence of fortune, which has slain many a man, I must be deprived of you, my joy, my solace, and my consort.' Surely this poetical monody speaks well for the tie which bound the two together being one of love, although the young Queen was not quite twelve years old, and is a proof that, though Richard may have been weak and passionate, he had a good and kind heart. That his dependence was not on his own power was shown in a solemn prayer which he put up to his heavenly Father in that his sore time of distress.

Bolingbroke's great desire seems to have been to get Richard into his keeping. He had heard of the great loss which the King had sustained soon after landing, therefore, to add to his pecuniary distress, he made himself master of two deposits of treasure, which had been made by the King, at Holt Castle, on the River Dee, in Denbighshire, and Beeston Castle, a few miles from Chester. Having thus crippled the King's means, and secured two of his best friends, he next sent the Earl of Northumberland, with a force of 400 men-at-arms and 1,000 archers, by fair means or foul to make him prisoner.

The Earl took possession on his way of the castles of Flint and Rhuddlan. Then, leaving a portion of his men in ambush, he went
Aug. 18. on with only five attendants to Conway. He was admitted without scruple and delivered to the King a letter, professedly from the Duke of Exeter, most probably written under compulsion, in which it was stated that the bearer might be fully believed and trusted. The terms he had to propose were that Richard should promise to govern more strictly according to law; that a Parliament should be summoned before which the Dukes of Exeter and Surrey, the Earl of Salisbury, and the Bishop of Carlisle, should be tried for their share in the death of the Duke of Gloucester; that Henry should be made grand justiciary; and that on these conditions the Duke would come to Flint and, on his knees, ask for pardon.

Richard, in consultation with his friends, said he saw no other way than to agree to the proposal, but that he would never abandon them to their enemies, 'some of whom,' he continued, 'I will flay alive, and would not take all the gold in the land for them if I continue alive and well.'

Mass was then celebrated at Percy's request, and he made a solemn oath on the Host that the terms should be observed. 'Like Judas,' says the narrator, Monsieur Créton, 'he perjured himself on the body of our Lord.' On taking his leave to make arrangements for the meeting at Flint, Richard said to him: 'I trust, my lord, to your faith. Remember your oath and Him who heard it.'

Soon afterwards the King, with his friends and servants, twenty-two in all, left Conway. They proceeded for some time until they came to a steep cliff named Penmaen Rhôs, when the King perceived a large band of soldiers with the Percy banners. 'I am betrayed!' he cried. 'Do you not see banners and pennons in the valley?' Northumberland and eleven others then rode up. 'Earl Percy,' said the King, 'if I thought you capable of betraying me, it is not too late to turn back.'

'You cannot return,' said the Earl, seizing the bridle of the King's horse, 'I have promised to conduct you to the Duke of Lancaster.'

By this time one hundred lancers with two hundred archers had come up, and Richard, seeing that escape or resistance was hopeless, exclaimed: 'May He on whom you laid your hand reward you and your accomplices at the last day.' Then, turning to his friends, he added : 'We are betrayed; but remember that our Lord was also sold and delivered into the hands of His enemies.'

There was nothing more that could be said or done—the King was a prisoner. After dinner, which was served at Rhuddlan, the march was continued to Flint, where they arrived in the evening. The King was too much overcome with melancholy to rest, and when alone with his friends, among whom was his ever-faithful Owain Glyndwr, he bitterly lamented his past indulgence to his cousin. 'Fool that I was!' he said. 'Thrice did I save the life of this Henry of Lancaster. Once my dear uncle, his father, would have put him to death for his treason and villainy. I rode all night to save him, and his father delivered him to me, to do with him as I pleased. How true is the saying that we have no greater enemy than the man whom we have saved from the gallows! Another time he drew his sword on me in the presence of the Queen, on whom God have mercy. He sided with Gloucester and Arundel; he consented to my murder, to that of his father, and of all my Council. By St. John I forgave him all; nor would I believe his father, who, more than once, pronounced him worthy of death.' There may be some exaggeration in this, but it is very clear that he had often acted leniently towards his cousin, and deeply felt his ingratitude.

That night, as Créton relates, he again bewailed his absent little Queen, in the presence of the Earl of Salisbury and the Bishop of Carlisle. 'My very sweet heart, my sister, to you I must say adieu! For your love I am detained here. I have never deserved to be so destroyed by my people. But if it please thee, O Lord, that I die, deign to conduct my soul to Paradise, for here there is no escape for me. . . . Alas! why did we believe Northumberland, who has delivered us into the hands of wolves? I doubt we be all dead men; for these men have no remorse or pity. May they be confounded!'

No one could have seen Richard or his friends, writes the chronicler, without feeling great sympathy for them. There was no sleep for any of them that night.

The unfortunate King rose early from his sleepless couch, and, after hearing Mass, ascended the tower to watch the arrival of his enemy. He soon saw the army, numbering between 80,000 and 100,000, marching along the sea-shore, with banners waving and trumpets sounding, until it reached and surrounded the castle. He shuddered and wept. Soon he was called down by the arrival of Archbishop Arundel, the Duke of Albemarle, and the Earl of Worcester. Tuesday,
Aug. 19.

They all knelt to Richard, who, without noticing the two recent traitors, held a long conversation with the Archbishop. It would appear that someone had betrayed to Northumberland, or one of his party, the threats which Richard had made when at Conway. Without defending Richard in this particular instance—for a promise is a promise, and ought to be kept—yet it may be pleaded that it was extorted through fear; that he had not made an oath to keep it, as Northumberland had done, and therefore might reconcile his conscience to a mental reservation. Be that as it may, Arundel upbraided him in no measured terms as being the most false of men. He went through the whole history of his brother and himself, and called to mind all the errors of the reign. Richard stopped him by saying in a most supplicating voice, 'Sufficit.' Then the Archbishop, seeing the King's misery, treated him with consideration, and endeavoured to comfort him. He tried to prove to him that resistance would be in vain, that his wisest course would be to resign the crown, when his life would be spared and he would be allowed to enjoy all the luxuries to which he had been accustomed. The Earl of Salisbury said afterwards that the Archbishop appeared to comfort the King very greatly, and the interview ended in a friendly manner.*

When the deputation had departed, the poor King reascended the tower, and, surveying the army of his opponent, he exclaimed: 'Good Lord God, I commend myself to Thy holy keeping, and cry Thee mercy that Thou would'st pardon all my sins. If they put me to death I will take it patiently, as Thou didst for us all.'

Dinner was now served, at which the King requested the Earl of Salisbury, the Bishop, and his other loyal friends to join him, saying they were all in like peril with him, and therefore should not be divided. They were not free from insults, however, for some of the Lancastrian faction entered the hall and threatened them with death.

When the meal, which Richard had prolonged as much as possible, although he himself scarcely ate anything, was at last over, he descended to meet the Duke. Henry entered the courtyard of the castle in full armour, save the helmet, and bowed low as soon as he perceived the King. When they approached each other, he bent his knee to the ground, with his cap in his hand.

'Fair cousin of Lancaster,' said Richard, taking off his bonnet, 'you be right welcome.'

'My lord,' answered the Duke, 'I am come sooner than you sent for me; the reason wherefore I will tell you. The common report of your people is that you have, for the space of twenty or two-and-twenty years, governed them badly and rigorously, and they are not well contented. But, if it please our Lord, I will help you to govern better.'

'Fair cousin,' replied the King, 'since it pleaseth you, it pleaseth us well.'

It must have been now, if ever, that a beautiful greyhound named Math, which belonged to King Richard, who was much attached to it, came bounding in, but instead of running to its master according to custom, it went to the Duke of Lancaster and leaped up, placing its paws upon his shoulders. Henry, being much surprised, enquired the meaning of this behaviour, as he knew not the creature. 'Cousin,' said Richard, 'it is a great good token to you, and an evil sign for me.'

* Dr. Hook's 'Archbishops.'

'Sir, how know you that?' asked Henry.
'I know it, cousin,' quoth Richard. 'The hound maketh you cheer this day as King of England, as you will be, and I shall be deposed. He hath this knowledge naturally; therefore take him to you; he will follow you and forsake me.' And so, indeed, it fell out. A similar incident is recorded as having happened at the battle of Auray, September 29, 1364, when a greyhound belonging to Charles de Blois forsook him to fawn upon Jean de Montfort.

The Duke now addressed a few words to the Bishop and the knights attending the King, but did not take any notice of the Earl of Salisbury, as he had not yet forgotten the errand of that nobleman to Paris. He then ordered horses to be brought. Two mean little hackneys, not worth forty francs, were produced for the use of the King and the Earl. This indignity must have sorely hurt Richard's feelings, as he had a great fondness for, and was a good judge of, horses. The bitterness of his fall was afterwards aggravated by hearing that his cousin and rival, when in London, rode his favourite steed.

> '*King R.* Rode he on Barbary? Tell me, gentle friend,
> How went he under him?
> *Groom.* So proudly as if he had disdain'd the ground.
> *King R.* So proud that Bolingbroke was on his back!
> That jade hath eat bread from my royal hand;
> This hand hath made him proud with clapping him.
> Would he not stumble? Would he not fall down,
> (Since pride must have a fall) and break the neck
> Of that proud man that did usurp his back?'

Having mounted these sorry jades, the captives were conducted to Chester, where a halt was made for three days. It is said that seven loyal Cheshire men each raised a body of seventy, wearing Richard's cognizance of the white hart, who formed a bodyguard, keeping a watch over their unfortunate monarch day and night. Possibly the Duke waited here to receive his son, whom he had sent for from the castle of Trim. Henry arrived, accompanied by his cousin Humphrey of Gloucester. To the last-named youth and to Thomas FitzAlan, then a young man not quite eighteen years of age, Henry gave the unfortunate Richard in charge, saying: 'Here is the murderer of your fathers, you must be answerable for him.' Whether Henry harboured the thought that they might wreak their revenge on the captive King can never be known. The words sound very much like an incentive to such a deed. It is not improbable that he would gladly have been spared any further trouble on Richard's account, and had anything happened to the King he would have been able to say: 'I am innocent of such a deed.' Humphrey died soon after reaching London, after a short illness. His mother, the widowed Duchess Eleanor, who had retired to Barking Abbey after her husband's death, did not long survive him, as she died on October 3 following.

Writs were sent out in the King's name to summon a Parliament, and proclamations issued for the preservation of the peace. Then, having dismissed a large portion of his army, Henry set out with his prisoners for London, taking the road through Nantwich to Stafford.

Sunday, Aug. 24. At Lichfield the unhappy Richard attempted to escape by letting himself down, when night came, through the window of his tower. Unfortunately the garden was surrounded by a high wall, so that he was soon recaptured, and afterwards more strictly guarded, having ten or twelve men in the room, who prevented him from having any sleep.

Lichfield appears to have been a favourite town with Richard. He was there in 1386, at the installation of Bishop Scrope, and in 1397 at that of Bishop Burghill. At the end of that year, when on his way to Shrewsbury, he spent Christmas there, when he held great tournaments and feastings in honour of the Pope's nuncio and many foreign noblemen.

The French chronicler records that a deputation arrived from London to request the Duke, on the part of the Commons, to cut off the King's head; to whom Henry replied: 'Fair sirs, it would be a very great disgrace to us for ever if we should thus put him to death; but we will bring him to London, and there he shall be judged by the Parliament.'

The cavalcade now proceeded to Coventry, Daventry, Northampton, Dunstable, and St. Albans.

At Coventry Castle, which had been a favourite residence of the Black Prince, the poor captive would be reminded of the last appearance there, in very different characters, of himself and his cousin of Hereford. At Northampton the castle would also probably be the resting-place, whilst at Dunstable the Priory would be chosen, as there was a gaol attached to it. If, when at St. Albans, quarters were sought in the Abbey, the difference between past and present times would again occur to Richard, as he had been there as a youth soon after the time of Wat the Tyler's insurrection and death. A portrait of the King was at one time in the Abbey.

Sept. 1. On leaving St. Albans, they were met by the Lord Mayor of London and a great number of the citizens, who paid much greater respect to Duke Henry than to the King, shouting with a loud voice: 'Long live the Duke of Lancaster.'

> 'The duke, great Bolingbroke,
> Mounted upon a hot and fiery steed,
> Which his aspiring rider seem'd to know,
> With slow, but stately pace, kept on his course
> While all tongues cried—God save thee, Bolingbroke!
> You would have thought the very windows spake,
> So many greedy looks of young and old
> Through casements darted their desiring eyes
> Upon his visage; and that all the walls,
> With painted imagery, had said at once,—
> Jesu preserve thee! Welcome, Bolingbroke!
> Whilst he, from one side to the other turning,
> Bare-headed, lower than his proud steed's neck,

> Bespake them thus,—I thank you, countrymen :
> And thus still doing, thus he pass'd along.'

Just before entering the city, at the hour of vespers, they separated. Henry rode in triumph to St. Paul's, where he dismounted, and proceeded first to the high altar, where he offered up a prayer, and then to the tomb of his father, which he had not before seen, over which he wept considerably.

Richard was sent to Westminster, and on the following day to the Tower.

Sept. 2.

> 'Men's eyes
> Did scowl on Richard ; no man cried God save him ;
> No joyful tongue gave him his welcome home ;
> But dust was thrown upon his sacred head ;
> Which with such gentle sorrow he shook off,
> His face still combating with tears and smiles,
> The badges of his grief and patience,
> That had not God, for some strong purpose, steel'd
> The hearts of men, they must perforce have melted,
> And barbarism itself have pitied him.'

The story was now revived of Henry's having a better right to the crown than Richard, from his great-great-grandfather Edmund, Earl of Lancaster. And as regards Richard himself, the report was spread that he was not the son of the Black Prince, but of a canon of Bordeaux. Poor fallen King ! at any and every cost your enemies sought to elevate your rival.

It was now determined by the Duke of Lancaster and his Council that Richard should be required to resign the crown, and that Parliament should then pass an act of deposition. Hardyng says that when the Percys became aware that Henry now aspired to be King, they withstood him, and called to his remembrance the oath he had taken in the White Friars' Church at Doncaster. But they stood alone ; all their forces had been dismissed, and they had to submit.

To obtain the required resignation from King Richard was a difficult matter. Although at times thoroughly dejected and in despair, he had flashes of the old Plantagenet spirit, before which many quailed. He was told to remember what had passed between him and Archbishop Arundel at their interview in Flint Castle ; but there is little doubt that a promise to abdicate was eventually wrung from him under threats of death. It should be borne in mind that he had now been nearly a month a close prisoner.

One day young Thomas FitzAlan, son to the late Earl of Arundel, and nephew of the Archbishop. was sent to summon him to meet the Dukes of Lancaster, York, and Albemarle.

'Tell Henry of Lancaster,' said Richard, 'I shall do no such thing. If he wants to see me, let him come to me.'

They came accordingly, but none showed any respect to fallen majesty except Henry, who doffed his cap and bent his knee, saying: 'Here are our uncle and cousin, who wish to speak to you.'

'Cousin, they are not fit to speak to me,' replied the King.

'But,' continued Henry, ' have the goodness to hear them.'

Upon which Richard turned with an oath towards York, crying: 'Thou villain! what would'st thou say to me? And thou, traitor of Rutland, thou art neither worthy to speak to me nor to bear the name of Duke, Earl, nor Knight. Thou, and the villain thy father, foully have ye betrayed me. In a cursed hour were ye born. By your false counsel was my uncle Gloucester put to death.'

'You lie!' called out Albemarle, throwing his bonnet at the King's feet.

'I am thy King and thy lord,' shouted Richard, 'and will continue King and greater lord than ever I was, in spite of all my enemies!'

Henry imposed silence upon Albemarle, but Richard was not to be silenced. 'Why,' he asked, 'am I in confinement? Why thus guarded? Am I your servant or King?'

'You are my King, sir,' replied Henry quietly; 'but the Council of the realm has thought proper to place a guard about you till the decision of Parliament.'

'Then,' with an oath the King said, 'let me have my wife.'

'Excuse me,' answered Lancaster; 'it is forbidden by the Council that you should see Queen Isabelle.'

The King, in great wrath, walked up and down the room, calling them false traitors, and offering to fight any four of them. Lancaster then fell on his knees and besought him to wait the meeting of Parliament, and did not leave until the King's temper had been soothed.

Sept. 29. On St. Michael's Day a deputation of prelates, barons, knights, lawyers, and some notable men of London proceeded to the Tower, and there alighted. Then King Richard came to them in the hall where they were assembled. He was apparelled in his robes, the crown on his head, the sceptre in his hand. Standing there alone, he thus spoke: 'I have been King of England, Duke of Aquitaine, and Lord of Ireland about twenty-two years, which royalty, lordship, sceptre and crown I clearly resign here to my cousin, Henry of Lancaster, and I entreat him here, in presence of you all, to accept this sceptre.' He then tendered the sceptre to the Duke, who, on receiving it, handed it to the Archbishop of Canterbury. King Richard next raised the crown from off his head, and said: 'Henry, fair cousin, and Duke of Lancaster, I present and give to you this crown and all the rights dependent on it.' And the Duke, accepting it, delivered it also to the Archbishop of Canterbury.

An authentic account of the proceedings was drawn up, and witnessed by all the prelates and lords present, and the assembly then broke up.

Sept. 30. On the morrow, the feast of St. Jerome, the two houses met in Westminster Hall. It had lately been repaired and freshly decorated by the unfortunate monarch whose deposition was to form its opening ceremony. The Duke of Lancaster sat, as one of the peers, in his usual place near the throne, which was empty and covered with cloth of gold. The resignation of the King was then read, and each member separately, beginning with the Archbishop of Canterbury, signified aloud his acceptance of it, amidst the shouts of the multitude outside.

Then came the act of deposition. The Coronation Act was first read, and afterwards thirty-three articles of impeachment against Richard for having violated it, and thus forfeited his title to the throne.

No opposition was looked for, but Thomas Merks, Bishop of Carlisle,
'Among the faithless, faithful only he,'
stood up and demanded for Richard the right of being confronted with his accusers, and for Parliament the opportunity of hearing from the King personally whether his resignation of the crown had been his own voluntary act or not.

> 'What subject can give sentence on his king?
> And who sits here that is not Richard's subject?
> Thieves are not judg'd, but they are by to hear,
> Although apparent guilt be seen in them :
> And shall the figure of God's majesty,
> His captain, steward, deputy elect,
> Anointed, crowned, planted many years,
> Be judged by subject and inferior breath,
> And he himself not present?'

Not one was found who would second him, and the house voted the deposition of Richard. Eight commissioners, specially appointed, ascended a tribunal in front of the throne, and in the name of Parliament pronounced the sentence of deposition which was afterwards written out and signed. The Chief Justice went with a deputation to notify the sentence to the captive Richard, who meekly replied that he hoped his cousin would be good lord to him.

The throne was now vacant. Who was to fill it? The direct heir was Edmund Mortimer, eldest son of Roger, who, as a descendant of Lionel, Duke of Clarence, had in 1387 been acknowledged presumptive heir to the throne. But Edmund was a boy, not yet eight years old, and no one ventured to speak on his behalf.

At length Henry of Lancaster rose from his seat, and, having formed the sign of the cross on his forehead and his breast, thus spoke : 'In the name of Fader, Son, and Holy Ghost, I, Henry of Lancaster, chalenge this rewme of Ynglonde, and the crown, with all the members and appurtenances, als that I am descendit be right line of the blode, coming fro' the gude lord King Henry therde, and throghe that right that God, of his grace, has sent mee, with helpe of my kyn, and of my frendes to recover it ; the which rewme was in poynt to be ondone for defaut of governance, and undoying of gude lawes.'

A most artfully-worded claim, but one which was, without any question being put, unanimously admitted by both houses. Henry then produced the ring and seal which Richard had previously given him, as confirming his right to the throne.

The Archbishops of Canterbury and York now approached, and led him to the throne. For a few minutes Henry prostrated himself on the steps in silent prayer. When he rose from his knees the two prelates seated him on the throne, amidst the acclamations of lords and commons, 'all the people shouting wonderfully for joy.'

Thus Henry of Lancaster became King. Better would it have been for him; better, far better, for his family, had he carried out his idea of going to the Holy Land, and had there either died in peace or fallen gloriously, sword in hand, in an endeavour, futile though it might be, to wrest the country from the grasp of the infidel.

Henry III., *ob.* 1272.

Edward I., *ob.* 1307.	Edmund, Earl of Lancaster, *ob.* 1296.
Edward II., *ob.* 1327.	Henry, third earl, *ob.* 1345.
Edward III., *ob.* 1377.	Henry, duke, *ob.* 1361.

Lionel, *ob.* 1368.   John, *ob.* 1399; m. Blanche, *ob.* 1369.

Philippa, *ob.* 1375; m.   Henry of Bolingbroke, b. 1366.
Edmund Mortimer, *ob.* 1381; æt. 30.

Roger Mortimer,   Edward.   John.
ob. 1398; æt. 24; m.
Eleanor Holland.

Edmund,   Roger.   Anne.   Eleanor.
b. Nov. 6, 1391.   *ob.* 1408.

SKETCH VIII.

THE LAST OF A LINE.

1399. ONE King being deposed and a new one elected, the power of Parliament also ceased. Writs were issued for a new one to assemble in six days, but as that was not possible, Henry took upon himself to summon the same men who had sat in the last one, only appointing new officers of the crown.

Oct. 6. The first act of this new-old House, obsequious to Henry as it had been to Richard, was to undo all the proceedings at Shrewsbury, and to confirm those of the 'Wonderful Parliament.'

Oct. 13. On the anniversary of the day on which he went into banishment, the Duke of Lancaster was crowned King as Henry IV. The ceremony used was the ordinary one, with the addition that the Earl of Northumberland bore, unsheathed, the sword which Henry had worn on landing at Ravenspur, and it was decreed that his descendants should in like manner bear the same sword at the coronation of succeeding Kings of the House of Lancaster. The Earl had been appointed Constable of England and he now received a grant of the Isle of Man. Ralph Neville, Earl of Westmorland, was at the same time made Earl Marshal of England. Henry of Monmouth, the eldest son of the King, was created Prince of Wales, Duke of Cornwall and Aquitaine, and Earl of Chester; and subsequently was declared Duke of Lancaster and heir-apparent to the throne, the name of Edmund Mortimer, the rightful heir, not being even mentioned. *Oct. 15.*

Richard's greatest fault—crime if you will—in the eyes of the nobles had been, that he was a lover of peace instead of war. War with them was love of gain. It meant wealth from captured cities and villages, and ransomed prisoners. Henry of Bolingbroke tacitly, if not openly, promised an end to such a state of things. The promise was kept, but not in the way he intended. For the greater part of his reign he was disturbed by insurrections at home, or troubles with his neighbours. It was but the commencement of wars, which should not end until above two-thirds of the old nobility and gentry, at least sixty princes of the blood royal, some hundreds of thousands of people, and the last Plantagenet King had been swept away.

Henry's great popularity with the people had been gained by siding with them against Richard. He therefore dared not impose taxes on them, but he would not remit the penalties which they had incurred, nor repay the loans they had made to the deposed King. Such power did they obtain, however, that, some years later, they presented a number of Articles, which he dared not refuse, although the conditions were far more dishonourable to him than any which had ever been imposed upon Richard. By these concessions the people won a higher position than they had ever held before, and did not obtain again for many years. The almost universal feeling appeared to be,

> 'Trust not him that once hath broken faith.'

The King's greatest reliance was upon the clergy, who were at all times his best supporters, under the leading of Archbishop Arundel. As that prelate had been mainly instrumental in opening for Henry the way to the throne, he could not do less than aid him now by obtaining contributions, which were generally forthcoming when needed. He would do this the more readily as Henry had to a certain extent always taken an interest in religious questions. Like his father, he had at one time favoured the doctrines of Wycliffe. But he felt obliged to withdraw his countenance from the learned doctor's followers, the Lollards, whose opinions he considered highly dangerous both to the Church and State. The statute 'De hæretico comburendo' was passed during his reign.

The next scene in Parliament was one of disgraceful riot, where the words 'liar' and 'traitor' were freely bandied about from one to another. All in any way connected with the proceedings against Gloucester, Arundel, and Warwick during the last reign—with the notable exception of King Henry, who, as Duke of Hereford, had *Oct. 19.*

taken as active a part as anyone—were called to account. All answered that they were no more guilty than the other lords who had condemned the appellees. The so-called confession of John Hall was then read, wherein the Duke of Albemarle was roundly charged with being an accomplice. Albemarle denied the fact. This brought up Lord Fitzwalter. 'The Duke,' said he, 'denies it, but I say that he was the cause of that murder, and will prove it with my body.' Or, as Shakspere puts it in Act IV. of 'Richard II.':

> 'I heard thee say, and vauntingly thou spak'st it,
> That thou wert cause of noble Gloster's death.'

He then threw down his hood as gage of battle, in which he was followed by twenty other lords.

'I never consented to the death of the Duke of Gloucester,' repeated Albemarle, 'and you lie falsely.' He, too, cast his hood on the ground.

In all the assembly only one stood up for the Duke of Albemarle, and that was the young Duke of Surrey, who declared that what Fitzwalter had said was false, and challenged him to combat in the usual manner.

The Earl of Salisbury was charged by Lord Morley with having betrayed the secrets of the Duke of Gloucester to the late King. Salisbury indignantly and flatly denied it, and both threw down their gages.

So the game went merrily on until the King ordered all the pledges to be collected, and placed in the custody of the Constable and Marshal. It was finally decided that the lords appellants should be deprived of the dignities conferred upon them as a reward by King Richard. Consequently the Dukes of Albemarle, Exeter, and Surrey became again Earls of Rutland, Huntingdon and Kent. John Beaufort, the King's brother, lost his marquisate of Dorset, and was once more Earl of Somerset, while the Earl of Gloucester descended to the ancient barony of Le Despenser.

The duel between the Earl of Salisbury and Lord Morley was appointed to be fought at Newcastle. The Earl, it will be remembered, had given great offence to the banished Duke of Hereford by his mission to Paris. Now that Henry was King, he had the opportunity of showing that merely personal matters did not weigh with him. The Earl was not included in the judgment against the other lords, from which it might be concluded that he was forgiven. On the other hand, the King, in his craft and subtlety, might consider that, in the permitted duel, the man he disliked had the chance of being got out of his way. If the duel took place, the Earl was *not* slain, for we shall hear of him again.

This John de Montagu, third Earl of Salisbury, had Plantagenet blood in his veins, being great-grandson of Joan of Acre, Countess of Gloucester, daughter of King Edward I. She took for her second husband Ralph de Monthermer, 'a squire of low degree,' but ennobled for her sake by her loving father. Hence the Earls of Salisbury derived their title of Barons de Monthermer. King Henry IV. and the third Earl were each fourth in descent from King Edward I., and were fifth cousins.

In contradistinction to these degradations the attainder of the Earl of Arundel was reversed, and his son, Thomas FitzAlan, became seventh Earl of Arundel. The Earl of Warwick was recalled from exile and restored to his honours and estates, but he did not enjoy them long, as he died on April 8, 1401. He was succeeded by his son, Richard Beauchamp, who, some years later, took for his second wife Isabel le Despenser, daughter and co-heir of Thomas, the Earl of Gloucester above-mentioned.

'Things bad begun make strong themselves by ill.'

A few days after this stormy scene, the Archbishop of Canterbury Oct. 23. stated to the lords spiritual and temporal that he had instructions from the King to charge them that the matter to be that day submitted to their decision must be kept an inviolable secret. The Earl of Northumberland then asked their advice as to how the deposed King was to be dealt with. Many urged that he should be put to death. They were informed that it was the King's will that his life should be spared. Henry was a reticent man, with great command of temper. If he at that time entertained any different thoughts, they were not divulged. It was finally decided that Richard should Oct. 27. be placed for safe keeping in some secret place, well guarded, and kept from all communication with any of his old servants.

On his first removal from the Tower, on the eve of All Saints, Oct. 31. King Henry sent him a black horse and a black dress complete. At the sight of black spurs Richard became indignant, and bade the attendant inform Henry of Lancaster that, as a knight, he was entitled to gilt spurs, and would not ride without them. The spurs were accordingly brought, also a sword, and then he set out under a guard of men of Kent.

The first place of detention was Leeds Castle, in Kent, but that was probably considered to be too accessible from London. The unfortunate King was therefore removed to Pickering, afterwards to Knaresborough, and finally to Pontefract, all situated in Yorkshire and belonging to the Duchy of Lancaster. Of Pickering Castle there are still some picturesque remains, but in a ruinous condition. The two rooms occupied by Richard at Knaresborough are still pointed out in the second story above the dungeon of the keep, as are also his apartments at Pontefract. Both these castles were besieged and destroyed by the Republicans during the Civil Wars.

The imprisonment of Richard did not prevent his friends from working for him, or increase their devotion to the reigning King. On the contrary, four of the degraded lords, with the Earl of Salisbury and some others, joined in a plot to dethrone Henry and reinstate Richard. They proclaimed a tournament to be held at Oxford on the festival of the Epiphany, at which the King had promised to be present. Great were the preparations which were made, and greater still the expectations roused in the country round about. At last Christmastide was over, when final touches had to be put to the design, and to each member of the plot had to be allotted a special part. The Earls of Huntingdon, Salisbury and Kent, and Lord le Despenser, were there; but there was one wanting—the Earl of Rutland. Without him they could not move, as he had undertaken a difficult task. Huntingdon therefore wrote him a letter, and despatched it by a messenger, with orders to use the greatest haste.

1400. Jan. 4. The letter, as to the purport of which he could make a shrewd guess, reached the Earl just as he was about to go in to dinner. It may be that he had already made up his mind to desert his friends, but he now formed the devilish design of betraying them, and of doing it in such a manner as to lead to the supposition that he had been coerced to it. He put the letter hastily into his breast, and showed plainly in his demeanour that something had unnerved him. His father, the Duke of York, observing this, questioned him closely, but did not receive any satisfaction. Glancing his eyes over his son, the Duke noticed a paper sticking out, and asked what missive he had there, but obtained only an evasive reply. This angered the old man so much that he snatched the paper away, and read it. Even the gentle Edmund fired up when he had finished. 'What devil's work are you up to now?' asked he. 'Tell me, lest I strike you dead.'

Rutland, 'of the coward heart,' then stammered forth the whole plot: that in the midst of the projected festivities they were to seize the King and his four sons, and butcher them all; then release Richard, and proclaim him once more as King.

'Thou, traitor to King Richard, wouldst now turn traitor to King Henry!' exclaimed the Duke. 'But thou shalt suffer for this, not I, who have become bound for thy loyalty in life and limb.' The Duke ordered his horses at once, with the intention of riding to Windsor, but was prevented by his son Rutland, who now realized in what peril he stood. He resolved that, if the tale were to be told, he would be the one to tell it. To do so, he must outstrip his father by using his fleetest steed and pursuing a different road. He thus accomplished his purpose of arriving first at Windsor. When, soon after arrival, he was admitted to the King's presence, he kneeled down, and humbly besought mercy and forgiveness. 'However heinous thy fault,' replied the King, 'if only in intent, not act, I pardon thee.'

Rutland then repeated the tale he had so recently narrated to his father. York, having grave doubts whether his son would reveal everything, had followed him very closely. He arrived just as the recital ended, and then handed to the King the paper taken from Rutland, which proved to be the indentures, sealed and signed by the whole of the conspirators, and set forth their designs in full.

Henry was for the moment paralyzed, as well he might be, but his resolution and activity soon reasserted themselves. It was the evening of a winter's day, but there was to be no tarrying. He ordered horses to be saddled instantly, and, declining any other escort than that of grooms to attend his younger sons, started at once for London, where they arrived late at night. This was Sunday, January 4.

Shakspere has introduced the Duchess of York in this scene as Rutland's mother. She was the Duke's second wife, Lady Joan Holland, daughter of Thomas, second Earl of Kent. Had she been present there would have been more need for her prayers on behalf of her brother Thomas, the third Earl, than of her stepson.

How fared it meanwhile with the traitors? They had not seen Rutland for some days, and had not yet received any reply to the note sent him. Knowing the man's character, they feared betrayal. Huntingdon, the King's brother-in-law, ever ready when mischief was afoot, proposed a change of plan. Laying aside all pretence of a tournament at Oxford, let them start for Windsor, and there accomplish their object. Accordingly, a number of men were despatched in carts to make their way there. The principal body, with the several leaders, took the road to Staines and Colnbrook. It is said that at the latter place they were joined by Rutland, late at night. If that be true, it must have been done to shield himself from suspicion; but it also shows that his meanness, treachery, and servility knew no bounds.

The King had lost no time in levying troops, and issuing writs Jan. 5. against his enemies. Thousands flocked to his banners, and with them, on Monday, he advanced towards Kingston.

At noon that day Huntingdon, with five hundred men, surprised and took Windsor Castle. He would not believe that Henry and his sons were in London, but not finding them after a strict search, he went back to his colleagues, leaving to the men the pleasing duty of ransacking the Castle.

The rebels, not daring to meet their King in arms, decided to go to the western counties. The Earl of Kent is said by some writers to have made a brave but ineffectual stand for some time at the bridge over the Thames at Maidenhead. Leaving that place, he and the Earl of Salisbury called in at Sonning, where the young Queen Isabelle was confined. Telling her that the usurper Bolingbroke had been sent to the Tower, and that they were now on the way to meet her husband, she gladly ordered the badges of Lancaster to be taken from her household and to be replaced by Richard's white hart, and willingly accompanied him. King Richard was proclaimed in every town and village as they marched along, through Wallingford and Abingdon, until they arrived at Cirencester, in Gloucestershire. Miss Strickland, in her 'Life of Isabella of Valois,' says: 'She was with the barons when they reached the fatal town, but, amidst the mysterious darkness which shrouds the termination of the insurrection, we lose sight of the actual manner in which the young Queen was recaptured by Henry IV.' She was sent, after quiet was restored, strictly guarded, to Havering atte Bower, which was afterwards her place of residence.

In some of the places through which they passed a priest named Maudelain, who bore such a striking resemblance to King Richard that he was by many believed to be an illegitimate son of the Black Prince, was dressed up as the unfortunate King, and made to personate him.

On arrival at Cirencester, the earls encamped their men outside, and then sought quarters for themselves in the town itself. A messenger, bearing the King's writ, had, unfortunately, preceded them, and the mayor had summoned the burghers to his assistance.

How the fray commenced is uncertain, but an attack, in which both men and women were concerned, was made on the inn where the leaders had found refuge. They manfully resisted, but what could five or six do against a multitude? After six hours' fighting they were compelled to yield, and were shut up in the Abbey. But misfortune still followed them. A fire breaking out there, which was attributed to their partisans, the mob broke in, dragged out the Earls of Kent and Salisbury—the rest had contrived to escape for a time—and struck off their heads.

Jan. 7. Thomas Holland, Earl of Kent, K.G., was a handsome young man, of great promise, and only twenty-five years of age. He had obtained the title Duke of Surrey after the execution of Richard FitzAlan, who was Earl of Arundel and Surrey. He was the founder of Mount Grace Priory, about nine miles from Northallerton, near Osmotherley, in the Hambleton Hills, Yorkshire, but the building was not finished until after his death. This is one of the few Carthusian establishments of which there are any good remains still left. At the earnest request of his widow, Lady Joan de Stafford, daughter of Hugh, second Earl of Stafford, the body of the unfortunate young man was brought from Cirencester and laid at rest here.

As Thomas died without issue, he was succeeded in the earldom by his brother Edmund, who was the last of the name of Holland to bear the title.

John de Montagu, Earl of Salisbury, and Knight of the Garter, was a most gracious man, worthy of a better fate. Créton says :

> 'Estait humble doux et courtois,
>   *   *   *   *
> Hardi estait et fier comme lions,
> Et si faisoit balades et chansons,
> Rondelaux et laiz,
> Tresbien et bel.'

Or, according to the translation of the Rev. John Webb, from whose version many quotations have already appeared :

'He was humble, gentle, and courteous in all his doings. . . . Bold he was, and courageous as a lion. Right well and beautifully did he also make ballads, songs, roundels and lays.'

Ballad-making was much in fashion at that period, and a man of cultivated tastes would not be likely to neglect it.

In Ireland and in Wales he had shown his zeal and attachment to King Richard. He was at one time a leader and supporter of the Lollards, and therefore removed all images from his private chapels. He was buried at first in the Abbey of Cirencester, but on the petition of his widow, Maud, the body was transferred to Bisham Abbey, in Berkshire, on the banks of the Thames, which had been founded by his grandfather, William de Montagu, first Earl of Salisbury of the name. John de Montagu was succeeded in the Earldom by his son Thomas, as fourth and last Earl.

John de Montagu left five children, who were reduced to great poverty by their father's attainder. They were relieved, it is pleasing to be told, by the generosity of King Henry IV.

The Lords le Despenser and Lumley had evaded the fate of their friends at Cirencester by climbing through a window of the inn, and thence over the roofs of adjoining houses, thinking to find an asylum in Wales. They contrived to get on board a boat which carried them to Cardiff. But the Earl of Rutland and Sir Thomas Erpyngham were on their track. Even in that strong castle of the Despensers they did not feel safe from pursuit. Collecting his treasures, the young Baron, with his companion and several attendants, put to sea, with the idea of escaping to foreign parts. He had evidently not consulted the captain, who refused to sail to any other port than Bristol. An altercation ensued, in the course of which as many as twenty men, fully armed, emerged from the ship's hold, and secured the whole party, who were accordingly conveyed to Bristol. It was a place of ill omen for Despenser, his ancestor, the Earl of Winchester, having perished there in the time of Edward of Caernarvon, and a similar fate now befell himself. He and his companion, Ralph, Lord Lumley, were given into the custody of the Mayor, who for two days refused to listen to the demands of the people that the traitors should be delivered over to them. At the end of that time the mob broke into the place where the prisoners were confined, dragged them forth and beheaded them in the market-place. Jan. 17.

Thomas, sixth Lord le Despenser, K.G., was the grandson of Edward, the second son of Hugh, the favourite of King Edward II., whose life and untimely end have already been related. He was fourth in descent from the Lady Joan of Acre by her first marriage with Gilbert the Red, Earl of Gloucester, and was therefore fourth cousin of the Earl of Salisbury. Henry Spencer, Bishop of Norwich, was his uncle.

Thomas had married Lady Constance, daughter of Edmund, Duke of York, and by her left two children—Richard, who died without issue at the age of seventeen, and Isabel, who succeeded to the family estates, and conveyed them to the house of Beauchamp by her marriage with Richard, fifth Earl of Warwick.

The unfortunate baron, who was only twenty-six years of age, was buried in the middle of the choir of Tewkesbury Abbey Church, where a lamp was kept continually burning before the Host. The family of Le Despenser can never be forgotten as long as the abbey exists, for some of the monuments, especially the one erected by Isabel, Countess of Warwick, are the finest objects in the church.

John Holland, Earl of Huntingdon, without attempting to confront his brother-in-law the King, dismissed his troops and fled into Essex. There he took ship, with the idea of crossing the sea for safety, but was beaten back by contrary winds. Some peasants discovered him lurking about as if after no good. One of the men, recognising him, caused him to be seized and carried to Pleshy. There they delivered their captive to the old Countess of Hereford, Jan. 15. mother-in-law of the King, by whose orders he was at once executed. His head was placed with those of the other rebels, on London Bridge, but was only allowed to remain there a day and a night, probably owing to his connection with the King. He left two sons and one daughter, Constance. The latter married Thomas, Lord Mowbray, son of the banished Duke of Norfolk. The widowed lady Elizabeth took for her second husband Sir John Cornwall, of whom we shall hear more later on.

Sir Thomas Blount and Sir Benedict Shelly were executed with some eighteen others at Oxford. It is related of Sir Thomas that, in his last moments, being insultingly addressed by Sir Thomas Erpyngham, the King's Chamberlain, he quietly answered, 'Blessed be this day, for I shall die in the service of my sovereign lord, the noble King Richard.' Richard Maudelain and William Feriby, two chaplains of the late King, were arrested on their way to Yorkshire, brought to London, hanged, drawn, and beheaded together.

As if all these horrors had not been sufficient, the climax was reached when that trebly-dyed traitor, Edward, Earl of Rutland, glorying in his shame, appeared, carrying on a pole, as if in triumph over him, the head of his young brother-in-law, Le Despenser.

The heads of the traitors were, by the King's orders, all sent to London and put up on London Bridge.

Thomas Merks, Bishop of Carlisle, who deserves all honour as the one true, faithful, and firm supporter of fallen royalty, had his reward in being sent as a prisoner to St. Albans at the time of Richard's deposition; but was liberated, after about a fortnight's detention there, at the request of the Pope. In consequence of this new insurrection the Bishop was again arrested, as an accomplice, and sent to the Tower. He was brought up and condemned to death as a traitor. King Henry, in his great desire of revenge upon his open foe, required that he should be at once degraded from his Orders. But the Pope had, in the meantime, translated him to the Bishopric of Cephalonia, and a respite ensued. He subsequently received a pardon, was appointed Vicar of Todenham, in Gloucestershire, and died there in 1409.

This conspiracy had a directly contrary effect to the one intended.

It certainly strengthened Henry's throne. It probably hastened the death of Richard. The feelings of consideration, either real or feigned, which Henry had once professed for his unfortunate cousin would seem to have turned to hatred and fear. 'Few are the steps between a prince's prison and his grave.'

Within a month from the last executions Richard was dead. How he died is a disputed point to this day. The probability is that he was starved to death. That he would voluntarily deprive himself of food, and so commit suicide, does not appear at all likely. His was not the nature to do such an act. His keepers could not have any motive of their own to urge them on to the crime of murder. Authorized by someone in power, they would probably regard it as an ordinary execution. Who would be the person whose orders they would implicitly obey? And who would derive any benefit therefrom? The reigning King. To him no event would be more welcome. When the Duke of Orleans, a year or two later, charged him with being the contriver, he denied having had any hand in it. But no one accused of such a crime would do otherwise. When the Percys rose in rebellion they roundly accused Henry, in the defiance which they issued, of having caused Richard, in Pontefract Castle, "to suffer from hunger, thirst, and cold for fifteen days and nights, and to be murdered." The chronicler Hardyng simply says:

'Men sayde forhungered he was.'

Créton writes: 'On receipt of the news' (the disasters of his friends) 'his heart was so troubled that he neither ate nor drank, and thus he died, so they say; but truly I do not believe it, for some say he is still alive and well shut up in their prison.'

Another account, the one which Shakspere adopted, and with which he concluded his play of 'Richard II.,' is that the captive King was assassinated by Sir Piers Exton and his followers, after hearing King Henry lament at being in continual fear of him. This account was believed on the Continent, but is now generally considered apocryphal by our historians. The story appeared to receive confirmation from the fact of the whole body, when brought to London being soldered in lead, except only the face. On the other hand, when Richard's tomb, some years since, was opened, his skull was found uninjured. Against this, Miss Strickland, in her 'Life of Isabella of Valois,' writes: 'Let the antiquaries consult medical authorities, and they will find that instant death may ensue from a concussion on the brain, without the bone of the head being broken.'

Some of Richard's firmest friends maintained that the body brought to London was not his, but Maudelain's. As already said, the likeness between them was remarkable. But he had been dead two months when the funeral took place, and his head, if not placed on London Bridge with those of the other rebels, was probably buried with the body. Only the head and face were left exposed on the car, the body was closely lapped in lead. If this head of Maudelain's had been used, as suggested, it would have required great medical skill to counteract the effects of time. Then it must have been sent to Pontefract, and this would involve the employment of too many persons to render such a scheme safe from detection, even had it been practicable. Supposing such a plan had been successfully adopted, the inference might fairly be drawn that Richard's flight from prison, with a mock funeral afterwards, had been long premeditated. On such an imposture Henry would scarcely dare to risk his throne and his reputation.

There is a story graphically told, and very ably supported by Mr. Tytler in his history of Scotland, that Richard escaped from prison and lived for nineteen years in Scotland. When the King was sent to Pontefract he was in charge of Sir Thomas Swinburn and Sir Robert Waterton, both of whom were in the confidence and high in the service of Henry IV. They felt great compassion for their prisoner and spread reports of his death. After that rumours arose that he was still alive and in Scotland. How, if he ever did so, he found means to escape, and who were his assistants, we are not told. His keepers were not the men likely to lend themselves to such a scheme. One day a poor, meanly clad, weary traveller arrived at the residence of the Lord of the Isles, and made his way to the kitchen, where he was hospitably entertained. There he was recognised by a lady, who was married to a brother of the then Lord Donald, as Richard of Bordeaux, whom she had seen and known in Ireland as King. The man himself constantly denied that he was the King, but many other persons as constantly affirmed that he was. It was decided to give him in charge to Lord Montgomery, who carried him to the Court of King Robert III. He was afterwards held for some time by the laird of Cumbernauld, and finally handed over to the Duke of Albany. Wyntown, prior of Lochleven, in his Chronicle writes :

> 'Quhethir he had bene king, or nane,
> Thare wes bot few, that wyst certaine.
> Of devotioune nane he wes,
> And seildyn will had to here Mes ;
> As he bare hym, like wes he
> Oft half wod or wyld to be.'

If this man was King Richard, either misfortune had for a time deranged his wits, or he had purposely adopted the ways of insanity. It was very unlike Richard not to wish to hear Mass, knowing as we do that he delighted in assisting at the service. But he might, for the sake of safety, deny his kingship, which an idiot would be proud to assume. Let the man have been whoever he may, he was treated with all courtesy and consideration, although nominally a captive, in the palace at Stirling, until his death on the feast of St. Luke, October 18, 1419. He was buried with the state and ceremony attaching to a king, in the church of the Dominican or Black Friars, at Stirling, on the feast of St. Lucy the Virgin, December 13. Above the tomb, which was on the north side of the high altar, was an epitaph setting forth his royal state and title. But tomb and church have been long since demolished. The most cogent arguments against this account are that Henry IV. tried to gain the hand of Isabelle, the young widowed Queen, for his son Henry of Monmouth, and that her father, King Charles VI., gave her in marriage to his nephew Charles, Count of Angoulême.

No man in England knew, or rather, no one admitted that he knew what had become of King Richard. But there was chance of a war with France, as King Charles refused to acknowledge any other King of England than Richard, his son-in-law. Suddenly his opinion changed. Having received an intimation of Richard's death, from a messenger who had been sent into Scotland, where he was convinced that the man at Stirling was an impostor, the King issued a manifesto that he would not disturb the truce concluded with his late dear son, but demanded the return of his daughter. It thus became necessary to show what had been the fate of Richard.

On a carriage covered with black cloth, with a banner at each corner, and drawn by two horses, placed one before the other—what we call now tandem—was placed a body with the face, from the forehead to the throat, exposed. One hundred men clothed in black attended on the car, and after leaving Pontefract a halt was made at all the principal places, in order that anyone desirous of doing so might have a view. On arrival at London the cortège was met by thirty men clad in white and bearing torches. By them the corpse was carried to St. Paul's, where it remained for two days, to give the people an opportunity of satisfying themselves that Richard, their late King, was indeed dead, and no less than twenty thousand, we are told, availed themselves of the privilege. After Mass, on the second day, March the 12th, which was attended by the King and all his family, the body was removed to Westminster Abbey, Henry himself acting as pall-bearer. If he had commanded the murder, his self-control, not to say hypocrisy, must have been marvellous. In any case, his was no enviable position. He might well say:

'Though I did wish him dead,
I hate the murtherer, love him murthered.'

At Westminster a dirge was chanted, and then the procession went on to Langley, once a favourite dwelling-place of Richard's, where he was interred in the Friary Church.

Créton wrote respecting this funeral: ' I certainly do not believe it was the old King, but think it was Maudelain his chaplain. If it were he, morn and night I heartily make my prayer to the merciful and holy God that He will take his soul to heaven, for, in my opinion, he hated all manner of blame and every vice. Never did I see anything in him save Catholic faith and justice.'

The ceremony at Langley was carried out in a very unostentatious, private, not to say paltry, manner. The Bishop of Chester was the only prelate present. With him were the Abbots of St. Albans and Walsingham. The customary hospitalities were wanting, and when the duties at the tomb were ended, there was not one who would invite them to dinner.

Thus the last legitimate Plantagenet of the elder line was, presumably, dead and buried. How, when, or where he died, as already shown, no one can positively affirm, but St. Valentine's Day, February 14, is on some theories the accepted time.

It is not known why Richard was not buried at Westminster. Did Henry begrudge his cousin a place even among dead kings, as he had deprived him of his status as a living one? Or did he believe that Richard was alive in Scotland, and therefore refrain from placing a stranger among the dust of kings? Like as in everything else connected with his disappearance, so also here all is mystery.

Whatever may have been Richard's real fate, the utter silence maintained regarding it by Henry of Bolingbroke 'will be a reproach to him for ever, as long as the world shall endure or the deep ocean be able to cast up tide or wave.'

Richard, in his will, had directed that his body should be buried beside that of his loved Anne of Bohemia. The noble-hearted Henry of Monmouth, when he ascended the Throne, thirteen years afterwards, as one of his first acts ordered the removal of the remains of the unfortunate Richard to Westminster, and their deposit in the tomb of the late Queen, he himself attending as chief mourner. He provided that four tapers should burn about the grave day and night for ever; that a dirge should be chanted once a week, and a requiem Mass on the day following, when alms were to be given to the poor; and that on the day of death, after Mass had been sung, £70 should be so distributed for his soul's health.

It is singular that the tombs of King Richard and his uncle the Duke of Gloucester are next to one another in St. Edward's Chapel.

SKETCH IX.

SOME FRUITS OF USURPATION.

1400. June.

IN order either to divert the minds of the people from dwelling on the recent tragedies, or to prove that, unlike his predecessor, he was not averse to war, King Henry now determined upon an invasion of Scotland. A large army was gathered together at York, with which he first marched to Newcastle, whence he issued a summons to King Robert III. to appear before him and do him homage, and then on to Edinburgh. The castle was under the government of David, Duke of Rothesay, who scouted Henry's claim of superiority, but offered to decide the quarrel by a combat of one, two, or three hundred knights on each side. This proposal was not accepted, and preparations were made for besieging the castle. The Duke of Albany, in the meantime, had raised an army with which he marched towards the capital, but it was not needed. Sickness and famine compelled Henry to retreat from an ill-advised, useless and inglorious expedition, which he did the more speedily as he had received tidings of an insurrection in Wales. It is to Henry's credit that he saved many innocent people from assault by granting to all who asked, whether in convent, castle, or country village, the protection of a royal banner to be hung from the walls.

This expedition is chiefly remarkable as being the last conducted by an English King into Scotland.

You will remember Owain Glyndwr, the faithful follower of Richard II. When the King was taken prisoner at Flint, Owain retired to his stronghold near Corwen, which was the central point of his domain in the region of the river Dee. Soon after the accession to the throne of Henry IV., Reginald, Lord Grey of Ruthyn, a powerful neighbour of Glyndwr's, took forcible possession of a tract of land which lawfully belonged to the latter. Owain appealed for justice to the King in Parliament, and was backed by the Bishop of St. Asaph, who warned the lords that, if some redress were not given, danger was imminent. They, however, rejected the suit with contempt, saying that 'they did not fear the rascally barefooted people.' Such an affront was sure to be taken ill by a chieftain of a proverbially passionate nation, proud of his descent on both father's and mother's side from a long line of Welsh princes, and notably from Llywelyn, the last Prince of Wales. In the same way he had from the ancestors of both parents Plantagenet blood in his veins, as shown in the table annexed. His grandfather was the great-grandson of King Edward I. through that King's eldest child. His grandmother was second-great-granddaughter of King John, third cousin of Edward I., and sixth cousin of her husband.

King Henry IV. was fourth in descent from King Edward I. Owain Glyndwr was fifth in descent from the same King, and they were consequently sixth cousins.

Strange as it may appear, it seems to be clear that if, at the deposition of Richard II., the crown of England was not to continue in the direct line of seniority, Owain might have put in a claim to it in opposition to Henry of Lancaster, although it could only be done as coming from the female side.

Owain had been well educated, entered at one of the Inns of Court at London, and became a barrister. He married Margaret, a daughter of Sir David Hanmer, one of the Justices of the King's Bench, by whom he had a family of five sons and four daughters. He probably soon retired from the profession of the law, as he was one of the squires of the Earl of Arundel, and soon afterwards entered the household of King Richard in a like capacity.

When King Henry was about to proceed to Scotland, among the writs of summons to his vassals to attend him, the one addressed to the Welsh chieftain was purposely withheld by Lord Grey, who represented Glyndwr's absence as an act of wilful disobedience of the royal commands. The King therefore sent the Lords Grey and Talbot to attack him in his own house of Glyndwrdy, which they did so suddenly that he had barely time to escape. His next appearance was at Ruthyn, the centre of Lord Grey's lands, which he took whilst a fair was going on; then, after plundering and burning the town, retired to his fastnesses among the mountains.

Sept. It was now that King Henry, on returning from Scotland, determined to march in person against Glyndwr, all of whose estates in North and South Wales he granted to his brother, John Beaufort, Earl of Somerset. But there was no enemy to be seen. Owain and his men were safe in the heights of Snowdon. All the King could do was to wreak his vengeance on a Franciscan monastery at Llanvais, near Beaumaris, putting some of the friars to death, and carrying away others because they had always been warm supporters of King Richard, and were presumed to be favourers of Glyndwr. After that he retired.

1401. In the spring Owain, bearing the title Prince of Wales, which he had assumed, and had himself so proclaimed as soon as the King had pronounced sentence of outlawry against him on September 20, 1400, marched to Plinlimmon, where he formed an encampment, and was joined by many enthusiastic young men from Oxford and other places. He sacked and burnt Montgomery and part of Welshpool, and took the castle of Radnor, where he beheaded the garrison to the number of sixty. The Flemings, who had been settled in Pembroke since the time of King Henry I., were objects of great dislike to Glyndwr, and they, in turn, were provoked at his incursions. They therefore raised a force of 1,500 men, with which they surrounded his camp. But honest Flemish weavers, though far outnumbering their opponents, were no match for sturdy Welsh mountaineers. Owain and his followers broke through their ranks, left 200 dead on the field, and dispersed the remainder.

The young Prince of Wales, Henry of Monmouth, was at the head of an expedition which attacked and destroyed Owain's house of Glyndwrdy, but for this injury ample revenge was taken by the rival claimant to the title.

June. The King again appeared on the scene, but only to signalize his presence by the destruction of another religious house, and the pillage of the county of Cardigan, when famine and tempestuous weather obliged him to withdraw, leaving Glyndwr triumphant.

> 'The Kyng Henry thryce to Wales went,
> In the haye time and harvest divers yere,
> In every tyme were mystes and tempestes sent,
> Of wethers foule that he had never power
> Glendour to noye.'

1402. A comet which showed itself this year was deemed a favourable sign for Owain, and fresh followers joined him. He made an attack on his original adversary, Lord Grey, whom he defeated on the banks of the Vyrnwy, not far from Ruthyn, and carried a captive to his camp amidst the wilds of Snowdon, where he remained for two years, and was only released on paying 10,000 marks, and giving an engagement to remain neutral in the future.

Glyndwr next turned his forces against those of his countrymen who had been induced by an offer of free pardon to desert him for the party of King Henry. But he had, near Knighton in Radnorshire, June. to encounter a large force under the leadership of Sir Edmund Mortimer, uncle of his namesake the young Earl of March. The followers of Mortimer were both English and Welsh. The latter refusing to fight against their countrymen, the Englishmen were totally defeated—upwards of a thousand were slain, and their commander was taken prisoner.

King Henry now determined upon a third invasion of Wales, from Aug. three separate quarters, he himself leading one division from Shrewsbury, Edmund, Earl of Stafford, and Richard Beauchamp, Earl of Warwick, leading the second from Hereford, whilst Henry, Prince of Wales, with Thomas FitzAlan, Earl of Arundel, were in command of the third, to assemble at Chester.

The great preparations were in vain. No foe was encountered; but the wind blew and the rain fell in torrents. One night, during a great hurricane, the King's tent was torn from its fastenings, and whirled away to a great distance. The whole of the tempestuous weather was attributed to the magical arts of Glyndwr, who was

'Not in the roll of common men.'

He might indeed say, in the words which Shakspere attributes to him:

'Three times hath Henry Bolingbroke made head
Against my power: thrice from the banks of Wye,
And bottom'd Severn, have I sent him,
Bootless home, and weather-beaten back.'

Henry was forced to return, once more discomfited by the weather.

'The King had never but tempest foule and raine,
As longe as he was ay in Wales grounde,
Rockes and mystes, windes and stormes ever certaine,
All men trowed ye witches it made that stounde.'

In addition to these Welsh risings, Henry had at this time great trouble on account of the persistent rumours that Richard was still alive. The air was full of them. Among the first to give them voice was a priest of Ware. He affirmed that Richard would shortly appear to claim his rights, and in consequence was hanged, drawn, and quartered. Not long afterwards Sir Roger Clarendon, a natural son of the Black Prince, who had been attached to the household of his half-brother the King, propagated the like reports. So did also some Franciscan friars. The Franciscans had always enjoyed the patronage of the late King. As they were continually going up and down the country, they might have seen the individual confined at Stirling, and have believed him truly to be King Richard. For so saying, nine of their number, along with Sir Roger, suffered the same barbarous punishment as the priest. King Henry published a proclamation against the authors of lying reports; but this brought up so many charges and prosecutions that even his cruel and unscrupulous nature was compelled to alter it, and make it applicable only to matters of rebellion.

One of the firmest believers in the existence of King Richard, who encouraged all others by every means in her power, was the old Countess of Oxford, Maud de Ufford, the mother of the ill-fated Duke of Ireland. She caused copies of Richard's device, the white hart, to be manufactured in silver, and conferred them upon various knights and powerful men to induce them to share and support her views.

Another, perhaps more important, personage who made no secret of his faith in the existence of Richard in Scotland was Sir John Oldcastle, Lord Cobham.

> 'If somewhere in the North, as rumour sang,
> Fluttering the hawks of this crown-lusting line—
> By firth and lock thy silver-sister grow,
> That were my rose, there the allegiance due.'

Fifteen years later, when placed on his tial for heresy, he declared he could not accept the authority of the Court before whom he was brought, so long as his liege lord, King Richard, was alive in Scotland.

At the same time King Henry was subjected to private accusations and challenges in reference to the death of King Richard.

Aug. 7. Louis, Duke of Orleans, sent him a challenge to meet, with one hundred knights and esquires, and combat until one of the parties should surrender.

Dec. 5. Henry answered that he was surprised to receive such a letter from a brother of the King of France during a time of truce between the two nations. Still more was he astonished, he continued, because a special alliance had been made between themselves when he was in Paris in 1396, which alliance must now, of course, be at an end. The King went on to say that he was not bound to reply to such a demand as the Duke's, except from persons of equal rank; that he should visit his own possessions at any time, and with as many followers as might be convenient, and that, should the Duke then desire a combat, so long as it might please God to suffer it, he should not be disappointed.

1403. March 26. The Duke's letter had evidently been addressed to Henry as Duke of Lancaster, and the King had expressed some doubt whether it was for him or not. Louis therefore wrote another letter, addressed to him as King of England, saying: 'I had not indeed given you your new titles at length, because I do not approve of the manner whereby you have attained them; but know that my letter was addressed to you.' He goes on to charge Henry with disloyalty to his cousin,

King Richard, and unmistakably evinces his own belief in the death of the latter having been brought about by Henry. He then goes on to the subject of Queen Isabelle, who, after great delay, had been sent back to France in the previous July, deprived of everything, down to her jewels, and burdened with a claim for 500,000 crowns said to be still unpaid of the ransom for King Jean after the battle of Poitiers. 'How could you suffer,' he writes, 'my redoubted lady, the Queen of England, to return so desolate to this country after the death of her lord, despoiled by your rigour and cruelty of her dower, which you detain from her, and likewise the portion she carried hence on her marriage? The man who seeks to gain honour is always the defender and guardian of the rights of widows and damsels of virtuous life, such as my niece was known to lead.'

Henry responded to this attack on his honour, as he says, April 30. 'although, considering the situation in which it has pleased God to place us, we are not bound to make you any reply.' 'In regard to the dignity we hold, we are surprised you do not approve it nor the manner by which we obtained it. We made you fully acquainted with our intentions before we left France, at which time you approved of them, and even promised us aid against our very dear lord and cousin, King Richard.' He then goes on to say that, as God had favoured his undertaking, so he hoped for His continued grace and mercy. He then proceeds: 'In regard to that passage in your letter where you speak of the decease of our very dear cousin and lord, adding: "God knows how it happened, or by whom caused," we know not with what intent this expression is used, but if you mean or dare to say that his death was caused by our order or consent, it is false, and will be a falsehood every time you utter it; and this we are ready to prove in personal combat if you be willing, and have the courage to dare it.'

Notwithstanding this war of words, they never personally met in the field. Henry complained to the French Government, which had not yet recognised him, with the view of silencing the Duke as an infringer of the truce. The reply received by his ambassadors was concise: 'Neither the King nor his Council have ever broken, nor will they ever break, their engagements. This is the only answer that can be returned.'

Valeran de Luxemburg, Count de Ligny and de St. Pol, who was Feb. 10. also a prince of the empire, sent a herald with a defiance of war against King Henry, 'as having been notoriously accused and severely blamed for the destruction of King Richard.'

To this announcement the King made answer that he held his menaces cheap, and that his will was that Count Valeran should enjoy his country and his subjects.

The Count began preparations for war, but first came a remarkable spectacle. He caused an effigy to be made of the Earl of Rutland, against whom he had conceived a great hatred. As with many others, he believed that the Earl had voluntarily betrayed the secrets of the Windsor conspirators. This figure, with an emblazoned coat of arms, was carried from his castle of Bohain, and, during the night, hung head downwards on a gibbet which his followers erected at the gates of Calais. The garrison, of course, cut it down on the following morning, and carried it into the town. Two or three years later they had their revenge, when they utterly discomfited him in his attack on the castle of Mercq, killed or took prisoners the greater part of the commanders on the French side, captured all the carts or engines of war, and obliged the Count to flee for his life, through St. Omer back to Therouenne.

Valeran Count de St. Pol died in 1415. He had by his wife, Maud Holland, only one daughter, Johanna, who had married Anthony Count of Rethel, afterwards Duke of Brabant, who was grandson of Jean le Bon, King of France. Johanna died in 1407, leaving two sons, Jean and Philippe, who were the last dukes of Brabant, the land and title going to their cousin, Philippe le Bon, Duke of Burgundy.

Far more serious opposition than that evinced by his two French correspondents was now manifested in a quarter where the King little expected it.

The nominal King of Scotland at that time was Robert III.; but almost the whole power was in the hands of a crafty and cruel man—his brother, Robert, Duke of Albany. He was jealous of his nephew David, Duke of Rothesay, an ardent and reckless young man, but with many good points about him, who could see through his uncle's schemes, but had not sufficient influence to thwart them. His life was somewhat irregular, and it was thought that a wife might be a check upon him. At Albany's instigation it was decided to put the hand of the heir-apparent to the throne at the disposal of the noble who should offer the highest price for it. The powerful George, Earl of March and Dunbar, was the highest bidder, and to his daughter Elizabeth (or Janet), therefore, the prince was contracted. This gave great offence to Archibald, third Earl of Douglas, who offered a larger sum with the hand of his daughter Marjory. The Duke of Albany, in true huckstering spirit, at once broke off the match with Elizabeth of Dunbar, and David was married to Marjory Douglas. The unfortunate Duke did not long survive his ill-starred marriage. His mother, Queen Amabel, and his father-in-law, who both had considerable influence over him, died in 1401. Then came a contest for power between David and his uncle. The prince was entrapped and carried to the castle of Falkland, belonging to Albany, where he was thrown into a dungeon. There for fifteen days he endured all the extremities of hunger and thirst until he died of starvation some time in March, 1402. The body was buried privately in the monastery of Lindores, and the report was spread that the prince had died of dysentery.

There is considerable analogy to be found between the fate of David, Duke of Rothesay, and that of Richard II., King of England.

The Earl of March, or Earl of Dunbar, as it may be well to call him, very naturally incensed at this breach of contract, renounced his fealty to his own King and did homage to Henry IV. of England, who gladly welcomed him, and granted to him and his heirs lands of considerable yearly value. In conjunction with the Earl of Northumberland, he totally routed a body of marauding Scots on Nesbit Moor, slaying June 22. their leader, Sir Andrew Hepburn, of Hales, and many other chiefs.

To avenge this loss, Archibald, fourth Earl of Douglas, who had 1401. received a grant of all the vast possessions of the Earl of Dunbar, collected an army numbering 10,000 men. With these followers he ravaged the country as far as Newcastle. On their return, however, laden with booty, they were met at Millfield, near Wooler, in the northern part of the county, by Northumberland and his ally, who had in the meantime increased their forces.

Douglas took up a strong position on Homildon Hill. The gallant Sept. 14. Hotspur was about to lead his men to the attack when Dunbar advised him to try what the archers could do. The advice was followed; shower after shower of arrows fell among the opposing force, all taking dire effect. Douglas, with his men-at-arms, tried to advance. The archers retired slowly, stopping occasionally to pour fresh volleys into the ranks of their foes. The Earl of Douglas fell from his horse, wounded in five different places, and the fight was over. It was won solely by the archers, not a blow being struck on the English side by either knight or squire. As many as 800 of the enemy are computed to have been slain or drowned in crossing the Tweed. The captives included the Earl of Douglas, one of whose wounds robbed him of an eye; Murdac Stewart, eldest son of the Regent Albany; the Earls of Moray and Angus, together with many French and Scottish knights, and several gentlemen of the first position.

Sir Walter Scott, in the dramatic poem of 'Halidon Hill,' celebrates some of the events of the battle on the day of the Exaltation of the Holy Cross at Homildon.

Among the prisoners was William Stewart, a knight of Teviotdale. This district had at one time been an English possession, but had been won back by the power of the Douglas family. On the plea, however, that he was the King of England's man, and, being taken in arms against him, was a traitor, Sir William was put upon his trial, together with his squire, Thomas Ker. One jury acquitted them, but Hotspur assembled another which was more subservient. They were condemned and executed as traitors, and their quarters set up on the gates of York. It was a lawless and unjust act, such as could not have been expected from the valiant Harry Percy. Wyntown writes that an Englishman prophesied as follows:

> 'Men may happen for to see,
> Ere a year be gone, that he
> Who caused that limb to be yonder set,
> Now upon that very gate,
> His own limb shall be right so,
> So may fare the game to go.'

This battle of Homildon Hill was the beginning of the end of the connection between the Percys and the man whom they had helped to a throne. What was the actual cause of complaint is not very clear. It may have been that the King kept back certain moneys which the Earl considered his due for the wardenship of the Marches; or that the King demanded the surrender to him of the prisoners taken at Homildon, whom Percy considered as his lawful prize, to Oct. ransom or retain as he pleased. Murdac Stewart, Earl of Fife, son of Albany, and six other captive knights were delivered up to Henry, who made a grant of the earldom of Douglas, with Eskdale, Liddesdale, Teviotdale, etc., to the Earl of Northumberland, who was to take possession of the lands—when he could. Northumberland made an alliance with Douglas, who, in lieu of ransom, was to aid him with a number of Scottish knights.

We must now return to Wales. Sir Edmund Mortimer, who had been taken prisoner by Glyndwr at Knighton, applied to King Henry for permission to obtain his liberty by payment of a certain sum to his captor. But the King, under the pretence that Mortimer had allowed himself to be made prisoner, forbade any attempts being made to release him, friendly or otherwise. There can be little doubt that this declaration was owing to a mean spirit of jealousy on the part of Henry, who knew that Edmund Mortimer was the uncle, and proper guardian of the rights, of his nephew, the younger Edmund Mortimer, the right owner of the crown.

'Wherefore he laye in feters and sore prysone,
For none payment of his greate raunsone.'

Nov. This decision led to very fatal results. Mortimer, from being suspected as a traitor, really became one. He married a daughter of Glyndwr on St. Andrew's Day, and leagued with him to restore Richard, *if alive*, or, in case he was dead, to place young Edmund on the throne.

Henry, Lord Percy, better known as Hotspur, who had married Elizabeth, the sister of the imprisoned Mortimer, having likewise had his request to ransom his brother-in-law refused, was so much embittered by the injustice that he also made an alliance with Glyndwr, which he induced his father, the Earl of Northumberland, and his uncle, the Earl of Worcester, to join. A formal treaty, it is said, was drawn up, whereby the kingdom was to be divided: Owain Glyndwr to have Wales and all the lands beyond the Severn; the Earl of Northumberland all the country north of the Trent; while the Earl of March was to hold the remainder.

The strangely-assorted allies, the Earls of Northumberland and Douglas, with their forces, set out on an expedition to recover the 1403. lands in Teviotdale, and James of Gladstanes, Laird of Cocklaws, May. sent to inform the Regent Albany that he had been compelled to promise to deliver up his castle or tower of Cocklaws unless relieved before Lammas Day, August 1. According to promise made,

Albany arrived before the date named—but Percy was not there. The object in view may have been to enlist the Duke of Albany on the side of the conspirators and get him to invade England. Or it may simply have been intended to divert King Henry's attention from their real design. The King set out to join the Percys, but June. had not completed half the journey when news reached him, at Burton-on-Trent, which caused his instant return.

On leaving Scotland the Percys made their way south as quickly July. as possible. The Earl himself was obliged, by indisposition, to remain at home, but the forces marched onward. In Lancashire and Cheshire Hotspur summoned men to rise and fight for King Richard, who was still alive. The very name of Richard was like a trumpet call, and they answered by assembling to the number of many hundreds to do battle against the usurper, Henry of Bolingbroke. They then marched on to Shrewsbury, and arrived at the gates very shortly after King Henry, who had departed in all haste from Burton-on-Trent, had entered the town.

A defiance was issued in the names of Henry Percy, Earl of Northumberland; Henry Lord Percy, his eldest son; and Thomas Percy, his brother, Earl of Worcester, in which they solemnly declared Henry to be a perjurer, usurper, murderer, oppressor, subverter of laws, and extortioner.

Briefly it was to the following effect:

1. 'Thou didst make oath on the Holy Gospels at Doncaster never to claim the crown, kingdom, or state royal, but only the inheritance of thyself and thy wife; that Richard, our King and thine, should reign during the term of his life whom yet thou didst imprison, and crownedst thyself King instead.

2. 'Contrary to thy oath, thou hast levied tenths and fifteenths on all manner of people by thine own authority alone.

3. 'Contrary to thine oath thou hast caused our sovereign lord and thine, King Richard, traitorously, within the castle of Pomfret, without the consent or judgment of the lords of the realm, by the space of fifteen days and nights, with hunger, thirst, and cold to perish, to be murdered.

4. 'Contrary to thy oath, when King Richard was, by that horrible murder, dead, thou didst usurp and take the kingdom wrongfully and unjustly from Edmund Mortimer, Earl of March and Ulster, the next and direct heir, by due course of inheritance.

5. 'Contrary to thy oath at thy coronation, thou didst cause letters to be written to every shire in England to choose only such knights as should be subservient to thy cause.

6. 'When Edmund Mortimer, brother of Roger Mortimer, Earl of March, was taken in mortal fight against Owen Glendore, cast into prison and laden with iron fetters for thy cause, thou didst proclaim him as willingly taken prisoner, and wouldst not deliver him thyself, nor suffer us his kinsmen to do so. When we, at our own costs, had agreed for his ransom, and for a peace between thee and the said

Glendore, thou didst proclaim us traitors, and hast conspired for the destruction of our persons.

'For which causes we defy thee, thy fautors and accomplices, as traitors and destroyers of the realm, and as invaders, oppressors, and confounders of the rights of the true and direct heir of England and France.'

King Henry replied that the charges were false and feigned, as the sword should prove. When the armies were drawn up opposite one another on Saturday, the eve of St. Mary Magdalen's Day, he sent two messengers with offers of conciliation. According to Shakspere, he said to the Earl of Worcester:

July 21.

> 'We love our people well; even those we love
> That are misled upon your cousin's part:
> And, will they take the offer of our grace,
> Both he, and they, and you, yea, every man
> Shall be my friend again, and I'll be his.'

The offers were declined, so it is said, by the advice of the Earl. It is not to be wondered at if he did give such counsel. Thomas Percy, Earl of Worcester, was a talented and accomplished man; he was, in addition, a great statesman and a chivalrous knight. He must have felt sure that, despite any promises or oaths, Henry was not the man to forget or forgive the framers of the charges made against himself.

The King ordered the advance of his army to the cry of 'St. George!' His opponents shouted 'Espérance! Percy!' and the fight began on Hateley Field, two or three miles out of the town. The archers on each side did deadly execution; the corpses strewed the ground 'like leaves in autumn.' The King, by the advice of the Earl of Dunbar, was arrayed as a private knight, while some knights had assumed the royal arms. Among these were Sir Walter Blount, and Sir Edmund de Stafford, the young Earl of Stafford, only twenty-six years of age, who had married Lady Anne Plantagenet, daughter of Thomas, late Earl of Gloucester. These two were both slain in an impetuous charge made by Harry Percy and the Earl of Douglas with some thirty followers upon the centre of the royal troops not far removed from the spot where the King was posted. The royal standard was overthrown, and the King unhorsed. At this time the battle appeared to be going in favour of the rebels. Henry, Prince of Wales had been wounded in the face by an arrow, though he would not quit the field, and many of the leaders among the royalists had been slain. Fortune, however, proved fickle. As the two chiefs, Percy and Douglas, were cutting their way back, an arrow from some hand unknown pierced the brain of the former, as he raised his visor for a moment's breath of fresh air, and he fell dead upon the spot. The King called out 'Victory! Harry Percy is dead!' and the rebels dispersed after three hours' hard fighting. It was the bloodiest battle which had ever taken place between Englishmen. Some fourteen thousand men were engaged on each side, and about one-third of the whole number are computed to have been slain. Among them were two hundred knights and squires of Cheshire.

The result might have been different if most of the lords who had promised their assistance to the Percys had not failed to keep to their compact, and if Glyndwr had been able to join forces. Unfortunately, the Welsh chief was at the other side of the river. The water at that time was so high that his men could not pass over by the ford, and the bridge was in possession of King Henry. Owain was therefore obliged to remain an inactive spectator of the defeat of his friends. Tradition says that he saw the battle from amid the branches of an oak-tree at Shelton. King Henry founded a church on the field of battle, of which some portion is still standing.

The Earl of Worcester was taken prisoner and beheaded at Shrewsbury, together with Sir Richard Vernon, an ancestor of the noted Dorothy, who, by her moonlight flitting with Sir John Manners, brought the far-famed Haddon Hall to the house of Rutland. The Earl of Douglas was also a prisoner, but, as a foreigner, treated with all consideration. Sir Robert Stewart of Durrisdeer, a friend of Douglas, was among the slain. *July 23.*

The gallant Hotspur was honourably buried, but the body was afterwards dug up, beheaded and quartered, and one of the limbs set up on the gate of York, thus verifying the prediction of the previous year. He left one son, Henry, who became second Earl of Northumberland.

Sir Edmund Mortimer fled into Scotland, and was made Laird of Craiggivar, Aberdeenshire. His brother, Sir John, was sent to the Tower, but, having made many attempts to escape, was removed to Pevensey and subsequently executed.

Owain Glyndwr had not given up his contest for the Principality. In the year following he attacked with success the castle of Harlech and several others. But in 1405, the rival Prince of Wales, Henry of Monmouth, marched against him, and, after a bloody engagement, in which 800 men were killed, captured Grosmont Castle, which was under the command of Glyndwr's son, Gruffydd. A month later Owain's forces were again defeated with still greater loss in Brecknockshire, when his son was taken prisoner and his brother slain. Owain's star was on the wane. His title of Prince of Wales was now, however, acknowledged by the King of France, who sent a force of several thousand men to his assistance. The joint forces took Caermarthen Castle, and compelled Henry of Monmouth to fall back for a time. On the return of King Henry from the north, the two armies remained watching one another, until the French, seeing no prospect of gaining much glory, and being dissatisfied with the provisions they could procure, thought it advisable to return to their own land.

Being thus abandoned, and left to his own resources, Owain could offer but feeble resistance. He had some successes, but more defeats. Finally his distresses were such that he often had to flee to the caves in the mountains of Caernarvonshire or Merionethshire for shelter.

But he resolutely maintained his independence until the close of the reign of King Henry IV. He died quietly, at the house of one of his married daughters in Herefordshire, about four months after his gallant opponent, the whilom Prince of Wales, as King Henry V. had won the glorious Battle of Azincourt.

The Welsh air 'Sweet Richard' is generally supposed to have been composed by Glyndwr in loving memory of the King, to whom he was so tenderly and almost romantically attached.

Although King Henry had won the Battle of Shrewsbury, his troubles were not by any means at an end. He sent the Earl of Westmorland to intercept the Earl of Northumberland, who, having recovered from his indisposition, had placed himself at the head of his retainers, raised, as he declared, on behalf of the King, while at the same time he disavowed the actions of his son. But nothing availed him. He was confined as a traitor and deprived, for a time, of all the honours which had been conferred upon him. At the same time, the King ordered that the Lady Elizabeth Percy, the widow of Hotspur, should be arrested and brought before him. Whether, as being a Mortimer, he had any special grudge against her, or whether he sought to gain from her facts criminating her late husband and her father-in-law, history telleth not, but the deed itself does not tend to exalt one's ideas of Henry's chivalry. The lords, many of whom in their secret hearts sided with Northumberland, claimed their right to pronounce judgment on him. They declared that the Earl had not been guilty of treason but only of trespasses, for which he ought to pay a fine at the King's pleasure. On swearing fealty to the King and all his sons, Percy was released, and all fines and penalties were afterwards remitted. He, and all in any way connected with him, most probably bitterly regretted their hostility to King Richard.

1404. Feb. A curious ceremony followed this act of mercy. At the request of the Commons, Henry Percy, Earl of Northumberland, and Ralph Neville, Earl of Westmorland, in full Parliament, thrice clasped hands, and as often kissed each other in token of perfect amity, promising, at the same time, that their men should do the like. It is not, however, recorded whether this promise took effect. It appears rather doubtful.

In the meantime the King had become less popular with the people, owing to his frequent though necessary demands for money. In the 'Lack-learning Parliament' the Commons suggested the resumption of crown lands and the appropriation of Church property, to which he assented. Thereby he incurred the distrust of the lords spiritual and temporal. The bill which the Lower House had prepared was unanimously rejected.

1405. The Earl of Northumberland, though pardoned, felt sure he was not forgiven, and would not again be trusted. Thomas Lord Bardolf had not, therefore, much difficulty in stirring him up to join another rising. Thomas Lord Mowbray, Earl of Nottingham, son of the banished and deceased Duke of Norfolk, smarting under the loss of the hereditary office of Earl Marshal, which had been granted by King Henry to the Earl of Westmorland, went with his armed forces to the well-beloved Archbishop of York, and avowed his purpose of obtaining satisfaction.

The Archbishop at that time was Sir Richard Scrope, a younger brother of the Earl of Wiltshire, who had been hanged, by order of Henry, Duke of Lancaster, at Bristol. He considered Henry a usurper, guilty of perjury and treason, and was a firm upholder of the right of the Earl of March to the throne. He preached a sermon, rehearsing all the ills under which the nation suffered, and exhorting all who heard him to assist in providing a remedy. A paper was affixed to the doors of all churches and monasteries in the city accusing Henry of perjury, murder, rebellion and usurpation, and a force of 8,000 men was soon collected and led to Shipton, about five miles from York.

The Earl of Westmorland, with whom was Prince John of Lancaster, a youth of sixteen years of age, the third son of the King, lay near them with an inferior force. The Earl, fearing to hazard an action, resorted to artifice. He sent to the Archbishop to request a conference. Scrope at once agreed, and, after some persuasion, so did also the more suspicious Mowbray.

The Archbishop stated to the leaders of the royal troops that his object was to bring about certain reforms, which he particularized. The Earl professed approval, agreed that all the demands were just, and promised that the King would give satisfaction. He then proposed a cup of wine, that they might drink to the renewal of concord, and suggested the dismissal of both armies. The Archbishop and Mowbray fell into the trap, sending a message to their troops that they might disperse, as there would not be any fighting. Westmorland had, however, not sent any such orders to his own army, and as soon as he knew that the opposing force had left, the Archbishop and the Earl Marshal were arrested as traitors and taken to Pontefract, where the King had arrived. From there they were carried in his train to Bishopthorpe, a manor belonging to the Archbishopric. It seems extraordinary that so clever a man as Scrope undoubtedly was, to say nothing of Mowbray, should have fallen so easily and completely into such a palpable snare.

King Henry ordered Sir William Gascoigne, Chief Justice of England, to sentence the prisoners to death as guilty of treason. But Gascoigne, the upright judge, absolutely refused, saying that no one could lawfully condemn a bishop to death, and that the Earl Marshal must be tried by his Peers. Foiled in this attempt, but determined to carry his point, Henry called upon a knight named Fulthorpe to take upon him the office. He, without any other authority than the King's word, without any pretence of justice or any form of trial, condemned the two unfortunates to death, and they were at once taken to execution in a field between Bishopthorpe June 8.

and York. The Archbishop was far more composed than his companion, whom he had to encourage to meet his end bravely. He himself declared that he had never intended any evil against the person of King Henry, and hoped that his death might not be revenged upon him or any of his friends. Both were buried in the cathedral, and at the eastern end of the Lady Chapel there is a stone monument to the memory of the Archbishop. The Earl Marshal's head was put on a pole outside the Micklegate Bar, which was the general place for the heads of those deemed rebels to the crown.

By his people the Archbishop was venerated as a martyr, and as many pilgrimages were made to his tomb, where miracles were supposed to be worked, the King ordered that they should be stopped. Nothing, however, could stop the feeling of horror which was excited all through the country at this execution, and when Henry shortly afterwards was attacked with leprosy, it was by great numbers of people regarded as a judgment of God for the crime.

Pope Innocent VII. issued a sentence of excommunication against all who were in any way implicated in the deed. The King, it is said, sent to his Holiness a portion of the armour which the deceased prelate had worn on the day of his arrest, with the message, 'Know whether this be thy son's coat or no.' It may be true, but, if so, there was not any originality about it, the same story being told of King Richard I. and the Bishop of Beauvais. Further back still, we learn that William the Conqueror had his brother Odo arrested, *not* as Bishop of Bayeux, but as Earl of Kent, both titles being borne by him. In the following year, 1407, when Gregory XII. sat on the papal throne, all the participators in the murder were allowed to receive absolution on condition of acknowledging their guilt.

Not satisfied with the success he had obtained, Henry endeavoured to induce the Peers to declare Scrope and Mowbray guilty of treason, but they declined to come to any decision. They, however, had no hesitation in regard to the Earl of Northumberland, Lords Bardolf and Fauconbridge, Sir Ralph Hastings, and some others, who, not being ready in time to join in the Yorkshire rising after giving up Berwick to the Scots, had retreated to Edinburgh, and they were unanimously declared to be traitors.

The King immediately took possession of Warkworth, the great stronghold of the Percys, and then marched against Berwick, which surrendered after considerable damage had been done to it. Fauconbridge and Hastings were taken prisoners and beheaded, together with seven other Englishmen. In returning, he seized the Castles of Alnwick, Prudhoe, and Cockermouth, and then started for Wales.

1407. The Earl of Northumberland and Lord Bardolf were in a state of perplexity. For a time they were in Scotland, but, hearing that King Henry had promised to set certain Scottish prisoners at liberty, on condition of his two rebellious subjects being delivered up to him, they fled into Wales. There they endeavoured to concert measures with Glyndwr for deposing Henry. Then they went to France and Flanders to try and raise men, but, not meeting with much success, they returned to Scotland. For a time they were living in the Castle of the Bishop of St. Andrew's; then at St. Johnston's, where the Duke of Albany entertained them nobly, and strenuously advised them not to return to England.

But they must needs rush on their fate. With a considerable 1408. force of Scottish mercenaries they entered Northumberland, and recovered some of the Earl's possessions. This encouraged them to proceed. The march was continued to Thirsk, where a proclamation was published that they were come as liberators from tyranny. Sir Thomas Rokeby, Sheriff of Yorkshire, went to bar their passage at Grimbald Bridge, near Knaresborough, but they eluded him and proceeded by Wetherby to Tadcaster. About five miles from that town, on Bramham Moor, they were brought to bay. The fight was stubborn and cruel, but victory remained with Feb. 19. Sir Thomas. The Earl was slain, Lord Bardolf was taken prisoner, when mortally wounded, and died almost immediately afterwards. Their heads, that of the Earl white with age, were set up on London Bridge. The body of the Earl was quartered, and placed upon the gates at London, Lincoln, Berwick-upon-Tweed, and Newcastle-upon-Tyne, but only remained until May, when, by order of the King, all were taken down and delivered to his friends.

The Bishop of Bangor and the Abbot of Hales were among the captives. The latter was hung, by order of the King, for having been taken when in arms.

The character of the first Earl of Northumberland is not one to be greatly admired, though there were few perhaps in those days who would have acted differently under the circumstances. He foully betrayed the King who had first advanced him to honour, and rebelled against the man he had helped to a throne. Among his own people he was greatly esteemed and beloved. They thought he had been harshly treated by King Henry, who became very unpopular with them, and, before many months had gone, with the whole nation.

The King himself was not the man he had been Nine years of rebellions had preyed upon his spirits and worn out his strength. His courage was still unabated, and he retained all his old vigilance, temper, and cautiousness. But he was suspicious, and soured by the discontent of his supporters at not being rewarded in accordance with their own ideas of their deserts, and by his inability to obtain subsidies when required.

In addition to his public troubles, Henry had foes in his own household. As early as the year 1401 we read that an iron, with three spikes, was laid in his bed, evidently with the intention that he should receive serious bodily injury. At other times his shirt and his hose were smeared with some venomous substance injurious to life, and poison was put both in his meat and drink.

He had cause enough to exclaim :

'Uneasy lies the head that wears a crown.'

Llwyelyn ap Owain,* Lord of South Wales, married Eleanor, d. of Henri, Comte de Bar, and Eleanor, eldest d. of King Edward I.

Llwyelyn, last Prince of Wales, slain at Builth, 1282; m. Eleanor de Montfort, gdau. of King John and cousin of King Edward I.

Catherine, m. Philip, Lord of Yscoed.

Thomas ap Llwyelyn, = Eleanor.
Lord of South Wales.

Eleanor, m. Gruffydd Vychan, Lord of Glyndurdy, lineal descendant of Llwyelyn ap Sitsylht, *ob.* 1021.
|
Owain Glyndwr.

Margaret, m. Meredyth ap Twdwr.

Owain Twdwr, m. Katherine of Valois. (Their grandson was King Henry VII.)

Eleanor de Montfort, who married the last Prince of Wales, was cousin of King Edward I. Eleanor de Bar, who married Llwyelyn ap Owain, was cousin of Edward III.

SKETCH X.

THE RIGHTFUL HEIR.

IT has been shown how the well-meaning but easily-influenced Edmund of Langley, Duke of York, was persuaded by his nephew Henry, Duke of Lancaster, to countenance proceedings against his other nephew, King Richard. What arguments Henry used to induce his uncle thus to betray his trust may never be known; but it is a striking instance of the mastery of a strong mind over a weaker one.

1402. The Duke did not survive the accession of King Henry quite three years, as he died August 1, 1402, aged sixty-one. He was buried by the side of his first wife, Isabel of Castile, in the church of the Friars Preachers at Langley, in Hertfordshire. This church, which was built in 1311, was destroyed in 1575, during the reign of Queen Elizabeth, and the tomb was then removed to the church of All Saints, at King's Langley. The vicar of the parish has kindly informed me that 'the tomb is a very beautiful one. It was transferred from a very awkward position in the chancel to a chapel which was built for it, to the expenses of which her Majesty Queen Victoria contributed, some fifteen years ago.'

Edmund was succeeded in his title and estates by his eldest son, Edward, Earl of Rutland. He left one other son, Richard, Earl of Cambridge, and a daughter, Constance.

Rutland in early life conducted himself in accordance with the

* This genealogy is from Burke's 'Royal Families.'

manners and customs of his mother's foreign kindred. There must have been something attractive about him, for he was loved by his cousin King Richard almost beyond any other man, and anything he had chosen to ask would probably have been granted him. The attachment was apparently reciprocal, and yet he deserted Richard and went to meet his other cousin, Henry of Bolingbroke, soon after his landing.

At the time of the quarrel between the Dukes of Hereford and Norfolk, the former affirmed to the Duke of Albemarle—Rutland's title at that date—that, according to what Norfolk said, 'the King, notwithstanding his fair countenance and great oaths, did yet intend to oppress the Dukes of Lancaster, Albemarle, and Exeter.' Albemarle might have thought there was truth in this assertion, and therefore have drifted away from Richard. At the lists of Coventry it may also be remembered that Albemarle was taken into the confidence of the Duke of Hereford.

Soon after King Henry came to the throne, the Earl of Rutland was appointed Lieutenant of Aquitaine. This may have been as a reward for his servility, or, on the other hand, the King may have desired to remove him from England.

He was suspected of being concerned in the Percys' conspiracy. Naturally, he denied it, but he had been connected with so many plots that it seems very probable he had agreed to join and had then deserted them.

Amid the conspiracies and rebellions which troubled the greater part of the reign of King Henry, he yet found time for the arrangement of family matters.

Soon after coming to the throne, he had caused masses to be sung for the repose of the soul of his wife, Mary de Bohun, under the title of Queen Mary. Yet in a year or two he thought it desirable to fill her place. The lady of his choice was Juana of Navarre, a descendant by both parents of the royal family of France, the widow of that John de Montfort who had been of such signal assistance to Henry in providing vessels for his return to England. Henry was probably struck with her appearance when he first saw her in Brittany. She would at that time be at the height of her beauty, very sweet-looking, but a woman of majestic grace and dignity. His first proposal appears to have been made a little more than a year after the death of her first husband. As they were distant connections, it was necessary that a dispensation should be obtained. But there were difficulties in the way. There was at that time a schism in the Church. Whilst Henry acknowledged Boniface IX. in Rome as Pope, Juana was on the side of Benedict XIII. at Avignon. Juana or her agents managed matters more adroitly, perhaps, than Henry could have done. A dispensation was obtained, which allowed her to marry anyone she pleased within the fourth degree of consanguinity, without any name having been mentioned.

The royal couple were married by proxy at Eltham on April 3,

1402. Henry may have expected to obtain great influence in Brittany, and even to have the guardianship of the young Duke—no more selfish or worldly-prudent man lived—but, if so, he was disappointed, for they were consigned to the care of Philip, Duke of Burgundy.

1403. Thomas FitzAlan, Earl of Arundel, was placed in command of the fleet which was sent out to escort the bride-elect to England. He was accompanied by two of the King's half-brothers, John de Beaufort, Earl of Somerset, and Henry de Beaufort, Bishop of Lincoln, also by Thomas de Percy, Earl of Worcester, Lord Chamberlain. The Duchess—or, rather, Queen, as she had already assumed the title—embarked on January 13, 1403, but the passage was unfortunate. The fleet was driven by storms on to the coast of Cornwall. All had to disembark at Falmouth, and proceed thence to Winchester.

There the King was found waiting for them. The marriage was celebrated in the cathedral with great magnificence on February 7, and the bridal banquet afterwards was a very costly one. The coronation of the new Queen took place on the 26th of the same month.

Queen Juana, or Joanna, as she is usually styled, brought with her two of her daughters, Blanche and Marguerite, leaving behind her two others, Marie and Jeanne, and four sons, Jean, Duke of Bretagne, Arthur, Jules, and Richard. Much cannot be said of the motherly affection of a woman who, at the call of ambition—it can scarcely have been love—would leave six young children, of whom the eldest was not more than fifteen, to wear the crown matrimonial of England, at the age of three-and-thirty. She was never popular in her new country.

The King also found husbands for his two daughters. Blanche, the elder, was married the same year to Louis III., Elector Palatine from 1410 to 1439, son of the Emperor Ruprecht, an active and energetic ruler, but unable, in his short reign of ten years, to effect much good during the time of confusion in which he lived. Louis is chiefly remarkable as being president of the Council of Constance when John Huss and Jerome of Prague, followers of John Wycliffe, were condemned to the flames in 1415 and 1416. When Huss was bound to the stake, the Elector offered him a pardon if he would recant, but he refused it.

Blanche died before 1417, leaving only one son, Ruprecht, who died in 1426, at the age of nineteen.

1405. Philippa, the younger daughter of King Henry, was married in 1405 to Eric X. of Pomerania, who in 1412 succeeded his great-aunt Margaret, the famous Semiramis of the North, as King of Denmark, Sweden, and Norway. But he was not a success. Being deposed in 1439, after a reign of twenty-seven years, he lived on for twenty years longer, and then died without issue.

Whilst on the subject of marriages, one may be mentioned as

taking place in this same year—that, namely, of 'a man whom the King delighted to honour,' Thomas FitzAlan, Earl of Arundel, and Doña Beatrix, a natural daughter of Joao I., King of Portugal. King Henry was present at the ceremony, which took place with great splendour in the Chapel Royal.

On February 14 in this year a female figure, enveloped in sable garments, entered the precincts of Windsor. She appeared rather to shun observation. Why should she do so? As Lady Constance of York, daughter of the late and sister of the then Duke, she had the right of entrée to the Castle, which none would have disputed. But she had come to play a desperate game, in which caution and secrecy were absolute necessities.

Constance of York was, in a manner, doubly related to King Henry. They were first cousins through their fathers; the lady's mother and the King's step-mother were sisters, and Henry's half-sister Catherine, Queen of Castile, was, of course, also first cousin to Constance. Nevertheless, she was determined to make an endeavour to oust Henry from his throne.

Like her brother Edward, she had followed in the steps of her Castilian relatives. For a time she had lived with Edmund, Earl of Kent, but left him to marry Sir Thomas le Despenser, who was soon afterwards created Earl of Gloucester. He, as we know, lost his life in trying to carry out the New Year's plot of 1400, and his widow, feeling that she and her children had been more harshly treated than the relations of others who were equally, if not more, guilty, panted for revenge.

When the shades of evening began to descend on that February day, the Lady Constance commenced her operations. Every room was, of course, well known to her, and she had no difficulty in passing from one to another, avoiding only those which were occupied, with one exception. She particularly desired access to a room in the Norman Tower, which was always kept fast locked. She had with her a bunch of keys, which had been made expressly for her by a cunning locksmith of Windsor. She gained an entrance to the Tower, and was soon at the door of the room she wanted. Again she found the key to fit the lock, and entered the chamber.

There she found the objects of her search, Edmund Mortimer, Earl of March, the rightful possessor of the throne, a boy about thirteen years of age, and Roger Mortimer, his younger brother. The boys both recognised their visitor, and gladly agreed to accompany her when she said she was come to take them to their uncle, Sir Edmund, who, with many others, including Owain Glyndwr, was preparing to make another attempt to depose King Henry. When darkness came on they descended, and found egress at a gate opening into the park. Mounting horses which had been provided beforehand, they rode away westward.

Next morning there was a hue-and-cry when the two captives could not be found, although every conceivable spot was searched. The question was as to who had let them out. As Lady Constance was also missing, and had not been seen to pass out, the inference was natural that she was with them. Horsemen were at once sent in pursuit of the runaways, who were found in the woods which at that time covered the Chiltern Hills, and brought back. The boys were again placed in their rooms in the Norman Tower, perhaps not sorry to have some rest after the hurry and fatigue of their bootless night journey. Lady Constance was taken before the Council for examination.

There she averred that her brother Edward was not only the originator of the scheme, but that he had also, some weeks previously, planned the murder of the King and his sons at Eltham, and, failing in that, had come to her for assistance now, and had provided the keys which she used on the occasion. She also named Thomas Lord Mowbray as an accomplice of her brother's.

Both the accused denied all knowledge of any such schemes as were laid to their charge. Constance produced a champion, William Maidstone, who was willing to do battle on her behalf against her brother, and, if he were defeated, she was ready, she said, to be burnt to death. The Duke of York, after considerable hesitation, accepted the challenge, but the King, for reasons of his own, would not give his consent to the combat.

The Duke had about this time ventured to send some love verses to Queen Joanna, and though no shadow even of suspicion could attach to the Queen, this may have contributed to the sentence passed upon him, which was confinement in the castle of Pevensey, in Sussex, during the King's pleasure. It was at one time reported that he had perished there, but, after a detention of a few months, he recovered both his liberty and his lands, and towards the close of the year following he was appointed Constable of the Tower.

He had at one time been with the Prince of Wales in his wars against Glyndwr, and there suffered under a charge of cowardice. It required all the energy of the Prince to vindicate his character in the Parliament of 1407, by declaring that he had shown both wisdom and gallantry in great emergencies. York's treacheries had made him odious to both sides, and yet Henry of Monmouth would appear to have had some attachment to him, perhaps in consequence of their relationship, and contrived to render him more useful and respectable. He closed a life of treachery and unrest, as we shall see later on,

'In glorious battle, fighting for the King.'

He founded the college of Fotheringhay, in Northamptonshire, in 1411, perhaps as an act of contrition for an ill-spent life, and there, according to a will made when at Harfleur, his body was laid to rest.

Thomas Lord Mowbray was left at large, but, as we have seen, he could not keep quiet, and lost his life in the Yorkshire rising very soon afterwards. The poor locksmith was the only one who suffered in life or limb. He had first his right hand chopped off, and then was hung for his share in the confederacy.

The Lady Constance was for a short time in captivity, but was soon released. It is not difficult to understand her feelings of resentment towards her brother, when it is borne in mind that he was the betrayer of the new year's plot of 1400, when her husband lost his life, and that, triumphing in his wickedness, he had carried his brother-in-law's head, exposed on a pole, up to London, to be a disgusting show to the mob in the city.

The warm-hearted Harry of Monmouth, Prince of Wales, commiserating the fate of his poor young cousins, the Mortimers—they were, in fact, his fourth cousins—prayed that they might be named his wards, and pledged his word for their loyalty. After events proved that he had judged them rightly. They were accordingly moved to more comfortable quarters in the royal house.

Edmund, who was five years younger than his protector, was a beautiful and gentle boy, without the energy of his forefathers, but given to music and reading, much as Harry himself had at one time been, and as he showed later on, when he delighted in having musical instruments and services of song in his private chapel, where the Psalms of David and other canticles were chanted. The love and trust which Harry evinced towards the boys they returned in full; but Roger, the younger one, died in 1408, and Edmund was left alone.

An important capture, destined to have consequences undreamt of at the time on the fate of the royal family, was made in this same year, 1405.

King Robert III. of Scotland, at length awakened to a knowledge of the intrigues of the Regent, the Duke of Albany, and, fearful lest the fate of his eldest son the Duke of Rothesay should befall his second and only remaining son James, Earl of Carrick, determined to send the boy, then eleven years of age, to be educated at the Court of France under the eye of the King.

Accompanied by the Earl of Orkney and a small suite of attendants, he embarked with a fair wind, and, as there was a truce then existing between England and Scotland, no apprehension was felt as to their safety. They had not, however, been many days at sea when they were captured by an armed merchantman. Most authors give Flamborough Head, in Yorkshire, as the place where the seizure was made; others state it to have been at Cley-next-the-Sea, on the north coast of Norfolk, a port now choked up with sand and annexed to Wells. It was not an action to be proud of, particularly when we know that, when carried to London, the young Prince and his attendants were committed to the Tower. It seems very probable that the whole plan of sending off the young Prince and his capture was a piece of villainy concocted between King Henry and the Duke of Albany. The latter, having in his hands the person of the supposed King Richard, gave the Prince of Scotland as a counterpoise into the keeping of the King of England, who had thus a guarantee that his reign would not be disputed by any pretender coming from Scotland.

Though this seizure was an act contrary to all right and justice, it probably was the saving of life to James. A double set of letters had been prepared, one to the King of France, the other to the sovereign of England. Henry, in reply to the entreaty of King Robert that he would be kind to his son if he found it necessary to land in his dominions, declared that, 'the boy could not have been sent to a better master, as he knew the French language indifferent well.'

Such was the effect of the news on poor old King Robert that he drooped from the day of hearing it, and died eventually of want of
1406. food and a broken heart, April 4, 1406.

King James was detained in the Tower for two years, when he
1407. was removed to the Castle of Nottingham. Though deprived of his liberty, he was treated with the greatest respect, and was instructed in all branches of useful knowledge then cultivated, and in all accomplishments of the period. He was good at throwing the hammer and putting the stone. He could wrestle and he could dance, and in the knightly sports of joust and tourney he was not excelled. He was a proficient on the lute, harp, and other musical instruments, which he would often accompany with his voice in songs of his own composing. His reading stood him in good stead when he eventually returned to his kingdom—many, many years later. He remained at Nottingham as long as Henry of Bolingbroke lived.

Affairs in France were in a very disturbed condition. Louis, Duke of Orleans, had been murdered at the close of the year 1407. The new Duke Charles, in order to obtain vengeance on his father's murderer, married Bonne, a daughter of the Count d'Armagnac, a determined opponent of Burgundy. At first they drove their enemy to his own dominions. Burgundy bethought him of applying to the
1411. King of England, who, his enemies at home being crushed, and his quondam antagonist, the Duke of Orleans, being dead, was not unwilling to show that he was made of different metal from King Richard. He therefore sent 800 archers and 1,000 lances under Thomas FitzAlan, Earl of Arundel, by whose aid the siege of Paris was raised.

1412. The Armagnacs, under the leadership of the young Duke of Orleans, the Dukes of Berri and Bourbon, and the Count of Alençon, in order to secure English support, now acknowledged King Henry as Duke of Aquitaine and bound themselves to serve him. He desired to go himself, but was totally unfit. His health was shattered; he could neither ride nor walk in comfort; epileptic fits frequently attacked him, and the fatal leprosy was spreading more and more. Thomas, Duke of Clarence, the King's second son, was therefore put in command. With Edward, Duke of York, Thomas de Beaufort, Earl of Dorset, his uncle of the half-blood, 8,000 men-at-arms and archers, he sailed in August for Normandy. The news of this expedition caused the opponents in France to make peace. Clarence demanded compensation, and, not receiving it, marched to the Orleanois, plundering Maine and Anjou on the way, which brought Orleans to his senses and he paid down 209,000 crowns. Clarence then continued his march to Bordeaux.

The young Earl of March, living at his ease in the royal castle of Windsor, contrived to fall in love with Lady Anne Stafford, a daughter of that Edmund, Earl of Stafford slain at Shrewsbury, and grand-daughter of Thomas, Duke of Gloucester, who had been lured from Pleshy to his death at Calais.

No choice more unacceptable to King and Council could have been made. If Edmund was rightful heir of the throne, the lady might, under certain possible circumstances, eventually have herself some claims to it. A match between the two could therefore never be sanctioned. Prince Hal thought otherwise, but, plead for them as he might, he was out of favour, and perhaps did more harm than good. Lady Anne was sent from court and Edmund was relegated to his old lodging in the Norman Tower.

Harry thought that where he had failed his step-mother might succeed. He knew that for love of him she would not do anything, but thought she might for love of gold. Joanna was avaricious. As he had not gold, he sent her an offer of a certain sum of money, to be paid to her whenever he should become King, if she would support his ward. She appears to have tried, but to have failed, as Harry himself had failed. He was apparently satisfied that she had done her best. The old King never knew of the transaction, but, in the first year of King Henry V., two sums of £100 each were handed over to Queen Joanna in part payment of a greater sum due on a private arrangement concerning the marriage of the Earl of March.

Two or three years before that time arrived, Richard, Earl of Cambridge, brother of Edward, Duke of York, had married Anne, the sister of Edmund Mortimer. Strangely enough, we are not told of any objections having been made to this match, and yet, the Earl of March dying as he did without issue, it was through it that the house of York, in the person of their son, Duke Richard, derived its claim to the crown.

1413

The sands of life for King Henry IV. were almost run out. He had sacrificed his King, his friends, his peace of conscience, his honour—everything that man holds dear, to wear a crown. He began his reign with the acclamations of the people. When the end came the same people were still louder in their demonstrations of joy. The various executions he had ordered appeared to them so many acts of cruelty and oppression. His popularity was utterly gone, and perhaps few kings were ever less loved or lamented.

His only claim to the throne was by the voice of the people. He had obtained it by lying, deceit and fraud. He kept it by means of the strong hand. The people's love and flattery could not save him from the stings of his own conscience, which must have condemned him.

'How I came by the crown, oh Heaven, forgive!'
is the prayer which Shakspere puts into his mouth in the last act of 'Henry IV., Part II.'

Bodily illness, combined with an uneasy spirit, brought him to an early grave, as he was only forty-six or forty-seven years of age. He said not a word of repentance for his usurpation, or of desire for the restoration of the right heir.

1413. When praying before the shrine of Edward the Confessor in Westminster Abbey, the King was seized with a fit. He was carried into the Abbot's lodging, called the Jerusalem Chamber, and there, on Sunday, March 19, he died.

> 'At his begynnyng full hye he was comende
> With coonm̄s then, and also lytell at the ende.'

The event was looked upon by Henry as the fulfilment of a prophecy that he should die in Jerusalem. It is very probable that he had expected to die in the Holy City itself, as he certainly at one time contemplated going there.

By his own wish the body was sent to Canterbury, to be buried near his uncle Edward, the Black Prince; and there is an altar-tomb in the Trinity Chapel of the cathedral to his memory and that of his Queen Joanna, who died in 1437.

Whether the body of Henry IV. really rested there is open to doubt. The corpse, placed in a coffin, was sent by sea. One of his attendants afterwards averred that, a great storm coming on, during which many accompanying vessels were lost, he and two others took the corpse from the coffin and threw it into the sea, when immediately the storm ceased; the coffin they carried to Canterbury. Only sixty-three years ago the coffin was examined. It was found to be stuffed with haybands, with a small cross formed of twigs lying on the surface. A body, lapped in lead, but much too small for the coffin, was found beneath. The lead was opened and the face was found in *perfect state*, but crumbled away on exposure to the air. Now it is well known that Henry's face, remarkable at one time as a perfect example of the manly beauty of the Plantagenets, had for years been disfigured by leprosy and other diseases.

It would be singular if some persons unknown occupied the tombs of both Richard II. and Henry IV.

King Henry endeavoured to introduce the Salic law into England by inducing the Parliament to pass a law settling the crown on himself and his heirs male without any mention of his daughters. The house, realizing the error which had been committed, in a subsequent session applied to him to make a new settlement. He yielded so far as to include the heirs of his sons without making any distinction between male and female, but his own daughters were passed over as before.

Henry did his best to bar his Beaufort brothers from the succession to the crown, not being able to foresee that his own usurpation of it was to be the cause of a hundred years' war, at the end of which all legitimate males of Plantagenet blood would be slain, along with a great part of the old nobility, and that the Beaufort blood, in the person of Henry Tudor, derived from the female side, mingled with that of the house of York, in the person of Lady Elizabeth, who also had Beaufort blood in her veins, was to hold sway in England for nearly a hundred and twenty years. That race came to an end when Queen Elizabeth died, 1603. But the Beaufort blood, once more derived from the female side, cropped up again when James I. ascended the throne.

Notwithstanding the frequent differences he had had with his father, Henry had sufficient filial respect to found a chapel and chantry opposite his tomb in St. Paul's Cathedral, some three or four years after becoming King. Six years later he made divers settlements on the dean and chapter for the celebration of Mass on the anniversaries of the deaths of his father and mother, as also on every great festival and Sundays for ever, which were to be attended by the Mayor and Sheriffs of London, when eight large tapers were to be lighted round the tomb.

Henry of Monmouth, Prince of Wales, was proclaimed King as Henry V. on March 20, St. Cuthbert's Day, and was crowned on Passion Sunday, April 9, in Westminster Abbey. The event was accompanied ' with stormes fell and haylestones greate also.'

One of his first acts was to free Edmund Mortimer from his restraint in the Norman Tower and restore to him all his possessions. He then took steps to legalize his marriage, and the Earl of March and Lady Anne Stafford were made man and wife.   1414.

In the following year Edmund discovered a plot which was hatched 1415. at Southampton, ostensibly in his favour, against his King, his friend, his benefactor, to whom he at once communicated it, as some return for the love and trust reposed in him. Truly, both Henry of Monmouth and Edmund de Mortimer were fine characters, and have left a noble example of disinterested friendship. It is difficult to tell whom to admire most.

The conspirators were Richard, Earl of Cambridge, Mortimer's brother-in-law, Sir Thomas Grey, and Henry Lord Scrope of Masham, a son of Sir Stephen, the elder brother of William, Earl of Wiltshire, and of Richard, Archbishop of York, but who had remained faithful to the interests of the late King Henry IV. and died February 10, 1408. Uncontrovertible evidence was given, witnesses were produced, and finally the three principals sent in a written confession. They were tried at Southampton, Cambridge and Scrope by a court of their peers—one of whom was Ralph Neville, Earl of Westmorland— Grey by a petty jury. They were convicted of treason, and beheaded August 5, 1415. The families were, however, not attainted, lands and honours descending to them in ordinary course.

The late King's firm friend Thomas Arundel, Archbishop of Canterbury, outlived him not quite a year. He died at the rectory of Halkyngton February 19, 1414.

SKETCH XI.

'THIS SMILING FRANCE OF OURS.'

1413. WHEN Henry IV. lay on his death-bed, it is said that he asked his son how he proposed to defend the ill-gotten crown.

'Fair son, what right have you to it? You know that I had none.'

'My liege,' replied the Prince, 'you won and held it by the sword, and it is my intent to hold and defend it in the same way.'

Harry was popular everywhere. He was young, not exactly handsome, but full of life and spirits, and delighting in all manly exercises. His youth, from the age of fourteen to early manhood, had been passed in the stirring life of an army, where he had given proofs of his bravery. But it was not an atmosphere favourable to the maintenance of a severe spirit of self-control, or of very moral behaviour. In person, when grown up, he was tall and slender, with an affable and winning manner. He loved a frolic, like most young men, and when recalled to London, living at Cold Harbour, being unused to Court life and its restraints, perhaps not on the best terms with his stepmother, it is very possible that he enjoyed the jokes of those whom he had been accustomed to lead in war. It is also very probable that he indulged in the follies which our greatest poet has connected with his name. He may have been wild and dissolute, but no gross acts of immorality have ever been laid to his charge. It happened, on one occasion, that one of his associates was brought before Chief Justice Gascoigne, the same who had set at nought King Henry IV.'s illegal orders at York, charged with felony. Harry tried to save the man and, failing in that, went up to the judge in a threatening manner, with his sword drawn. Gascoigne committed him, for contempt, to the King's Bench Prison, and Harry obediently submitted. When the affair was reported to the King, he is said to have given thanks 'that he had a judge resolute to minister justice and a son so willing to obey.' The biographers of the Prince claim that this story is, at best, doubtful, but it is too characteristic to be omitted, and it exhibits all the principal characters in a good light.

> 'His addiction was to courses vain;
> His companies unletter'd, rude, and shallow;
> His hours fill'd up with riots, banquets, sports;
> And never noted in him any study,
> Any retirement, any sequestration
> From open haunts and popularity.'

> 'The strawberry grows underneath the nettle;
> And so the prince obscur'd his contemplation
> Under the veil of wildness.'

The change came when his father died. No sooner had the breath left the old King's body than Henry retired to contemplation and prayer in his private chamber. There we cannot follow him. But we are told that he sought his confessor. From him he would doubtless obtain absolution and encouragement in his resolution to lead a new life.

Listen again to Shakspere:

> 'The breath no sooner left his father's body,
> But that his wildness mortified in him,
> Seem'd to die too; yea, at that very moment,
> Consideration like an angel came,
> And whipp'd the offending Adam out of him.'

Any levities in which he may have indulged were at once and for ever put aside when Madcap Hal became King HENRY V. The companions of his late indiscretions were dismissed, with gifts indeed, but under strict injunctions never again to appear near the Court.

Henry signalized the commencement of his reign by recalling Henry Percy, son of Hotspur, from Scotland and restoring him to the honours and estates of his grandfather. He was created Earl of Northumberland, March 16, 1415. The King's two brothers, John and Humphrey, were created respectively Dukes of Bedford and Gloucester on May 16, 1414. No notice was, however, taken of the unfortunate James, King of Scotland, who was still maintained in captivity.

The first trouble of Henry's reign was occasioned by the Lollards. When Prince of Wales he had endeavoured, but ineffectually, to save one of their sect, Thomas Badby, from the flames. This action may have inclined them to think that he would protect and defend them. In that they were disappointed. Their leader, Sir John Oldcastle, Lord Cobham in right of his wife, instigated them to preach and commit other irregularities without the license of the Archbishop. He, moreover, set forth opinions directly opposed to the teaching of the Church, for which Convocation asked that proceedings against him might be taken. The King delayed these by offering to see Oldcastle, who had formerly been his friend and companion in war, and endeavour to induce him to cease his opposition. In this he was unsuccessful, and Cobham was therefore committed to the Tower. Under the law passed in the preceding reign, he was, after conviction of heresy, liable to be burnt. A respite of forty days was, however, granted him, in the hope that he might recant. That hope proved futile, and before the time had expired the prisoner had made his escape.

The Lollards had arranged for a large meeting to take place in St. Giles' Fields, which they expected would be attended by thousands of London apprentices. It was rumoured about that their design was to seize the King and his brothers, perhaps put them to death; destroy all monasteries and other religious houses; and proclaim Oldcastle as President or Regent of the country. The King had been spending the Christmas with his brothers at Eltham, but, hearing of the intended proceedings, he returned to Westminster. On the

Jan. 7. day following the Festival of the Epiphany, he ordered all the gates of the city to be closed and marched with a strong body of men to the place of meeting. The rebels were thrown into confusion at sight of the armed force. Some few were killed, many were taken prisoners, but the assembly dispersed as precipitately as it could. Of the prisoners about thirty, with one of their leaders, Sir Roger Acton, were condemned and hanged. If Oldcastle had been present, as anticipated, he made his escape, and a large reward was offered for his capture. Four years later, he was taken in Wales, and, under the old sentence, was burnt in St. Giles's Fields on Christmas Day, 1417,

> ' Rose of Lancaster,
> Red in thy birth, redder with household war,
> Now reddest with the blood of holy men,
> Redder to be, red rose of Lancaster——'

Henry IV. sided alternately with the Orleanists and Burgundians in their desolating quarrels for supremacy in France. His son adopted a more decided tone, and one which gave infinite satisfaction to the nobles as well as to the people generally. A little more than a year
July. after his accession he renewed the claim of Edward III. to the Crown of France. Richard Beauchamp, Earl of Warwick, the Bishop of St. David's and others were sent as ambassadors. But all discussion of such a subject was indignantly rejected. Henry then waived his claim to the crown, but demanded Normandy, Anjou and Maine in full sovereignty; the lordship over Aquitaine and all that had been ceded at the peace of Bretigny to his great-grandfather, together with several towns; the hand of the King's daughter Katherine, with a portion of 2,000,000 crowns; and the immediate discharge of the remainder of the ransom of King John. The Duke of Berri made answer that, for the sake of peace, the King agreed to give his daughter with 600,000 crowns, and the ancient Duchy of Aquitaine comprising Gascony, Guienne and Poitou. Henry was not satisfied; but the truce for twenty-eight years concluded by Richard II. on his marriage with Lady Isabel had not yet expired, and the ambassadors
Nov. were recalled, the truce being prolonged for four months.

1415. About this time the King's uncle, Thomas Beaufort, Earl of
Feb. Dorset, with the Bishops of Durham and Norwich, Richard Lord Grey of Codnover and a retinue of six hundred horsemen entered Paris, where they were lodged in the Temple. The magnificence of their appearance seems to have been the cause of considerable astonishment to the Parisians. King Charles, soon after their arrival, gave a grand festival, at which the English ambassaders were present.

Another prolongation of the truce was soon agreed upon. Then a fresh proposal for peace was made. The claim on Normandy, Anjou and Maine was abandoned, and the dowry required with the Lady Katherine was reduced to one half. The Duke of Berri gave the same reply as before, except that he offered eight instead of six hundred thousand crowns as the young lady's marriage portion.

April. King Henry announced to the Council his determination to recover what it pleased him to call 'his inheritance.' The claim made by Edward III. to the Crown of France was, to say the least, very questionable. Many other descendants from former kings of that country might have put one forward with more justice. If Henry of Monmouth was rightful King of England he would hold the same position in regard to France as his great-grandfather. That, however, we know he was not. The Earl of March, had he so chosen, could have made a demand for the crowns of both England and France. But he had virtually acquiesced in Henry's sovereignty by taking his seat as a peer of the realm next after the Earl of Arundel, and not as one of the royal blood. Writers of the present day stigmatize Henry's claim as most unreasonable. He himself undoubtedly thought his position a just one, and was prepared to maintain it with the strong hand. He looked to a war to consolidate the dynasty of his family. War was evidently desired by the country. The nobles wished for it as a time for making money through the ransom of prisoners, the lower orders, down to the serfs, as a means of raising their condition of life.

Shakspere, following some of the chroniclers, has represented Henry Chicheley, Archbishop of Canterbury in succession to Thomas de Arundel, as one of the principal inciters to war. He makes him promise

> 'To give a greater sum
> Than ever at one time the clergy yet
> Did to his predecessors part withal.'

It is most probable that he did advocate it as being for the good of the country. He raised a subsidy from the clergy. He also suspended the payment of Peter's pence into the Papal treasury and devoted it to the service of the King. On his recommendation the possessions of alien priories were sold and forfeited to the crown, and the profits arising from wardships were also applied to war purposes. Moreover, at his instigation, the clergy undertook to see to the defence of the south coast when the army left the country.*

Parliament granted two-tenths and two-fifteenths; the barons and knights agreed to furnish troops to the extent of their power; Henry Beaufort, Bishop of Winchester, the King's uncle, provided the considerable sum of £20,000; and the King himself, by pawning his jewels, and contracting loans both at home and abroad, also gathered together a large amount of ready money.

The King was at Winchester when the Archbishop of Bourges and June. the Count of Vendôme arrived to endeavour to prevail on him to accept the terms offered by the Duke of Berri. The Ambassadors were entertained by the King and the Bishop in the Castle, but failed to shake Henry's resolution.

In order to explain his proceedings to the other crowned heads of July. Europe, Henry wrote to them letters setting forth the disturbed condition of France, and his own right to interfere. He then made his

---

* See Dr. Hook's 'Lives of the Archbishops of Canterbury,' vol. v.

will, of which Archbishop Chicheley was appointed one of the executors.

Aug. The army had assembled at Southampton, and the King had gone there to superintend the embarkation, when the conspiracy of Cambridge and others was discovered. About five days after they had met their deserts, the King went on board his ship, the *Trinity*, and on the following day the whole fleet of 1,200 to 1,500 vessels, carrying 30,000 men, set sail. John, Duke of Bedford was appointed Regent of the kingdom, and due arrangements were made for the defence of the country against Scotland and Wales.

On the third day, August 13, the fleet entered the mouth of the Seine, and landed at Clef de Caux, situated between Honfleur and Harfleur. As soon as all the men, the camp equipage and provisions, had been disembarked, the fortress of Harfleur was invested both by land and water. Harfleur is not any more a port; what was once the harbour is now seen as pasture land. A small river, a tributary of the Seine, divided the town into two parts. The King was on one side, and his brother Thomas, Duke of Clarence, on the other. The entrance was defended by a strong chain extended from a tower on either side.

After King Henry had in vain demanded the surrender of the town to him as lawful Duke of Normandy, the siege was commenced in due form on August 18. The defence of the town was in the hands of the Lords Gaucourt, d'Estouteville, and others, who had a force of some two or three thousand men under their command.

The rough cannon of the period were employed in casting stone balls against the town, but the damage thereby occasioned was almost as quickly repaired. The besieged in return discharged missiles against the foe, which did no little damage; and they made some sallies, with little effect, however, as they were generally repulsed with loss; Humphrey, Duke of Gloucester, who was occupied in mining, was met by countermining, and conflicts underground were of frequent occurrence. This means of attack was therefore discontinued:

> 'Once more unto the breach, dear friends, once more;
> Or close the wall up with our English dead!'

For thirty-six days the siege went on. During that time the besieging army suffered severely. Provisions were scarce, as, of the supply brought from England, a large proportion had been ruined in transit, and it was with great difficulty that stores could be procured from the surrounding country. The weather was wet, the ground whereon they were encamped was marshy, and the exhalation from putrid matter in the camp was specially noxious. An epidemic of dysentery attacked the forces, and some thousands fell victims to it. Among the number may be mentioned Michael de la Pole, Earl of Suffolk, who died on September 14. He was the son of the unfortunate minister of King Richard. Another victim, on the day following, was Richard Courtenay, Bishop of Norwich, a trusted counsellor of the King, who nursed him tenderly and watched over him carefully until the end came. It may be that Henry did this, in part, in consequence of their relationship. The Bishop's grandmother was Margaret de Bohun, great-aunt of Mary de Bohun, the King's mother; the two men were therefore fourth cousins. The Bishop's body was brought to England and buried in Westminster Abbey.

The town had suffered equally with the enemy, so that, when Henry sent them another summons to surrender, the leaders promised to do so if they did not receive succours within three days. One of their number, the Sire de Bacqueville, was sent to lay their case before King Charles, who was with his son, the Duke of Guienne, at Vernon-sur-Seine. All the answer he received was that the forces were not assembled, and no such speedy succour could be given. On Sunday, September 22, therefore, the town surrendered unconditionally.

On a hill opposite the town King Henry sat on his throne in a pavilion, surrounded by the nobles and other leaders in the army, his crowned helmet being held upon a lance point by Sir Robert Umfraville. A lane was thence formed by the troops up to the principal gate, along which came the leaders and the chief townsmen, carrying the keys of the town, which they humbly presented to the King and threw themselves on his mercy. The whole of them afterwards attended a feast given by the King.

The banner of St. George was hoisted over the gate, and next day the King made his entry into the town. He dismounted at the entrance and walked thence barefooted to the Church of St. Martin, there to offer up his prayers and thanksgiving for his success. Such of the inhabitants as elected to take the oath of allegiance were allowed to remain. All others had to depart. The men-at-arms, after taking an oath to yield themselves to the governor of Calais, had to march out in their doublets. The men, women and children, who did not choose to remain, were ordered to leave at once, with only a portion of their clothes, and with five sous given to each one for subsistence on the journey.

Most of the possessions left in the town were distributed among the conquering army, some portion of the booty being sent to England, along with the sick and wounded and the warlike engines. Thomas Beaufort, Earl of Dorset, was appointed Lieutenant of Harfleur with 500 men-at-arms and 1,000 archers under his command.

The question was now, What was to be done? The capture of one town was not a great step towards the object in view. Many, the Duke of Clarence among the number, advocated a return to England with the sadly diminished forces. But, even had Henry been willing, there were not ships left to transport them there, as the greater part had gone back. 'We must see a little more,' he said, 'of this smiling France of ours.' He sent a challenge to the Dauphin to settle the dispute in single combat, but, even had Louis been a young man of spirit, bold and hardy enough to accept it, there were people around him wise enough to prevent it, and no reply was vouchsafed. It was too late in the year to attempt laying siege to other towns and fortresses as originally intended But lest his returning home at once should be construed into running away, Henry declared his resolution to march overland to his town of Calais. Rash it may have been, chivalrous it certainly was, and after events justified it. 'His trust,' the King said, 'was in God. If it please Him we shall go without hurt or damage. If the enemy dispute our passage we will frustrate them, and receive victory and honour.'

On first landing King Henry had issued strict orders against looting of any kind. Nothing was to be taken without being paid for. The property of the Church was especially to be held sacred. No violence or injury was to be offered or inflicted on any private individual, especially women. The punishment for disobedience was to be instant death. These orders were now repeated. Notwithstanding this, one of the soldiers was detected when at Corbie with a copper-gilt pyx, probably the spoil of some church, concealed in his sleeve. He was instantly hanged. Shakspere makes Bardolph the culprit, and King Henry says with regard to him :

'We would have all such offenders so cut off; when lenity and cruelty play for a kingdom, the gentler gamester is the soonest winner.'

Oct. On Tuesday, October 8, the King commenced his march, with forces reduced to 900 men-at-arms and 5,000 archers. Hardyng, who was present, mentions 9,000 men; he probably included camp followers of all kinds. Monstrelet, writing from hearsay and, of course, with a strong bias, says 2,000 men-at-arms, 13,000 archers, and numbers of other men.

The direct distance to Calais would be little over a hundred miles, but, as we shall see, that was considerably exceeded. The enemy watched each step and took every opportunity of cutting off stragglers. Great difficulty was experienced in getting food, and frequently the troops had to pass the whole day without any.

Oct. 11. After crossing the small river Bresle, they were attacked by the garrison of the Castle of Eu, who were, however, soon compelled to seek the shelter of the fortress. Eu is the frontier town of Normandy and is about two miles from Tréport, at the mouth of the river.

The Somme had yet to be crossed, and Henry thought to do so at Blanchetaque, as Edward III. had done. But he received intelligence that the ford had been rendered impassable by palisades, whilst men-at-arms and archers guarded the banks on the opposite side of the

Oct. 13. river. He therefore went to Airaines, where he passed the night, as his great-grandfather had done before him. His troubles now really began. The French under the Constable D'Albret were on the opposite side of the river watching his movements. Every bridge was ordered to be broken down and every ford destroyed.

On the 17th the English were at Corbie, and next day at Nesle. Oct. 17. It was at this time the order was given that each archer should provide himself, from a wood near by, with stakes sharpened at each end, to be used in case of attack by cavalry. Some writers affirm that this suggestion was made by the Duke of York. If that be a fact, then he must be credited with having materially contributed to the victory which ensued a week later. Nesle is about four miles from the Somme, with marshy ground intervening. Here Henry received the joyful news that fords had been discovered between Bethencourt and Voyenne, which were only partially destroyed, through the neglect of the people of St. Quentin. On the 19th the day was passed in removing the obstructions placed in the fords and repairing the causeways. The King was active in superintending these works, and in seeing to the passage over of the troops. It was fortunate that all the cannon had been sent back to England, for it would have been difficult, if not impossible, to have dragged them over the river. Before nightfall the whole army was on the right bank of the Somme. Onward marched Henry to Peronne, which had but just been left by the French who were on his track, and took up his quarters at Monchy la Gache.

Meanwhile the French, who had hitherto watched the English progress with mingled anger and contempt, had met King Charles in council at Rouen, and decided, by a large majority, to give battle to their foes. They went so far as to fix upon Friday, October 25. Three heralds were sent on the 20th to announce the result of their deliberations to King Henry, who thus answered them: 'I seek not your master, but, if he or his seek me, I will meet them. If any one attempts to stop me on my peaceable journey towards Calais, they do it at their own risk, and I do not desire them to be so ill-advised as to try it.'

The army continued its weary march through a hostile country, though enfeebled with sickness and suffering many privations. Constant alarms were caused by the enemy hovering round about, so that the men were deprived of their natural rest. The weather, too, was unpropitious. Rain in the daytime, and frost at night, with fuel so scarce that it was with great difficulty any fire could be had. The hardship was terrible. Money was there in plenty, but there was not anything which could be bought with it.

At length Blangy, on the river Ternois, was reached, just in time Oct. 24. to prevent the French demolishing the bridge. Large masses of the foe, with their glittering pennons, were seen on the marshy plain. Henry then gave orders to form into line of battle. On this first appearance of the immense host, soon to be opposed to them, Sir Walter Hungerford expressed a wish for more men, to which the King replied: 'I do not wish a man more here than I have; we are few indeed compared with the enemy, but if, as I trust, God shall favour us and our just cause, we shall speed well enough.'

In Shakspere's 'Henry V.' it is the Earl of Westmorland who says :

> 'O that we now had here
> But one ten thousand of those men in England
> That do no work to-day !'

To whom the King replies :

> 'No, my fair cousin ;
> If we are marked to die, we are enough
> To do our country loss ; and if to live,
> The fewer men the greater share of honour.'

Both Westmorland and Hungerford may have expressed the wish, but it is a doubtful point whether the Earl was there at all, as he had been appointed a Councillor of Regency in the spring of that year. Dr. Sparrow, in his charming book 'De Nova Villa' sees no reason to doubt his presence on the field, and, in support of that opinion, quotes a paragraph from Surtees' 'History of Durham,' to the effect that he had in his train five knights and one hundred and thirteen men.

The English host remained until dusk, when, following up a road on rising ground, they arrived in less than half an hour at the village of Maisoncelles. Here the King took up his quarters for the night. Better food and more comfortable accommodation was found than the troops had enjoyed for many days, yet the shelter they obtained was not impervious to the rain which fell almost continuously during the night. They had every confidence in their leader, but, not knowing what might happen to them next day, they deemed it right for each one to make his confession, and for such as required it to draw up their wills. They also had music to cheer them up and make the time pass joyously. The King himself had little rest. He was up the greater part of the night, visiting the various quarters of the troops, examining the ground, and arranging the operations for the morrow.

The French, on the other hand, in certain anticipation of victory—for did they not number at least ten times as many as their opponents ?—passed the time in throwing dice for the prisoners they fondly anticipated taking next day. They had no lack of anything to cheer them in the shape of food or drink, or great fires to keep them warm. But they had no music to inspire them, and as Monstrelet relates, scarcely any horse neighed the whole night long, which was looked upon as a bad omen.

The first to attack the English lines was Arthur of Brittany, Count de Richemont, the second son of King Henry's stepmother. With a force of some 200 men-at-arms and archers he advanced during the night, hoping, probably, to take the English by surprise. But they were on the alert and a smart skirmish took place, after which the French retired as they had come.

Oct. 25. King Henry rose early on this day of SS. Crispin and Crispian and
Friday. summoned all to attend Matins and Mass. That duty done, he

mounted a grey horse and led them to the field. On his helmet he wore a crown of gold, which sparkled in the sun. His face was lit up with smiles even brighter still. 'Either this day I shall win honour,' said he, 'or it shall be made famous by my death. No ransom shall be paid for me, nor shall France triumph over me in life.'

He arranged his men about a mile from the village, between two woods, in two divisions with two wings, the archers being placed in advance in the form of a wedge, with the pointed stakes fixed in the ground before them. Another small body of archers was also stationed in a wood on the left hand. To the Duke of York, at his special solicitation, was given the command of the vanguard, while the young Earl of Suffolk, son of the Earl who died at Harfleur, had the rear-guard. In addition to others already named, there were with the army Edmund Mortimer, Earl of March; Richard de Vere, Earl of Oxford, cousin of King Richard's favourite; John FitzAlan, Earl of Arundel; John Mowbray, Earl Marshal and Earl of Nottingham, brother of Thomas, beheaded after the rising in Yorkshire; John Holland, Earl of Huntingdon, cousin of King Henry and son of the Earl concerned in the conspiracy of 1400; Gilbert Umfraville, Earl of Kyme; Richard de Beauchamp, Earl of Warwick and Baron le Despenser; and Edward Courtenay, son of the second Earl of Devon, and brother-in-law of the Earl of March, whose sister Eleanor he had married; together with bannerets, knights and esquires with such of their respective followers as were left after the troubles they had undergone.

The French, whose forces are variously estimated at from 60,000 to 150,000 (Hardyng calls them 100,000), were drawn up behind the village of Azincourt, and across the direct road leading to Calais. They had a wood to their rear, and also to their right, but do not appear to have made any tactical use of them. D'Albret, Constable of France, was in command. His object was simply to remain on the alert, but inactive, knowing that his forces could not suffer anything by delay, while his tired opponents would probably have to endure more fatigue and privation. For some hours, therefore, each army remained inactive, and Henry took advantage of the interval to order refreshment to be given to the men. Some proposition for a truce was made by the French, but nothing came of it, as the King was not one likely to alter his views at such a moment.

At length, towards noon, King Henry cried 'Advance banners.' Sir Thomas Erpingham, a bold and fearless knight with snow-white hair, threw his truncheon into the air, and, according to Monstrelet, called out 'Nestrocque,' which was probably 'Now strike.' Such a shout as the French had seldom heard then arose from the English army. With one accord all now threw themselves on the ground, with a prayer to Heaven for protection, and rose each one with a fraction of soil in his mouth, in token of their submission to Him in whom they trusted.

The archers now advanced in front of the stakes, obliquely planted before them in the ground, and having discharged their arrows, returned to their station. The French cavalry, clothed in complete steel from head to foot, made a furious charge upon them. The arrows of the archers in front, as well as those in the wood, were however, rained upon them with such velocity, that the horses, from sheer pain, became unmanageable. Some were gored to death on the pointed stakes. Others rolled with their helpless riders on to the clayey ground, which, owing to the heavy rain and continued

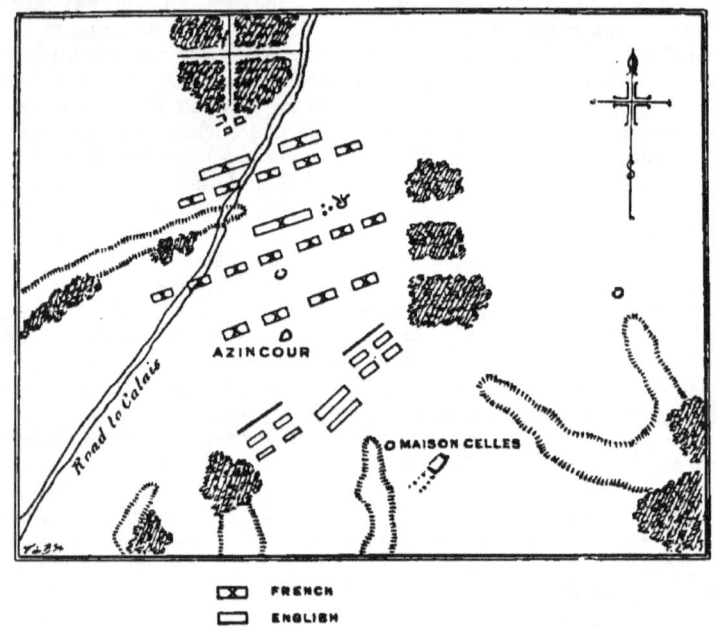

FROM JOHNES' MONSTRELET

trampling, had been converted into a sea of mud. The archers, slinging their bows behind them, with swords or hatchets, knives or anything that they had at hand, bare-headed and half naked, many of them without shoes to their feet, boldly attacked what horsemen there were left and drove the few remaining alive back on to the first division, which was thrown into great confusion. The Constable D'Albret was among the slain.

King Henry with his men-at-arms now marched against the second division. They were encountered by Anthony, Duke of Brabant, a brother of John 'the Fearless,' Duke of Burgundy, who, for two hours maintained an obstinate defence, but, when he and his brother Philip, Count of Nevers and Rethel, were slain, the battle was virtually over, for the third division began to fly.

A few stout hearts were still left, who, if they could not change defeat into victory, at least would try for partial revenge. A party of eighteen knights, with the Sire de Croye at their head, swore either to kill King Henry, or, failing that, make him prisoner. One of them succeeded in striking him so hard a blow that he fell upon one knee, but was almost instantly up again. Of his opponents all were slain. The Duke of Alençon came forward with a fresh troop of knights to the number of sixty, and making way to the King, with one blow of his axe struck off the crown from Henry's helmet, and with another he beat the Duke of York to the ground, and he, having become very corpulent, was trampled to death, as he was unable to rise. The Duke of Alençon had so many opposed to him that, in despair, he at last called out : ' I yield me to the King, I am Alençon.' Henry at once stretched out his hand to save him, but was too late to do so, as his rival in love and war fell under a shower of blows.

About this time some hundreds of Picardy peasants came to plunder the baggage left at Maisoncelles. It was reported to the King that a large force of fresh foes had appeared in the rear and he hastily gave orders that all the prisoners taken should be put to death. Large numbers were accordingly massacred in cold blood. Henry has been severely blamed for this, but it was an act of self-preservation, which no one could more sincerely have regretted than did he. As soon as the error was discovered the carnage was at once stopped. The leader of the peasants Robinet de Bournouville and some others were afterwards imprisoned and severely punished by John, Duke of Burgundy, notwithstanding they had made a present to the Count de Charolois of a precious sword ornamented with diamonds, that had belonged to the King of England.

The last charge made against the English was by the Counts de Fauquemberg and de Marle, who, with 600 men belonging to the third division, rushed gallantly on their foe, and either met captivity or death, and—the victory was won, as acknowledged by Montjoye the French herald.

The field of battle lies between the communes of Azincour and Tramecour, and is eight miles north of Hesdin, which in turn is eight miles north of Créci, the scene of the famous battle sixty-nine years previously. The road from Calais to Abbeville and Amiens passes the sites of both these celebrated spots.

The English lost about 1,600 men, including the young Earl of Suffolk. The body of the Earl, who was only three-and-twenty, was taken home and buried in the Priory Church of Butley, three miles from Orford in Suffolk. He was succeeded in the title by his brother William, then about nineteen years old. It is a little singular that the leaders both of the van-guard and the rear-guard should thus be among the slain. Another noticeable death was that of a Welshman named Sir David Gam, who is remembered specially on account of his reply to a question as to the number of the enemy. 'There are enow,' said he, 'to be killed, enow to be taken prisoners, and enow to run away.'

The loss to the French in slain must have been at least 10,000 men, including 300 lords and 8,000 gentlemen. Large numbers were taken prisoners, the most noticeable being the Dukes of Orleans and Bourbon; the Counts of Richemont, Eu and Vendôme, and Marshal Boucicault.

On this Saturday and the four following days the corpses of all the slain, who could be recognised in their state of entire nudity, were well washed and taken for burial in various churches. The bodies of the Dukes of Brabant and Alençon, the Counts de Nevers, de Vaudemont, de Fauquemberg, the Lord de Dampierre, the Constable d'Albret and one or two others were carried to the Church of the Friars Minors at Hesdin, and there buried.

The Abbot of Roussainville, at the instigation of Philippe Count de Charolois, measured out a square of twenty-five yards, and, in three trenches which were dug, the remaining bodies, to the number of 5,800, were interred.

This square was afterwards consecrated by order of the Bishop of Therouenne, and was surrounded by a strong hedge of thorns.

King Henry decreed that the battle should be known by the name of Azincour, after a castle which at that time stood near by, but has now disappeared as a building, though some loose stones still remain.

He then ordered all to join in offering their thanksgiving for the great success vouchsafed to them.

The troops left Maisoncelles on the following day and resumed the march to Calais, where they arrived on October 29, and it was then determined to return to England as soon as possible.

Nov. 17. When Henry reached Dover the crowd rushed into the water to meet him, and carried him in their arms to land. It was one long triumphal procession up to London. On arrival in the capital pageants were exhibited in the streets, the conduits ran with wine, music resounded from all quarters, bands of children were everywhere singing songs in the King's praise, and a general intoxication of joy took possession of all the people. Henry, in fact, grew tired of hearing so much about the glorious battle of Azincour, and a formal edict was passed forbidding any more songs or recitations in honour of the event. But he did not disdain the more substantial offering of Parliament, where similar enthusiasm was felt. It ordered the immediate levy of the subsidy granted in the previous one, voted another tenth and fifteenth to be raised within twelve months, and settled on him for life the duty on wool and leather.

SKETCH XII.

THE REGENT AND HEIR OF FRANCE.

THE EMPEROR SIGISMUND brother of the late 'good' 1416. Queen Anne, who held the noble idea of bringing about unity in the Church, had convened for that purpose a council of ecclesiastics, who had met at Constance about a year before this time. He also entertained the hope of being able to mediate a peace, and heal all the differences then existing between France and England. For this purpose he first paid a visit to Paris, where he was well received and suitably entertained. On one of the occasions when he was present in the Court of Parliament, it happened that there was a dispute for the seneschalship of Beaucaire between two persons, one only of whom had received the honour of knighthood, which was a necessary qualification for the office. The Emperor thereupon dubbed the esquire a knight, so as to put both claimants on an equal footing. In appearance, it was the act of an Emperor claiming authority over the king of another country, but it was not deemed advisable or necessary to take any notice of it.

Soon afterwards the Emperor crossed over to England. But the news of his action at Paris had been received, and before he was allowed to land at Dover, he was required to give an assurance that he had not the least intention of claiming, in any way, imperial jurisdiction in the country. Then he was accorded a right royal reception, was escorted by the King's brothers to Windsor Castle, where he was welcomed by King HENRY and at the next festival of St. George, which was attended by the King's two sisters, Blanche and Philippa, made a Knight of the Garter.

Sigismund was a noble-looking, finely-grown man, with a well-informed mind. It is said that he could speak six languages. His learning, however, must have been but shallow, and his vanity excessive, if we are to believe the following anecdote. One day, at the Council of Constance, he made a Latin speech in which the word *schisma* occurred. One of the Cardinals observing quietly that *schisma* was a neuter, not feminine word, Sigismund exclaimed : 'Not feminine! I, as King of the Romans, am above the laws of grammar.' His biographers say he was honest and true-hearted, lively and active; but fickle and undecided, and hence unable to carry through his many well-conceived plans. He was also a bad man of business, and continually in trouble through want of money, which caused him to descend to many acts of meanness.

King Henry had a just appreciation of the character of his visitor, and, by giving him and his numerous band of followers free entertainment wherever they went, caused him eventually to change his character of a mediator into that of an ally.

In the meantime the state of Harfleur was becoming critical. The commandant, the Earl of Dorset, in making an incursion towards Rouen, had been attacked and defeated, with considerable loss, by the French under the Lord de Villequer. Next day, however, the tables were turned, when the French were put utterly to the rout and their commander slain. In retaliation the Count d'Armagnac, who had assumed the office of Constable of France on the death of the Dauphin Louis, December 18, 1415, laid siege to the town by sea, and even sent a fleet into the English Channel. King Henry desired to go himself to the relief of the place, but was dissuaded by the Emperor, who deemed the enterprise might be conducted by some

Aug. 14. one of inferior rank. The Duke of Clarence, having with him John, Earl of Huntingdon, was therefore entrusted with the command of the expedition, consisting of 300 vessels which sailed from Sandwich. The ships of the blockading force were principally Genoese and higher by some feet than the loftiest of the English. Undismayed by this difference, and trusting to English pluck, the Admiral bore down on the enemy, the ships were boarded, many of them taken,

Aug. 15. some sunk, others driven away, and before nightfall of the second day Harfleur was saved.

Sept. The Emperor, having brought his visit to a satisfactory close, crossed with King Henry and William VI., Count of Holland and Hainault, to Calais, where they met John 'the fearless,' Duke of Burgundy. A truce which already existed between England and the Duke's counties of Flanders and Artois for the protection and regulation of trade, was now prolonged for two years. The mere fact of the meeting was of great disservice to Duke John with the party in power in France. But he had his own ends in view, the suppression of the Armagnacs, and went quietly on his way.

The Emperor returned to Constance, where he had the satisfaction of seeing an end put to the division in the Church. The Cardinal of Ostia, Otto of Colonna, was elected Pope, and took the name of Martin IV. On April 22, 1418, the assembly was closed. But the French were still not satisfied.

1417. The Count of Hainault died, from the bite of a mad dog, on May 13, a few months after his arrival at home, and was succeeded by his only child Jaqueline, a girl of nineteen, whose life reads like a romance. She had been married to the Dauphin Jean, who died,

April 5. as it is said, of an abscess in the ear, on Palm Sunday, April 5, when at Compiègne, and was buried in the Abbey of St. Corneille. He had but just united with the Duke of Burgundy to remove the Armagnacs from power. This sudden death of the Dauphin Jean, as well as that of his elder brother Louis, was commonly reported to be due to poison, administered by someone who had power over the King. Many did not scruple to attribute to Queen Isabeau 'the deep damnation of their taking off' in order to make way for her better-loved son Charles.

About this time Sir Louis de Bourdon, when returning from a visit to the Queen at the castle of Vincennes, passed King Charles without the usual signs of submission or veneration. The Count d'Armagnac more than hinted at gallantries between the Queen and Sir Louis. Whether there was any truth in such report is uncertain. But, considering the former behaviour of Isabeau with the King's late brother, the Duke of Orleans, there was grave cause for suspicion. Sir Louis was arrested, imprisoned, and then drowned in the Seine. The Queen was banished to Blois in the first instance, and thence to Tours, in Touraine, where she was placed under guard. This treatment induced her to make common cause with the Duke of Nov. Burgundy, who, at her request, came to see her, attended by a considerable number of men-at-arms. Together they took possession of the town and castle. After appointing a governor and leaving 200 men as a garrison they departed to Chartres. Thus the Queen, Regent of France, and the Duke of Burgundy, the murderer of her quondam lover, were arrayed against King Charles and the Dauphin Charles, husband and son of the guilty woman, whilst the enemy was conquering a portion of the country.

Having appointed his brother JOHN, DUKE OF BEDFORD, guardian July 25. of England, King Henry, with his brothers of Clarence and Gloucester, and an army of twenty to thirty thousand men, with necessary artillery and the usual body of supernumeraries, sailed again for Normandy.

They landed at Touques, now a mere village, dwarfed by the Aug. 1. better-known Trouville. The castle was immediately assaulted, but did not surrender for four days.

As at his first appearance in France, so now, strict orders were issued against violence and plunder. All ecclesiastics, and any private individuals who might elect to own the King's authority as Duke of Normandy, were taken under royal protection, and any insult offered to them was punishable with death. Henry's known firmness in carrying out such regulations was almost equivalent to a guarantee against their infringement.

Harcourt, Evreux, Domfront, and many other places surrendered after but slight resistance, and garrisons were established in all of them.

About the middle of the month the siege of Caen, one of the most interesting towns in Normandy, was commenced. The suburbs were occupied by a strong force under the Duke of Clarence, and St. Stephen's Abbey, which had been founded by William the Conqueror, was saved from destruction by the monks admitting an English force. The castle, under the command of the Lord de la Fayette, was surrendered on condition of the garrison being allowed to march out in security with their bag and baggage, and the town was then strongly occupied after some hundreds of people had been sent out as useless.

The town and castle of Cherbourg were besieged by the Duke of 1418. Gloucester for ten weeks, and eventually surrendered by the governor, Jan. 2. Sir John d'Engennes, on condition that he should receive a stipulated sum of money. Monstrelet relates that Sir John retired to Rouen after its capture by the English, and was beheaded, to the great joy of the French, because he stayed there when the term of his passport had expired.

Feb. 15. Falaise, so celebrated as the birthplace of William the Conqueror, surrendered, through famine, after a siege of about fifteen weeks. Bayeux, Lisieux, Avranches, Coutances, and many more towns quietly submitted, although many of the inhabitants betook themselves to Brittany and other parts of France, rather than own an English duke.

The greater part of Normandy was by this time in possession of the English, but Rouen, the most interesting city in the duchy, perhaps in France itself, if Paris be excepted, had yet to be approached, and King Henry was gradually drawing nearer. He advanced to Louviers, which submitted, and quartered himself at the Cistercian Abbey of Bomport, near Pont de l'Arche, on the banks of the Seine. This abbey, it is said, was founded by Richard 'Lion Heart,' in accordance with a vow made while swimming his horse across the river in pursuit of a deer, that, if saved from drowning, he would build a monastery to Our Lady there.

The town of Pont de l'Arche takes its name from the fine stone bridge which here crosses the Seine. In view of Henry's meditated attack upon Rouen, the possession of this bridge for the passage of his troops to the opposite side was a necessity, but it was strongly guarded by the French. Resort was therefore had to a ruse. About three miles lower down the river there is a small island in the middle of the stream. Sir John de Cornwall with his son, a boy of fifteen, one horse, and about sixty men, embarked in eight small boats and landed on the island in the very sight of the French, who never even made an attempt to dislodge them. What had been done by so small a party was imitated by a thousand or more men. Henry now had the footing he needed, and to join his two camps he made a bridge of boats. After three weeks' siege, Sir John de Graville, the governor, surrendered the town and castle of Pont de l'Arche, on condition that he and his men might depart in safety with their baggage. Leaving here a sufficient garrison, Henry at once pro-
June. ceeded to the investment of Rouen, which was eight miles lower down the river.

The whole town lay then on the right bank of the river, and not, as now, on both sides. It was enclosed by a wall in which were six gates with the necessary fort to each.

The King's object was not to assault the place, but to invest it by land and water, and patiently wait for the time when necessity should compel a surrender. The six gates of the town, viz., St. Hilaire, Caen, Martinville, Caux, Beauvais and the Castle, were guarded respectively by the forces under the Duke of Gloucester; the Duke of Clarence; the Earl of Warwick; the Earls of Huntingdon, Salisbury and Kyme and John, Lord Neville, eldest son of Ralph, Earl of Westmorland;

the Duke of Exeter; and John Mowbray, the Earl Marshal, with Sir John de Cornwall. Deep galleries were dug to afford communication between one quarter and another, and the banks were thickly planted with hedges of thorn so as to render the passages free from assaults of cannon or other warlike engines.

To prevent boats from bringing provisions into the town, chains were slung across the river at two different spots, one three miles up, the other three miles down, the stream. In each place there were three chains, one a foot or two below the surface, another on a level with the water, and a third two feet above.

According to Monstrelet, there were in the English camp a large number of Irish, mostly on foot, who had only one stocking and one shoe, the other leg being bare of covering. They had for arms a short javelin and a knife, with a target for protection. Those on horseback, instead of saddles, had panniers, such as are used to carry provisions in. They rode their small ponies exceedingly well, and did infinite damage by making excursions into the country round about, whence they returned laden with booty of all kinds.

Fortunately for the city, the magistrates at the first appearance of the English forces had counselled all who had not a sufficient supply of provisions for a year to take their departure, and thus the number of inhabitants was considerably reduced. As a precautionary measure the suburbs were burnt, and the surrounding land reduced to a wilderness. The garrison consisted of 5,000 men and 15,000 militia, under the immediate command of Sir Guy le Bouteiller, and Alain Blanchard was the governor. Sorties were occasionally made, but generally much to their disadvantage. Once a force of 10,000 men, under their brave leader, resolved on a sally, but it resulted so disastrously that Sir Guy was severely blamed for his temerity.

The first place to surrender, at the end of a month, was the fort on Mont St. Catherine, and the garrison were allowed to go out in safety, but without any baggage.

Month after month went by, and still there was no other sign of yielding, though the inhabitants were suffering sorely from want of proper food. They were reduced to eating dogs, cats, mice, and vermin of all kinds. Twelve thousand poor people, men, women, and children, were driven out of the city, and, as they were not permitted to pass through the English lines, they had to remain under the walls until they died of hunger. Babes newly born were drawn up in baskets to the top of the wall to be baptized, and then returned to their mothers, who had nothing to give them, and so, of course died miserably. Oh! it was pitiful.

Messengers were sent to the King of France to explain the terrible state the city was in and to demand succour. In consequence, an embassy went to King Henry to treat of peace, but though negotiations lasted for fourteen days, nothing came of them. A portrait of Lady Katherine had been brought to him for inspection, and he was well pleased with it. But it did not cause any diminution in his demands, which still were so much money for the young lady's dower, with such and such portions of the kingdom of France. The envoys from Rouen were therefore informed that before the fourth day after Christmas it would not be possible to send the required relief. The day dawned and waned, but the expected succours came not to the starving multitude. An army had indeed been collected, and ordered to repair to Beauvais, but, in consequence of quarrels between the Dauphin and the Duke of Burgundy, no use was made of it for relieving the town.

France was indeed a country divided against itself. The junction of the Queen and Burgundy was viewed with great disfavour by the Armagnac party, who resented it as treason. This roused the anger of the Parisians, who were generally at heart Burgundians. They secretly admitted a number of the Duke's followers, whom they joined in a rising against the men in power. The Count of Armagnac himself, with some bishops and officers of the Government, were massacred, together with some thousands of men, women, and children. The Dauphin was only saved by a faithful friend and follower of the late Duke of Orleans, Tanneguy du Chastel, who folded him in a blanket, and carried him to the Bastille, whence he was conveyed to Melun.

Seeing no prospects of relief, the inhabitants of Rouen now resolved to treat with their adversaries. Archbishop Chicheley, who was present in the English camp in the capacity of confessor to King Henry, and chaplain-general of the army, together with Richard Beauchamp, Earl of Warwick, had been appointed to receive a deputation. But they had only been empowered to accept an unconditional surrender, and this was refused as entirely inadmissible. It was therefore resolved by the inhabitants to undermine a portion of the wall, and support it by wooden props inside to which they would set fire, and, when the wall fell, sally out *en masse* and take whatever fate might be in store for them.

1419. Jan. 16. On learning this determination, Henry, who did not wish the destruction of the finest city in Normandy, caused other terms to be offered. All had free leave to depart, but leaving everything behind them except their ordinary clothing. The men-at-arms, having first deposited their weapons in a specified place, were to swear not to bear arms against England for a year. All who remained must swear faith and loyalty to the King of England and his successors, and, in return, would be maintained in possession of all the liberties and privileges which they had obtained in the days of St. Louis. Finally, 365,000 crowns were to be paid to King Henry, and Alain Blanchard, with two other leaders, were to be delivered up to be dealt with according to his pleasure. Alain was executed four days afterwards, but the other two were let off. Sir Guy le Bouteiller and several of his followers took the oaths of allegiance to the King, and Sir Guy received an appointment under the governor of the city.

Jan. 19. On Thursday afternoon, amid the ringing of all the church bells,

King Henry entered the city, attended by his brothers and all the nobles in the army. He was followed by a page, mounted on a fine charger, and bearing a lance which had a fox's brush attached to its point. All the mitred abbots and other clergy met the King and escorted him to the cathedral of Our Lady, where he offered up his thanksgiving at the high altar. He afterwards took up his lodgings in the castle.

The greater part of the other Norman towns now submitted to the conqueror without making any further resistance. The inhabitants adopted the red cross of England and many of them even joined the army. Henry's demeanour towards them subdued the hearts of all the people.

Notwithstanding the successes of the English, the French factions were as far as ever from coming to an understanding. A deputation, headed by the Earl of Warwick, went to King Charles and the Duke of Burgundy, who were at that time at Provins, in the Isle de France. On the way there they were attacked by Tanneguy du Chastel and the Dauphinois or Armagnacs, who were, however, dispersed with a loss of forty men. *April.*

After the return of the ambassadors, it was arranged that a meeting between the two kings should take place at Meulan. The French were to assemble at Pontoise and the English at Mantes. The place of meeting was to be a space of ground on the banks of the Seine. The other three sides were guarded by a deep ditch and a palisading of boards, to prevent the presence of interlopers. Outside the hoarding, on each side, sumptuous tents were erected for the accommodation of the royal parties and their followers, and near the centre of the ground were two rich pavilions, in front of which was a mast, where the actual assemblage was to take place.

On the day appointed King Charles was too unwell to appear. But Queen ISABEAU, with the Lady KATHERINE, the Duke of Burgundy and the Count de St. Pol, attended by an escort of 1,000 men, arrived and took up their quarters in the tents on the right hand. King Henry, with his brothers of Clarence and Gloucester, the Earl of Warwick and also an escort of 1,000 men, came soon afterwards and entered the tents on the left hand. *May 30.*

At a given signal, the Queen and King, with their immediate friends entered the enclosure at the very same moment.

Having saluted the Queen, King Henry then kissed her and Lady Katherine. The Duke of Burgundy saluted the King by bending his knee slightly and inclining his head, but Henry took him by the hand and embraced him. All then entered one of the pavilions, the King and Queen leading the way.

Henry was undoubtedly struck with the beauty of Katherine, who had regular features and a brilliantly fair complexion, though expression was lacking, and there was a certain vacuity which might be inherited from her unfortunate father, but he was not, therefore, disposed to lower his terms.

June 1. Only compliments passed on the first day. Two days later all met again, with the exception of the fair Katherine. Queen Isabeau had noted the impression made by her daughter on King Henry, and calculated that 'absence would make the heart grow fonder,' and that to obtain her hand he would give up many of his claims. She did not know the man she had to deal with. Henry did not abate one jot in his demands. He required full sovereignty over Normandy, and all the places which had fallen to his arms, together with all lands ceded at the peace of Bretigny, and the hand of Katherine. The French did not raise any objections, but put forward several counter-demands, raised doubts here, required explanations there, and so worked matters that, when a month had elapsed, things were *in statu quo ante:* the whole proceedings had been a sham. When

July 3. Henry went to keep the last appointment at Meulan he found all the paraphernalia had been removed, and only the Duke of Burgundy was there to meet him. 'Fair cousin,' said Henry, stung by this premeditated insult, 'we wish you to know that we will have the daughter of your King, and all that we have asked, or we will drive him and you out of the kingdom.'

'Sire,' replied the Duke, 'you are pleased to say so, but before you can drive my lord and me out of the kingdom, I make no doubt that you will be heartily tired.'

The reason of all this comedy is to be found in the fact, that, by the intervention of Tanneguy du Chastel, and Madame de Giac, a favourite of the Duke, a reconciliation had been effected between the Dauphin Charles and John 'the Fearless' of Burgundy. A meeting

July 11. between the two took place near Pouilly le fort, about a league from Melun, when a treaty was signed. They separated with every mark of affection, the Dauphin going to Tours and the Duke to Corbeil. If this pacification had been sincere, it would have tended materially to the best interests of France, but it was the prelude to a tragedy which laid the country at the feet of the conqueror.

This peace, far from dispiriting King Henry, only made him more determined to prosecute his enterprise with greater energy. He decided to attack Pontoise in the Isle de France, the strongest town between Normandy and Paris. The expedition was led by Gaston de Foix, the Captal de Buch, a distant connection of the Captal de Buch so celebrated as a friend of the Black Prince. With not more

July 31. than 3,000 men he arrived before sunrise on July 31, at one of the gates. As it was closed, some of the men scaled the wall and opened it from the inside without alarming the guard. The army immediately entered to the cry of 'St. George! the town is ours.' The governor, the Lord de l'Isle Adam, who was in bed asleep at the time, on being informed of what had taken place, went out to make a personal inspection. Having satisfied himself that resistance would be useless, he had all his money and effects packed up, and, with some thousands of the inhabitants, who followed his example, took the road towards Paris. The place was treated as a conquered town.

John de Foix, the son of Gaston, was, many years later, in the time of Henry VI., created Earl of Kendal.

An army led by the Duke of Clarence appeared before the walls of Paris, and the court removed in all haste to Troyes, in Champagne.

The town and castle of Gisors, on the frontiers of Normandy, towards France, were besieged by the Duke of Clarence, and at the end of three weeks, surrendered through want of provisions. The garrison had leave to march away with all their baggage, whilst the inhabitants were required to swear allegiance to the King of England.

The castle of Gisors was erected during the reign of William Rufus by his friend Robert de Belesme. An elm, standing about a mile out of the town, was often the place fixed upon for a meeting between the Kings of France and England. There, amidst great festivities, were treaties made, only to be infringed, sooner or later, by one or both. One of the most celebrated of these meetings was that between Philippe Auguste and Henry II., a year before the death of the latter, on receiving the news of the capture of Jerusalem by Sultan Saladin. Both Kings took the cross, and vowed to march against the conqueror. There is a sculpture on one of the walls of the castle dungeon, said to have been done with a nail by some unfortunate man confined there. This formed the subject of a painting called 'The prisoner of Gisors,' which was afterwards engraved. The castle is now in ruins, but there are considerable remains yet left.

Two other castles, among the strongest in Normandy, were also besieged about this time.

Chateau-Gaillard had been built and strongly fortified by Richard 'Lion Heart,' in defiance of Philippe Auguste of France. It was situated on the rocks above Les Andelys, and considered almost impregnable. But during the reign of Richard's pusillanimous successor, John, it was taken by the French, after being blockaded for more than a year. Now it was besieged by the English, under the Earl of Huntingdon, and was defended by the gallant Sir Ollivier de Manny. For sixteen months the castle was held, and only surrendered at last in consequence of being unable to obtain any water, the cord by which the supply had been hitherto drawn up being quite worn out. There are considerable remains of the castle still standing, which are well worth a visit.

The castle of La Roche Guyon, not far from Mantes, also on the Seine, was defended by the widow of Guy IV. Sire de la Roche Guyon, who had been slain at Azincour. It held out for two months, but at length surrendered. King Henry gave the castle in charge to Sir Guy le Bouteiller, and desired him, at the same time, to take the lady in marriage. But the lady was not willing, and marched out with all her men.

Charles, Duke of Touraine and Dauphin of France, with 20,000 men marched to Montereau-sur-Yonne, and thence despatched

Tanneguy du Chastel with an invitation to the Duke of Burgundy to come and consult with him on public affairs.

After considerable hesitation, the Duke set out, attended by his council and escorted by 500 men-at-arms and 200 archers. On Sunday, September 10, they were at Braye-sur-Seine. On approaching Montereau, at three o'clock in the afternoon, three of the Duke's dependents came thence to warn him that several barriers had been erected on the bridge where the conference was to take place, and advised him to be very wary and careful. A council was called, but opinions were divided. Some suspected evil intentions on the part of the Dauphin. Others contended that a son of the King of France could not harbour thoughts derogatory to his dignity. The Duke decided to proceed, feeling convinced that, if anything afterwards occurred to delay the peace and reformation of the country, the blame would be laid on his shoulders if he did not appear. The march was therefore continued until they reached the gate of the castle of Montereau, which had been appointed for the Duke's residence, while the Dauphin lodged in the town on the other side of the river. The Duke accordingly dismounted, with several of his principal lords, his favourite, the Lady of Giac, his trusted attendant Jossequin—in whom, as well as in the lady, he placed unlimited confidence—200 men-at-arms, and 100 archers.

Tanneguy du Chastel came to inform the Duke that the Dauphin was already on the bridge waiting for him. Accompanied by Charles, eldest son of the Duke of Bourbon, and nine other nobles, the Duke set out.

On arriving at the first barrier, they were met by some of the Dauphin's people and urged to hasten, with promises of perfect safety in doing so. Still the Duke hesitated. But his companions saying he might proceed without danger, and that they were willing to run the same risk, he consented to do so. They therefore passed through the first barrier, which was at once closed and locked behind them.

Other men of the Dauphin's still urged them on, with renewed assurances of safety, until the second barrier was passed, and, like the first, securely fastened behind them. Here the Duke met Tanneguy du Chastel, whom he clapped on the shoulder, saying: 'This is a man in whom I trust.'

Advancing still further, the Duke observed the Dauphin leaning against the third barrier, and therefore bent his knee to the ground in salutation. But the ungracious boy—he was then seventeen years of age—made no return, showed no sign of affection, but reproached him with not keeping to his engagements. Being urged to rise, he tried to remove his sword, which had got between his legs and prevented his at once doing so. One of the knights attending on the Prince called out: 'What! do you put your hand on your sword in the presence of my lord the Dauphin?' At the same moment Tanneguy du Chastel, saying, 'It is now time,' struck the Duke with a battleaxe to his knees, and cut off a portion of his head. The Duke tried to rise and draw his sword, but Tanneguy repeated his blow and, assisted by others, laid him dead. The Lord de Nouailles, one of the Duke's attendants, alone tried to render him assistance, but was slain, after a scuffle, with the Viscount de Narbonne.

Thus died JOHN 'THE FEARLESS,' of Burgundy, in the forty-ninth year of his age, trusting to the promises and securities of a weak, frivolous, and dissipated youth, governed by worthless favourites. Whether the Dauphin was actually cognisant of the intended murder from the first is an open question, but probabilities are against him, and a stain must ever attach to his memory on that account.

The victim was stripped of everything excepting his doublet and drawers, and left on the bridge until midnight, when the body was carried to a mill near by. Next day it was interred in front of the altar of the church of Our Lady at Montereau, and twelve masses were hastily said for the repose of the soul of the defunct.

Of the other nine attendants on the late Duke, one only, the Lord de Montague, escaped; the others were made prisoners. The garrison in the castle were forced to surrender it. The Lady de Giac and Jossequin remained behind of their own accord, and it is much to be feared that these trusted companions of the Duke were not unaware of the fate to which their advice would lead him.

The Dauphin, Charles, sent letters to Paris and other places, with a very garbled account of the affair. He stated that on reproaching the Duke with not having waged war against the English in accordance with his engagements, he had answered vaguely, and 'put his hand to his sword as if about to attack us, but we were saved by our loyal friends, and he died.'

Universal horror was excited all through the country, and revenge on the murderers was loudly called for.

PHILIP, Count of CHAROLOIS, the only son of the murdered Duke, was also son-in-law to King Charles, having married his eldest daughter. He was at Ghent when the news reached him. 'Michelle,' said he, turning to his wife, 'your brother has murdered my father.' She was fearful lest on that account she might lose his affection. But he reassured her on that point, only saying that he was obliged to seek his revenge on the assassin. He at once applied to King Henry for aid, offering him his friendship and co-operation on any terms.

Queen Isabeau was now as much incensed against her last remaining son as she had ever been against his brothers, and she instilled the same feeling into her husband, the King. She assured Henry of her support, and the consent of the King to anything he might require.

Under these circumstances Henry was not backward in naming his terms. He required the hand of Katherine, the regency of the kingdom during the lifetime of King Charles, and the assured succession to the crown at his death.

Everything he demanded was assented to without scruple. Before the middle of November the preliminaries were arranged, but it required six months to settle all the minor points.

At length King Henry, accompanied by his brothers, some of the chief nobles and a small army of men-at-arms, set out from Rouen by way of Pontoise, Charenton, and Provins for Troyes. Outside the latter city they were met by Philip, Duke of Burgundy, who conducted the King and his friends to the hotels set apart for them, whilst the army was quartered in the villages round about.

1420. May 20.

May 21. Next day, Henry in complete armour, with the fox's brush in his helmet, went to the Church of Our Lady. There, on the high altar, Queen Isabeau and the Duke of Burgundy, acting for poor King Charles, who was suffering under one of his attacks, swore to observe 'the perpetual peace of Troyes,' whereby the Dauphin Charles was declared incapable of succeeding to the crown, and Henry, King of England, was pronounced 'regent and heir of France.' Queen Isabeau and King Henry then affixed their seals to the document. At a subsequent meeting of the estates of the kingdom at Paris, the treaty received unanimous approbation. And yet it was altogether an unjust proceeding. Even if the 'some-time Dauphin' Charles were unworthy of wearing the crown of France, there were other princes of the houses of Orleans, Anjou, Bourbon, even Burgundy, who had more just claim to it than Henry of England.

On the day of the ratification of the treaty, the betrothal of HENRY and KATHERINE took place, 'when,' according to Miss Strickland, 'he placed on her finger a ring of inestimable value, supposed to be the same worn by our English queen-consorts at their coronation.'

June 3. The marriage was solemnized in the Cathedral on Trinity Sunday, when the Archbishop of Sens officiated. Such great pomp and magnificence were displayed by Henry and his princes, says Monstrelet, as if he were at that moment King of all the world.

The honeymoon did not last long. In accordance with his undertaking, Henry had now to conquer the places held by the Dauphin Charles against his father. On the Tuesday after his marriage he marched to the siege of Sens in Bourgogne, which capitulated in ten days on favourable conditions.

June 5.

Montereau-sur-Yonne was the next to be approached, and in this he was joined by Philip, Duke of Burgundy. On St. John Baptist's Day an attack was simultaneously made on several quarters of the town, and a detachment of Englishmen was quartered in it, fronting the castle. On the morrow a party of Burgundians took up the body of the late Duke John from its resting-place, put it into a leaden coffin, filled with salt and spices, and sent it to be interred in the Carthusian Convent at Dijon by the side of his father, Duke Philip the Bold.

June 24.

Some of the prisoners taken in the town were promised their lives on condition of their persuading the governor to surrender the castle. They tried, but failed, and were hanged accordingly. Eight days later the castle was surrendered, on condition of the lives and fortunes of the garrison being spared. The governor, Sir Pierre de Guitry, was severely blamed for allowing the unfortunate townsmen above named to be put to death, and holding out so short a time afterwards.

Melun, which commanded the passage of the Seine, was the next place to be besieged. King Henry, with his brother-in-law, the Elector Palatine Louis, was at one side, and Philip of Burgundy, with John Holland, Earl of Huntingdon, and other nobles, at the other. A bridge of boats connected the two camps and prevented the relief of the town by water. Mining was attempted and met by countermining on the part of the garrison. On one occasion Henry encountered and engaged in personal combat with a stranger to him in one of the mines. After a while they paused, and Henry enquired who his antagonist was.

'I am Barbasan, the governor,' said he; 'and you?'

'You have fought,' replied Henry, 'with the King of England.'

It is not often we hear of Henry taking any actual part in fighting. The duty of superintendent was a sufficiently onerous one of itself. But he probably was not averse to the excitement of exchanging blows with another stout man-at-arms.

As the place was apparently about to hold out for a long time, King Charles and Queen Isabeau were brought there, and established in a house which King Henry had caused to be erected not far from his tents, but away from any danger to be feared from cannon shots. There they remained for about a month, and every day at sunrise and nightfall were regaled by melodious music from eight or ten clarions and divers other instruments provided by their son-in-law. Henry was not deprived of the presence of Queen Katherine, who was at Corbeil along with Margaret Holland, Duchess of Clarence, grand-daughter of the Fair Maid of Kent, and widow of John Beaufort, first Earl of Somerset, the King's uncle of the half-blood.

The besieging army suffered severely from an epidemic disease, Dec. and many died daily. But, within the town itself, they were sore oppressed by famine, everything eatable having been used up. On receipt, therefore, of a message from the Dauphin that he could not attempt a relief, and advised the making the best possible terms with the enemy, Barbasan, after holding out eighteen weeks, proposed to capitulate.

Those only who could give security not to serve again against the King of France, or the Regent, the King of England, would have their life and liberty; all others would be treated as prisoners. All in any way concerned in the murder of the Duke of Burgundy were specially excepted from any act of mercy. Among these was Barbasan, the governor, who, on that account, was kept for nine years a prisoner.

When the surrender of Melun was completed, the King of England and the Duke of Burgundy, having disbanded a portion of the army, marched to Corbeil. Thence, with King Charles and the two

Queens, they rode to Paris, where an enthusiastic welcome was accorded to them.

Henry's court at the Louvre was far more splendidly attended than that of the actual King at the Hôtel de St. Pol. Every office was at his disposal, and all men flocked to the rising sun. Among others who presented themselves were the Lords d'Albret, who came to offer their homage to Henry as Duke of Aquitaine.

The Regent's measures for the reform of abuses and redress of grievances were so much appreciated, that, in Paris as in Normandy, all were favourably impressed, and rejoiced in the prospect of having a firm yet just ruler.

Having made various appointments for the safe keeping of the different towns, and the good governance of the country, King Henry, with his Queen, his brothers and many of his barons, set out, soon after Christmas, for Rouen, where he remained a considerable time until he returned to England early in the new year.

SKETCH XIII.

THE KING OF FRANCE AND ENGLAND.

1421. THE home-coming of King Henry with his bride was hailed with joy unspeakable by people of all ranks. They landed at Dover on February 1, and were conducted in triumph to London.

Three weeks later the coronation of Queen Katherine took place in Westminster Abbey. Archbishop Chicheley placed the crown on her head, and the bearers of the two sceptres were EDMUND MORTIMER, Earl of March, and JOHN MOWBRAY, Earl Marshal. 'Such was the magnificence displayed,' says Monstrelet, 'that the like had never been seen at any coronation since the time of that noble knight Arthur, King of the English and Bretons.'

The banquet was given in Westminster Hall, but, as it was the season of Lent, it consisted almost entirely of fish of different kinds, served up in various styles, and interspersed with subtilties or ornaments. Upon the Queen's right-hand sat the Archbishop of Canterbury, and Henry Beaufort, Bishop of Winchester, the King's uncle. On her left hand sat JAMES I., King of Scotland. The noble Earl of Warwick, RICHARD BEAUCHAMP acted as deputy steward. William de la Pole, Earl of Suffolk, was cupbearer, and Sir RICHARD NEVILLE, afterwards Earl of Salisbury, eldest son of RALPH, Earl of WESTMORLAND and JOANNA BEAUFORT, the King's aunt, was the carver.

Progresses were then made by the King and Queen through the country. Their joy was suddenly damped, when at York, by the receipt of the direful intelligence of the battle of Beaugé.

THOMAS, Duke of CLARENCE, who had been appointed Lieutenant in France and Normandy, made an incursion on Easter Eve into Anjou, which owned the authority of the Dauphin Charles. The Constable la Fayette assembled an army of Frenchmen, which was joined by five to seven thousand Scots under JOHN STEWART, Earl of Buchan, and ROBERT, his brother, sons of the late Regent of Scotland, Robert, Duke of Albany; Archibald, Earl of Wigton, son to the Earl of Douglas; and JOHN STEWART, Lord Darnley.

CLARENCE, in his great desire to meet the foe, of whose numbers he does not appear to have been aware, hurried on with only some of his knights and men-at-arms, without his archers, who had great difficulties in crossing the river, thinking to surprise the enemy. Instead of that he and his followers fell into an ambush.

The Duke was conspicuous by the coronet of gold studded with March 22. precious stones which he wore on his helmet.

> 'Swinton laid the lance in rest,
> That tamed of yore the sparkling crest
> Of Clarence's Plantagenet.'

After being wounded and unhorsed by the lance of Sir John Swinton, he was beaten down by Buchan with a large mace which he held in his hand. So died a brave and stalwart knight, Henry's best beloved brother, and nearest to him in age, there being only a year between them. The coronet worn by Clarence was taken by a Laird of Lennox, and sold by him to Stewart of Darnley for a thousand golden angels.

The fight was a stubborn one, but it ended in the first defeat of Henry's troops, of whom 1,200 were slain and 300 taken prisoners. Of the enemy between 1,000 and 1,100 are reputed to have been killed.

Among the slain were Gilbert Umfraville, Earl of Kyme; Sir John Grey of Heton, Earl of Tancarville, in Normandy; and Lord Ross.

The principal among the prisoners were JOHN BEAUFORT, Earl of Somerset, and his brother THOMAS; JOHN HOLLAND, Earl of Huntingdon, and Lord Fitzwalter. Somerset, who was then only seventeen years of age, remained a prisoner for nearly the same number of years, until December, 1437, when, on the death of his mother, Lady Margaret, Duchess of Clarence, he was ransomed for an immense sum of money, and so returned to England.

The body of the unfortunate Duke of Clarence was recovered by the archers under the command of Thomas de Montague, Earl of Salisbury. It was sent over to England and interred in Canterbury Cathedral. A fine tomb was erected to his memory by his Duchess Margaret, who died nineteen years later, in December, 1440, and was laid to rest beside him.

In token of gratitude for the service thus rendered him, the Dauphin nominated the Earl of BUCHAN Lord High Constable and Count D'EVREUX. Lord DARNLEY was at the same time declared Commander during the absence of the Earl of Buchan, and was created Lord d'Aubigni. This title, with the château in Berri, remained in the family until the death of Charles Stewart, Duke of Richmond, Earl of Darnley, Lord d'Aubigni, etc., in 1672. It was then given, at the request of King Charles II., to Louise de Querouaille, Duchess of Portsmouth, one of his numerous mistresses, and after her death, in 1734, it descended to her grandson, Charles Lennox, her son, Charles, the founder of the present ducal house of Richmond, having predeceased her.

This defeat and death of his brother must have been a sad blow to King Henry. We are left to imagine the effect upon him, and are only told that he hastened on preparations for a return to the seat of war against his adversary Charles, Dauphin of Vienne. The Parliament and Convocation readily confirmed the treaty of Troyes; loans were raised, the clergy voted him a tenth, and fresh troops were everywhere being raised.

James of Scotland was with the royal pair when the intelligence of Beaugé came to hand. Henry requested him to forbid his subjects to fight against the English, to which he replied that, as a captive, he could scarcely hope that such commands would be obeyed. But he added that, as a private knight, he would gladly accompany the foremost warrior of the time, and learn the art of war under so competent a commander. He only stipulated not to be employed against his own subjects.

Soon after Henry ascended the throne, he had removed James, whom he had always befriended as far as he was able, from his six-year-long captivity at Nottingham to a freer life on the heights of Windsor, where he was placed in honourable captivity in the Devil's Tower, and treated with great consideration.

Beneath this tower, stretching to the outer fosse, was a garden with hawthorn hedges, and a green sward intersected by alleys, which were furnished with arbours.

One day, after rising as usual at daybreak, James sat at his window gazing on the scene and listening to the songs of the birds, while he meditated on the art and nature of love.

'The fairest and the freshest young floure' suddenly appeared before him. At once 'in captivity he is captive.' His imagination is fascinated. The object of his wishes, the queen of his world of fancy, is there before him. Who could the lady be?

Next day she came again, with two female attendants and a little dog with bells round its neck. The radiance of her beauty, the richness of her dress, were enhanced tenfold by comparison with her followers. When she left, he was afraid it might all be a dream. But she came again—and yet again.

Bolder grown, though keeping out of sight, he one day took his lute and sang. She, on her part, came oft to pace the garden, to gather flowers, or sit in the arbour and read. She, too, could, and did sing, and the conquest was complete.

Still, who could the lady be? Having entrance to that garden, he knew she could only come from the lodging of the Maids of Honour. Her bearing, her dress, her whole appearance proved to him that she was of high degree.

Next to Queen Katherine there was, at that time, no higher lady in the land. She was Lady JOAN BEAUFORT, daughter of John, first Earl of Somerset, and therefore cousin-german to King Henry, who took great interest in her, and placed her with his consort.

To Katherine soon came the knowledge of how matters stood, and she was not one to cross affairs of love. James had made such a good impression on her at the time of her coronation feast that, as a token of her favour, she gave him the gilt cup which he had held for her when she laved her fingers. She also begged her husband to set free his prisoner-guest; and it is said to have been the only instance known of the fair Queen actively interesting herself in anyone's favour.

At Windsor Castle on St. George's Day King James was knighted April 23. and admitted into the Order of the Garter. He accompanied King Henry on his next expedition to France, under a promise that he should revisit his own kingdom within three months of his return.

Archibald, Earl of Douglas, had also agreed, in consideration of an annuity of £200, to serve under Henry with 400 men, but, on receipt of the news of the battle of Beaugé, he transferred his services to the Dauphin.

An unexpected visitor came about this time in the person of JAQUELINE, Countess of Holland. As a lady in distress, King Henry received her honourably, and made her the very handsome allowance of £100 per month. Queen Katherine also gave her a hearty welcome.

Like many other countries, those which owned her sway were troubled by two opposition parties, the Hoeks and the Kabbeljaus. On the death of her father in 1417 the former upheld her cause, while the latter, objecting to female rulers, chose her uncle, John, Bishop of Liège, as their ruler.

> 'A clerk nocht clerklike aperand,
> Nocht all commendit of gud fame,
> Bot hey and haltane, prowd and stout,
> As nane his Pere was hym about.'

He resigned his bishopric and tried to compel his niece to marry him. But she would not listen to him, and appealed to the Pope, who granted her permission, in 1418, to marry her cousin-german, JOHN, Duke of BRABANT, son of Anthony, slain at Azincour, she having, for some woman's reason, declined a much more advantageous match with John, Duke of Bedford, which had been proposed to her by his brother, King Henry. The ex-bishop found a wife in Elizabeth of Luxemburg, and then carried on a war against his niece. But she marched in person to meet him, and defeated him at Gorcum, when Philip, Count de Charolois, endeavoured, but vainly, to make peace between them. King Henry was, however, more fortunate, as he supported her rights, and effected a reconciliation.

Her first husband, JOHN, the DAUPHIN of France, had been a poor sickly youth, and her second was not much better. He was a puny boy, five years her junior, weak in body and mind, bad-tempered, and much addicted to companions of low degree, by whom he was governed. His whole conduct during the past year had been so unpopular to his subjects in the Duchy of Brabant, that the nobility and gentry sent for his younger brother Philip, whom they declared governor of the country in his stead. She was a young and fine-looking woman, well formed, and accomplished, but with a will of her own, sharp in tongue and bold in action. They were an ill-matched pair, and were always quarrelling. After three years of cat-and-dog life, she accordingly left her home and returned to her mother at Quesnoy le Comte. Margaret, her mother, was aunt to Philip, Duke of Burgundy. They both tried, but in vain, to bring about a reconciliation between the divided couple. Jaqueline absolutely refused to return to her husband, and declared her intention of seeking for a divorce.

She left her mother to visit Valenciennes, and one fine morning in early summer she started, ostensibly, on a visit to Bouchain. But her stay there was only of a few hours' duration. Next morning she rode out, and was met by a knight of Hainault, named Escaillon, with a body of sixty men. Under their escort she travelled that day to Hesdin, thence to Calais, and soon afterwards crossed over to England, where we must leave her for the present.

June 10. On St. Margaret's Day King Henry embarked at Dover, with about 5,000 men-at-arms and 24,000 archers, the most numerous army he had ever collected, and landed in the afternoon of the same day at Calais.

Reinforcements of 1,200 men, under John, Lord Clifford, were sent to the Duke of Exeter at Paris, his position not being by any means a safe one, as the party of the Dauphin had been for some time gaining ground.

Henry marched by the seashore to Montreuil, and at the hotel of the Crown there had an interview with Philip of Burgundy, in order to confer as to future proceedings. During a stay there of two or three days he amused himself by hunting in the forest of Créci. Henry desired to cross the Somme at Abbeville, but could only obtain the permission of the authorities for the passage of his troops through the town on Duke Philip promising that any expenses incurred should be duly paid. The route was then continued through Beauvais and Gisors, whence Henry went to the Château de Vincennes, and was cordially welcomed by King Charles and his Queen.

With a considerable force, added to that he had brought over, Henry now marched to Nantes. He hoped to have a battle with the Dauphin, who had been seven weeks investing the place. But Charles was not willing to meet his great adversary, and retreated to Tours. In the same way the Dauphin and his party retired from the siege of Chartres as soon as the English appeared, and went to Bourges. It seemed as if the policy of Charles V. was being revived: to keep on the alert, harass the enemy, but never to hazard a battle.

The siege of Dreux had been entrusted to James, King of Scotland, who had with him Humphrey of Gloucester. On the Aug. 20. approach of the King the town capitulated.

A hermit, quite unknown to Henry, came to him at Dreux and told him he brought great evils upon Christendom by his unjust ambition in usurping the kingdom of France, and threatened him, in the Holy Name, with a severe and sudden punishment if he desisted not from his enterprise. Henry heeded not the exhortation; but within a very few months it was verified.

Villeneuve le Roi was taken, then Beaugency. At the end of September the headquarters of the army were at Lagny-sur-Marne, where Henry began his preparations for the siege of Meaux. He Oct. 6. encamped before it on October 6.

The defence of the city was in the hands of the Bastard of Vaurus, who had acquired an unenviable notoriety for barbarity, as it was his custom to hang, on an elm-tree outside the walls, any prisoner who could not pay a ransom. A great insult was offered by the besieged to the English troops, and more particularly to the King, who did not, however, deign to take any notice of it. An ass was led on to the walls, and by dint of beating made to bray. The party in charge of it then cried out to the English that it was their King calling for assistance, and bade them go to him. It was a very puerile trick, and scarcely worth recording, but Monstrelet gives it a place in his chronicles, and you may like to know it.

The town itself was taken by the middle of December, but the Dec. garrison retreated to what was called the market-place, which was strongly fortified and on the other side of the river.

The English army had been considerably reduced by an epidemic during the campaign on the Loire, in addition to losses in the field. King Henry therefore applied for assistance to JOÃO I., King of Portugal, who had married his aunt Philippa, and to the Emperor Sigismund. The King was then very glad to welcome ARTHUR, Count de RICHEMONT, who had been released from his imprisonment, and now brought a large body of men-at-arms to join the army.

Another source of joy to Henry was the news he received of the birth of his son HENRY on St. Nicholas' Day, December 6. His Dec. 6. first enquiry was as to where the boy was born. On being told it was at Windsor, he said, with a sigh, to his chamberlain, Lord Fitzhugh: 'I, Henry of Monmouth, shall small time reign and much get; Henry, born at Windsor, shall long reign and lose all.' It seems that

Henry had specially requested his Queen not to let their firstborn see the light at Windsor Castle. Katherine did not obey as she should have done, and the prophecy, whether an old one or one of Henry's composing, was singularly fulfilled.

1422. April. Towards the end of April the defenders of the market-place, having been disappointed of relief by the Dauphin, at last offered to come to terms of capitulation; but it was not until after a fierce assault, and May 10. when compelled by famine, that it was decided. The commander and three of his officers, who were accused of having assisted at the murder of the Duke of Burgundy, together with any English, Scottish, or Irish soldiers, were exempted from mercy. The others, to the number of eight hundred, were sent prisoners to Paris, Rouen, and England. The Bastard of Vaurus was beheaded. His body was hung on his favourite tree, and his head, put on a lance-point, was fixed over it. The officers were sent to Paris, and after due trial were beheaded.

RICHARD BEAUCHAMP, Earl of WORCESTER, a cousin of the Earl of Warwick of the same name, was killed by a stone cast from a sling April 16. during the last few days of the siege, on April 16. The Earl's body was sent home, and interred in the choir of the abbey church of Tewkesbury, where his widow, Isabel le Despenser, daughter and heiress of that Thomas, Earl of Gloucester, who had been executed in the beginning of the reign of Henry IV., erected a chapel to his memory. Sir JOHN CORNWALL, a young man of great promise, was also killed. Monstrelet calls him a cousin-german of King Henry. His father, of whom you have read elsewhere, had certainly, after 1400, married the King's aunt, ELIZABETH, Countess of Huntingdon, but, according to genealogists, there does not appear to have been any issue of the marriage.

After the fall of Meaux many other towns and castles submitted. Yet even now only the country north of the Loire, from which Maine and Anjou must be excepted, acknowledged the authority of the Regent, the King of England. To the south of that river the Dauphin was supreme, and kept his court at Bourges in Berri.

May 21. QUEEN KATHERINE, without her boy, escorted by the Duke of Bedford, arrived at Harfleur, and at Vincennes, whither she proceeded to visit her parents, was joined by her husband, 'who received her as if she had been an angel from heaven.' The two May 30. courts went, on Whitsun Eve, to Paris, where the festival was to be celebrated. Shows and pageants were organized for the amusement of the people, who were admitted to the Louvre to see King Henry and Queen Katherine sitting at table, with crowns on their heads, and arrayed in their royal robes. But, neither meat nor drink being offered them, which had been the custom of the Kings of France when keeping open court, they went away highly offended. They murmured at the great display made by the Regent, while their own King, Charles 'the well-beloved,' appeared to be in a subordinate position at the Hôtel de St. Pol, deserted by everyone.

From Paris the two courts went to Senlis, and, during their stay June 18. there, the town of Compiègne, which had held out for the Dauphin, submitted, in accordance with the terms of a treaty made by the governor.

The Dauphin CHARLES had not been idle. He had won the town of La Charité, and closely besieged Cône-sur-Loire, in Bourgogne, which had agreed to capitulate on August 6 if not relieved. The Duke of Burgundy sent to request the aid of some men-at-arms and archers from King Henry, who replied that he would bring them himself. The army was sent forward under the command of the Duke of Bedford and the Earl of Warwick.

HENRY had long been suffering from some disease, called, variously, dysentery, pleurisy, or fistula, which had baffled the skill of all his physicians. He went with the army as far as Melun, but his illness compelled him to take to a litter, and be carried after them. He grew so much worse that he had to transfer the command to his brother John, and be taken back very slowly to Vincennes. The mere appearance of the Duke of Bedford with his forces so much alarmed the Dauphin that he retreated in all haste to Bourges, and Cône was relieved. The Duke, hearing of his brother's danger, started off at once for Vincennes.

Henry was perfectly aware of his critical position. He knew that 'the rider on the pale horse' was coming, and he prepared to meet him as calmly as ever he had gone to the field of battle. As soon as the Dukes of Bedford and Exeter, the Earl of Warwick, and others had assembled round his bed, he told them that he had not much longer to remain in this world.

He besought his brother John 'to comfort his dear wife, who would be the most afflicted creature living,' and to continue towards his son the same loyalty and affection which had ever been evinced for himself. He desired that the Regency of France might be offered to the Duke of Burgundy; but, in case he declined, that Bedford might undertake it. At the same time, he charged him on no account whatever to make peace with the Dauphin unless full sovereignty over Normandy was assured to the crown of England. It would appear from this that Henry's ambition was really restricted to having possession of the cradle of the race of English kings, and did not extend to the whole of France. To the brave and loyal Earl of Warwick, Richard Beauchamp, he preferred the request to take over the charge of his little son. He then prayed them all ever to keep on good terms with Duke Philip of Burgundy. Especially he charged that this should be impressed on Humphrey of Gloucester, whom he appointed Regent of England, but whose hasty and choleric temper he much doubted would breed mischief, as it will be shown later on that it did. Finally, he gave strict injunctions that the Duke of Orleans and other French prisoners should not be released until his son had come to full age. All were deeply affected, and promised to fulfil his wishes to the best of their ability.

He then enquired of his physicians how long he had to live. They hesitated for a moment, but then said that 'it was in the power of the Almighty to restore him to health.' This did not satisfy him, and he required to be told the exact truth. 'Sire,' then said one of them, falling on his knees, 'think of your soul. Unless God should will otherwise, you cannot live more than two hours.'

In no ways dismayed, he sent for his confessor and chaplains, and received the last rites of the Church. Then they began the Penitential Psalms. When they came to the words at the end of Psalm li., *muri Hierusalemi*, 'build thou the walls of Jerusalem,' he stopped them, saying that 'it had been his purpose, after restoring peace to France, to have gone to the deliverance of Jerusalem from the Saracens.' The priests then proceeded with the Office, and soon after they had come to an end he passed quietly away, between two and three o'clock in the morning, in his thirty-fifth year.*

Aug. 31.

Thus died Henry of Monmouth,

> 'The flower of kings past,
> And a glass to them that should succeed.'

When a boy of eleven years of age he had been a student at Oxford, where at one time in a stained glass window there was an inscription calling him: *Hostium victor et sui*—'Victor over his enemies and himself,' which very tersely describes his character.

As a man, he was pure in life, high-minded, merciful, religious.

> 'He was a true lover of the Holy Church,'

and as such never omitted any of her ordinances. He founded monasteries for the Carthusians at Shene, and was a great benefactor to Westminster Abbey. In 1414 he founded a nunnery for Bridgettines at Twickenham, which was removed in 1432 to Isleworth, where now stands Sion House, belonging to the Duke of Northumberland. He was opposed to the Lollards, as the disturbers of the peace of the Church and country.

He was not a mere soldier, but an able general—a diplomatist and politician of no mean order. He was stern and rigid in exacting the most perfect obedience to orders, but was never needlessly cruel. His self-reliance was great, his intrepidity and coolness unsurpassed.

As a king he was the noblest, and certainly most popular, who had ever reigned. He was the idol of the people. By his talents and energy he caused them to forget the crimes by means of which his father had climbed into his cousin's throne.

As Mr. Hallam says, 'He was loved throughout his life, as, indeed, a temper so intrepid, affable, and generous well deserved. His successes, more dazzling even than those of his great-grandfather, Edward III., only added to the feeling.'

> 'King Henry the Fifth too famous to live long!
> England ne'er lost a king of so much worth.'

---

* He was born, according to Doyle's 'Baronage,' September 16, 1386.

He believed so firmly in the justice of his cause, that he laid the blame of all the miseries which followed his invasion of France upon those who opposed him.

The funeral of the great King, in its pomp and ceremony, proved the great esteem and affection in which he had been held by all manner of men. The body, after being embalmed, was placed in a leaden coffin, which was deposited in a car drawn by four powerful horses. On the car was an effigy of the King in royal robes, with a golden crown studded with jewels on the head, a sceptre in the right hand, and in the left a golden orb with a cross. Over it was a canopy of crimson silk, heavily embroidered with gold.

On either side of the car marched a number of men, clothed in white surplices, bearing torches, and 500 men-at-arms, in black armour, followed, with reversed lances.

Owing to the absence of the Duke of Bedford, who was compelled to remain at his post in France, James of Scotland, arrayed completely in black, acted as chief mourner, and was attended by princes of the blood, the nobility and officers in the army.

At the church of Nôtre Dame, in Paris, a solemn service was performed, and then the procession moved on to Rouen, where the body lay in state for some time. Here the mourners were joined by Queen Katherine, who had not known of her husband's dangerous illness and death until a day or two after it occurred.* She had with her a large retinue, but was usually a league in the rear of the main body.

From Rouen the procession moved on to Abbeville, where the body was placed in the church of St. Ulfran, and requiems were chanted over it incessantly until the next morning. The march was then resumed through Hesdin and Montreuil to Calais. There a fleet was ready to convey the party to England.

At Dover the mournful cortège was joined by Henry Chicheley, Archbishop of Canterbury, and fifteen suffragans, in full pontificals, and the route was continued through Canterbury and Rochester to London, where they arrived on Martinmas-Day, and were met by Nov. 11. several mitred Abbots, clergy, and a large concourse of persons of all ranks. The priests chanted the service for the dead as they went through the streets, and the inhabitants stood at the doors of their houses, each one bearing a lighted torch.

In every town through which the body had passed masses were sung from early dawn until nearly noon.

The Archbishop officiated when the corpse of the great hero and King was laid to rest in the chapel of St. Edward the Confessor, in Westminster Abbey.

On his tomb was placed, by his Queen, a silver-plated statue, with a head of solid silver; but all the silver has disappeared, and nothing but a headless, mutilated figure of wood remains. In the

* Miss Strickland is of opinion that Katherine and her mother attended the last hours of Henry V.

chantry above can be seen the helmet, shield, and saddle, which are supposed to have been used by the hero at Azincour.

The autumn of this year was a time of deep mourning for Queen Katherine. In addition to the loss of her husband, she had to deplore the deaths of her sister and her father.

During the time that preparations were being made for the relief of Cône, Michelle, her sister, wife of Philip of Burgundy, fell ill at Ghent, and died there suddenly, greatly to the grief of all who knew her, for she was much beloved for her goodness, and her husband's subjects adored her. She was buried in the church of the monastery of St. Bavon. It was reported that she had been poisoned by Ourse de Viefville, one of her ladies, who had been at one time highly in her confidence, but had lately been dismissed from her service. The Duke did not, however, lend any countenance to such a tale, and nothing was ever done in the matter.

Oct. 22. CHARLES, King of France was taken ill but a few weeks after his son-in-law, and died on October 22, at his hôtel of St. Pol. The Duke of Bedford—who had been appointed Regent, as the Duke of Burgundy did not wish to undertake the office—being absent at the time in Normandy, the body of the King was placed in a leaden coffin and deposited in the private chapel of the hotel until his return.

Nov. 11. On November 10 the late King's body was carried in great state to Nôtre Dame, and, after mass had been chanted, it was removed to the church of St. Denis. Next day, after celebration of mass and the service for the dead, the body was laid in the sepulchre of his ancestors, in the presence of the Duke of Bedford and a great multitude of the inhabitants of Paris, who loudly lamented a gracious King, whose like they never expected to see again. Monstrelet especially adds that not one of the princes of the blood royal of France was in attendance. The sergeants-at-arms and ushers broke their staves and threw them into the grave, when Berri, king-at-arms, cried out: 'May God show mercy and pity to the soul of the late most puissant and most excellent Charles VI., King of France, our natural and sovereign lord!' Immediately adding: 'May God grant long life to Henry, by the grace of God King of France and England, our sovereign lord!' The sergeants and ushers then shouted: 'Long live the King! long live the King!'

Charles was in the fifty-third year of his life and the forty-third of his reign.

At the very same time, in England, over the grave of Henry V., garter king-at-arms proclaimed HENRY VI. King of England and France.

Charles, the only surviving son of the late King Charles VI., was living at the castle of Espally, near Puy, in Auvergne, when he heard of his father's death. By the advice of his ministers, prominent among them being Tanneguy du Chastel, he at once put on mourning. But next day he appeared in chapel in a vermilion robe, attended by officers in emblazoned coats, and, the banner of France being displayed, all present shouted 'Vive le Roi!' He was afterwards crowned at Poitiers, but was only acknowledged as CHARLES VII. by members of his own party. He narrowly escaped death when holding a council at La Rochelle. Owing, perhaps, to the great concourse of people, the floor fell in, and John de Bourbon, with some others, was killed. Charles was extricated from danger, having received only some slight abrasions of the skin.

SKETCH XIV.

FRANCE AND SCOTLAND.

THE new King of England, HENRY VI., was an infant not a 1422. year old at the time of his father's death.

Almost from the commencement of the reign trouble was caused by a man from whom, as a close relation, better things might have been expected. As long as he lived he was a thorn in the side of his nephew and his government. That man was HUMPHREY, DUKE OF GLOUCESTER, the late King's youngest brother, and at that time thirty-one years of age.

The title of 'Gloucester' was not one of good omen. The De Clares, among the earliest bearers of it, had frequently been unruly subjects, though the last of the line fell fighting for his King at Bannockburn. Of Thomas of Woodstock, and Thomas le Despenser the story has been told. That of Humphrey has now to be set forth.

Humphrey had the good looks of the family perhaps in a greater degree than any of his brothers. He was a well-read man, a patron of science and literature, and the possessor of a good collection of books, which he is said to have given to a Divinity School at Oxford. More credit has, however, been given to him on that account than circumstances warranted, to judge from an account in the 'Pictorial History of England.' It appears that the Duke of Bedford, as Regent of France, in 1425, sent the whole of the library at the Louvre, consisting of 853 volumes, into England, where perhaps they became the groundwork of Duke Humphrey's library.*

If, out of these, he gave 600 books to Oxford, he apparently obtained, without purchase, what was intended by his brother for the good of the country; and to Bedford, rather than to Gloucester, thanks should therefore be rendered.

To his equals, and the nobility in general, Humphrey's demeanour appears to have been haughty. But, like his father, he always showed every possible mark of courtesy to the people in general. With them, therefore, he was a great favourite, and with them obtained the

* Vol. ii., p. 205.

name of 'the good Duke'; but in no sense of the word did he deserve it, with the one possible exception that he was an assertor of the independence of the Church. Even that attitude might have been adopted out of sheer opposition to Cardinal Beaufort, who was zealous for Rome and all her interests when he was aiming at the papal tiara. His private life was corrupt in the extreme, and he gave way to excesses which damaged his health. In his actions he was utterly unscrupulous when he had any special ends to gain. To him, more than anyone, must be attributed the beginning of the decline of the English power in France, as his narrow and selfish ambition to increase his own power and dominions, without regard to the welfare of either kingdom, first put the alliance between England and Burgundy in jeopardy. He was an inordinately ambitious man, and his pride was touched when, on claiming to exercise the authority of Regent, in accordance with his brother's appointment, he was informed by the Lords in Parliament that such appointment was contrary to law, and his demand could not be complied with. In order to conciliate him it was agreed to appoint him President of the

Dec. Council, with the title of *Protector of the Realm and Church of England* during the absence of the Duke of Bedford. With that he had to appear content; but his dissatisfaction was great.

1423. JOHN, DUKE OF BEDFORD, the Regent of France, was a man of distinguished presence, but unlike any of his family in having a prominent Roman nose. He was in every respect an amiable man, a sage counsellor, prudent manager, and devoted servant of his nephew, the young King. He had not hitherto had much to do with military matters, but he proved himself to be an able organizer and commander.

At the commencement of this year the town of Meulan was captured by a party of Frenchmen, under Sir John de Grasville, and shortly afterwards the Duke of Bedford led an army to lay siege to

Feb. the place. The Earl of Buchan and others marched to its relief with some 6,000 men; but, in consequence of quarrels breaking out among the leaders, the expedition was given up. The garrison were so much enraged that they flung to the ground the banner of the Dauphin, Charles, tore off his badges, and agreed to surrender

March 1. the town to my Lord Duke of Bedford, or his commissaries. Among these were Thomas Montague, Earl of Salisbury, Sir John Fastolfe, and Sir Richard Wydeville, whose name now appears for the first time, but of whom we shall hear more.

Bedford had a meeting at Amiens with the Duke of Burgundy and

April 27. John VI., Duke of Brittany, when a triple alliance was formed, and confirmed by a treaty wherein they mutually agreed to aid each other in bringing about peace and tranquillity in the distracted country. In ratification of their amity two marriages were agreed upon with the sisters of Duke Philip. The DUKE OF BEDFORD was to marry ANNE; and ARTHUR, COUNT OF RICHEMONT, who had come with his brother of Brittany, was to marry MARGUERITE, the widow of

Louis, the eldest son of the late King Charles. The Regent then entertained the whole company at dinner in the Bishop's palace where he was staying. The Duke of Brittany returned home, after being paid his expenses, and his brother Arthur accompanied his prospective brother-in-law to Burgundy, where his marriage took place a few months later.

The marriage of the Duke of Bedford was solemnized, with great splendour, at Troyes, in Champagne, whither the bride was brought by a number of the great barons of Burgundy and their ladies. The happy pair set out for Paris. On the way the Duke stopped to commemorate his honeymoon by the storming of the town of Pont-sur-Seine, which was soon taken. Then the journey was continued to Paris, where the Hôtel des Tournelles had been prepared for the reception of the bride and bridegroom.

The town of Crevant, six miles above Auxerre, in Burgundy, was besieged by the Constable of France, the Earl of Buchan, who had with him the Count de Ventadour and many other noble lords. The English, under Thomas de Montague, Earl of Salisbury, William de la Pole, Earl of Suffolk, Lord Willoughby d'Eresby, and others, marched to its relief with 4,000 men. At Auxerre they were joined by the Marshal of Burgundy and his forces. Some curious orders and regulations were agreed upon between the commanders of the combined forces. [July.]

It was ordered that all should march away at ten o'clock on Friday morning; that, when arrived near the probable place of battle, every one should dismount—those refusing to be put to death—and the horses be left half a league in the rear; that every archer should be provided with a stake pointed at both ends, thus copying the plan adopted at Azincour; that no prisoner should be taken until the field was won, on pain of such prisoner being put to death, and the captor also if he refused obedience; that each one should keep the station assigned him under pain of corporal punishment; and other injunctions of like character.

Next day, Saturday, at ten o'clock, they were before the town, but separated from it by the river Yonne. The French and Scots were posted on a hill facing the town. For three hours the armies stood facing each other; then the English and Burgundians gained possession of the bridge. The enemy descended from the hill, and were attacked by the townspeople in the rear, and the fight began in earnest. The battle was won by the attacking forces, and of the Scots at least 3,000 were killed or taken prisoners. The two leaders, the Earl of Buchan and the Count de Ventadour, were among the latter, each with the loss of an eye, and with them was Stewart d'Aubigni. The victors entered the town in triumph amidst the rejoicings of the inhabitants.

About this time many persons were astonished to hear of the marriage of HUMPHREY, Duke of Gloucester, and JAQUELINE of Hainault.

When Henry of Windsor was born, Jaqueline, as being the lady of highest rank near the Queen, was chosen as his godmother. The proceedings she had instituted for a divorce were still going on, and in looking out for a third husband, she cast her thoughts on Humphrey of Gloucester. Gloucester, who had a craving for riches and power, was not an unwilling wooer. He ignored his dying brother's special message to him to avoid all quarrels and dissensions, or even the giving occasion for such, with the Duke of Burgundy. He paid no heed to the personal warning King Henry had given him, which the Duke of Bedford had since repeated, against a matrimonial alliance with Duchess Jaqueline. He wanted the lady's broad lands of Holland, Hainault, Friesland and Zealand, and, when the marriage between John of Brabant and Jaqueline of Hainault was pronounced null and void, although it afterwards appeared that it was only so done by the Anti-pope Benedict XIII., in order to obtain those lands he married her in March, 1423. It is questionable whether love on his side had much or anything to do with the match. Humphrey was, at the time, living with Eleanor Cobham, the beautiful but wanton daughter of Lord Cobham, of Sterborough, whom he had the effrontery to name as one of the ladies of his duchess.

Great alarm was caused in Hainault, when the news of this marriage reached there, for fear of a war between Jaqueline's two husbands, each of whom styled himself lord of the country. Opinions among the nobility were divided on the matter.

1424. The Dukes of Bedford and Burgundy met at Amiens in the month of January following to endeavour to adjust the differences, having with them several of the nobles, as well as commissioners from the rival dukes, but nothing could be decided upon, except that they would meet again about Trinity Day. In the month of October, 1424, Humphrey and Jaqueline landed at Calais with 5,000 men, under the command of John Mowbray, Duke of Norfolk, and Earl Marshal, for an invasion of Hainault. Thereupon the two dukes with their advisers had another meeting at Paris. They agreed on terms, including a reference to the Pontiff, which were submitted to Humphrey of Gloucester and John of Brabant. The former sent an absolute refusal, while the latter declared his willingness to accept the terms. Philip of Burgundy then informed his brother-in-law that he should assist his cousin, the Duke of Brabant. Now Jaqueline was even more closely related to him, being his cousin both on the father's and mother's side. It seems probable that he sided with the former as being the weaker and more pliant character. He had his own ends in view. The Duke of Bedford was moved to anger against his brother of Gloucester, fearing that the alliance with Burgundy would be put in jeopardy, and the power of the English in France be destroyed, which actually came to pass.

Towards the end of November Humphrey and Jaqueline marched with their army into Hainault. They were well received at Bouchain and Mons, and most, if not all, of the principal towns soon pronounced for Jaqueline and the Duke of Gloucester, her husband, as she declared he was.

The Duke of Burgundy was very indignant, and, in accordance with his announced purpose, summoned his men-at-arms to serve him against the Duke of Gloucester, and in support of John, Duke of Brabant, under the command of Philip, the brother of the latter. A bitter war now commenced.

Humphrey wrote to Duke Philip from Mons on January 12, 1425, saying that he asked for nothing but what was his own in right of his wife, and would guard and preserve it as long as she should live.

Burgundy answered in a letter of March 3 that Gloucester had refused equitable terms, which had been accepted by the Duke of Brabant. He called upon Humphrey to retract certain charges made against his honour and fame, or to meet him in personal combat in the presence of the Emperor, or of the Duke of Bedford.

Writing from Soignies on March 16, Humphrey accepted the challenge, and named St. George's Day for the day of combat. Soon afterwards he returned to Mons. There, in conference with the Countess Dowager of Hainault and some of the nobles, it was agreed that he should go to England to make preparations for the duel in prospect. They requested him, however, to leave Jaqueline behind, and to this he agreed on their swearing to defend her against anyone who might attempt to injure her. That being done, he departed, but not alone; he took Eleanor Cobham with him. Poor Jaqueline was dissolved in tears, foreseeing many evils, which, indeed, too surely came.

About this time JOHN OF BRABANT received an official letter, dated February 15, from Pope Martin, which was afterwards read to the people from all the pulpits. His Holiness denied having judged the marriage between the said John and Jaqueline of Hainault invalid, and having confirmed the union of Jaqueline with Humphrey of Gloucester. Open war then commenced between the partizans of Duke John and the towns professing obedience to Jaqueline and the Duke of Gloucester.

The Countess Dowager interviewed the Duke of Burgundy and the ambassadors of John of Brabant. It was agreed to restore Hainault to John, and to put Jaqueline under the wardship of her cousin of Burgundy, with certain specified sums for her establishment, until the definitive sentence of Rome should be promulgated. Contrary to their oaths to the Duke of Gloucester, the deputies of Mons, on June 13, delivered up their liege-lady Jaqueline to the Prince of Orange, by whom she was taken to Ghent or Gand, and lodged in the ducal palace. It seems strange that her own mother should thus intrigue against her. It may be that Margaret of Burgundy was more concerned for the advancement of the interests of her own family than for those of her daughter, who had no prospect of having any children. She may also have believed, with many others, that Jaqueline had acted very wrongly in deserting her lawful husband for another man.

Before leaving Mons, Jaqueline wrote two letters, on June 6, to the Duke of Gloucester, one addressed to him as her 'very dear and redoubted lord and father,' and the other as her 'very dear and well-beloved cousin,' in which, with many loving words of hope and trust in him, she told of her betrayal 'by the false citizens of Mons,' and besought his help. The letters never reached their destination, but came into the hands of Philip of Burgundy.

The Duke of Gloucester had to submit to a severe reprimand from the Duke of Bedford and the English Council for undertaking his expedition into Hainault. That, however, did not prevent his raising another force next year (1426), which he placed under the orders of the Earl of Salisbury, and was only prevailed on by the urgent entreaties of his brother of Bedford to give up his intention of sending it to the help of his Duchess, as he still called her. It may be added here that it was by the wise management of the same Duke that the projected duel had been prevented.

Jaqueline did not long remain quiescent. In September, arrayed as a man, and accompanied by one of her women in similar attire, she escaped on horseback, under the escort of two men, to Antwerp. There she resumed her own dress and drove on in a car to Breda, where, as well as in other towns, she was well received. But the Duke of Burgundy, hearing of her escape, followed her, and a serious war began between the two cousins. In December a force of 500 men under Lord FitzWalter arrived in Zealand to the support of Jaqueline, but they were defeated by Burgundy, who then returned to Flanders. Jaqueline marched northward and blockaded Haarlem. She attacked and defeated a body of men from Flanders, who had come to the assistance of the town, but eventually, not having forces or material sufficient, she had to raise the siege.

About Mid-Lent, 1426, the Duke of Burgundy returned to Holland and was generally successful against Jaqueline, who, being driven northward, tried to surprise the town of Hoorn, on the Zuider Zee, but was repulsed.

At length came the bull from Pope Martin, who declared the marriage between Gloucester and Jaqueline null and void, and added that if John of Brabant should die, they could not legally marry each other.

John of Brabant died on April 17, when his brother Philip succeeded to Brabant, and, notwithstanding the Pontiff's sentence, Jaqueline called herself Duchess of Gloucester and appealed to Humphrey to come for her and take her back. All in vain. What Humphrey called love was now bestowed on his mistress, ELEANOR COBHAM, whom, five years later, he made his wife.

John 'the Pitiless,' of Bavaria, once Bishop of Liège, died this year, and, being childless, declared Philip of Burgundy the heir and successor to the lands he called his, totally ignoring his niece Jaqueline.

The war between the cousins still continued, but Burgundy was getting the upper hand. For some time Jaqueline had been residing at Gouda in Holland. That town was in 1428 besieged by her opponents. She was wearied out, and, in council with her friends, agreed to acknowledge Philip of Burgundy heir to all her lands in Holland and elsewhere, and to appoint him guardian of them. She also promised not to marry without his consent. Philip and Jaqueline then went together into Hainault, where the people were not satisfied with the arrangements made, but, seeing no remedy, had to acquiesce in them.

Jacqueline's troubles were not yet over. In despite of her promises she this same year married a private gentleman, FRANZ VON BORSELLEN. Philip, mistakenly named 'the Good,' seized him by craft. In order to secure his release, Jaqueline was compelled to cede all her rights in and over Hainault, Holland, Friesland and Zealand, to her cousin, in return for a yearly pension.

Real happiness had, until now, been a thing almost unknown to JAQUELINE, but, as she disappears from history, it is fair to conclude that during her last years she enjoyed it.

At her death, childless, in November, 1436, when only thirty-eight years of age, all her lands were incorporated with the other possessions of the Duke of Burgundy, who six years previously, on the death without heirs of Philip, Duke of Brabant, at Louvain, on August 4, 1430, had succeeded also to that dukedom.

After the Battle of Beaugé, the Earl of Buchan and the Earl of Wigton went back to Scotland, where the latter remained, being invalided. Buchan, on the other hand, not only raised an additional force of 8,000 men, with which he returned to France, but induced his father-in-law, Archibald, Earl of Douglas, to promise to follow him, which he did, accompanied by his second son James and 5,000 retainers. King Charles was so much delighted with this latest accession to his supporters, that he created Douglas Duke of Touraine, and named him Lieutenant - General of the kingdom. Buchan's power was so great, that, even after the disastrous result of the Battle of Crevant, he obtained a renewal of the ancient league between Scotland and France, which was ratified in Parliament by the regent Murdac, Duke of Albany, the nobility and prelates of Scotland. 1423.

The English Council, in order to put an end, if possible, to this constant supply of succour to the enemy, deemed it advisable to treat with King James for his release from captivity, and return to his own country. Envoys came from Scotland whom James first met at Pontefract, and it did not take long to come to terms. It was agreed that James should promise to forbid any more of his subjects to enter into the service of France; and to pay for his maintenance while in England—it could not be called ransom, as he was not, properly speaking, a captive—the sum of £40,000. Certain hostages were to be left in England until the sum should be paid, and four of the chief towns in Scotland engaged to defray the amount, should the King be unable to do so.

1424. Feb. 2. Still further to ensure the King's attachment to England it was resolved that JAMES' long attachment to Lady JOAN BEAUFORT should be rewarded by making them man and wife. The marriage was celebrated in the church of St. Mary Overie, Southwark, now St. Saviour's, with all the feudal pomp and ceremony of the age, and was graced by the presence of James' constant friend, Queen Katherine. The wedding-feast was given by the bride's uncle, HENRY BEAUFORT, Bishop of Winchester. On the following day £6,000 was remitted from the sum agreed upon, as the dower of his wife.

The newly-married pair set out in March, accompanied by a cortège of English noblemen as far as Durham, where they were met by the chief of the Scottish nobility. From there they were escorted by the Earl of Northumberland as far as Melrose.

James was received by his subjects with every manifestation of joy and affection after his long captivity of nineteen years. On May 21, he and his Queen were crowned in the abbey church of Scone.

James proved himself a King of whom any country might be proud. He was a great blessing to Scotland, and her most gracious Majesty Queen Victoria may look back to him as among the most illustrious of her ancestors. From him she is lineally descended.

In the meantime, the struggle for supremacy was still going on in France. Towards the close of 1423 the town and castle of Ivry, one of the border towns on the south-east of Normandy, situated on the river Eure, which was garrisoned chiefly by Bretons and held out for Charles VII., or the 'King of Bourges,' as the English usually styled him when they gave him a higher title than that of Dauphin, was being besieged by order of the Duke of Bedford.

This town of Ivry is the spot where, in 1590, Henry IV. of France won the great battle which decided the struggle of the League, and gives the title to the stirring battle-song by Lord Macaulay, of which the first two lines are here given :

'Now, glory to the Lord of Hosts, from whom all glories are !
And glory to our sovereign liege, King Henry of Navarre !'

Some of the French, on going to its relief, met with Sir John de la Pole, brother to the Earl of Suffolk, who was Governor of Avranches. He was returning from some marauding expedition, had dismissed a portion of his men, and being attacked by the enemy, was taken prisoner. The French then thought to take Avranches by surprise, but were utterly defeated by the remainder of the garrison and the townspeople, and forced to retreat.

Arthur of Richemont, being dissatisfied because he failed in obtaining from the Duke of Bedford as important a command in the army as he anticipated, showed an inclination to go over to the French, and the garrison of Ivry, learning this, thought themselves justified in holding out, which they did until August 8, when they were obliged to surrender to the Duke of Bedford, who had also some months before recovered Compiègne and Crotoy.

Jean, Duke d'Alençon, son of the Duke who was slain at Azincour, with other noble lords and 18,000 men, had marched to IVRY as if to relieve it. But on perceiving how matters stood there, they turned about and marched to Verneuil, another frontier town of Normandy about forty miles to the south-west, which was then in possession of the English. Here they gave out that they had completely defeated the English army and forced the Regent to fly. In consequence of that misstatement the gates were opened and they were admitted.

The Earl of Suffolk on the capture of Ivry was detached with some 1,600 men to watch the movements of the French army. He had reached as far as Breteuil, which is about twenty miles from Verneuil, when he learnt that the French were in possession of that town. He therefore sent off messengers at once to the Duke of Bedford, who had in the meantime gone, with the remainder of his army, to Evreux.

The Regent did not lose any time in putting his army in motion towards VERNEUIL. He at the same time sent a message to the Earl of Douglas, who used to ridicule the Duke by calling him '*John with the leaden sword*,' that 'he purposed coming to dine and drink wine with him,' to which the Earl replied that 'he should find the cloth laid.'

On arriving before the town all were ordered to dismount, as had been done before at Crevant, and to send their horses to the rear, where they were tied together by the collars and tails, and thus formed an almost impenetrable barrier. The pages and supernumeraries, together with the baggage, were also placed there, and 2,000 archers were detailed to guard the whole. The fighting-force formed one body, without van or rear-guard. The archers, again with their pointed stakes, were posted some in front, some on either flank, and in that position they patiently awaited the attack of the enemy.

The army of the allied French and Scots contained also some 600 lances and 1,200 foot-soldiers, Lombards and Milanese, contributed by Filippo Maria Visconti, Duke of Milan. All were assembled outside the town. Observing that the Englishmen had dismounted, they did the same, with the exception of the Italians, and sent their horses into Verneuil. In this position all remained for a considerable time. Unfortunately for them, there was disagreement among the leaders. The Duke of Touraine, or Earl of Douglas, to give him the more familiar title, recommended remaining where they were to receive the English attack. The Viscount de Narbonne, on the contrary, insisted upon the wisest plan being to march forward. He thought himself sure of revenge on his adversaries. It was then Aug. 17. about three o'clock in the afternoon. Snatching up a standard, he called upon his countrymen to follow him. By their impetuosity some of the English archers were for a time disorganized, but soon recovered themselves. Douglas felt himself obliged to follow, although his men were slightly in disorder.

A fierce hand-to-hand fight ensued, and the ground was contested foot by foot, nay, almost inch by inch, as for a long time no advantage appears to have been gained by either side.

The Italian cavalry made a sudden onslaught on the English rear, with a view to plunder. They fell into a trap. They could not break a way through the horses, and could not recover the road they had come, and thus fell a prey to the English archers, who were then at liberty to join their friends in front.

Their appearance decided the fate of the battle, which, after an obstinate fight of three hours, resulted in an unmistakable victory for the English, and the total rout of the allies.

The enemy lost all their baggage and treasures, and had to retire beyond the Loire. Between four and five thousand, three thousand of whom were Scots, were slain, and two hundred nobles and gentlemen taken prisoners.

Chief among the slain were the Earl of Douglas, and his son; the Earl of Buchan, and his brother Robert Stewart; the Counts of Aumale and Tonnerre; the Count de Ventadour; the Viscount de Narbonne; the Earl of Moray; Sir Alexander Home, of Wedderburn, a great friend of the Earl of Douglas; Sir Walter Lindsay, and many others whom it would be tedious to particularize.

This Earl of Douglas was the same of whom you have read at Homildon and Shrewsbury, and, from the number of battles in which he had been beaten, had acquired from his countrymen the name of *Tineman* or *Lose-man*. He was buried with his son-in-law, the Earl of Buchan, and Robert Stewart, with great pomp, in the church of St. Gratian at Tours.

The body of the Viscount de Narbonne was quartered and hung on a gibbet, he having been an accomplice in the murder of John Duke of Burgundy.

The principal prisoners were the Duke d'Alençon, the Lord de la Fayette, and various others.

The Scots were almost annihilated. They never again appeared as a distinct corps. About five years later the few then left were taken by King Charles VII. as a bodyguard, under John Stewart, Lord d'Aubigni, and for many years the troop was kept up by his successors. You will find them taking a prominent part in that capacity in Sir Walter Scott's romance of 'Quentin Durward.'

When the battle was over the Duke of Bedford assembled all his officers round him on the field, and returned humble thanks to God Aug. 18. for the great success He had given him. The town of Verneuil surrendered on the following day, August 18.

It had indeed been a great victory. the greatest since Azincour, though it had cost the English 1,600 lives. It fully established the Duke's right to be considered one of the ablest commanders of the time, and not unworthy to rank with his great brother Henry. Hardyng writes :

> 'The regent was there that daye, a lion,
> And faught in armes, like any champion.'

Yet the position of affairs was not much changed from that of two years ago, and for want of men the Regent was unable to make any forward movement. The position of the indolent and pleasure-loving Charles was even worse. He was poverty-stricken, unable to raise any money, and with a Council so divided that they only 'agreed to disagree.' For three or four years there was comparative peace.

SKETCH XV.

THE MAID OF ORLEANS.

AFFAIRS in England were not progressing smoothly, and it is as well that we should now direct our attention for a short time to that country.

Henry V. had constituted his uncle HENRY BEAUFORT, Bishop of Winchester, joint guardian of his infant son—probably only until the boy was old enough to be taken in hand by the Earl of Warwick.

Hardyng says :

> 'Of his soonne Henry, he made custode,
> Thomas Beaufort, his uncle, dere and trewe,
> Duke of Exeter, full of all worthyhode.
> * * *
> 'With helpe of his other eme,* then full wise,
> The Bishop of Winchester, of good aduise.'

Henry was the second of the three sons of John of Ghent bearing the name of Beaufort. When only about twenty-two years of age he was consecrated Bishop of Lincoln, and seven years later (1405), on the death of the celebrated William of Wykeham, he was translated to Winchester. About the same time he was made Chancellor by his brother, Henry IV., and presided in the Lack-learning Parliament. In 1417 he resigned the Chancellorship and started for the Holy Land, but whether he went there or not is uncertain. He attended the Council of Constance, and it was in great measure owing to him that Martin V. was elected Pope. In the month of November following he was nominated a Cardinal, but was told by the King, his nephew, that he could not hold his bishopric at the same time, and therefore had to let the cardinalate go. Beaufort was not a favourite with the people, probably because he was always opposed to their idol, the Duke of Gloucester. They looked upon him as a miser, because, unlike the latter, he did not squander his money on unworthy objects, but was frugal in all his habits, and thus

* Uncle.

enabled to come to the help of his nephew as we have already seen. He also furnished some £12,000 when men were required abroad for the service of that nephew's son. Later on in life he was a great benefactor to the Church. He completed the work commenced by 'Wykeham, the Great Bishop,' in Winchester Cathedral. He was the second founder, almost rebuilder, of the Hospital of St. Cross, near Winchester, originally founded by Henry de Blois, brother of King Stephen. This 'Almshouse of Noble Poverty,' as he called it, is still in existence, one of the most charming spots in England. He also repaired Hyde Abbey, which had been founded by King Alfred, and he made liberal provision for the relief of poor prisoners, which is an especially good trait in his character.

1424. In 1424 the Bishop had again been appointed Chancellor, and, in that capacity, had been strongly opposed to Gloucester's claim on the possessions of his wife Jaqueline. During the Duke's absence the custody of the Tower was committed by Beaufort and the Council to Sir Richard Wydeville, with orders 'to admit no one greater than himself.'

1425. On GLOUCESTER'S return, he required admission to the royal fortress, and, on being refused, called upon the Mayor to close the gates of the city against the Bishop, to whose ill-feeling against himself he attributed his exclusion, and to furnish him with five hundred men as an escort, that he might visit the King at Eltham.

Oct. 30. Next morning, when prepared to set out on his journey, he found his way barred. Beaufort's retainers had possession of London Bridge. They blocked up the road, occupied the houses on each side with archers, and declared that, if the Bishop might not enter the city, the Duke should not leave it.

The Bishop wrote at once to the Duke of Bedford, requesting him to come to England, for 'an ye tarry long we shall put this land in jeopardy with a field, such a brother as you have here. God make him a good man !'

Pending the arrival of Bedford, Archbishop Chicheley and PEDRO, Duke of COIMBRA, the second son of IOAO I., King of Portugal, and PHILIPPA of Lancaster, who had come on a visit to England, did their best to reconcile uncle and nephew. They made no less than eight journeys from one to the other before they could persuade them to keep the peace until the Duke of Bedford should be there to judge between them.

Towards the end of the year the Duke of Bedford arrived. He made it pretty evident that his private opinion was in favour of his uncle rather than his brother, and he did not show any good-will to the Londoners who had abetted the latter; but he thought it was a matter which the Council ought to settle.

1426. A Council was accordingly called together at Northampton in January, but the Duke of Gloucester declined to attend.

Parliament was therefore summoned to meet at Leicester on February 28. Strict orders were issued that no weapons were to be carried by anyone. Swords or daggers being thus forbidden, the retainers of the nobles brought clubs or bats with them. These being also disallowed, they concealed stones and plummets of lead in various parts of their dress. This meeting has hence derived the name of the 'Parliament of Bats.'

The Duke of GLOUCESTER having refused to make his appearance, it became necessary to issue a royal summons, which he was obliged to obey.

The little four-year-old King was sitting on the throne when the Duke condescended to appear. He impeached the Bishop of Winchester for shutting him out of the Tower, for having attempted the life of the late King when Prince of Wales, and having prompted him to usurp his father's throne. The Bishop, in reply, said that he had good cause for the personal offences of which the Duke complained; and as to the other two charges, he thought it sufficient to point to the good esteem and confidence in which his dear nephew King Henry had always held him as a complete and sufficient refutation of them.

The affair would appear to have been now referred to what we should call a sub-committee, consisting of Archbishop Chicheley and eight other persons. The Bishop appeared before the King, again seated on the throne, and declared his innocence in the most solemn manner. The Duke of Bedford replied for the royal infant that 'the King had no doubt of it, and held him to have been a true man to the late King.' 1426. March 12.

Turning to the Duke of Gloucester, the Bishop said 'he had never intended him any injury in person, honour, or estate, and hoped he would be good lord to him, never having given occasion to be otherwise.' To which Gloucester replied: ' Fair uncle, since you declare yourself such a man, I am glad it is so, and take you for such.' Then they shook hands.

It was 'a lame and impotent conclusion,' and doubtless the Bishop thought so, as next day he resigned the seals, and asked permission to travel. John Kemp, Bishop of London, was appointed Chancellor in his stead, and retained the office for six years.

The Council, whether judging from the Duke of Gloucester's demeanour at the late trial or from some other cause does not appear, seemed to think that he aimed at more power than the constitution warranted. It was decided to summon both him and the Duke of Bedford to their presence. The lords cannot have feared anything from Bedford, but they may have thought it would look less invidious if both brothers were called up together. 1427.

BEDFORD willingly appeared. After a long preamble, the Chancellor stated that, the King being under age, all power belonged to the Council, acting together, and not to any individual member, except in one or two special cases, where such power had been delegated. He went on to say that, unless they were free to govern in accordance with the authority they had received, the members of Jan. 28.

the Council had resolved to resign their commissions. Bedford calmly and courteously replied, declaring himself quite ready to be ruled by the assembled lords. With tears in his eyes, he made oath on the Gospels that, if at any time his actions were deemed to require amendment, he would gladly undertake to see to it.

The Duke of Gloucester pleaded illness for not attending when called upon. A convenient illness! or it may have been that he was suffering from the effects of one of his usual debauches. But he was not to escape. The Council went next day to his inn, and had anything but a gracious reception. The Chancellor paid him in kind, and complained of certain replies sent by the Duke to the Council. Gloucester said he would not be accountable to anyone save the King when of age. 'Let the Duke of Bedford do as he will while here,' he continued ; 'but when he returneth to France I will govern as seemeth to me good.' He changed his tone when the Chancellor told him of Bedford's submission. Perhaps he feared that his brother might remain in England. At any rate, he expressed his willingness to submit to the King's authority as exercised by the Council ; but he did not take any oath as his brother had done. Later on he had the position of principal adviser of the Crown in *Council* conceded to him, but in Parliament he simply ranked as Duke of Gloucester. ' He was a man utterly devoid of principle, and careless of the public good when it conflicted with his own ambition, comfort, or caprice.'

Feb. Having seen matters well settled, as he hoped, the Duke of Bedford returned to France, accompanied by his uncle, the Bishop of Winchester. At Calais the Bishop received the news of his having, in the previous June, again been named a cardinal by Pope Martin, and he was invested with the insignia of his high office in the presence of the Duke of Bedford. Henceforth he figures in history as Cardinal Beaufort.

1426. During the absence of the Regent, Arthur, Count of Richemont, had been bribed by the Constable's staff to join the party of the Dauphin. He did this with the consent of his brother-in-law, the Duke of Burgundy, who had at that time not yet forgotten the Duke of Gloucester's conduct in marrying the Duchess Jaqueline. Arthur now induced his brother Jean, Duke of Brittany, to allow him to levy troops in his territories, and to promise to break off his alliance with England as soon as Burgundy should do so.

The Regent induced the Council in England to declare war against the Duke, in consequence of his meditated treachery. Troops from Normandy, under the Earl of Suffolk and Sir Thomas Rampstone, were hastened into the duchy, which was despoiled up to the walls of Rennes. After trying the fortune of war for some time, the Duke was at length compelled to sue for peace. He made a treaty with the Regent, which was signed by himself, his two sons, his barons, and prelates, wherein he acknowledged Henry VI. as his rightful sovereign, and undertook to pay homage to him for his duchy.

THE MAID OF ORLEANS

If the Duke of Bedford had not succeeded in adding to the con- 1428.
quests of his brother, he had at least maintained the English
supremacy north of the Loire. Thomas de Montague, Earl of Salisbury, had recently come over from England with 6,000 fresh troops. June.
It was therefore proposed to cross the Loire and lay siege to Orleans.
Bedford was opposed to making the attempt, as it would very severely
tax the English resources; but in the council of war the majority of
voices was against him. He yielded, but against his better judgment.

The Earl of Salisbury, who was Captain-General of the army, and
one of the foremost warriors of the time, had the command of the
expedition. With him were William de la Pole, Earl of Suffolk,
Lords Talbot and Scales, who to the forces he had brought added
another 4,000 men. After reducing Nogent le Roi, Jargeau, and
one or two other small places, they arrived before Orleans. Oct. 12.

The city of Orleans is situated on the right or north bank of the
Loire. The French had provided themselves with stores of all
kinds, and, being determined to defend themselves and the place to
the utmost, had destroyed all their beautiful suburbs, including at
least a dozen churches, so as to be able to use their cannon freely
against the enemy.

The English were on the south side of the river, and the headquarters were on the site of a ruined convent. The first object of
attack was the tower called Les Tournelles, at the end of a bridge
over the Loire leading into the town. This was stormed and taken Oct. 23.
in spite of the discharge of cannon and frequent sallies of the besieged. The French had taken the precaution to shatter one of the
arches of the bridge, and to erect a second castle at the other end,
so that ingress to the city was impossible by that way.

Three days later SALISBURY, with Sir Thomas Gargrave and Oct. 26.
William Gladsdale, ascended the Tournelles for the purpose of taking
an observation of the place. There was a window, or aperture, with
iron gratings, through which they were reconnoitring. They were
seen from the walls by the son of the master-gunner, who had been
eyeing them for some time. Though but a boy, he had often watched
his father's operations, and, his father being away for the moment,
thought this a good opportunity to try his hand. He took the match
and fired the gun at them. So well was it aimed that the grating
was shivered to pieces; one fragment struck the Earl on the cheek,
carrying part of that and one of his eyes away. He had to be
taken to Meuny-sur-Loire, about ten miles south-west of Orleans,
where he died eight days afterwards. Sir Thomas Gargrave, who Nov. 3.
was standing close to the Earl, was likewise struck, and died within
two days.

The Earl's body was taken home, and buried 'with greate wor-
shippe and hie solempnitee,' in Bisham Abbey, the resting-place of
his forefathers. THOMAS DE MONTAGUE was the last of his name.
His daughter ALICE, or ELEANOR, was married to RICHARD NEVILLE,
eldest son of Ralph, Earl of Westmorland, and his second wife, Lady

Joan Beaufort, who, in right of his wife, was created EARL OF SALISBURY a few months later. They were the parents of the more famous Richard Neville, known as the 'King-maker.'

The EARL OF SUFFOLK, by order of the Regent, now took command of the besieging forces. His first care was to erect blockhouses, or wooden towers, called *bastilles*, all round the town, on the north as well as the south side of the river, in which detachments of men were posted. It being winter time, this gave the men employment. Only occasionally were sallies made from the beleaguered city, which were easily repulsed. There the supplies were becoming scarce. Convoys of provisions occasionally reached the place, but more frequently were stopped on the way. All things looked well for the besiegers, though even they, having to obtain their supplies from a distance, were often in want.

1429. The Duke of Bedford despatched 500 carts, containing a good supply of Lenten food, principally herrings, under the escort of Sir JOHN FASTOLFE, with 600 men-at-arms and 1,000 archers, besides carters and others. They left Paris on Ash Wednesday, and by short stages arrived safely at Rouvray, in Beauce, a small village between Genville and Orleans.

The French had by some means received notice of this supply coming, and it was thought to divert it for the use of the inhabitants of Orleans. Under the Count de Clermont, son of Charles, Duke of Bourbon, at that time a prisoner in England; John Stewart, Lord d'Aubigni, and his son; De la Fayette; La Hire; Dunois, the Bastard of Orleans, and others, 5,000 men marched to intercept it.

The English, in their turn, soon heard of this movement. Fastolfe formed the wagons into a square, to which there were but two openings, guarded by archers and supported by men-at-arms. The horses and non-combatants were placed in the most secure positions. For two hours they waited the pleasure of the enemy. It was now the night of the first Sunday in Lent.

The delay was caused by disagreement among the attacking party. The French wanted to remain on horseback, the Scots to fight on foot. It was at length decided that each nation should take its own way. Lord Charles de Bourbon and some others were first Feb. 12. knighted by the Lord de la Fayette, and three hours after midnight the affray began.

The horsemen could not protect themselves against the archers, and were soon forced to retreat. The Scots made their way to the front, but, by the incessant shower of arrows, were decimated, and the 'Battle of the Herrings,' as it is called, was won.

Lord d'Aubigni, an old man over seventy years of age, was slain, together with his son, 120 gentlemen, and 500 common men, principally Scots. DUNOIS was wounded. The English only lost one man of note, and only one man, a Scot, was taken prisoner.

Fastolfe went to the camp with his precious charge, and was received with great joy.

The English power had actually attained its culminating point. The Dauphin Charles, on hearing of this latest blow to his power and prestige, was considerably depressed. Affairs, indeed, looked gloomy, and he anticipated their growing worse. He felt that, if Orleans should fall, it would be his finishing stroke. Many of his nobles abandoned him, and he meditated a retreat into Provence, or Dauphiné. It was proposed to give up Orleans to the Duke of Burgundy. But the Duke of Bedford refused to agree. 'He was not the man,' he said, 'to beat the bush, that others might catch the game.' What had been won by English blood and treasure should, he contended, be handed over to English keeping. Burgundy apparently acquiesced, but it was treasured up in his mind as another grievance against his allies. The darkest hour is that preceding dawn :

> 'Things at the worst will cease, or else climb upward
> To what they were before.'

To himself unknown, Charles's calamities had reached their climax. Help came from an entirely unexpected quarter, and the wheel of Fortune took a turn.

In the village of Domremy, on the Meuse, about ten or fifteen miles south of Vaucouleurs, in Lorraine, in the year 1412 was born a girl named JEANNE D'ARC. She was the only daughter of Jacques and Isabel d'Arc, poor but honest and religious peasants, who gained a scanty living by the work of their own hands and the aid of a few cattle and sheep.

Jeanne, taking after her parents, was of a highly religious nature. She had great love for the Blessed Virgin and the saints, particularly St. Margaret and St. Catherine. She was also a dreamer of dreams and a seer of visions, in which St. Michael appeared to her and bade her go to the help of the King. There was an old prophecy, she remembered, that out of Lorraine should come a maid to deliver the fair realm of France. Could it be possible that she was the appointed one? When she was sixteen a band of Burgundians fell upon Domremy, and the whole population had to flee for very life. The family of Arc went to Neufchateau. While there the son of the innkeeper asked Jeanne to be his wife, but she declared she had a higher mission, and should never marry. Her father was very angry at this, but tried in vain to shake her resolution. On their return home a fortnight later they found the entire village a wreck. Again Jeanne's Voices spoke to her, bidding her 'go to the King and restore to him his realm.' She resolved at last to go to the Governor of Vaucouleurs and seek his assistance in her project. Sir Robert de Baudricourt laughed at her. But she persisted that she was bidden to conquer the English and carry the Dauphin to his coronation 'It is not work of my choosing,' she said, 'but my Lord wills it.'

'Who is your Lord?' asked Baudricourt.

'He is the King of Heaven,' replied the maid.

The rough captain was touched, and promised to write about her to the King, from whom a favourable reply was received. Two knights of the neighbourhood agreed to accompany and protect her, and her youngest brother, Pierre, threw in his lot with her. The people of Vaucouleurs, who had been won over to her side, provided her with a horse and a man's suit of steel armour, covered with a gray woollen jacket, her Voices having prescribed such a dress for her.

On the very day that the Battle of the Herrings was fought, Jeanne, with the three companions above named and four attendants, set out on the perilous ride to Chinon, on the river Vienne, in Touraine, twenty miles south-west of Tours. The road led through a hostile country, where they were exposed to the attacks of the English and Burgundians, and also of plunderers, who are never wanting in time of war. We have no particulars of the journey, but we do know it was fortunately accomplished, and on the eleventh day from leaving Vaucouleurs the little party arrived at Fierbois, near Chinon, 250 miles distant as the crow flies.

The two knights went to ask permission for Jeanne to wait upon the Dauphin. But Charles felt dubious, and would not agree until a commission had been appointed to report upon her. This proving favourable, a time was specified when she would be admitted to an interview.

She was ushered into a hall lighted by fifty torches, and filled with some hundreds of nobles, splendidly arrayed, among whom stood Charles in plain attire. Without a moment's hesitation she walked straight up to him, and, bending the knee, said :

'God give you good life, gentle King.'

'I am not the King,' said Charles, pointing to someone more finely dressed ; 'there he stands.'

'It is not he ; but you are King,' said Jeanne, and repeated her greeting. 'Gentle Dauphin, I am Jeanne la Pucelle ; sent by the King of Heaven to tell you that you shall be crowned in the city of Rheims.'

Charles now took her aside, and afterwards affirmed that she had told him things concerning himself with which no one else was, or could be acquainted. But he wanted something more to convince him, and therefore, as soon as the court removed to Poitiers, an assembly of theologians was convened, who pronounced the maid's mission undoubted and herself inspired. The Queen, Marie of Anjou, and her mother, Yolande of Aragon, as well as their ladies, were unanimous in speaking of her modest, pure and religious life. In preparation for her appearance in public Jeanne caused a banner to be worked with a representation of the Saviour in gold, surrounded by fleurs-de-lys. She also asked for a sword which her Voices told her was buried at the back of the altar of the church of St. Catherine at Fierbois. She described it as being engraved on each side with five of the same lilies that were on her standard. No one, not even those attached to the church, had ever heard of such a weapon, but it was found at the indicated place, and though very rusty, the flowers were plainly discernible.

At length, after two months of dreary waiting, Jeanne's opportunity came. It was determined to make another effort to send a supply of provisions to Orleans, which was suffering from famine, and Jeanne obtained permission to go with it. She joined the expedition at Blois, and virtually took the direction of it. She began by expelling all loose characters from the army, and by calling on the men to betake themselves to prayer and confession. She promised complete success to the commanders if they would only keep to the north bank, where the bulk of the English army was, and march through their midst. Dunois preferred his own judgment, and, knowing the English to be weakest on the south bank, without letting her know, marched on La Sologne. Not till she arrived within sight of Orleans was she aware how she had been deceived, and she naturally felt hurt at the distrust the commanders had shown. And she was in the right, after all, for the river was too low and the wind too high to permit heavily-laden boats to cross, and the relieving party had to retrace their steps, cross the bridge to Blois as Jeanne had first advised, and then march thirty-five miles to Orleans. [April.]

Jeanne's entry into the city at nightfall, arrayed in full armour, with her banner borne in her right hand, and mounted on a white charger, was greeted with the joyous acclamations of the whole population. Her fame had preceded her, and they looked upon her as a deliverer sent from heaven. She wrote to the Regent Bedford, and to the English commanders that she had been sent by the Most High to restore King Charles to his throne, and ordered them to evacuate all the places which they had taken. [April 29.]

The next convoy of provisions was taken through Beauce without any resistance by the besiegers. The soldiers had by that time begun to believe in the maid's mission, as several towers had been already captured. They became depressed, lost all spirit, and declared it was no use fighting against more than human power. . Things went from bad to worse.

The tower of St. Loup was successfully attacked, and 300 of the English forces were slain or taken prisoners. On the following days other forts fell in like manner. On one occasion, when the French were wavering, as if about to retreat, the maid rushed forward, unfurled her banner, and led them on to victory. At the storming of the famous bastille Les Tournelles, Jeanne was in the act of planting a ladder against the wall when she was struck by an arrow between the neck and shoulder. She fell into the ditch, but was carried away by some of her faithful followers. As soon as the arrow was extracted and the wound dressed, though weak from loss of blood, she again rushed to the front, and the soldiers were so much inspired by her bravery that in a very short time the fort was won. [May 4. May 7.]

When Gladsdale saw that the day was going against the English, he and a number of his followers retired to the base court, and thence on to the bridge and to the arch, which had been shattered. The great weight imposed upon it caused the whole structure to crash together. All who were on it were either crushed to death or drowned.

May 8. The English were dispirited. Above 6,000 men had been slain. The courage and confidence of the remainder had completely vanished. The Earl of Suffolk and his council, under these inauspicious circumstances, thought it most prudent to raise the siege. After setting fire to the forts which were left, the remains of the army marched away to Meuny-sur-Loire, and thence to Jargeau. It being Sunday, the maid forbade any pursuit, as the day ought to be spent in prayer, not fighting.

Suffolk's hopes of being able to hold his own till he could receive help from the Regent were not to be realized. The maid followed him with 6,000 men, and invested JARGEAU. The assault was successful, although Jeanne at one time received so severe a wound in the head from a stone, that she was only able to cheer on her followers with her voice, bidding them not to fear as 'the Lord was with them.' Two of the Earl of Suffolk's brothers were slain, along

June 12. with 300 men. He himself was taken prisoner. Before yielding, he enquired of a young Frenchman named Regnault if he were of gentle blood. Being answered in the affirmative, he next asked, 'Are you a knight?' The reply was, 'Not yet.' 'Then I make you one,' said Suffolk, and, having given him the accolade, he surrendered his sword. It would have been derogatory to his dignity to yield to one of lower rank.

MEUNY and BEAUGENCY soon after fell. The remains of the English army, under JOHN LORD TALBOT, with Lord Scales and Sir John Fastolfe, on their way towards Paris, were encountered at PATAY by the French, led by the Maid of Orleans—this title was now given to her—with whom were joined the Constable Richemont, La Hire,

June 18. and Xaintrailles. There was division among the English leaders. Fastolfe

'Cowardly fled, not having struck one stroke,'

and made his way to Corbeil. Talbot disdained to turn his back upon the enemy,

> 'Having full scarce six thousand in his troop,
> By three and twenty thousand of the French
> Was round encompassed and set upon :
> No leisure had he to enrank his men ;
> He wanted pikes to set before his archers ;
> Instead whereof, sharp stakes, pluck'd out of hedges,
> They pitched in the ground confusedly,
> To keep the horsemen off from breaking in.
> More than three hours the fight continued ;
> Where valiant Talbot, above human thought,
> Enacted wonders with his sword and lance.'

This is Shakspere's graphic account of the battle; but he rather underrates the odds, which are believed to have been five or six to one. Over 1,800 men were slain, and 100 were taken prisoners, including Lords Talbot, Scales and Hungerford, and Sir Thomas Rampstone.

Fastolfe, for his cowardice, had the order of the Garter taken from him. He pleaded that the men had not the power of contending against a witch, and he thought it better to save their lives. The Regent accepted his excuse, and readmitted him. A more material loss to him was the sum of over £4,000, which he had expended in the service of the State, and which was never repaid to him.

Jeanne called to the recollection of the Dauphin that it was necessary for him to proceed to his coronation. He therefore collected together 10,000 or 12,000 men at Bourges, and, accompanied by the Maid, marched with them through Gien to Auxerre. The town supplied his force with provisions, but would not open the gates and admit them until it was seen what other towns would do. Troyes, after three days of hesitation, opened its gates. Chalons voluntarily sent its keys. Rheims did the same, in opposition to the wishes of the Lords de Chastillon and Saveuses, who held the place for King Henry, and Charles made his public entry into the town.

On the following day Charles was crowned and anointed King by the Archbishop, Renaud de Chartres, as Charles VII. of France. There was neither pomp nor display of any kind. Not one of the princes of the blood royal was present; but some private individuals, dressed up in coronation robes, acted as representatives of the absent ones.

June 28.

July 16.

July 17.

Jeanne stood by his side holding her standard in her hand. Unlearned peasant girl though she was, with her well-made, graceful and slender figure, her bright eyes shining with the light of inspiration, her flowing tresses black as the raven's wing, her maiden modesty, yet martial bearing, she was the noblest figure there. When the ceremony was over she knelt at Charles's feet, saying:

'Gentle King, the will of God is done.'

She wrote on the same day to the Duke of Burgundy, calling upon him not to fight any more against France.

> 'One drop of blood, drawn from thy country's bosom,
> Should grieve thee more than streams of foreign gore;
> Return thee, therefore, with a flood of tears,
> And wash away thy country's stained spots!'

are words which Shakspere puts into her mouth in a supposed personal interview with the Duke.

As a reward for her services King Charles ordered that, for her sake, Domremy should thenceforward be exempt from taxation. She wished now to go home, but he did not want to lose her services. She had been of more use to him than all his nobles and army combined, who had no faith in themselves without her aid. A few months later Jeanne received a patent of nobility for herself and her family in the name of De Lys, with a grant of income sufficient to support their dignity.

The Duke of Bedford was dismayed but not disheartened. He recalled some of the garrisons from Normandy. He wrote home that the tide of success had been turned by a 'limb o' the fiend,' and that he required reinforcements. At the same time he recommended that young Henry should be crowned, which was accordingly done a few months later. In order to secure the waning friendship of Burgundy, he made him some concessions of territory, which had the desired effect. John Holland, Earl of Huntingdon, brought 1,000 archers to his aid. Cardinal Beaufort, who, by a lavish expenditure of money had raised an army of 5,000 men with the intention of leading them to a crusade against the Hussites in Bohemia, diverted the force to the service of his nephew the Regent. With these additions Bedford thought it well to make an advance. Before doing so he wrote a

Aug. letter, in not very courteous terms, to King Charles, offering to meet him and treat as to a peace, or, if that were found impossible, then to continue the war. No reply was given.

After his coronation Charles went to Soissons, Château Thierry, and many other towns, which all opened their gates to him. Crespy received him as King, and thence he marched to Senlis. There the two armies came in sight of each other. There was a slight skirmish in which some 300 men were slain, but no general engagement ensued, and after two days all departed.

Monstrelet relates that about this time Château Gaillard was taken by the Sire de Barbasan, who had been captured by Henry V. at Melun, as you may remember. The place was, however, afterwards retaken by the English.

Sept. King Charles had often wished to try and regain Paris, but had been dissuaded. He now determined to make the attempt. He marched to St. Denis, where he was well received and where he remained. The army went thence to Montmartre. In the first attack made on the city the maid was wounded and left lying helpless and in great pain for nearly a whole day, until one of the leaders came with a party to her relief. The assault failed, and was abandoned by order of the King, in opposition to the advice of Jeanne and some of the best captains. She thought that her commission was ended, and she hung up the armour she had been wearing as an offering to the Blessed Virgin, in the abbey church of St. Denis.

Charles dismissed his army and retired to Bourges. There, in listless and indolent enjoyment, he passed the time, while the English were gradually retaking many of his towns.

1430. Jeanne felt the state of inactivity irksome. Though she had
May. presentiments of evil happening to herself, she set out, accompanied by her brother, her knights, and a small force, on her way to Compiègne. At Lagny-sur-Marne, not far from Paris, they were attacked by 300 Burgundians under Franquet of Arras, a valiant freebooter, whom they defeated, and the leader, being taken prisoner, was instantly beheaded.

Compiègne was being besieged by the allied English and Burgundian

armies under the command of Duke Philip. Jeanne threw herself
and her little company into the town. A sortie was made by the May 23.
French on Ascension Day as far as Marigni, but they had to retreat.
Jeanne took the post of honour, the charge of the rear. On their
return to the town it was found shut against them. Orders had been
given by someone—perhaps the governor, Guillaume de Flavy, who
had been dissatisfied at seeing a woman come to share his office—to
close the gate and raise the drawbridge. The enemy was upon them.
The Maid was dragged from her horse by an archer, carried back to
Marigni, and handed over to the Bastard of Vendome. He sold
her to Sir John of Luxemburg. a nephew of the Duke of Burgundy,
who took her first to his castle of Beaulieu, and afterwards to Beau-
revoir, near Cambray. There she remained some months, but was
finally sold to the Regent Bedford. and removed to Rouen. There Nov.
she was imprisoned in one of the towers of the castle, which one
appears to be uncertain ; some say the Bigot Tower, but the whole
castle has been long since destroyed.

'The Earl of Warwick, Richard de Beauchamp, had the chief
command of the castle. He seems to have lost all his ordinary
nature in dealing with her. He caused her to be chained by the feet
to a log of wood by day, and to her bed at night, and three guards
always watched her.' 'The Duchess of Bedford sent ladies to visit
her, and tried to enforce respect for her. She also sent her a petti-
coat to put over her man's dress, but to this Jeanne objected.'*

The Bishop of Beauvais, Pierre Cauchon, a man devoted to the
English cause, who had fled from the seat of his bishopric for fear of the
Maid, now claimed the right of trying her as a sorceress and impostor.

There was not one voice raised on her behalf. Charles, the indolent and pleasure-loving King, whose kingdom she had regained,
and on whose head she had put the crown, not only did not offer to
ransom her, but concerned himself no more about her. showed not
the slightest interest in her doings, did not even so much as mention
her, but abandoned her to her fate.

The commanders in the army, being jealous of her actions and her
fame, were probably glad to be rid of her. But from the common
soldiers, whom she had always befriended, and the ordinary people,
from whose ranks she had sprung, and whom she so entirely
loved, better things might have been expected. But discipline must
be maintained in the army. The people might fear to be implicated
with her, and therefore, perhaps, we do not hear of any protest or
petition in her favour.

At length the mockery of a trial commenced, before a man who 1431.
was at one and the same time accuser and judge. True, he had Feb.
others sitting with him equally credulous with himself. These
learned men for sixteen days badgered and baited a plain country
girl, who had nothing but her simple, pure, brave, ardent character

* Miss Yonge's 'Cameos,' II., 381.

to support her—there were no witnesses, and she had no counsel; it is not therefore to be wondered at that she was found guilty of heresy and schism, and condemned to the stake. The University of Paris confirmed the sentence.

May 24. When brought on to the scaffold, near the Church of St. Ouen, and in sight of the pile where she was to be sacrificed, the Bishop of Beauvais read the sentence of condemnation. Jeanne's spirit failed her, and in terror she cried, 'I submit.' She was made to sign an act of renunciation to any claim of Divine mission, and then to promise not any more to wear man's attire. Then her sentence was commuted to perpetual imprisonment on bread and water. Life is dear to most people, but mere existence on such terms is surely harder to bear than sharp but sure death, even if by fire. 'The tender mercies of the wicked are cruel.'

Jeanne was taken back to her prison and clothed in her old peasant costume. Her spirits soon revived. She had said on her trial that by torture they might force her to incriminate herself, but that truth and fact would ever remain. It is very possible that torture was actually employed to bring about her recantation. Her male attire was one day purposely left in her prison by order of some one in authority. The sight of it was more than she could withstand. She put it on. Again she had faith in her Voices, and her old enthusiasm returned to her. This act was reported to her judges, and the Bishop of Beauvais gladly declared that, as a relapsed heretic, she must die by fire.

May 30. In the old market-place of Rouen a scaffold was erected whereon sat the Bishop of Beauvais, and, sad to say, the Cardinal Bishop of Winchester, with many others, to witness the end of the 'English scourge.' It has, however, been said that the Cardinal left before the actual execution.

Jeanne was brought in, wearing on her head a cap on which were the words, '*Hérétique, Relapse, Apostate, Idolâtre.*' She was then dragged to the pile of wood already there, and the fire was kindled. Some kind onlooker, at her request, furnished her with a simple cross, made from two pieces of wood. Two monks stood as near to her as they could, holding up a large crucifix. She repeatedly declared her innocence, pronounced her Voices real, and with the holy name of 'Jesus' on her lips, resigned her spirit to God who gave it.

Thus died a girl of simple and sincere faith, a victim to cruelty and superstition. Cardinal Beaufort, to his shame be it said, ordered her ashes to be thrown into the Seine.

Twenty-five years later (July 7, 1456), under Pope Calixtus III., this judgment was reversed. Four hundred and twenty-five years after that Jeanne was declared a saint.

Streets and squares have been named after her, statues and monuments have been erected to her memory. But nothing can cancel the irrevocable past; nothing that has been or can be done can wipe off the shame and disgrace which, as long as time shall last, must ever attach to those in any way connected with this direful tragedy. The Burgundians, who sold her; the French, who betrayed and deserted her; the English, under whose orders she was condemned and executed—all were guilty, and all must share the opprobrium.

In the Place du Martroi, Orleans, about forty years ago, a bronze statue, thirty feet high, was erected, when an older statue was removed to the south bank of the river, and a few yards from this a cross marks the site of the Fort des Tournelles, captured by Jeanne, as already related.

In the Place de la Pucelle, Rouen, on the spot where she was burnt, a fountain was raised to her memory, but it was destroyed during the Revolution, and a statue now stands in its place.

Pierre Cauchon, the infamous judge, as an act of atonement for having pronounced an unjust sentence, erected the Lady Chapel in the Church of St. Pierre at Lisieux.*

SKETCH XVI.

THE BROKEN ALLIANCE.

WHEN HENRY BEAUFORT returned to England with his new rank of CARDINAL, towards the close of 1428, or the beginning of 1429, he was met by the Lord Mayor and a large number of the inhabitants of London, who conducted him in triumph to his palace in Southwark.

In council, however, an attempt was made by Gloucester to deprive him of his bishopric, and force him to refund the revenues which he had received, urging as a reason that a cardinal was a servant of the Church, a vassal of the Pope. But his enemies failed in their purpose, except so far that the Cardinal had to promise to abstain from attending the Chapter of the Garter until the King should be of age.

Later on, his transfer of men from the service of the Pope to that of the country, though it offended His Holiness, gave great satisfaction at home. His loyalty was commended, his popularity re-

---

* In the 'Book of Days,' edited by Robert Chambers, there is a strange story told, under the date May 30, that Jeanne la Pucelle was not burned in 1431, but was liberated from prison after the Duke of Bedford's death, another criminal having been substituted for her at the execution. The account states that Jeanne married a certain Chevalier Robert d'Amboise at Mentz, in 1436, when her brothers Jean and Pierre De Lys, who had been invited by the authorities for the purpose, at once recognised her, and the happy pair received numerous presents from the inhabitants of the city. Three years later, in 1439, they visited Orleans, where great rejoicings were held in her honour, and the council of the city made her a gift of 210 livres for the services she had rendered during the siege. It reads like a romance, but the author asserts that there is documentary evidence in support of all the statements.

established. He was requested to resume his seat at the Council, only to absent himself when affairs in connection with the court of Rome came under discussion. The Commons were loud in their praises of his services.

1429. Nov. 6. The young King was crowned at Westminster as HENRY VI., on St. Leonard's Day, Sunday, November 6. John Holland, Earl of Huntingdon, bore the sceptre; and Humphrey Stafford, Earl of Stafford, the sword of State. John Mowbray, Duke of Norfolk, acted in his hereditary office of Earl Marshal; and Richard Neville, Earl of Salisbury, was Constable of England for the occasion.

Henry was then not quite eight years old, but appeared grave for his years. He was meek and gentle, and with a look of care about him not fitted for one so young. It seemed, even then, that not his father's strength of will, but his unfortunate grandfather's weakness had descended to him. Alice Boteler, his governess, had but just given up charge of him. His tutor, and great-uncle, Thomas Beaufort, Duke of Exeter, having died December 30, 1427, Richard Beauchamp, Earl of Warwick, had been appointed to succeed him. It is possible that his treatment was a little too rough and rude for the boy's timid nature, as we read of the Council being entreated to soften his severity.

Hardyng writes :

> 'Therle Richard, in mykell worthyhead,
> Enfourmed hym, but of his symple head
> He could litle within his brest conceyve,
> The good from eivill he could uneth* perceyve.'

'Alice was allowed to slap the child; and Warwick was allowed to flog him. Nurse and governor both exercised their powers on the deserted boy.'†

Truly he was a deserted boy. His mother had left him. After the Parliament when Queen KATHERINE sat on the throne with the King on her knee, she suddenly disappeared from all State functions and all records. She had formed other ties. It is hoped, rather than known, that she married OWEN TUDOR, her 'clerk of the wardrobe,' at one time 'squire of the body' to her late husband, King Henry V., under whom he had fought at Azincour.

Burke in his 'Royal Families' shows Owen to be descended from Rhodri Maur, King of All Wales, 843-847.

Of this union there sprang three boys and one girl. The eldest son, EDMUND of Hadham, was, many years later, created Earl of RICHMOND, and Premier Earl of England by his half-brother King Henry. By his marriage with Lady MARGARET BEAUFORT he became the father of the first of our Tudor Kings. JASPER of Hatfield, the second son, was at the same time created Earl of PEMBROKE. OWEN, the third son, became a MONK. Margaret, the only daughter, died young.

After the coronation it was decreed, much to the vexation of

---

* Not easily.   † Hepworth Dixon's 'Royal Windsor,' vol. ii., p. 308.

Duke Humphrey, that the King, having taken upon himself the protection of the country, the title of Protector and Defender of the realm had ceased, but that the Dukes of Bedford and Gloucester would henceforward be principal counsellors. It was some compensation to Gloucester's ruffled feelings that, when the King went over to France, he was appointed Guardian and Lieutenant of England. 1430.

The Duke of Bedford had wished Henry to be crowned in France as soon as that ceremony had been performed in England, but want of means prevented it. At length the time had arrived. Accompanied by Cardinal Beaufort, John Stafford, Bishop of Bath and Wells, the Earl of Warwick, and other nobles, with a guard of archers, the King sailed from Dover and soon arrived at Calais, where a stay of a month was made. The party afterwards proceeded to Rouen, just about the very time that the heroic Maid was taken prisoner. It is satisfactory to learn that before the tragedy was consummated, the Regent and his Duchess removed with the little King to Pontoise, having been at Rouen about a year. April 23. 1431. April.

Rheims was the usual place of coronation of the Kings of France, but there appeared little probability of being able to get there with safety. Ultimately it was decided that the coronation should take place in Paris.

About the end of November the King set out for St. Denis, having with him, in addition to those already named as forming his escort from England, RICHARD, DUKE OF YORK; John FitzAlan, Earl of Arundel; the Earls of Stafford and Huntingdon; Richard Neville, Earl of Salisbury; the Earl of Suffolk, recently ransomed; many great lords of France, including three or four bishops, with 3,000 archers to act as guard, so that, on the whole, the cortège was a brilliant one. Nov.

On the way they were met at various intervals by the provost of Paris and a numerous attendance of burghers; the commandant of the watch, the provost of merchants and officers of the Court; the President and all the lords of Parliament, followed by all the public functionaries; the whole of them being in flowing robes of state, silk and satin forming the material, and the colours principally crimson or scarlet, which must have had a dazzling effect. Monstrelet adds ' with regard to the common people, they were numberless.'

The entertainments prepared in Paris were varied. Mysteries were represented. Doves and other small birds were let loose to fly about the boy King; and flowers were plentifully thrown over him and his lords. Pageants with living figures, both religious and secular, were exhibited. Fountains were running with hippocras, of which all were free to partake. Among the living pictures was a stag-hunt. An artificial forest had been erected, but the stag, dogs, and huntsmen were real. After a long chase the poor animal took refuge near the feet of the King's horse, and Henry saved its life. It is the only instance in which any personal action of his is mentioned.

No other sign did he give of pleasure or satisfaction, but went through everything as if it were a task.

One of the last representations was of Henry sitting with two crowns on his head, while the Duke of Burgundy and the Count de Nevers, standing at his right hand, presented him with the shield of France, and the Duke of Bedford, with the Earls of Warwick and Salisbury, at his left hand, presented him with the shield of England. The Duke of Burgundy would not have been well pleased had he known this, as, although Hardyng says he was present at the coronation, he was then meditating, if he had not even actually agreed upon, a truce with King Charles.

When the procession passed the Hôtel de St. Pol, that disgrace of womanhood, Queen ISABEAU, from a window of her residence, kissed her hand to her little grandson. Therefore Henry, after he had dined at the Regent's Hôtel des Tournelles, went to pay her a visit of ceremony, being the first and last occasion on which they ever met.

As she will not appear again, it may be added that this unfaithful wife, unnatural mother and treacherous Queen died September 30, 1435, deserted by all, and was buried without any show in the church of St. Denis.

The day following his public entry into Paris, the King and his court went to the Château de Vincennes, where they remained until December 15, when they returned to the Louvre.

Dec. 17. The CORONATION took place in the Church of Nôtre Dame at Paris, when Cardinal Beaufort officiated, and also chanted Mass, much to the disgust of the Bishop of Paris. Altogether the ceremony did not give satisfaction to the French who were present, as the English 'Use,' which was different from their own, was followed in every detail.

> 'Henry the Sixth, in infant bands, crown'd king
> Of France and England,'

was the only one of all our kings to be so crowned, although the title was borne by all succeeding monarchs until the reign of George III., who adopted the title 'King of Great Britain.'

Dec. 18. A grand dinner at the palace followed, when more pageants were introduced. On the following day a tournament was held, at which the Earl of Arundel and the Bastard of St. Pol gained the prizes, amidst the applause of the ladies.

Notwithstanding all their public demonstrations of joy, the general public of Paris would appear to have been ill at ease. A week later Dec. 25. the King was taken back to Rouen, where he remained a few weeks, 1432. and then returned, viâ Calais, to England. He was welcomed with Feb. 9. every demonstration of joy by the people, who seemed as if they could not sufficiently express their pride and exultation at seeing the first King of England who had been also crowned King of France.

Feb. 3. During his stay in Rouen, the city ran a great risk of being captured by the French. Some of the inhabitants had become disaffected, and tampered with the garrison of the castle to admit a man named Richarville, with 150 men, who had been detached for that purpose from a larger force led by the Marshal de Boussac. 1432. The Earl of Arundel, the captain of the castle, had not sufficient followers to withstand them, and had to retreat into the town, but not before a considerable number of the enemy had been slain. Having gathered his forces together, he surrounded the castle. The French shut themselves up in the great tower, which they resolved to hold to the last extremity, but their friends not coming to their relief as they expected, they were in a few days compelled to submit, and many of them were beheaded.

On the return of King Henry to his dominions, the authority of Feb. 9. the Duke of Gloucester as Guardian and Lieutenant naturally ceased. He had maintained tranquillity in the country, but he had not been willing to work for nothing. His insatiable craving for money would not admit of that, poor though he knew the treasury to be. He was utterly selfish. He obtained at different times from the Council 1,000 marks for doing his duty, and afterwards a yearly salary of 6,000 marks, subsequently reduced to 4,000. His machinations against his uncle Beaufort were continued, and he tried all he knew to oust him from his see.

After the coronation at Paris, the Cardinal obtained permission to pay a visit to Rome, and he did not return to England until three months after the King. On landing at Dover all his plate and jewels May. were seized, by order of the Duke of Gloucester. Restoration of the property was ordered in Parliament, but the Cardinal had to forego some claim he had on the Government. He at the same time made another loan of £6,000 to the King. Some writers estimate that during his life he thus advanced as much as half a million of money. He had still another victory over his opponent. In his place in Parliament he said that, having heard he was to be accused of treason, he had come home to meet the charge. Gloucester and his party, after consultation, answered that no one appeared to make the charge, and the King held him to be a true and faithful servant. He succeeded this year in obtaining a bill of indemnity relieving him from the penalties of a præmunire for accepting the red hat without securing royal permission. Archbishop Chicheley had protested, not against the dignity of Cardinal being conferred upon the Bishop, but against his assumption of the powers of a *legate à latere;* and when he was satisfied that Beaufort had no intention of interfering with his functions as primate he did not prolong the controversy.*

Gloucester never, as long as he lived, ceased his efforts to injure his rival. But he was a man of violent and headstrong temper, which he indulged, regardless of its effect upon the affairs of the kingdom, Beaufort, with his wisdom and his calmness, gained a manifest advantage over him, yet for some reason, perhaps his being a churchman, he failed in gaining the confidence of the mass of the people as the Duke had done.

* Dr. Hook's 'Archbishops of Canterbury,' vol. v., p. 105.

A year or two before this, the Duke of Gloucester, in opposition to the house of Beaufort, introduced RICHARD, DUKE OF YORK, and placed him in the royal house at Windsor as a companion to the King, and we have seen that he went with him to France. He is an important character in history. Gloucester evidently considered him as, after himself, undoubtedly the nearest heir to the throne, while the Cardinal was in favour of his own nephew.

Richard was the grandson of EDMUND OF LANGLEY, Duke of York, through his second son, Richard of Coningsburgh, who was executed in 1415 for treason against his King and benefactor. by whom, only a year before, he had been created Earl of Cambridge. That Richard of Coningsburgh had fallen in love, during the reign of Henry IV., with Lady ANNE MORTIMER, the sister of Edmund, fifth Earl of March, the 'legal heir' to the throne. Richard, like his brother Edward, was a cunning and a tricky man. He knew that the Earl of March, for dynastic reasons, had been prevented from marrying. He must have known that, for similar reasons, all the King's counsellors and all prudent men of the time would be opposed to his own marriage. It has been conjectured that Henry of Monmouth, disregarding all chances of danger, favoured the union, and thus

'Wrought for his house an irredeemable woe,'

as their son was born in 1412.

Richard, the son of this traitor Earl, succeeded his uncle Edward, who fell childless at Azincour, in the dukedom of York, and on January 19, 1425, to the earldom of March and Ulster, *jure matris*, on the death of his uncle Edmund Mortimer, who had become very lame, and had long been confined to the house. At the time of which we are now treating, Richard was nineteen years of age, nine years older than his father's cousin's grandson, his fourth-cousin, Henry VI., and represented two branches of the line of King Edward III., Clarence and York. Of his childhood nothing is known. He must, at a very early age, have been deprived of a mother's care. She may, possibly, have died in giving him birth. His father had certainly taken a second wife before entering on his conspiracy. It appears that Richard was made a ward of the Earl of Westmorland. and thus came to marry CECILY NEVILLE, 'Proud Cis of Raby,' the youngest of the Earl's twenty-three children. He was a young man of medium height, of slight build, with the usual good looks of his race, but with dark hair and eyes. He had a frank and open countenance, was gracious in behaviour, mild in disposition, prudent in conduct; but he was liable to be led by wills stronger than his own. Thus we shall find that his father's unquiet and daring spirit, which had descended to him, but had for a time lain dormant, and the unruly blood of some of his Mortimer ancestors ere long manifested themselves.

Affairs in France were not going well for the English. The Regent was not supported as he ought to have been, but was left to sustain his nephew's cause by the influence of his own name. In consequence of the treachery of the inhabitants, the city of Chartres was won by the French under the Bastard of Orleans and the Sire de Gaucourt. April 20.

The Earl of Arundel captured several castles held by the French on the borders of the Isle de France, and then marched to the siege of Lagny-sur-Marne, whence bands of plunderers often made inroads on the city of Paris. He succeeded in destroying some of the bulwarks, but could not gain the town. The Duke of Bedford went with additional forces to his assistance. The garrison was on the point of capitulating when the French, under the Marshal de Boussac and Dunois, arrived with additional forces. After several gallant deeds had been done, and many persons killed and wounded on both sides, the siege of four months was raised. and on St. Laurence's Day the English marched away. The Duke of Bedford tried afterwards, but in vain, to bring his opponents to a regular engagement. Aug. 10.

A much severer blow fell on the Duke personally, three months later. His Duchess, Anne of Burgundy, had long been suffering under some disease which baffled the skill of several physicians, and she succumbed to an epidemic which visited Paris at the close of this year. She had been of great service to her husband in keeping her brother Philip staunch to his engagements. She was laid to rest in the chapel of the Célestines, where Louis, Duke of Orleans, had been interred. 1432. Nov. 14.

The Duke and all his party were very much afflicted at this death, says Monstrelet. It may have been so. But in less than six months he married again. His choice this time fell on a girl of seventeen, handsome, well made and lively, but not a fit mate for staid John of Bedford, a man twenty-seven years her senior. She was JAQUETTA OF LUXEMBURG, eldest daughter of Pierre, Count de St. Pol, and niece of Louis, Bishop of Therouenne, principal minister and adviser of the Duke, who had indeed recommended the match. 1433. April.

'Hasty marriage seldom proveth well.'

The death of his sister had considerably weakened the attachment of Philip of Burgundy to the English cause, but this hurried union with a vassal of his own showed, as he thought, such scant respect for that sister's memory that the tie was soon broken.

Cardinal Beaufort, knowing well how disastrous to the interests of his country would be the estrangement of Burgundy, laboured hard to bring about a meeting between the two Dukes. He first tried his nephew, John of Bedford, who was indignant because Philip of Burgundy had expressed his surprise at not having been consulted on the matter of a marriage with a member of a house connected with that of Burgundy. Eventually the Cardinal succeeded in persuading both Dukes to promise to meet at St. Omer, at that time part of Flanders. Both arrived accordingly. But they stood on their dignity: neither of them would make the first advance. Bedford thought that, as a son of Henry IV., a brother of the late and uncle of the present King of England, he had done sufficient in coming into the Duke's territories, and that Philip should now visit him. Burgundy held that his rank as a sovereign prince, with, perhaps, more power, certainly more wealth, than the King of either England or France, entitled him to expect the Regent to call upon him. Despite the intervention of the Cardinal, and that of various lords, nothing could move either of them, and they actually left St. Omer without meeting, and more discontented with each other than before.

The failure of these negotiations does not appear to have affected the relations between the Duke of Burgundy and the Cardinal. The Duke for his third wife had married ISABEL, the only daughter of IOÃO I., King of Portugal, and PHILIPPA OF LANCASTER, sister of King Henry IV., and also of the Cardinal. When their first son was born, therefore, Henry Beaufort stood as godfather to the boy, along with the Counts de St. Pol and Ligny. The child was christened by the unusual name of Josse (or Jodocus), but died young.

April 14.

At this time the Duke of Gloucester was in power in England, therefore the war must be carried on. The Duke of Bedford was inclining more to his late brother's idea of being satisfied with Normandy as an absolute possession. The nation was almost ruined, and supplies were grudgingly granted. Yet Gloucester's rapacity for wealth even now prompted him to add to his means by grants from the Crown. Cardinal Beaufort, on the other hand, though in favour of peace, made loans to the Government, and conducted negotiations with foreign powers; his popularity in consequence began to increase.

To particularize the various military movements of the next two years would be both tedious and uninteresting. The town of St. Valery was twice taken by the French and as often regained. In like manner Crespy was once won, and lost to John, Lord Talbot, who now returned to France and took also Creil and Avalon. On the other hand, Hamme was gained by the French.

1435.

The small town of Rue, near the mouth of the Somme, had also been taken by the French. The Regent therefore instructed the Earl of Arundel, who was stationed at Mantes, to march with 800 men through Gournay, Neufchatel, and Abbeville, to besiege the place. On the way he heard that the French were restoring the castle at Gerberoy, which is situated between Gournay and Beauvais, and at the instance of the inhabitants of these two towns he resolved, in disobedience to orders, to attack it. At midnight the force started, and at eight o'clock next morning the van came in sight of Gerberoy. The men were posted in a field surrounded by hedges, and a hundred were detailed to go towards the castle and give notice of any movements there. The main body of the English was still some distance in the rear, with a long train of wagons.

The French leaders, Poton de Xaintrailles, La Hire, and Sir Regnault de Fontaines, decided not to shut up themselves and their followers in the castle, but at once to make the attack. The leaders, with sixty men, were on horseback, the rest, between 2,000 and 3.000, on foot, were ordered only to appear by degrees. They fell upon the van of the English, who were taken by surprise, and defeated them. The French horsemen then galloped against the main body of the English, and so threw it into confusion that many were slain or made prisoners.

With the remnant of his men the Earl posted himself in a corner of the field, a hedge to the rear and the usual pointed stakes in front. The French, being unable to break through this position, brought a culverin out of the castle to bear upon it. At the second shot the Earl had his leg shattered just above the ankle, and fell to the ground.

La Hire with his cavalry and other forces, returning from pursuit of the runaways, now charged the faithful few remaining, and soon gained the victory. The French only lost twenty men. The losses of the English were 200 slain and 100 taken prisoners, among the latter being John FitzAlan, Earl of Arundel, Sir Richard Wydeville, and Sir Ralph Standish.

The Earl was carried to Beauvais, where, happily for him, he died, June 12. at the early age of twenty-seven, and was buried in the church of the Cordelier Friars. Authorities differ as to the final resting-place of the body. One account says that the Earl had previously selected his own place of interment, and a cenotaph of beautiful design in the chapel at Arundel still marks the spot. But, owing to the neglect of his wishes by his executor, the soldier was not permitted to find rest in the sepulchre of his fathers.* Another writer says the body was brought home by an Englishman named Elton, who kept it for twenty years, until the family reimbursed him 1,400 marks for the expenses which he had incurred. Then the body was interred with all ceremony in the family chapel.†

The year previous to his death he had been created Duke of Touraine. His son Humphrey succeeded to the earldom, but not the dukedom. He, however, died an infant three years later, and was succeeded by his uncle, William FitzAlan, as eleventh Earl of Arundel.

Under the sanction of the Pope, Eugenius IV., the Council of Basel recommended a conference of the principal powers of Europe to endeavour after a pacification between the contending nations.

The Congress was fixed to take place at Arras, and is noteworthy as the first meeting ever held for such a purpose.

The first to arrive were the Cardinal of Santa Croce and the July. Cardinal of Cyprus, as representatives respectively of the Pontiff and the Council of Basel, who, with a numerous following, were handsomely received by the Bishop of Arras, the clergy, and the inhabitants generally.

* Beattie's 'Castles and Abbeys,' quoted from Mr. Tierney.
† Finlason's 'Hereditary Dignities,' as quoted in Timbs's 'Abbeys and Castles.'

The English ambassadors came next, with John Kemp, Archbishop of York, at their head. He was accompanied by the Bishop of St. David's, the Earl of Suffolk, Sir John Ratcliff, Lord Privy Seal, Lord Hungerford, and two hundred knights. They were welcomed by the Burgundians with great cordiality.

July 28. When Duke Philip arrived the whole English Embassy went a league beyond the walls to meet him. He was preceded by the archers of his bodyguard, all in rich uniform, and the people sang carols as he passed along.

July 31. On the Sunday came the French legation of twenty-nine noblemen and four or five hundred horsemen, at their head being Charles, Duke of Bourbon, and the Count de Richemont. The Duke of Bourbon only came to the title in the previous year, on the death of his father, John, who had been taken prisoner at Azincour, and had remained in England ever since. Charles was married to Agnes, the youngest sister of the Duke of Burgundy, who sent the Count d'Estampes with knights and squires as far as St. Quentin to meet them, and conduct them to Arras. When they arrived Philip went some quarter of a league out of the town to join them, and embraced his two brothers-in-law with great affection. Their entrance into the town resembled a triumphal procession, and the evident concord existing between the ally of England and the representatives of 'our adversary of France' augured ill for the English cause.

Aug. 3. The next to appear was Isabel, Duchess of Burgundy, with a numerous attendance of ladies, all in gala array. She was met by the English and French ambassadors, and loyally escorted to the hôtel of her husband, who afterwards gave a grand entertainment, at which, from all accounts, it would appear that the English were not present. Ambassadors and envoys came from all the powers of Europe; from the city of Paris, and all the towns under the sway of Duke Philip. Archbishops, bishops, and abbots arrived from all quarters; feastings and tournaments followed one another in bewildering succession.

Aug. 15. On Monday, the festival of the Assumption, Duke Philip and all the French lords, with their attendant knights, went to hear Mass, and afterwards to a sumptuous banquet given by the Duke at his hotel. But again there were no English there, and their suspicions of some secret understanding to their disadvantage became stronger.

Aug. 19. At length the Cardinal Bishop of Winchester arrived, attended by John Holland, Earl of Huntingdon, and 300 horsemen. The Duke of Burgundy, with the greater part of his nobles, went out to meet him, and they mutually paid each other the greatest respect.

The place of meeting for the Congress was fixed at the Abbey of St. Vaast. The Cardinal of Santa Croce opened the proceedings in a long harangue; but it was evident from the first that no result satisfactory to the English would be attained. They offered to Charles all that the French at that time possessed, but claimed that Henry was King of France. The Archbishop of York made a proposal in the name of the Regent, who was then lying sick unto death, for a truce of twenty years, to be ratified by a marriage between a daughter of King Charles and Henry, King of England, who was to retain Normandy. The French offered Guienne, Gascony, and that portion of Normandy then in the hands of the English, to be held as fiefs from Charles, King of France. The Cardinals of Santa Croce and Cyprus and Duke Philip's ministers had been won to their side by the French. As a natural consequence, the English terms were considered quite inadmissible.

Cardinal Beaufort and the whole English Embassy left Arras, Sept. 6. much incensed at the perfidy of the Duke of Burgundy, and returned by way of Calais to England.

When the news of this failure reached the DUKE OF BEDFORD at Rouen 'his high heart broke.' He had struggled bravely on, often under most disheartening and disadvantageous surroundings, to maintain his brother's conquests, his nephew's rights, but now he was worn out.

'A braver soldier never couched lance,
A gentler heart did never sway in court.'

He died when only a few months over forty-six years of age, and was Sept. 14. buried with all possible solemnity in the cathedral church of Nôtre Dame, on the north side of the high altar, under a sumptuous and costly monument of black marble, which was destroyed at the Revolution. A tablet in the pavement now marks the spot.

Some years later it was proposed to Louis XI. to remove his remains to a less honourable position. The King angrily replied: 'I will not war with the remains of a prince who was once a match for your fathers and mine, and who, were he now alive, would make the boldest of us tremble. Let his bones rest in peace, and may God have mercy on his soul!'

In order to give popularity to English rule, the Duke, in January 1431, founded the University of Caen, for the study of canon and civil law, to which, a few years later, King Henry added faculties for arts and medicine, and Pope Eugenius gave his sanction to it in 1439. It grew and flourished until the Revolution, when its name was changed to an academy.

One week later a treaty of peace was signed between Charles, King Sept. 21. of France, and Philip, Duke of Burgundy.

The great wonder is that a prince of the blood-royal of France should for so many years have aided the rule of strangers in opposition to his own kith and kin. For fifteen years he had had full revenge for the murder of his father.

King Charles deplored the accident. He averred that it took place without his approval, and when he was too young to prevent it. He engaged to found a chapel in the church at Montereau, where Duke John's body had been buried; also a church and convent for Carthusians in the same town, where Mass should be daily sung for the repose of the soul of the deceased, and to erect a cross on the bridge. As compensation for jewels and other articles, the property of the late Duke, which had been stolen, he promised to pay the sum of 50,000 golden crowns, in two instalments. Finally, he added to Philip's already immense possessions counties, towns, and castles—Artois, Auxerre, Bar-sur-Seine, Peronne, and many others, and absolved him from the duty of doing homage or service for the lands he then held in France.

Before the sacrament on the altar, Philip swore on the cross never more to call to remembrance the death of his late father.

The Duke of Bourbon and the Constable of France then fell on their knees, and, touching the cross, begged pardon in the King's name for the said death.

Duke Philip having granted it, the Cardinals of Santa Croce and Cyprus absolved him and many other lords from any oaths they might have taken to the English. Among these was the Lord de Launoy. When it came to his turn, he said : 'Five times during this war have I taken oaths for the preservation of the peace, not one of which has been observed. But now I promise, before God, that this shall be kept by me, and, whatever others may do, I will not infringe it.'

SKETCH XVII.

PEACE OR WAR?

OWING to dissensions in the Council at home, the war in France was not supported with energy.

Disaster on disaster, rout on rout, followed each other in quick succession. Harfleur, the first conquest of Henry V., surrendered to the French, and Normandy generally was being reconquered by them. Pontoise was taken by the Lord de l'Isle Adam,

1436. who had gone over soon after the Duke of Burgundy, and Paris
April. quickly followed.

Then RICHARD, DUKE OF YORK, with 8,000 men, was sent out as Lieutenant and Governor-General of France and Normandy. He had some successes, but had not much opportunity of showing either statesmanship or military capacity, as he was recalled in little more than a year (July 16, 1437), and his offices filled by Richard Beauchamp, Earl of Warwick.

June. The Duke of Burgundy, with a large army, undertook the siege of Calais. But, owing to a mutiny among his Flemings, he had to
July 31. march back again, after destroying large stores of provisions and war materials, which they had brought with them.

The Duke of Gloucester, who had persuaded his nephew to create him Earl of Flanders, sent a herald to inform Duke Philip that he was coming to seek him, either at Calais or in his own territories.

When he arrived, with 10,000 men, of course there was no enemy to be seen. He marched into Flanders, where the people usually retreated before him, so that he had few skirmishes, if any. But he burnt towns and villages, and made great waste generally wherever he went. Numbers of cattle were driven away by his army of freebooters, which they could not keep, owing to want of water, and were glad enough to exchange for bread, of which they had scarcely any. It was an inglorious expedition, in which the poor, inoffensive people of Flanders and Artois, and perhaps the Church, were the most considerable sufferers.

'When Henry was on his throne, presiding in Parliament,' writes Miss Strickland, in her 'Life of Katherine of Valois,' 'news was brought to him of his mother's death.' She had long been ailing, and 'Henry never forgave his uncle Gloucester the harsh usage she had experienced.' Only two days before he had sent her, in token of affection, a tablet of gold, on which was a crucifix studded with pearls and sapphires. He may have heard that she was ill, but this sudden announcement must have been a great grief to him. 1437. Jan. 3.

KATHERINE died in the Abbey of Bermondsey, and her two eldest boys were placed under the care of Katherine de la Pole, Abbess of Barking. She was buried, with the usual funeral show and pomp, in the Chapel of Our Lady in Westminster Abbey. But, as her life had been a chequered one, so in like manner even her remains were, for many years, not destined to rest in peace. When her grandson, Henry VII., built his chapel, the glory of the Abbey, the remains were removed, in a wooden chest, and placed near the tomb of Henry V., in the Chapel of St. Edward. At the same time, the tomb erected to her memory by her son Henry VI. is supposed to have been purposely destroyed, because it bore a Latin epitaph representing her as *widow* of Henry V.

It was probably in St. Edward's Chapel that Samuel Pepys saw the body, on February 23, 1669. He writes, in his Diary, on that day, 'being Shrove Tuesday, we did see, by particular favour, the body of Queen Katherine of Valois; and I had the upper part of her body in my hands, and I did kiss her mouth, reflecting that I did kiss a queene. I did see that the body was buried in a leaden coffin, which was laid in a wooden coffin.'

It was not until 1776, when George III. was King, that the body was finally deposited under the tomb of Sir George Villiers, in the centre of the Chapel of St. Nicholas, so that nearly three centuries and a half had elapsed from the time of the first burial.

A few weeks later a dreadful tragedy occurred in Scotland, when KING JAMES I., in whose fortunes Queen Katherine had once taken the liveliest interest, was foully murdered in the Dominican Monastery at Perth. Feb. 20, 21.

'Murther most foul, as in the best it is;
But this most foul, strange, and unnatural.'

All the perpetrators and abettors were connections of the King. The prime mover and chief of the assassins was Sir Robert Graham.

The first ostensible cause of complaint was that King James had deprived Malise Graham, his own second cousin, of the earldom of Strathern, conferring the life-rent thereof upon the Earl of Athole, and creating a new earldom of Menteith in favour of Malise, a youth at that time in England.

Sir Robert Graham, the uncle of Malise, a man of fierce and vindictive character, had been included in the proceedings against Murdac, Duke of Albany, in the first year of the King's reign, and had then made a vow to have his revenge. This new act of what he called tyranny roused his anger to the extent of stigmatizing it as such in Parliament. He was imprisoned, his estates confiscated, and, upon his escape to the Highlands, declared an outlaw. He sent a letter to the King renouncing his allegiance, and avowing his intention to slay him as his mortal enemy. He contrived to seduce Walter, Earl of Athole, the King's uncle, an old man of about seventy years, to his side, by citing the prediction of some Highland seer that Athole should one day wear a crown.

The Earl of Athole's grandson, Sir Robert Stewart, who was chamberlain to the King, and high in his confidence, was allured by this prospect of greatness, and, entering eagerly into the plot, did as much as anyone to ensure its success. It was through his instrumentality that the body of conspirators obtained entrance into the monastery.

The brave action of Catherine Douglas in barring the door against them with her arm, when she saw the bolt was removed, has often been portrayed, as, indeed, has the whole sad story, both by pen and pencil. But her heroism availed not. When the King had for a time eluded the vigilance of his foes, one of the villains attacked and wounded Queen Joan, and might have proceeded to murder had not a son of Sir Robert Graham ordered him to leave the women alone and look after the King. James made a desperate struggle for existence, but he was overpowered by numbers, and, after his arms and hands had been severely cut—he himself had no weapon of any kind—and he had received fully twenty wounds, death came to his relief.

Thus, after a reign of twelve years, in his forty-third year, died the first James, the brightest and best of his family. He was buried in the Church of the Carthusians, at Perth, which he had himself founded. His only son, James, then six years of age, succeeded to the throne.

James left six daughters. The eldest, MARGARET, was contracted, when almost a baby, to Louis, the Dauphin, son of Charles VII. of France. In 1434, when she was ten years old, it was resolved to complete the marriage. A fleet of forty ships and barges was accordingly fitted out. Accompanied by a train of nobility, waited on by 100 young squires, and guarded by 1,000 men-at-arms, she left her native land for that of her betrothed. Although there was at the time a truce between England and Scotland, the Duke of Gloucester and the Council determined to try and intercept her, much in the same way that her father had been captured. A fleet was accordingly sent to the coast of Brittany, but was turned aside in the hope of making prize of some merchant-vessels, and so the young Princess was safely landed at Rochelle, where she was received by the Archbishop of Rheims and other dignitaries of the Church. The marriage was celebrated at Tours, with great magnificence, on July 6, 1435. It might have been better for her had her father's fate been hers, rather than marry a youth like Louis, with whom she never had any happiness. Her father- and mother-in-law loved her; her ladies looked up to her with respect; all France revered her. Her husband alone, though he might esteem her virtues, never loved her.

> 'O, sweet pale Margaret,
> O, rare pale Margaret,
> Of pensive thought and aspect pale,
> Of melancholy sweet and frail.'

Fortunately for her, she inherited, with her younger sister Eleanora, the literary tastes of her father, and many weary hours were passed in cultivating them.

> 'A fairy shield your genius made,
> And gave you on your natal day.'

But it did not shield her from calumny.

Alain Chartier, who had been high in the service of King Charles VI., was, at the same time, the most distinguished man of letters and the ugliest man in France. He was remarkable for his patriotism, which shone forth in both prose and verse.

It chanced one day that he lay asleep on a bench in a room through which the Dauphiness and her ladies had to pass. Margaret stopped, and kissed him on the mouth. When remonstrated with by one of the bevy of attendants, she replied, with a smile: 'I do not kiss the man, but the precious mouth whence issued such wise words and virtuous sentences.'

Not long afterwards reports injurious to her reputation were set afloat. The King and Queen entirely disbelieved them, but the Dauphin, for purposes of his own, appeared to credit them, if he had not even been their originator. She struggled hard against them; but they ruined her health.

Thus, when only twenty years of age, in 1445, died the Dauphiness Margaret Stewart,

> 'Done to death by slanderous tongues.'

She was first buried in the church at Chalons-sur-Marne where she died. When her husband came to the throne, as Louis XI., out of respect to her memory he caused the body to be removed to the abbey church in Thouars, Poitou, where it now lies. There were not any children of this loveless marriage.

ELIZABETH or ISABELLA—the names at that time were almost indiscriminately applied—the second daughter of James, was the beauty of the family, of an elegant figure, and in possession of vigorous health. But in mind she was far inferior to her sister. John VI., of Brittany, sent over ambassadors to treat of a marriage between her and his son Francis. On their report of these facts, with the addition that she was remarkably silent—as it seemed to them, from extreme simplicity, or, to put it more plainly, because there was nothing in her—the Duke said: 'Return and bring her at once; she is the very woman I have been seeking.' He continued: 'A wife is sufficiently knowing if she can tell the difference between her husband's shirt and his shirt ruffles.' She was accordingly brought over in 1441, and became the second wife of Francis, who, in the following year, succeeded his father, John VI., as Duke of Brittany. Elizabeth had two daughters only, so that her issue did not rule in Brittany.

Jean, the third daughter, married three times. Her daughter by her third husband, George Gordon, Earl of Huntley, was the beautiful Catherine Gordon who married Perkin Warbeck, the pretended Richard, Duke of York, son of Edward IV. MARY and ELEANORA went over to France on a visit to their sister, the Dauphiness. On their arrival they first heard of her death, at which they were naturally much grieved; but King Charles did his best to console them, and gave them establishments equal to their late sister's, until they were married.

Eleanora, the fifth daughter, was the first wife of Sigismund *der Münzreiche*, or The Moneyed, Archduke of Austria. He was one of the richest rulers of the time, owing to the recently discovered silver mines of Tirol. But he was so open-handed, and of such an easy disposition, that he was constantly in debt. One of his great hobbies was the building of castles or hunting-seats, of which there are still many remains scattered up and down Tirol. One of the items of extravagance charged against him was that he wore silk stockings, so contrary to the simple manners of the people.

Of Eleanora we do not hear much, and may justly conclude that she led a quiet, happy life. Her literary talents were employed in translating old romances into German for the amusement of her husband. She died childless in 1480.

At the request of his people, Sigismund resigned in 1493, in favour of the Emperor Maximilian I., and died March 4, 1497, at the age of sixty-nine.

MARY, the fourth daughter of James, married a son of the Lord of Campvere in Zealand. Arbella, the youngest, died unmarried.

After the horrible tragedy of the King's murder, Queen JOAN fled with her boy to Edinburgh. Subduing, as far as possible, her terror, her grief, suppressing even her tears, she did all that lay in her power to pursue and bring the miscreants to justice.

Within forty days all of them suffered a painful and ignominious death. The Earl of Athole's torture lasted three days. On the second day he was exhibited crowned, in fulfilment of the prophecy, with a hot-iron crown bearing the inscription '*Here stands the king of traitors.*' On the third day he was beheaded, declaring to the last moment that he was innocent of any participation in the conspiracy, but not denying that he had heard of it.

Sir Robert Graham, after having the flesh torn piecemeal from his limbs, was hanged and quartered. In the midst of his agony he averred that his memory would be blessed for having rid the country of a tyrant. The people evidently were not of that opinion. To show their abhorrence of his misdeeds they went about chanting this rhyme :

> ' Robert Graham,*
> That slew our king,
> God give him shame !'

Sir Robert Stewart was hanged and quartered, as were also some of the minor conspirators.

The murder was an atrocious act, but it must be admitted that the executions which followed were merciless in the extreme, only to be accounted for by the prevailing cruelty of the age.

About the same time that these tragedies were being enacted in Scotland an event occurred in England which caused considerable stir at the time, though no one could anticipate the serious influence it was destined to have over the fate of the country, and the tragedies of which it was to be the forerunner. JAQUETTA, of Luxemburg, Duchess of Bedford, married Sir RICHARD WYDEVILLE, one of the handsomest men and best captains of the age, but not considered fit to mate with the widow of a royal duke. He was put in prison, but released on payment of a heavy fine.

Towards the close of this year, when King Henry was nearly sixteen, he claimed the right to sit in the Council, and learn in what manner the affairs of the country were conducted. A similar demand had been made and refused three years before. Now, it was ruled that the pardon of criminals, the presentation to benefices, and special graces should be left to him ; that he should be informed of all debates of importance ; and that the decision in all matters where the minority in the Council was above one-third should be in his hands. This arrangement continued in force until he became of age.

Henry was of a most gentle, amiable, and unassuming character; studiously inclined, though not perhaps over endowed with intellect. He had, however, a great desire to promote the learning of others. To that end he founded on the banks of the Thames the college of Eton, the first stone being laid on his birthday, December 6, 1441, and, in connection with it, King's College, Cambridge, which was only open to scholars from Eton. He was eminently religious, never

---

* Pronounced Graeme.

so happy as when reading holy books, or attending the services of the Church. Pure in thought, word, and deed, it is told of him that he rebuked certain females who came to him immodestly dressed, saying: 'Fie! fie! forsooth ye are to blame.' So perfectly free was he from vice of any kind that it is no wonder if he held aloof as much as possible from his uncle of Gloucester on account of his immoral life. His religious feelings taught him to love peace rather than war, and therefore he put great trust in his great-uncle of Winchester as long as he lived. Years went over his head, but his capacity for government did not increase, and we shall therefore find him trusting implicitly in those around him, whom he considered his friends. To a certain extent he was in advance of his times. He was born four centuries too soon. Had he lived in these days, when it is an axiom that 'monarchs reign, but do not govern,' he might have been a very good head of the State.

Charles VII. of France, Henry's uncle, was for a long time a lazy, listless, dissolute prince, governed by favourites such as Tanneguy du Chastel, Pierre de Giac, la Tremouille, and others, who reigned in turn. The one pure figure of the time, Jeanne d'Arc, had, as we have seen, roused him for a space, but he sank back to his old life, and appeared to take no interest in anything but frivolous dissipation. La Hire once said to him: 'I did never know any prince who delighted himself more with his losses than you do with yours.' His wife, Marie of Anjou—the sister of René—as noble a woman as then lived, who would have made the happiness of any other man—strove to instil into him feelings of patriotism, and stir up his sluggish nature. But it was all in vain. If he did make one or two spasmodic efforts, he immediately suffered a relapse. It was another woman who strengthened the impression which the Queen had succeeded in making. That woman was AGNES SOREL, *la belle des belles*, of Fromenteau, in Touraine. She came to court with Isabelle of Lorraine, the wife of Duke René, and such was the impression made on Charles at first sight of her—so visible the improvement in his manner and spirits, that Queen Marie and her mother, Yolande of Arragon, joined him in requesting Duchess Isabelle to leave her with them. To Agnes, therefore, should all honour be given for influencing her weak lover to show himself a man, and fight for his country.

The war dragged on its weary way. Lord Talbot prevented the recapture of Rouen by defeating a body of Frenchmen, whom some of the inhabitants had agreed to admit into the town. He regained Pontoise by a clever manœuvre. It being winter time he dressed his troops in white. Thus accoutred, they made a night march through the snow, which lay thick on the ground. On arriving at the ditch it was found, as the gallant leader no doubt anticipated, to be frozen over. The walls were soon escaladed, and the town was won. Thence he swept the country towards Paris, and the capital itself had nearly been regained. But Crotoy was being besieged by Philip of Burgundy. Talbot, with 4,000 men, crossed the Somme at Blanchetaque, though the water was as high as their breasts, and the Duke retired to Abbeville.

> 'The warlike Talbot, for his acts
> So much applauded through the realm of France,'

> 'England's glory, Gallia's wonder,'

was at that time the greatest leader on the English side.

King Charles in person marched against Montereau-sur-Yonne, which surrendered in about six weeks. On Tuesday, November 12, he made his first entry into Paris, accompanied by his eldest son, the Dauphin Louis, then thirteen years of age, and a great number of nobles. Great preparations, in the way of pageants and mysteries, had been made, and the people were enthusiastic in their welcome. But Charles had no pleasant recollections connected with his last appearance there; consequently, as soon as he well could, he returned to Tours.

In December of this year Charles of Artois, Count d'Eu, who had been taken prisoner at Azincour, was exchanged for John Beaufort, Earl of Somerset, who had been captured at Beaugé. Charles was brother-in-law of Philip of Burgundy, who had taken his sister Bona for his first wife. He was also uterine brother of Charles, Duke of Bourbon, their mother being that same Marie of Berri whom Henry of Bolingbroke had unavailingly sought for his wife forty years before, as told in a former sketch.

In addition to the war, both France and England were visited by 1438. famine and pestilence. To continue the contest with France seemed hopeless. The wisest party, with Cardinal Beaufort and the 1439. Earl of Suffolk at their head, advocated peace. The Duke of Gloucester strongly opposed them, but the treasury was empty, and without means the war could not be carried on. Unwillingly he had to yield. We have had peace parties and war parties since that time, but fortunately they have not been embittered, as were those of Henry VI.'s reign, by ill feeling and personal hatred of one leader towards another of the opposite side.

A meeting took place between Calais and Gravelines of Cardinal June. Beaufort and Isabel, Duchess of Burgundy, to deliberate on peace between the contending countries. On the part of England appeared the Bishops of Norwich and St. David's, John de Vere, twelfth Earl of Oxford, Humphrey de Stafford, sixth Earl of Stafford, and Henry Bourchier, Earl of Eu. France was represented by the Archbishops of Rheims and Narbonne, the Bishop of Chalons, the Count of Vendôme, Dunois, the Bastard of Orleans, and the Lord de Dampierre. The Duchess, as became her stateliness, was attended by ten ladies of position, the Bishop of Cambrai, and several lords. The same state and ceremony were observed as at the meeting at Meulan twenty years previously, and therefore it is needless to recapitulate. The English offered to Charles the whole of the territory beyond the Loire, with the exception of Guienne. The

French, on the other hand, claimed the whole of France, but agreed that Henry might hold Normandy and Guienne as a feudatory of King Charles. The Duchess Isabel, seeing no prospect of agreement, proposed a peace for a limited period. The only result arrived at was that another meeting should be held, to which Charles, Duke of Orleans, should be brought over, on pledging his word to return to his captivity, in case nothing satisfactory to all parties could be
July. determined upon. The conference then separated, but not before the Cardinal, with his usual magnificence, had feasted his niece, the Duchess, and all the company on more than one occasion. For this special purpose he had brought with him sumptuous pavilions, with abundance of gold and silver plate, fine napery, and all the necessaries and luxuries of the table. If good entertainment could have brought about the result at which he aimed, that end would surely have been attained; but it was not to be.

1440. A year later another meeting of the ambassadors was held at Calais, at which the most interesting figure was that of the Duke of Orleans, who stood on the soil of his native France for the first time after a lapse of over twenty-four years. He joyfully embraced his valiant bastard-brother John, the hero of France, whom he had last seen a mere boy. At various conferences, many proposals were made, but no articles of peace could be agreed upon, and the ambassadors separated. The Duke of Orleans was carried back to England, but he had not much longer to wait for his freedom.

July. At this time RICHARD, Duke of YORK, went over again as Lieutenant and Governor-General of France and Normandy, in succession to RICHARD BEAUCHAMP, Earl of Warwick, who had died on April 30 at Rouen;

> 'For whom great mone was made and lamentacion,
> For his wisedom, and for his manhode ay,
> For his norture and communicacion:
> He stode in grace of hie commendacion,
> Emong all folke unto the daye he died,
> Regent of France, full greately laudified.'

In his will the earl left directions for the building of the Beauchamp chapel at Warwick, which is almost equal in beauty to Henry VII.'s chapel at Westminster. There is a large marble tomb to the 'Good Earl,' as he has been styled, with an effigy in brass gilt, as large as life. It was of him that the Emperor Sigismund, after seeing him at the Council of Constance in 1414, said that 'no Christian prince had another such a knight for wisdom, nurture and manhood, and if all courtesy were lost, yet it might be found in him.' The Earl had married, for his second wife, Isabel le Despenser, the widow of his cousin, the Earl of Worcester, of the same name as himself, whose death at Meaux has been already mentioned. The Countess Isabel retired to the monastery of Southwick, in Hampshire, but died on June 24 following, less than two months after her husband. She was buried at Tewkesbury Abbey, to which she had been a great benefactress, and there is a beautiful tomb to her memory in the abbey church. She left two children : HENRY, who succeeded his father as sixth Earl of Warwick, and ANNE, who eventually became heiress of the BEAUCHAMP and DESPENSER properties, and carried the whole to the Neville family, by her marriage with RICHARD, son of Richard, Earl of Salisbury.

Arthur, Count of Richemont, laid siege to the city of Meaux. John, Earl of Somerset, with the title of Lieutenant-General of France and Normandy, together with Lords Talbot and Falconbridge and Sir Richard Wydeville, marched to its relief with 4,000 men. They tried, but in vain, to force on a battle ; Richemont was much too wary for that. All they succeeded in doing was to throw some few of their men into the market-place, and then they withdrew their forces as supplies were running short. Three weeks later the garrison capitulated. Sept.

Cardinal Beaufort, feeling more and more convinced that peace was an absolute necessity for the country, suggested the liberation of the Duke of Orleans as a means to that end, although knowing that it was contrary to the last advice of the late King Henry. The Duke of Gloucester tried to circumvent him by delivering to the young King a strong memorial, going over all the old ground against him. Henry read it, but it did not induce him to change his opinion. He perfectly agreed with his great-uncle in the expediency of releasing Orleans, and negotiations were accordingly commenced.

The trade with Flanders had suffered so much since the termina- April. tion of the alliance with Burgundy, that it was thought advisable to approach Duchess Isabel on the subject of a peace between the two countries. She was by no means unwilling, and, with her assistance, an armistice for an indefinite period was arranged.

Harfleur, which had been taken by the French eight years before, was attacked by the Earl of Somerset, his brother Edmund, Earl of Dorset, Lord Talbot and others, with a force of 4,000 men. They lay so long before the town that the Countess of Somerset and other ladies went to the camp to wait for the surrender. The Bastard of Orleans and others went to the relief of the town by land, the Count d'Eu made a fruitless attempt from the sea. The French made many endeavours, but vainly, to break through the strong intrenchments. Equally vain were their attempts to bring on a general engagement. At the end of four months they withdrew their forces, and the town Aug. surrendered, the inhabitants being allowed to depart in safety, each bearing a white staff in hand.

In the meantime the compact with the DUKE OF ORLEANS, thanks to the good offices of the Duchess of Burgundy, had been brought to a satisfactory termination. Orleans agreed to pay a ransom, never to bear arms against England, and to use his influence at the French court in favour of peace. The Duke of Gloucester was still opposed to the release, but his influence was less now than it had ever been. When, therefore, Orleans came to swear on the sacrament Nov. 13. to fulfil all his engagements, Gloucester lodged a solemn protest against the whole proceeding, and went away to his barge.

The Duke of Orleans, after taking leave of King Henry, set sail for Calais, and at Gravelines met his kind friends the Duke and Duchess of Burgundy.

1441. June. A blow still heavier to bear fell soon afterwards upon the Duke of GLOUCESTER. The chaplain of his household, Roger Bolingbroke, a learned man of science, well versed in astronomy and astrology, was charged with necromancy, in conjunction with Thomas Southwell, a canon of St. Stephen's Chapel, Margery Jourdemain, called the Witch of Eye, and others. Bolingbroke was summoned before the Council for trying to bring about the death of the King by arts magical. He declared that he had studied these arts at the suggestion of the Duchess of Gloucester.

On learning this, the Duchess, or Dame ELEANOR, as she was styled, an ambitious, proud, and avaricious woman, at once fled into sanctuary. She aped royalty, and gave herself airs as wife of the man who, should Henry die unmarried or childless, stood next in succession to the throne of the House of Lancaster.

July 25. On Sunday Bolingbroke was taken, clothed in the garb he wore when he worked his necromancy, to hear a sermon at Paul's Cross. He was placed in a chair on a high platform, bearing a sceptre in one hand and a sword in the other. There he had to sit, the gaze of all beholders, who would probably pay more attention to this fantastic figure than they did to the preacher. It appeared on his trial that a wax image was made in the likeness of the King, which was expected to melt away under force of spells, or fire, and as it did so the King's life was in like manner to decay.

Dame Eleanor and Margery Jourdemain were then cited before an ecclesiastical court, which was opened by Chicheley, Archbishop of Canterbury, though he was too infirm and old to take part in the proceedings. Cardinal Kemp, Archbishop of York, presided in his place, Adam Moleyns, Dean of Salisbury, acting as assessor for Archbishop Chicheley. According to some writers, a meeting, perhaps a preliminary one, took place at Leeds Castle, in Kent.

The accused were charged with necromancy, witchcraft, heresy, and treason. Bolingbroke was called up to witness against them. He avowed that all his proceedings had been taken at the promoting of the Duchess, who 'wanted to know to what estate she should come.'

Margery admitted having made love-potions ten years before for Dame Eleanor, in order that she might secure the affection of Duke Humphrey.

Dame Eleanor admitted some of the twenty-four charges against her, others she denied, but finally submitted herself to the mercy of the court. She was convicted as an accessory of the others, Nov. 13 and sentenced to walk from Temple Bar to St. Paul's church bareheaded and barefooted, with a lighted candle in her hand. This penance was to be gone through twice in different parts of the city in the ensuing week. She was not a favourite with the populace as her husband was. Many years previously a deputation of citizens' wives had actually gone to Parliament and presented a petition against her, for alluring Duke Humphrey from his then wife, Duchess Jaqueline, but no attention appears to have been paid to them. Perhaps it was not to be expected that they would now show any great favour to her, yet her apparent humility gained her a good deal of sympathy. Her penance done, she was handed over to Thomas Lord Stanley, to be imprisoned for life in the Isle of Man, one hundred marks being allowed to her annually.

The Duke, though not implicated, must have severely felt this disgrace of his wife. He retired for a time from court, whether to hide his shame or plot mischief none can tell. Shakspere, in the Second Part of Henry VI., has a scene in which the Duke meets her in the street, and endeavours to soothe her. It is poetical, if not historical. But the whole of the three plays are full of anachronisms. This trial, for instance, is made to occur subsequent to the marriage of King Henry, which did not take place until more than three years later. Margaret therefore could not have had any share in the proceedings.

Bolingbroke was hanged and quartered at Tyburn, denying to the last that he had ever intended any treason to his King.

Southwell, who was accused of having prostituted his office of priest by blessing the instruments used by Bolingbroke in his necromancy, died in the Tower. John Hum, another priest in some way implicated, received a pardon. Margery Jourdemain was burnt at Smithfield as a relapsed witch.

There is one scene in the Second Part of Henry VI. which is founded on fact. As a relief from an account of unsatisfactory proceedings abroad, rivalries and dissensions at home, it may be as well shortly to tell the tale, more particularly as showing the cleverness and ready wit of the Duke of Gloucester.

When the King and the Duke were at St. Albans, they saw a beggar, who professed to have been born blind and to have suddenly recovered his sight at the shrine of St. Alban. The Duke called the man up to him, and, looking at his eyes, asked 'if he had never in all his life seen anything before.' 'Never before,' said the man; and so said his wife also. 'Can you see well now?' queried the Duke. 'Yes, sir, I can now see as well as any man.' 'Then tell me,' quoth the Duke, 'the colour of this man's gown.' The man told it correctly. 'And my gown and my neighbour's.' He told these also, without staying or stumbling, and the names of all the colours that could be showed him: and when the Duke saw that, he made him to be put openly in the stocks.

SKETCH XVIII.

DUKE AND CARDINAL.

1441.
May.

July.

KING CHARLES of France, having effectually crushed a rising known as 'La Praguerie,' which was headed by his son, the Dauphin Louis, again turned his attention towards ridding his country of the invaders. With a large force he undertook the siege of Pontoise. Lord TALBOT several times threw supplies into the town, and at length the Duke of York, with Lord Scales, Sir Richard Wydeville, and some 6,000 men, marched to its relief. But no battle was hazarded by either side. It was resolved to cross the River Oise, and advance into the Isle de France, Boats were provided, made of wood covered with leather. In one of these three or four men passed over, carrying with them strong ropes which were securely fastened into the ground with staves of wood. Other boats and ropes soon followed. On these were placed hurdles, so that the whole formed a rough kind of pontoon bridge, over which cars and carts with provisions and stores were passed. But all contrivances, all bravery, were useless. Charles knew how to wait and tire out his opponents. Various skirmishes, but none worth recording, took place.

Sept. 16. At length, the Church of Our Lady outside the walls was stormed and taken, and all the English found in it put to death. This happened on a Saturday, and on the Tuesday following the town was won.

1443. Charles then marched to Guienne, where he stayed some months and conquered some castles, and at the beginning of 1443 he assembled a large army to march into Normandy to the relief of Dieppe.

Aug. 28. JOHN BEAUFORT, Earl of SOMERSET, with a considerable force, marched into Anjou, Touraine, Maine, and thence into Brittany, where he had some successes. In the autumn of this year he was created Duke of Somerset and Earl of Kendal, but he did not long enjoy his new dignities. According to one of the continuations of the 'Chronicle of Croyland,' he was soon afterwards sent on another expedition abroad, and being, on his return, accused of treason, and denied admission to the King's presence, he was so indignant, and so utterly unable to bear up under his disgrace, that his high heart broke, and it was generally said that he put an end to his own existence on May 27, 1444, when but forty years of age. He left only one daughter, then about three years old, that gracious Lady MARGARET, who lived to be the last of the line of John of Ghent, Duke of Lancaster, and to see her son, Henry Tudor, on the throne as founder of a new race of kings.

John was succeeded in the earldom of Somerset by his brother Edmund, Marquis and Earl of Dorset, who was married to Eleanor, second daughter, by his first wife, of Richard Beauchamp, fifth Earl of Warwick.

It was now thought to be high time that King HENRY should marry. When he was a boy only eleven years of age the hand of Margaret, the eldest daughter of King James of Scotland, had been asked for him by Lord Scrope, when it was also proposed to give up Roxburgh and Berwick. This would have secured peace with Scotland, but the Council, to which the question was referred, rejected the proposal, and when Sir Robert Ogle, a few months later, made an infraction of the truce then existing, by openly assisting some Scottish lords then in rebellion, the original treaty was carried out with France, and, as we have seen, Margaret was married to the Dauphin Louis. It would almost certainly have been better for Margaret could she have married Henry, and it may be that affairs in England would have gone more smoothly. But it was not to be.

Some years afterwards, when the question of peace with France was first mooted, it was proposed that Henry should marry Catherine, one of the daughters of King Charles, but this was dropped, perhaps in deference to Henry's scruples as to marrying his first cousin. The young girl became the first wife of Charles, the son of Philip, Duke of Burgundy.

The Duke of GLOUCESTER proposed a daughter of the Count of Armagnac, who offered a handsome dower, with possession of certain towns and castles in Gascony, and ambassadors were sent from England to conclude the contract, May, 1442. The Count's object was to obtain assistance against King Charles in maintaining some of his rights in Gascony, which would surely have led to an embitterment of the war between France and England. But Charles was beforehand with him. In June the Dauphin, with considerable forces, invaded the Count's territories. The people, hearing that no succours would come from England, had to submit, and the Count, with his family, were taken prisoners. That project therefore came to an end.

The most clear-headed statesman of the time, Cardinal Beaufort, who was, with John Stafford, Archbishop of Canterbury and Lord Chancellor,* as much as ever in favour of peace, thought he saw a way of achieving that end, and at the same time of finding a suitable consort for his great-nephew, by entering into a treaty with RENÉ, titular King of Sicily, Naples and Jerusalem, Duke of Anjou, Lorraine, and Bar, Count of Provence, etc., for the hand of his daughter MARGARET. As she was also a favourite niece of Marie of Anjou, the Queen of Charles VII., and as the King likewise evinced great partiality for her, it was hoped that through her a permanent peace might be established.

After one or more preliminary meetings, a decisive one was held 1444. at Tours. England was represented by WILLIAM DE LA POLE, Earl May 28. of Suffolk, who was at that time the Cardinal's chief supporter. Adam Moleyns, Dean of Salisbury, Sir Robert Roos, and others;

* Stafford was the first to bear the title Lord Chancellor.—Dr. Hook's 'Archbishops of Canterbury,' vol. v.

France by Charles, Duke of Orleans, Louis de Bourbon, Count of Vendôme, and others. There were likewise representatives there of the Duke of Burgundy and the principal towns.

The Earl of Suffolk had great scruples about undertaking negotiations which were beset with so many difficulties. In order to satisfy him King Henry gave him full authority to conduct the treaty to the best of his ability, and granted him pardon beforehand for any errors in judgment he might make. This was afterwards approved by Parliament, and it is well to bear it in mind, in view of subsequent events.

A truce for two years was agreed upon, which was afterwards prolonged to five years. The marriage of Henry and Margaret was also arranged. René, with all his high-sounding titles, was a pauper, and could not find the money to get a proper outfit for his daughter, much less could he give her any dower. Still, he asked that his ancient possessions, Maine and Anjou, might be restored to him. In this he was supported by his brother-in-law, King Charles. Suffolk hesitated considerably, but at length agreed to it, and then returned to England to render his report to the King.

Margaret was considered to be the loveliest, best educated, and most fearless maid in Christendom. In person she was small and slight, but well proportioned. Her complexion was fair, and she had long golden hair, with bright blue eyes. Henry was delighted when he saw her picture, and heard the description of her various charms of person and manner set forth by his ambassadors. She was then fourteen years of age, having been born on March 23, 1430.

The majority of the Council signified their approval of the treaty and the marriage. But the Duke of Gloucester was vehement in his opposition, as he desired that the war should be continued to the bitter end. The country was, however, almost bankrupt, and the cessation of hostilities for a time was an absolute necessity.

Sept. 14. The Earl of Suffolk was created a Marquis, in order to give
Oct. greater lustre to his vicarious authority, and sent back to marry Margaret by proxy.

Nov. The espousals took place at Tours,* in the church of St. Martin, at the beginning of November. The Bishop of Toul officiated on the occasion, and the ceremony was graced by the presence of the King and Queen of France, the Dauphiness, Margaret Stewart; with bishops, dukes, earls, and knights too numerous to particularize.

The rejoicings afterwards at Nancy lasted eight days, and tournaments were held, in which the Kings, Charles and René, the Count de St. Pol, and Ferri of Lorraine, who was married to Margaret's sister Yolande, were the principal competitors.

King Charles and Queen Marie escorted their niece for a couple of leagues, and then took leave of her with tears. Her father and

---

* Miss Strickland, and most historians, give Nancy, but Mrs. Hookham in her 'Life of Margaret of Anjou' gives Tours.

mother, King René and Queen Isabelle, went as far as Bar le Duc, when they also parted from her with fervent prayers for her welfare.

King Henry had been anxiously waiting for his bride, but he had first to summon a Parliament in order to raise funds for all necessary expenses. When it met, the Archbishop of Canterbury, as Lord Chancellor, opened the proceedings in a long speech, or rather a sermon, from all accounts. He gave an account of all the proceedings in connection with the marriage, and asked for a supply to defray the costs, which was at once granted. The Duke of Gloucester, after approving all that had been done, then fell on his knees, and seconded a request which had been made, that some special mark of approval should be bestowed upon the Marquis of Suffolk. 1445. Feb. 25.

The progress of the young bride, which had been so long delayed, now continued uninterruptedly. The route traversed appears to have been a most erratic one, but at every place where she stopped she was received with great rejoicings. At Pontoise she was met by the Governor-General of Normandy, Richard Duke of York, who must have been then at the height of his manly beauty. It would be interesting to know what impression these two noble personages, who were in after years opposed in deadly conflict, made on each other, but there is not any record, and it would be useless to speculate. The cavalcade went through Mantes to Rouen, where a halt was made for eight or ten days. March 18.

Margaret made many new friends during her progress, but she was deeply grieved and saddened by the news of the sudden death of her lovely, amiable, and accomplished friend, Margaret Stewart, so much esteemed by all who knew her, except her husband, the Dauphin Louis, and who, as we have seen, had been present at the rejoicings at Nancy. It was the one cloud amidst her anticipated joys. Two lasting friendships were made by Margaret: one with the Marquis and Marchioness of Suffolk; another with the Earl and Countess of Shrewsbury. The Marchioness was ALICE CHAUCER, a granddaughter of the poet, and widow of the Earl of Salisbury who had been killed at Orleans. She was second-cousin of Cardinal Beaufort. The Earl was the celebrated Lord Talbot, who had been so created in 1442, and the Countess was Lady Margaret Beauchamp, eldest daughter of Richard, 'the good' Earl of Warwick, by his first wife; therefore half-sister of Anne, Countess of Warwick, who married Richard Neville. The Earl of Shrewsbury was a great admirer of Queen Margaret's learning and accomplishments, and as long as he lived showed her great respect. JAQUETTA, Duchess of Bedford, who had gone over to France to welcome her Queen, may also be reckoned among Margaret's first friends, and her daughter, Elizabeth Wydeville, subsequently became a maid of honour.

About the same time, September, 1444, that De la Pole was created a Marquis, HUMPHREY STAFFORD, Earl of Stafford, a grandson of Lady Anne, the daughter of Thomas of Woodstock, Duke of

Gloucester, was raised to the dignity of Duke of Buckingham. A still greater honour was bestowed on HENRY BEAUCHAMP, Earl of Warwick, son of the King's old tutor, and half-brother of the Countess of Shrewsbury. He was declared premier earl of England, raised to the rank of duke, made a Knight of the Garter, and crowned King of the Isle of Wight by King Henry's own hands. In the following year he was created Lord of Jersey, Guernsey, Alderney and Sark. He did not long bear this accumulation of dignities. He died, when only twenty-two years of age, on June 11, 1446, and was succeeded by his little daughter Anne as Countess of Warwick. She died, a child of five years old, June 3, 1449, and was buried at Reading Abbey, near her great-grandmother, Constance of York, Lady le Despenser. Thus her aunt Anne became her heiress, as told in another sketch.

April 10. At length Queen Margaret, with her noble escort, arrived at Portchester, in Hampshire, where she found King Henry awaiting her. She was unwell when she landed, and her first greeting to the shores of England was a terrific storm of thunder and lightning. Her illness proved to be a mild species of small-pox, which delayed the marriage for some days.

April 22. In the Priory Church of Southwick, originally an establishment of Austin Canons, of which there are still some scanty traces, on Thursday, April 22, Henry VI., King of England, was wedded to Margaret of Anjou, then just turned fifteen years of age. Cardinal Kemp, Archbishop of York, officiated, assisted by the King's confessor, William Aynscough, Bishop of Salisbury, who made a long discourse before giving them his blessing. The ring used on the occasion was formed out of one which had been put on Henry's finger when he was crowned King of France.

May. One of the first to greet the happy pair on their way to London was the Duke of Gloucester, who met them at Blackheath with 500 of his followers, and conducted them to his palace at Greenwich, where he did his best to prove that the charms of the King's young consort had impressed him equally with all who had seen her since her landing.

It may be worth while to advert to the curious coincidence that Thomas, Duke of Gloucester, had, in like manner, as already told, been the first to greet Anne, of Bohemia, the first Queen of Richard II.

May 30. The young Queen was crowned on the first Sunday after Trinity by the Archbishop of Canterbury, and the splendour of the show on the occasion must have drained the coffers of the King, who appears to have thought he could not sufficiently show his love for her. The principal nobility vied with one another in the magnificence of their array. By apparently universal consent, everyone wore the daisy—'the wee, modest, crimson-tipped flower' which Margaret had chosen for her badge on the day of the tournament at Nancy.

The newly-married pair were happy in one another, and the affection subsisting between them endured to the end of their lives. A long life of happiness appeared to be before them, and yet, almost from the first, it was brimful of misfortune.

'Famed for mildness, peace and prayer,'

Henry, so good at heart, so desirous of the love and good-will of all, was so easy tempered that he appeared to have no will of his own. Margaret, so bright, so lively, so winning in manner, charmed him. Ambitious she probably was, and gifted with a courage beyond most women. She soon saw her husband's weakness, and was in a manner compelled to act his part, and rule. Young and inexperienced, it was only to be expected that she should make mistakes. The principal one was that, there being two factions in the State, she leant towards the one which had advanced her to power. It was, perhaps, a natural choice, but it was in opposition to the voice of the people, and the man who posed as the people's friend, the Duke of Gloucester; and led to her being involved in the charges made against her friends.

An embassy arrived from France for the purpose of endeavouring July. to convert the existing truce into a lasting peace. It was headed by Louis de Bourbon, Count of Vendôme, and the Archbishop of Rheims, who were accompanied by representatives of Juan II., King of Castile—father of the celebrated Isabella the Catholic—and of René of Anjou, the father of Queen Margaret. The Count of Vendôme, it may be remembered, had been taken prisoner at Azincour, but released six years later. He died December 20, 1447. He was the direct ancestor of Henri le Grand, King of France.

The ambassadors were conducted to Westminster Hall. There July 15. they found the King, dressed in a robe of red cloth of gold, which trailed on the ground, sitting on his throne, with the Lord Chancellor, the Archbishop of Canterbury, and the Marquis of Suffolk on his right, and the Cardinal Archbishop of York, with the Duke of Gloucester, on his left. On the approach of the ambassadors, the King rose, descended a few steps, slightly raised his hat, and took each member, as he was introduced, by the hand. The Archbishop of Rheims, after a complimentary speech in French, presented a letter from King Charles. Archbishop Stafford then spoke in Latin, and expressed his King's pleasure at hearing from 'the noble Prince, his uncle, of France.' After reading the letter apart, the Chancellor intimated that a conference with the embassy would be held as soon as possible. In taking leave, the Archbishop of Rheims assured the King that, 'next to the Dauphin, the King of England was nearest to the heart of King Charles, who desired nothing so much as to promote peace between his nephew and himself.' Henry, it is said, gazed with a well-pleased smile at Suffolk, saying: 'St. Jean, merci!' while he looked triumphantly at Gloucester. The Chancellor returned thanks for the expression of a wish for peace by King Charles, and stated that a time and place for the next meeting would be notified in due course. The King appeared disappointed that more cordiality had not been expressed. He took each of the ambassadors by the hand, and desired Suffolk to inform them that they must consider themselves as much at home in his house as in that of their own King.

On another occasion, in private audience, when the King appeared only in his ordinary robe of black velvet, the ambassadors enquired after the health of Queen Margaret, and wished them both a long life of prosperity, with a perpetual friendship between the kindred families of France and England; Henry bade Suffolk tell them that 'it gave him great joy to hear of the King his uncle, whom he loved better than anyone else in the world, except his own wife, and that he desired the continuance of peace between the two kingdoms.' When the Marquis had concluded, Henry exclaimed, 'St. John, yes!' and talked familiarly with the ambassadors.*

This speech appears to have been but a necessary reply to the complimentary one made previously by the French Archbishop. It was, however, later on brought as a charge against Suffolk, as if he had made it on his own account.

It was once proposed that a personal interview should take place between the uncle and nephew; but, after all, the business was not brought to any satisfactory conclusion, and the ambassadors returned home about the end of the month.

It will be observed that Cardinal Beaufort did not take any part in these proceedings. Having, as he hoped, accomplished his desire for peace by bringing about the King's marriage, he retired from active participation in the government of the country, and went to reside at Wolvesey Castle, his palace in Winchester, a few scattered fragments of which only remain, where he employed his time and his money in making improvements in the cathedral, and performing divers acts of charity among the prisoners and other people in distress.

1446. We are told by some writers that, about this time, the Duke of
Aug. Gloucester was accused of having, during his protectorate, illegally put people to death on his own authority; of having increased the sentences passed upon others; and of having unjustly enriched himself at the expense of the crown. We are further told that when John de Foix, son of Gaston, the Captal de Buch who fought for
Aug. 22. England at Azincour, was created Earl of Kendal, and married to Elizabeth de la Pole, a niece of the Marquis of Suffolk, the Duke was compelled to resign to him some possessions in Guienne. Though it is said that the Duke, before the Council, replied to the charges against him, and was acquitted, yet both these circumstances, taken together, must have caused serious annoyance to the proud and ambitious Humphrey.

The King and Court went to Bury St. Edmunds to spend Christmas.

* Dr. Hook's 'Archbishops of Canterbury,' vol. v., and Miss Strickland's 'Life of Margaret of Anjou.'

Whether they remained there afterwards is not very clear, but it is believed that their stay lasted until Easter. Dec.

But a Parliament was summoned to meet there, instead of at Westminster. The knights of the shire were ordered to come well armed, and the people of Suffolk were called upon to form a guard for the King, as if there were great apprehension of danger from some quarter. The Duke of Gloucester, with only a small escort, arrived from his castle of Devizes, where he was then residing, though it is understood to have formed a part of the dowry of Queen Margaret. The present castle is only a modern structure. 1447. Feb. 10.

On the day after his appearance in Parliament, the Duke was arrested on a charge of treason, at his lodgings in St. Saviour's Hospital, of which there are still some few remains, by John Beaumont, Viscount Beaumont and Constable of England. The very next day, he was found dead in his bed.* There were no visible signs of violence on his body, which was exposed to public view, and it was reported that he died of apoplexy; but public opinion declared it a murder. Feb. 11.

Hardyng writes:
> 'In parlesey he died incontynent
> For heuynesse, and losse of regyment;
> And ofte afore he was in that sykenesse,
> In poynt of death, and stode in sore destresse.'

Whethamstede, Abbot of St. Albans, who was a great friend of the Duke's, and bitter against his enemies, says he fell ill and died of his illness and of sorrow within a few days. Some authors say 'within eighteen days.'

Nowhere is it stated that a coroner was called in to view the body, which is much to be regretted. It would then have been shown that the deceased was a very intemperate man, of an exceedingly passionate temper, who had led a corrupt life. He was undoubtedly at the time of his arrest in a bad state of health, and that affront might so affect him as to cause his death. Doctors say that, under the circumstances, such a man might die in a fit, when his countenance would be distorted; or, if his heart were weak, he might faint and die in a moment. It must be borne in mind that all the family had been short-lived. His father, King Henry IV., died at forty-seven years of age, and his mother at twenty-one. Of his brothers, Henry V. only reached the age of thirty-four, and John, of Bedford, forty-five. His elder sister, Blanche, died at thirty-three, and Philippa, the younger, at thirty-eight; while Humphrey himself lived to be fifty-six.

King Henry was fully persuaded of the guilt of his uncle, and was of opinion that he died a natural death. It would be going too far to say that Henry felt much regret at the removal of his kinsman, his feeling towards him having always been more one of fear than of either love or esteem. But, out of gratitude to God for protection

* Croyland Chronicle Continuator.

from imminent danger, he subsequently pardoned some of the Duke's followers, who had been convicted of conspiracy to kill the King and raise the Duke to the throne. This death of Gloucester was, there is little doubt, the beginning of the end of the house of Lancaster.

Shakspere's plays are delightful reading, but his historical ones, particularly the three parts of 'Henry VI.,' founded as they are on the old chronicles, are not to be taken as absolute fact, as many young people, and some older ones, are apt to do. In act iii. of the second part he exhibits the Queen, Cardinal Beaufort, York and Suffolk as plotting the destruction of Humphrey of Gloucester, and makes Margaret the chief instigator. A French historian boldly asserts her guilt, without any proof. Indeed, there is absolutely no proof that any murder was committed. If there were, it is very unlikely that Margaret would be entrusted with the secret. She would have revealed it to her husband; and no one has ever ventured to include the gentle Henry in the charge boldly preferred against others.

Humphrey was selfish, turbulent, and wrong-headed. Individually he was no loss. But the rivalry between York and Somerset then became of importance. He may, perhaps, have purposed trying to compel the King to declare Richard of York the next heir to the throne, instead of Somerset, as he was always opposed, as his father had been, to the house of Beaufort being considered to have any claims to the succession. For a long time after his death the supporters of the late Duke brought forward motions in Parliament for the reversal of his attainder and for declaring his loyalty. But no arguments could shake the King's belief in his guilt, and the Bills were accordingly always thrown out, until the Duke of York usurped the power of government.

The body of Duke Humphrey was buried in St. Albans Abbey, where a beautiful shrine tomb, in the south aisle of the church, was erected to his memory during the time of his friend Abbot Whethamstede. In a vault beneath the chancel the corpse was discovered some time early in the last century. The leaden coffin in which it was contained was filled with a strong pickle which thus preserved the body. But being left exposed, the pickle evaporated, the body crumbled away, and various bones were carried off by curiosity-hunters and others. There was at one time a painting of the crucifixion on the wall at the foot of the coffin, with the inscription, 'Blessed Lord, haue mercy upon mee,' traces of which are still visible.

Cardinal Beaufort had, assuredly, no hand in the fall and death of his nephew and great opponent, the Duke of Gloucester. He was lying sick at that time in his own palace at Winchester. He did not 'die and make no sign,' as Shakspere has pictured in that fearful last scene of act iii., filling up the outline he had derived from the old chronicler. On the contrary, as the Cardinal on the day before Passion Sunday lay on his bed of sickness, he was surrounded by the clergy and monks—not by the King and his nobles—while the

Prior of St. Swithun's chanted the Requiem Mass. He then caused his will to be read over to him. A few days later the Prior, in full pontificals, again went through the whole of the funeral service. The will was then read aloud, and, when some corrections had been made and codicils added, the dying Cardinal, in an audible voice, confirmed every disposition. That being done, he took leave of his friends, and, on the day following, went quietly to his rest, at the age of seventy-one. April 11.

The greater portion of his money was left to charities. To the principal cathedrals and monasteries he bequeathed plate and jewels. He had always been open-handed to the King and Queen, and materially assisted the young pair on many occasions. To Henry he left a dish of gold and a cup enamelled with images; to Margaret he left the bed, with hangings of cloth of gold of Damascus, in which she had slept on the occasion of her visiting him at his house at Waltham.

There is a beautiful chantry with a grey marble tomb in Winchester Cathedral, to the memory of the great statesman-bishop, who, though he might be proud and haughty, was not actuated by selfish reasons, but did his best for the King and kingdom under difficult circumstances. He was the King's great mainstay. Henry always declared 'he was a most kind uncle to me while he lived,' and he honoured his memory when dead. It was a great blow to his power, one, indeed, from which he never recovered.

Dr. Hook, in his 'Archbishops of Canterbury,' very justly remarks: 'The extreme denunciation of Cardinal Beaufort is as unjust as is the glorification, also in the extreme, of the Duke of Gloucester.'

SKETCH XIX.

NORMANDY AND GUIENNE.

THE removal of the Cardinal-Bishop and the Duke of Gloucester stirred up the latent ambition of the protégé of the latter, RICHARD, Duke of YORK. He felt slighted when, after holding the governorship of France and Normandy for over seven years, he was called upon to resign the office. It␣was the more galling to him because the post was conferred upon a member of the family for whom collectively, he expressed great contempt—EDMUND Beaufort, third Earl of SOMERSET—who was soon afterwards created a Duke. An active ill-feeling was thereby aroused in York, and also in the people, who appear to have adopted him as their favourite in place of Humphrey of Gloucester. 1447. Dec. 7.

Richard was appointed Lieutenant of Ireland in succession to the Earl of Shrewsbury, and went to the seat of his government with his beautiful wife, Cicely Neville. He was liked by both races, but did Dec. 9.

not identify himself with either. Thus he won 'golden opinions from all sorts of people'; or, as Hardyng writes :

> 'And greate thanke there, and love of all the land,
> He had amonge the Iryshe alwaye,
> And all the Iryshe beganne him to obey;
> He ruled that lande full well and worthely,
> As dyd afore his noble auncetrye.'

When his son GEORGE, in after years, the

> 'False, fleeting, perjur'd Clarence,'

was born at Dublin Castle, October 21, 1449, the two great Earls of Desmond and Ormond were requested to act as sponsors, and joyfully complied. The attachment of the Irish to the cause of the White Rose was mainly attributable to the Duke's rule for the five years he was in the island.

The new Duke of Somerset had not by any means such an easy seat as he probably anticipated, and the Duke of York must, in his heart, have felt very much gratified at having been spared the humiliation which his rival had to undergo.

1448. The cession of Maine had not yet been made, and King Charles, tired of waiting, in spite of the truce then existing, sent an army to besiege the city of Le Mans, which was forced to capitulate. Adam Moleyns, Bishop of Chichester (he had been so consecrated February 6, 1446), was then sent over to surrender the province, and the truce was renewed for two years. At the same time it was asserted that Henry only resigned possession to his father-in-law, and maintained his own sovereignty. Compensation was also promised to those Englishmen who had received grants of land there.

It unfortunately happened that Sir Francis Surienne, an Arragonian, but a Knight of the Garter, with 700 men, who had thus been driven out of Maine, in search of adventure and subsistence attacked and March 24. captured the town and castle of Fougères, in Brittany, on the borders of Normandy, where they did a considerable amount of damage. The Duke of Brittany, Francis I., sent his herald to demand restitution and compensation from the Duke of Somerset, who denied all knowledge of the matter. At the same time he agreed to send commissioners to Louviers, to treat with others on the part of King Charles, who warmly espoused the cause of his nephew and ally. The French estimated the damage done at 1,600,000 crowns, a sum impossible to be raised, as Charles well knew, and its non-payment would give him a pretext to continue the war.

1449. While the commissioners were meeting at Louviers on the Eure, May 16. then, as now, a trading and manufacturing town, one of its travelling merchants, assisted by some men-at-arms owing allegiance to the Duke of Brittany, surprised, and took by stratagem, the town of Pont-de-l'Arche, on the Seine, about five miles north of Louviers. A body of 400 or 500 horse was posted in the forest between the two towns, and some men on foot were in ambush near the gate of St. Ouen. After dark, the merchant, by name Jacques de Clermont, presented himself at the drawbridge, having with him only a cart, with the necessary driver, and two men dressed as carpenters, each having a hatchet suspended from his shoulder. The merchant asked the porter to let him pass, on the plea that he wished to go on to Rouen and be back in Louviers next day, and offered to pay him for his services. The temptation to earn a little money was too great for the porter to resist, and, calling another man to his assistance, the bridge was let down. In taking out his purse to pay the man, the merchant let one small piece drop to the ground. In stooping to pick it up, the porter was stabbed to death by the carter, whilst the assistant was despatched by the two seeming carpenters. The horse and foot were called in, and the town was won to the cry of 'St. Ives for Brittany,' all the inhabitants being in bed asleep. The English, to the number of a hundred or more, were made prisoners. Among these was WILLIAM, Lord FAUCONBERG, second son of Ralph Neville, Earl of Westmorland, and Lady Joan Beaufort, who had been sent by King Henry as ambassador to France, and had arrived only the preceding day. He was apparently ransomed two or three years later on.

The French now offered to restore Pont-de-l'Arche and Lord Fauconberg to England, in exchange for Fougères, *plus* the 1,600,000 crowns. There was no option but to refuse, and the war was continued to the bitter end, with the significant difference between this and former ones that the losses were always on the English side.

Gerberoy, about twelve miles from Beauvais, was taken, and the English, to the number of thirty, put to the sword. Conches, four miles from Evreux, Coignac on the Charente, St. Maigrin, and other small places were won back.

Another conference was held at the Abbey of Bonport, when the French offered to surrender all, together with Lord Fauconberg, for Fougères and the estimated damage, as before. This being again refused, as he doubtless anticipated, King Charles declared war, and appointed the Count of Dunois, heretofore known as the Bastard of Orleans, Lieutenant-General of the armies.

The town of Verneuil was captured through the treachery of one of the inhabitants, in revenge for some ill treatment he had received from one of the English garrison. Being on guard at night he dismissed the usual watch on some pretext, and allowed the French to fix their scaling ladders to his mill, so that they entered the town unsuspected by anyone. The greater part of the garrison were either killed or made prisoners, but the remainder took refuge in an almost impregnable tower, which they held until August 23, when want of provisions compelled a surrender. On the 27th of the same month King Charles made his public entry into the town, amidst great demonstrations of joy on the part of the inhabitants. *July 29.*

Mortain, which once belonged to Robert, the half-brother of William the Conqueror, Lisieux and Mantes, all surrendered, apparently without any demur, and Gournay soon followed their example. *Aug. 26.*

Vernon was divided in opinion. The inhabitants generally were for surrender; the governor, John Butler, son of the Earl of Ormond, was opposed to it. He had only some 200 men under him, too few to withstand a discontented population inside and a large army outside. He made the best terms he could: that he and the garrison might march out in safety, with all their baggage.

Sept. 3. The castle of La Roche Guyon was surrendered by the governor, John Howel, who became a Frenchman and took the oaths of allegiance to King Charles. Monstrelet accounts for this act of perfidy by saying it had come to Howel's knowledge that the Duke of Somerset, on hearing of the proposed surrender, had tampered with the messenger who brought the news to introduce four-and-twenty men into the castle to murder him. In that case there was treachery all round, for the messenger must also have betrayed the Duke's design if he ever entertained such a one. It is more probable to suppose, though the age was a most faithless and unscrupulous one, that Howel could see which was the winning side, and, having married a Frenchwoman with landed property, in order to secure that, he deserted his own country and her cause. His was not a solitary instance of change of sides. The governor of Gisors, Sir

Oct. Richard Merbury, betrayed the trust reposed in him, turned to the French interests, and was appointed by King Charles governor of St. Germain-en-Laye.

Somerset, unable to obtain money from home, was so far from having an army ready to send assistance to the various places attacked, that he had even been obliged to dismiss a large number of men for want of means to pay them, and had retired to Rouen with the remainder.

Charles's forces, on the other hand, were augmenting day by day. The tide of victory had turned, and rolled ceaselessly onward, without an ebb, until every foreign invader had been swept from the soil of France. The Duke of Brittany, with his uncle, Arthur, Count of Richemont, and a considerable army, entered Normandy, laid siege to St. Lo, which surrendered, and afterwards won Coutances, Carentan, and many of the surrounding towns, villages and castles. The Duke of Alençon conquered Essay, and Alençon the town whence he had derived his title. The Count of Dunois marched to the siege of Argentan, a little over twenty miles from Alençon. Here, as elsewhere, the inhabitants were in favour of their own countrymen, and opened the gates to them. The garrison retired to the castle, and, a breach being made in that, then to the donjon, which they were soon obliged to surrender, but had to give up their arms before being allowed to march away.

An irruption had also taken place in Guienne, headed by the Count de Foix and others, with between two and three thousand men. Siege was laid to the town of Mauléon. The usual course was followed even in that far-away spot. The inhabitants, out of fear, agreed to surrender. The garrison retired to the castle, a very strong position, but want of provisions obliged them also to submit.

Seeing towns, castles and villages returning once more to their allegiance, Charles determined upon the reduction of Rouen to obedience. The army sent against it suffered at first so severely from continued rain and cold wind that it had to be marched back again to Pont-de-l'Arche.

Some of the citizens, having gained possession of two towers, sent an offer to the King to admit a detachment of French soldiers into them.

The Count of Dunois went in command of the expedition, and had the satisfaction of seeing thirty of his men scale the wall, and so gain an entrance into the town. But gallant Talbot, to give him his more familiar title, charged upon them and slew the traitor guards and most of the assailants, the rest being flung into the ditch.

Somerset had but 1,200 men to oppose a large army outside, and a disaffected population inside, the town. A mob of furious people once surrounded him, and tried to compel him to agree to a surrender. Failing in that, the citizens held a meeting at the palace of the Archbishop, when it was resolved to send a deputation, with the Archbishop at the head, to treat with King Charles. At an interview Oct. 18. with Dunois and other nobles it was agreed that, when the city gates were opened, a general amnesty should be proclaimed, and permission be given to all to choose whether to remain or go away in safety. Somerset, Talbot, and all the English protested against such terms, and there were great dissensions, each side taking up arms.

The fort on Mount St. Catherine was surrendered to Count Dunois Oct. 20. by the governor on being allowed to march away in safety with the garrison. Monstrelet says that when on their way they met King Charles, who bade them not take anything from the poor people without paying for it, and gave them 100 francs to pay their expenses.

The gates were opened by the citizens to admit the French, who Oct. 21. invested the castle and palace, in which all the English were collected.

Somerset sought an interview with the King, who was at St. Oct. 25. Catherine's, and requested permission for himself and all under his orders to march out, according to the terms of the general amnesty. Those terms had been refused, said Charles, and then added that Honfleur. Harfleur, and all places in the Pays de Caux, must be delivered up before they could be allowed to depart.

The terms were bitter, too bitter to be at once accepted. Three Oct. 28. days later, Somerset again tried his best to change the King's resolve, but was not successful. A truce, meanwhile, from day to day was concluded with the Count of Dunois, who was besieging the castle, and a week later SOMERSET had a third interview with King Charles. He then agreed to deliver up the castle of Arques, a few miles south Nov. 4. of Dieppe; Honfleur and other towns and castles; to pay a ransom of 56,000 crowns within a year; and to leave Talbot, with other noble personages, as hostages for the due fulfilment of these engagements.

Nov. 10. The French flag again waved over Rouen, and King Charles made his triumphal entry into the ancient city, where he was welcomed with all possible pageantry and display by the clergy and inhabitants in general. At the entrance of the King to the Church of Our Lady, the English hostages, with Talbot at their head, stood at a window to see the show, which, one would think, could not have been one to cause them much gratification.

Dec. 8. The siege of Harfleur, the first conquest of Henry V., was commenced. On Christmas Day negotiations for surrender were completed and signed. A week later the keys of the town were delivered to the Count of Dunois, and the English standard was displaced for the French one.

1450.
Jan.

King Charles then retired to the Abbey of Jumièges, and went thence to pay a visit to the fair AGNES SOREL, who had so effectually stirred him up to the recovery of his kingdom, but who was now lying ill at her house, Mesnil-le-bel, in the neighbourhood. It proved to be a final leave-taking, as the King had to return to his army, and Agnes died on February 9, after giving birth to her fourth daughter, who only survived a short time. Her body was sent to Loches in Touraine, and interred in the Church of Our Lady. Her heart was buried in the chapel of the Virgin in the Abbey of Jumièges, with a black stone over it, which may still be seen, though not entire, as the abbey itself was destroyed at the time of the Revolution. Agnes bore a good character for charity and liberality to the poor and the Church. The inscription on her tomb styles her 'Agnes Seurelle Dame de Bréauté, d'Issodun, et Vernon-sur-Seine. Piéteuse aux pauvres.'

Mr. Johnes, in the notes to his translation of Monstrelet, gives a quotation from the French historian Du Clos: 'She never abused her influence over the King, but was a tender lover, a sure friend, and a good citizeness.'

1450.
Jan. 17.

During the time that Charles was at Jumièges, the siege of Honfleur, which had not surrendered in accordance with the terms of the treaty, was commenced. He arrived when the blockade was complete, and took up his quarters at the Abbey of Grestain. Being in want of provisions, the garrison agreed to capitulate if not relieved before February 18. When that day arrived they marched out.

March. At length the English Government contrived to ship off a small reinforcement for the Duke of Somerset, who was then at Caen. There were but 3,000 men, under the command of Sir Thomas Kyriel, one of the old commanders of the time of Henry V. They landed at Cherbourg, and soon laid siege to Valognes, about twelve miles distant, which held out for three weeks, but was then taken.

April 12. The force was increased by additions under Sir Robert Vere, Sir Henry Norbury, and Sir Matthew Gough, so that it now amounted to about 6,000 men. They marched on until they reached the village of Fourmigni, about ten miles from Bayeux. Here they took up their quarters, with a small river and orchards to their rear. A detachment of French under the Count de Clermont, who had April 18. received intelligence of this movement, came up with them early in the day, and though somewhat outnumbered, after three hours' skirmishing, a regular engagement was commenced, but the French were sharply repulsed. Help was, however, coming to them from another quarter. The Count de Richemont, just returned from Brittany, had arrived at St. Lo, where he also heard of this fresh stir. He set out before daybreak with a force of some thousands, and arrived at Trevières, a small town about two miles south of Fourmigni. His army came in sight when crossing a bridge over a stream, and no sooner were they perceived than a panic seized the men who had been drafted from Caen and Bayeux. They fled, to the number of 1,000, with their leaders Vere and Gough. The English were now hemmed in between two armed forces, in front and flank, and a battle soon raged on the plains between the town and village. In three hours the English were utterly defeated, with 3,773 men slain. who were buried on the spot; and the rest taken prisoners, including Kyriel, Norbury, and other officers. It was the first victory the French had gained in the open field for nearly twenty years, and it was accordingly greeted with universal applause. Not far from the church of Fourmigni a monument was erected to record the event, which is a memorable one, as it settled the fate of Normandy.

There was no more fighting. Place after place surrendered. July 15. Valognes at once reverted to France. Avranches and Bayeux opened their gates. Caen was indeed besieged, but Somerset agreed to capitulate if not relieved, which he was not. Falaise surrendered, and the Earl of Shrewsbury, who was there, was released without a ransom, owing to the admiration which King Charles entertained of his valour. At the same time the King made his gallant enemy many valuable presents, including richly-caparisoned horses, on learning his wish to attend the Jubilee which was to be held that year at Rome. When Cherbourg, the last stronghold in the hands Aug. 12. of the English, was delivered up, the whole of the Duchy of Normandy was again French, and only a few days over a year had been occupied in effecting the change.

Contrast that with the thirty years occupied in conquering the country; the millions of money expended, the thousands of lives lost in so doing, and it must be admitted that the French inhabitants had never been in favour of their English rulers. It may also be claimed that the policy of Cardinal Beaufort and the Duke of Bedford, to be satisfied with the retention of Normandy alone, would have been the wisest and the best.

King Charles, having recovered Normandy, resolved also to become master of Guienne, which had been an English possession for three hundred years, ever since Henry of Anjou married Eleanora of Aquitaine in 1152.

No time was lost in deliberation. A force was despatched under Sept.

the Count de Penthievre, and the first place to surrender was Bergerac on the Dordogne, the town from which Henry, first Duke of Lancaster, derived a title in the reign of the great King Edward. Chalais and other places were taken.

The nobles of the country, as a class, were in opposition to England. One instance has been given already. Now, Lord d'Orval, son of the Lord d'Albret who thirty years previously had gone to Paris for the express purpose of doing homage to King Nov. 1. Henry, had an engagement on All Saints' Day with the Bordelais, whom he defeated, and carried away many prisoners to Bazas, forty miles distant from Bordeaux.

The people of the country did not hold the opinions of the nobles. They considered themselves almost a race apart from Frenchmen, and were in many respects essentially different. They had enjoyed more liberty under English rule than they could ever hope for under a French one. Their peculiar privileges and customs had been respected by England, and, above all, their trade had been encouraged, and had flourished accordingly.

1451. Troops were poured into the country under the Count of Dunois,
May. as Lieutenant-General, who had with him the Count of Angoulême, brother of the Duke of Orleans, the Count of Nevers, the Count of May 20. Armagnac, Poton de Xaintrailles and others. Blaye, on the Garonne, was taken, and within a few days Le Bourg, a village June 2. near Bordeaux; Libourne, on the Garonne; Castillon, on the June 26. Dordogne, and St. Emilion were assaulted and carried. Dax, on the June 25. Adour, and Rions surrendered. On St. John Baptist's Day the town of Fronsac, with the strongest castle on the Dordogne, had to yield for want of reinforcements. Other places also declared for Charles.

This invasion of the country had been one totally unexpected, and many men having been transferred to the north to fight in Normandy and elsewhere, it is no wonder that the towns fell one after another. The inhabitants generally held out until good terms could be secured, and gradually most of the English were gathered together in Bordeaux. When that city was besieged, the mayor, at the head of the garrison and from 8,000 to 10,000 citizens, made a sortie. It was a plucky thing to do, but, with perfectly undisciplined troops, only failure could be expected to follow. They were routed with great loss in dead and prisoners, and the city fell on the same day as Fronsac.

Of all the principal towns only Bayonne now remained true to July 6. England. After a siege of over six weeks it also surrendered, and Aug. 21. Guienne was lost.

1452. It was very soon discovered what a great misfortune had happened. Nobles and burghers alike were dissatisfied with the change of rulers. They found taxation now much heavier, their treatment by the officers placed over them much harsher, and, perhaps more than all, their wine trade was languishing and like to perish. An embassy, with the Lord de l'Esparre at the head, was accordingly sent to

England to express great regret at all that had happened, and to promise perfect obedience to King Henry for the future, if he would but assist them in their endeavours to relieve themselves of the yoke which the French had imposed upon them. Their application was successful.

TALBOT, Earl of SHREWSBURY, was appointed Lieutenant-General Sept. 1. of Aquitaine. With 4,000 to 5,000 men he landed at Medoc, and Oct. 18. his son, by his second marriage, John, Lord Lisle, Lord Moleyns and others soon afterwards came with additional forces.

On his appearance before Bordeaux the city council deliberated as to whether the French garrison and civil officers should be sent to prison, or be permitted to retire. They were prevented coming to any decision by the gates being opened to Talbot, who made them Oct. 23. prisoners of war. Most of the places around returned to their old allegiance, and, when spring came in, the flag of England was again 1453. paramount in Guienne.

The Count de Clermont as Lieutenant-General was despatched in all haste, by orders of King Charles, to carry fire and sword into what he denominated his revolted province. He was joined by the Counts de Foix and d'Albret and had an army of over 20,000 men under his command. They carried out their instructions to the letter and particular severity was shown to any Frenchmen found in the towns they retook.

Siege was laid to Castillon, an important town about twenty miles July 13. from Bordeaux, which Talbot had recaptured. The old hero, it would appear, was in Bordeaux at the time, and had some doubts whether it might not be wiser to await there the arrival of the French.

Eventually he sallied out before daybreak with 800 or 1,000 horse, July 20. leaving others to follow on foot. He surprised and cut to pieces a body of franc-archers who were posted in an abbey outside the town, and drove the remaining few into the camp. While waiting for the infantry to come up, he caused a cask of wine, which was discovered in the enemy's quarters, to be broached and distributed, along with other provisions, among his men, whom he ordered to dismount, but he himself remained on his small hackney. He now advanced boldly against the barriers which the French had raised, and had nearly carried his point when a fresh body of Bretons came up to the relief of their friends, and the English began to give way, but were cheered on again and again by their truly valiant leader and the fight continued fiercely. The French had also cannon at their command, which did great execution. One of the balls of these culverins struck down Talbot's hackney, and the Earl, with his thigh broken, fell under him. Some cowardly ruffian killed him as he lay there disabled. He entreated his son, Lord Lisle, who came up just as he was dying, to escape while there was time, but the young man refused. He chose rather to share his father's fate than quit the field, and was slain with many others, guarding that father's corpse.

> '"Fly, to revenge my death when I am dead;
> The help of one stands me in little stead.
> 'Tis but the short'ning of my life one day.
> In thee thy mother dies, our household's name,
> My death's revenge, thy youth, and England's fame;
> All these, and more, we hazard by thy stay;
> All these are sav'd if thou wilt fly away."
>
> '"Before young Talbot from old Talbot fly,
> The coward horse that bears me fall and die:
> And if I fly I am not Talbot's son:
> Then talk no more of flight, it is no boot,
> If son to Talbot, die at Talbot's foot."'

Thus, at the age of sixty-three—not eighty as generally stated—died

> 'The scourge of France,
> The Talbot so much fear'd abroad
> That with his name the mothers still their babes;'

after he had, as Hall says, with much fame, more glory, and most victory served his King and country for twenty-four years.

The body of the Earl was sought for by his herald for a long time in vain, but at last he discovered it in a pitiable plight. 'Alas, my lord! is it you?' he said. 'I pray God to pardon you all your misdoings. I have been your officer of arms for forty years or more; it is time I should surrender to you the insignia of my office.' Then, with the tears trickling down his cheeks, he threw his coat-of-arms over the corpse, thus performing the hitherto accustomed rites at funerals.

The Earl was first buried at Rouen, together with his son, and the inscription on the stone set forth all his titles in full. The body was afterwards removed to Whitchurch in Shropshire, and in the church of that town a mutilated effigy of the great warrior may still be seen. Peace to his ashes!

> 'A stouter champion never handled sword.'

One of his ancestors was living at the time of the Conqueror. Thus he was

> 'Of ancient name, and knightly fame, and chivalrous degree.'

He was great-grandson of Richard Talbot and Elizabeth Comyn, who was the daughter of John Comyn, 'The Red,' and Joan de Valence, niece by the half-blood of King Henry III.

For his first wife he took Maude Neville, daughter of Thomas Lord Furnival, a brother of Ralph, Earl of Westmorland, and in her right was summoned to Parliament as Lord Furnival, and after that he was also styled Sir John Talbot of Hallamshire, as part of his wife's inheritance was the castle of Sheffield, so noted, under his descendant George, sixteenth Earl of Shrewsbury, as the place of detention of the unfortunate Mary Queen of Scots. He became sixth Lord Talbot in 1421, on the death of his niece Ankaret, the only child of his elder brother Gilbert. He had been twice Lieutenant of Ireland, where the English, at least, expressed great approval of his government, and he was created, perhaps in consequence thereof, Earl of Wexford and Waterford, and Lord of Dungarvan.

When the leader was slain the battle was soon at an end. A great many of the English army were slain, fighting their way back to Bordeaux. A thousand were made prisoners, either in the French works, or in Castillon, to which many had retreated when the town fell, as in a short time it did. The most noticeable among the prisoners were: Sir Robert Hungerford, Lord Moleyns, in right of his wife, the daughter of William Lord Moleyns, slain at Orleans in 1429; he was kept a prisoner for seven years; and John de Foix, Vicomte de Castillon, Earl of Kendal and Knight of the Garter, son of Gaston, Captal de Buch, who fought on the English side during the reign of Henry V. ' He had large possessions in Guienne, and, on the reduction of Bordeaux he sold all to his nephew, the Count de Foix, and retired to Spain.'*

There was no second army—no Talbot; town after town again fell. After a siege of four months famine compelled the yielding of Bordeaux. The English garrison were allowed to depart. Such of the inhabitants as wished were told they might do the same. Many availed themselves of the privilege, and the city was comparatively deserted. Oct 10.

All hopes of ever recovering Guienne were crushed at once. The only possession remaining to England on the Continent was the town of Calais, with a few marshy tracts round it, and France was greater and more powerful than she had ever been before.

SKETCH XX.

TROUBLOUS TIMES.

IN England the people were still clamouring for the war to be carried on, while, at the same time, they would not vote one penny piece for the purpose, because, led by the Duke of York or his friends, they would not place any trust in the Duke of Somerset, the King's lieutenant in France; or the Duke of Suffolk, the minister at home. They were full of complaints against the government, and generally in an unsettled state of mind. Among the nobility each one was looking after his own interests, and meditating or carrying out schemes of revenge for private injuries. The court was divided into factions; in short, the whole kingdom was a prey to discord—a state of things which was, unfortunately, to go on increasing. 1448.

The King, meanwhile, does not appear to have taken any concern

* Burke's ' Royal Families.'

in political affairs, but to have left the guidance to his council, while he continued his placid course, and devoted a great portion of his time to the performance of his religious duties.

Sept. 26. He visited the tomb of St. Cuthbert, at Durham, and remained at the castle until the end of the month as the guest of Robert Neville, Bishop of Durham, the fifth son of Ralph, Earl of Westmorland, by
Sept. 29. his second wife. On the feast of St. Michael and All Angels, he assisted at vespers. Thence the King went to Lincoln, where also, most probably, he would reside with the Bishop of the diocese,
Oct. 19. William Alnwick. During his stay there he wrote, on the morrow of St. Luke the Evangelist, expressing the great pleasure he had derived in Durham from the noble manner in which the services were conducted, the evident faith of the people, and the reverence they had shown to himself. Queen Margaret, who generally accompanied the King, tried to introduce the manufacturing of woollen and silk articles into Norwich when they visited that city this same year. In emulation of the piety of her husband in establishing his colleges at Cambridge and Eton, she commenced the erection of another at Cambridge, to be called Queen's College, of which the first stone was laid this year, and the King showed the great interest he took in it by his subsequent gifts, which were many and varied.

Mutual love ever existed between Henry and Margaret from the day on which they were made man and wife. Yet the old chroniclers have not scrupled to assert, and Shakspere has unfortunately followed them, that an unholy attachment existed between Margaret and the Duke of Suffolk, a man old enough to be her grandfather, as there was a difference of thirty-three years in their ages. Suffolk, it must be remembered, was her first English acquaintance, and had acted as proxy for the King at the marriage. He was the principal minister of the kingdom, and, as such, brought into constant communication with the Queen, who really had the direction of affairs. He was, besides, a married man, and the Duchess, as told already, was even a greater friend of Margaret's than the duke himself. Discard therefore, as only a poetical licence, Shakspere's description of Margaret being taken prisoner by Suffolk, and as most improbable and ridiculous the scene where she avows herself a very wanton.

This year was the last of comparative peace which Henry was ever to know.

1449. As a sign of the point towards which men's thoughts were tending, it may be observed that a lawyer stood up in Parliament, and moved that, the King having no child, an heir to the throne should be selected, and nominated the Duke of York for the office. He was promptly sent to prison for his speech.

Towards the close of the year the Duke of SUFFOLK was attacked in both houses. A man named Tailbois was charged by Lord Cromwell, the Treasurer, with coming to the House with a band of armed followers, in order to murder him. Suffolk tried to protect the man, and thus brought himself into suspicion, as the Treasurer was one of his most noted enemies. Notwithstanding this intervention, Tailbois was sent to prison, and condemned to pay a fine of £3,000.

This was a terrible year. 1450.

The first sign of coming trouble was the resignation by Archbishop Jan. Stafford of the Great Seal, which, as Lord-Chancellor, he had held for thirteen years. Cardinal Kemp thereupon accepted the office.

Adam Moleyns, who was in Portsmouth preparatory to going Jan. 9. abroad—having resigned his see of Chichester—was engaged by the government to pay certain soldiers and sailors who were about to be sent to France. It being bruited abroad that he was the man who had sold Maine to the French, he was attacked and brutally murdered. In order to save himself, if possible, it is said that he averred Suffolk to have done it, and to have boasted of being as greatly trusted by the King of France as by King Henry himself. It was reported that this murder was committed at the instigation of the Duke of York. The Duke was, however, at that time in Ireland, and he does not appear to have been a man at all likely to have prompted such an unnecessary crime. Could he have foreseen the consequences, there is no telling whether he might not have thought it a wise step to take. The King evidently believed in the Duke's guilt, and two years later, in reply to a communication from him, distinctly charged him with it.

The Duke of Suffolk thought it necessary to repel the insinuations which were, in consequence, being publicly and in all quarters made against him. He defended himself, before the King and Parliament, Jan. 22. in a most brilliant speech. He recapitulated the services of his family: that his father had died at the siege of Harfleur, his eldest brother had been slain at Azincour, his two next brothers at Jargeau, while he himself had been taken prisoner and had to leave his youngest brother as hostage, who died before he could collect the 20,000 crowns demanded for ransom; that he had been a Knight of the Garter thirty years; had served the King abroad for eighteen years, and had been a privy councillor for the same number of years. He declared that all his interests and those of his family lay in England, that he had always been true to his King and country, and asked how it was possible that for any consideration he could become a traitor.

The Commons, guided by Lord Cromwell, requested that the Duke Jan. 26. might be committed to the Tower; but the lords replied that could not be done without some specific charge being made against him.

They brought a paltry charge against the Duke of having stored Jan. 28 provisions and military requisites in his castle of Wallingford with the object of assisting the King of France, who, they pretended, was about to invade England. He was then arrested and sent to the Tower.

A Bill of impeachment in eight articles, containing all the rumours Feb. 7. current with the people, was brought up. The most important was the one charging him with a design to marry his son John, then a boy seven years of age, to Margaret Beaufort, only child of John, late Duke of Somerset, depose and murder the King, and then declare the young girl heir to the crown. The liberation of the Duke of Orleans was another item, and also the very measures for which, five years previously, he had received the thanks of King and Parliament.

March 7. To replace the original Bill the Commons brought in a fresh one of sixteen articles, one of which was for screening William Tailbois from the pursuit of justice.

March 13. The Duke was again brought before the Council, when he declared it would have been an act of treason to look on Lady Margaret Beaufort as having any claim to the crown, and that it was well known he had purposed marrying his son to Lady Anne Beauchamp, Countess of Warwick, if she had not, unfortunately, died. As to the cession of Anjou and Maine, he affirmed that all the lords of Parliament were equally responsible with himself. Of the rest of the charges he said that they were frivolous and needed no reply.

No case had been made out against him, but the populace had been won over to the side of a party who hated him, and they called loudly for his blood as the author and contriver of everything that had gone wrong in the country. The old nobility were for the most part opposed to him. His great—unpardonable—crime in their eyes, as had been that of his great-grandfather, the first Earl, during the reign of Richard II., was that he could only claim a merchant-prince as the founder of the family.

March 17. The King and court now sought to save the Duke's life. He was therefore brought from his prison to the King's apartment in the Palace of Westminster, where the Lords Spiritual and Temporal had been summoned to assemble. He fell on his knees when he first appeared, and so remained the whole time. Being asked what he had to say to the charges made against him, he replied that all were false and some impossible, but that he threw himself on the mercy of the King. The Chancellor then said that, as he did not claim the privilege of the Peerage, but submitted himself to the Royal will, he was commanded to inform him that the King did not hold him guilty, or innocent, of the treasons charged against him in the first Bill. As regarded the second Bill, the Chancellor continued, the King, of his own judgment, and on the grounds of the Duke's submission, commanded him to leave the country before the 1st of May, and not set foot in it again for five years.

It was a bold course for the King to pursue, and, as Dr. Hook writes in his 'Lives of the Archbishops,' it was probably suggested by Cardinal Kemp, at the instigation of Queen Margaret. But it unfortunately failed in securing the Duke's safety. Parliament was then prorogued, but through John Viscount Beaumont it first protested against the whole proceedings as unconstitutional and tending to deprive the Peers of their undoubted right to be the judges of one of their own house.

In reference to this trial, Dr. Lingard writes: 'In neither of these impeachments is there any allusion to the death of the Duke of Gloucester, a pretty plain proof that there was no evidence of his having been murdered.'

The populace were fearfully exasperated when they heard the result of these proceedings. They cordially hated the Duke, on whose shoulders they laid the whole blame of the poverty of the King and country, of every grievance on the part of the people, and of every error in the government. They worked themselves up into such a state of excitement that two thousand of them gathered together in St. Giles' Fields, in the hope of intercepting him before he could leave London. There would have been but scant mercy for him had they succeeded. Fortunately for them and for himself he contrived to evade them, and arrived safely at Wingfield, his place in Suffolk.

It must have been a sorrowful meeting between the Duke, his wife and son. Into the particulars of it we need not seek to pry. He left behind him a most beautiful letter addressed to his son, with rules for his conduct in after-life. In it he impressed upon the boy the duty of honour and obedience towards God, his King, and his mother; such a letter as none but a man good at heart could write. Whoever reads it must be convinced that he was neither a disloyal man nor a bad one. His last act was to assemble the knights and gentlemen of the county around him; and, in their presence, he swore on the Sacrament that he was innocent of all the crimes which had been laid to his charge by his enemies.

The Duke sailed from Dunwich* with two ships and a little spinner; and on Thursday, April 30, arrived at Dover. The little spinner was sent on towards Calais to learn how the Duke would be received there, and on the way met a vessel called the *Nicholas of the Tower*. The master thereof learnt from the men in the spinner of the Duke's coming. Therefore, when he saw the two ships, he sent men to enquire what they were, and the Duke himself answered that he was going to Calais by command of the King. The men then said that he must speak to their master, and so the Duke, with two or three more, got into the boat. When they reached the *Nicholas*, the master saluted the Duke with: 'Welcome, traitor!' On learning the name of the vessel, the Duke remembered having been told that, if he could avoid water and escape the danger of the Tower, he would be safe, and so his heart failed him, for he thought he had been deceived.

April 30.

The prophecy as to water is thus noticed by Shakspere. Suffolk, asking to be held to ransom, says:

> 'Look on my George, I am a gentleman;
> Rate me at what thou wilt, thou shalt be paid.

---

* Ipswich is generally given as the port of embarkation, but historians of Suffolk point out that Dunwich was his nearest port.

> *Whit.* And so am I ; my name is Walter Whitmore,
> How now? Why start'st thou? What, doth death affright?
> *Suff.* Thy name affrights me, in whose sound is death.
> A cunning man did calculate my birth,
> And told me that by *Water* I should die ;
> Yet let not this make thee be bloody-minded ;
> Thy name is *Gualtier*, being rightly sounded.
> *Whit. Gualtier*, or *Walter*, which it is I care not.'

The prophecy was held to have been fulfilled.

May 2.   'On Saturday, in sight of all the men in his own ships, the Duke was put into a boat, and one of the meanest of the crew bade him lay his head on a block, which was there provided, and he should be fairly dealt with. The man took a rusty sword, and, after six strokes, smote off his head.'*

> 'Great men oft die by vile bezonians.'

After taking away the gown of russet and the doublet of velvet mailed, which the Duke wore, the man laid the body on the sands at Dover. Some say the head was set up on a pole.

Watch was kept over the body until the Duke's chaplain came to claim it. It was carried to Wingfield, about six miles from Eye, and buried in the chancel of the church, where a fine altar-tomb to the memory of the first Duke of Suffolk was erected, with many others of his family.

This blood-shedding was the first of the revolutionary horrors that were to come upon England.

Who was the real instigator of the crime was never known. Some have supposed it to have been Lord Cromwell, who, as we have seen, originally commenced the attack upon the Duke ; some again have pointed out the Duke of York as the man, as in the case of the Bishop of Chichester. From the employment of a ship of war on the occasion, it seems clear that some one in authority was concerned in the matter. Henry Holland, second Duke of Exeter, was, in 1447, according to Doyle's 'Baronage,' Admiral of England, and joint Constable of the Tower. But at this time he was not quite twenty years of age, and he would scarcely venture to take such a responsibility upon himself of his own accord. He was, however, married to Anne of York, eldest daughter of Duke Richard ; and there is a possibility that, in order to please his father-in-law, or at a hint from him, he may have given the order for the sailing of the ship. It was imperative that Suffolk, the faithful minister, should be got out of the way before York could announce the claim to the throne which he was even then meditating. But the young Duke of Exeter was the grandson of John Earl of Huntingdon, executed in 1400, and great-grandson of John of Ghent, therefore third cousin of King Henry, and we know that he espoused the King's cause later on. Lord Say de Sele was Constable during the young Duke's minority. The secret was well guarded, and everything is wrapped in mystery.

* The Paston Letters.

The murdered Duke's grandson was declared heir to the throne when Richard III. was King.

The distress caused to the King and Queen was very great. This was considerably increased by the news, just received, of the disastrous battle of Fourmigni, and, at the same time, of a rising in the county of Kent. Riots were mentioned as taking place in many counties, but in Kent, particularly, the people were roused by a report that vengeance was to be taken on them for having manned the ships which went in pursuit of Suffolk.

JOHN CADE, an Irishman of fine stature and noble bearing, who May. had served in the wars in France, on one side or the other, returned home about this time. He there assumed the name of Sir John Mortimer, thus claiming relationship with the Lieutenant of Ireland, Richard of York. It was believed by many that the man's proceedings were instigated by some of the Yorkist party, if not by the Duke himself. Any way, they played his game for him. Some of Cade's followers, after the suppression of the insurrection, confessed that it had been their intention to place the Duke of York on the throne.

Cade came over to England and placed himself at the head of the men of Kent. He appeared with 20,000 men at Blackheath, and June 1. thence issued two papers: 'The Complaint of the Commons of Kent,' and 'The Requests by the Captain of the Great Assembly in Kent.' The complaint was that Kent was to be destroyed, as report said, for the death of the Duke of Suffolk, of which they were guiltless; that the goods of the people were taken without payment for the service of the King; that the princes of the blood were kept out of the government, which was filled by men of low degree, oppressors of the people; that they had been overtaxed by the sheriffs and collectors, who were extortioners; that they had been deprived of the right of electing the knights of the shire; that the administration of justice had been seriously interfered with and delayed. The requests were: that the King would banish all the relations of the Duke of Suffolk, call to his presence the Dukes of York, Exeter, Buckingham and Norfolk; punish the traitors who had brought about the deaths of the Duke of Gloucester, of their holy father the Cardinal, and others, as well as those who had caused the loss of Maine, Anjou, Normandy and Guienne; that all extortions should be abolished, and the extortioners brought to justice.

If Cade drew up these papers, he must have been a man of considerable knowledge and cunning. He erred, however, in writing of the murder of Cardinal Beaufort, who, as we have seen, died a natural death. Some of the complaints were doubtless just, and, though not at once, were ultimately remedied.

An army of 15,000 men was raised and led by the King in person June 11. to Blackheath; but Cade, knowing that his men had not any ill-feeling against Henry personally, thought it prudent to retreat to Sevenoaks, twenty miles away, where he took up a strong position in a wood. The King returned to London, happy in the belief that his subjects would not fight against him. The command of a detachment of the royal forces was then entrusted to Sir Humphrey Stafford and his brother William, great-nephews of the Archbishop, who followed the rebels. But though Sir Humphrey was a gallant knight, and led his men courageously to the attack, superiority of numbers prevailed.

June 24. Cade gained a complete victory, and both the Staffords were slain.

This victory had a demoralizing effect upon the rest of the army. The men began to ask why they should fight against their countrymen, who only required a redress of grievances. The King and Council were alarmed lest Cade should now advance upon London, for he soon returned to his old position at Blackheath. As a concession to public opinion, one of the obnoxious ministers, James Fiennes, Lord Say de Sele, lord-chamberlain of the household, was sent to the Tower.

June 29. Disaffection also showed itself in other parts of the country. William Ayscough, Bishop of Salisbury, had become unpopular, owing partly to his frequent absence from the diocese, rendered necessary by his attendance on the King, and partly to avarice and inhospitality which were alleged against him. He had retired for safety to Edington, about three miles from Westbury, in Wiltshire. Some of Cade's men followed him there. After plundering his house, they dragged him from the altar of the magnificent church, while he was in the act of celebrating Mass, took him to the top of a hill in the neighbourhood, and there did him to death by stoning. He was buried in the chapel attached to the house of the Bonhommes.

The King and Queen retired, out of harm's way, to Kenilworth. Of the disbanded army 1,000 men were selected as trustworthy, and sent, under the command of Lord Scales and Sir Matthew Gough, to defend the Tower, which it was feared might be soon attacked.

At the request of Chancellor Kemp, Archbishop Stafford, who was a popular man, undertook to go to the camp at Blackheath as a mediator. He took with him his kinsman, Humphrey, Duke of Buckingham. When brought to the presence of the rebel leader they found him arrayed in the splendid armour of the slain Sir Humphrey, which must have been a galling sight to them, but they could not complain of his using the spoils of war.

Pardon for the rebels, and redress of all grievances was promised. But Cade would not treat with any one, save the King in person, to whom he professed himself perfectly loyal. He would not lay down his arms, he declared, until the incompetent ministers were dismissed, and wiser ones chosen, evidently meaning the Duke of York and his friends. The brave old Archbishop then went back, and joined the forces in the Tower.

July 1. Cade advanced to Southwark and then demanded entrance into London, which, after slight demur, was granted to him. The gates

July 3. were opened, and he led his followers over the drawbridge in the centre, cutting the rope which held it in position with his sword as he passed. He rode through the streets, keeping all his followers in good order, till he came to London stone, and striking it with his sword, said: 'Now is Mortimer lord of this city.' The same evening all returned quietly to Southwark. Next day he caused Lord Say to July 4. be brought from the Tower. How that nobleman came to be surrendered by the Tower authorities there is not anything to show. But he was arraigned for treason before the mayor and judges, whom Cade compelled to sit in the Guildhall, as were also the widowed Duchess of Suffolk, the Bishop of Salisbury, who, as we have seen, had been already murdered, and others. None of the accused. fortunately for them, were present except Lord Say, who claimed a trial by his peers. Cade ordered his men to take him from the officers who had him in charge, and carry him to the standard in Cheapside, where his head was cut off and set on a pole. Lord Say's son-in-law, William Cromer, Sheriff of Kent, who was one of those specially named as extortioners in the 'Complaint,' was captured at Mile-end, and, without any other accusation or trial, was beheaded, and the head fixed on a pole. These two heads were carried about, and made to kiss each other, much to the disgust of all honest citizens. With these examples before them the mob became ferocious; neither property nor life was safe; Cade himself pillaged the house in which he had dined that day. It was therefore resolved not to allow them to re-enter the City. Some of the soldiers in the Tower were set to guard the bridge; the insurgents received news of this move and determined to try and force an entrance. A conflict July 5. ensued that lasted the whole of Sunday night, and cost many lives, including Gough, the leader of the loyalists. At nine o'clock in the July 6. morning a truce for a short time was agreed upon by mutual consent.

The Archbishop of Canterbury seized the opportunity. He drew up a general pardon for all, including prisoners released from the gaols of the King's Bench and Marshalsea, who would return quietly to their homes, and after having the Great Seal attached,* went into Southwark with Waynflete, Bishop of Winchester. The offer was joyfully accepted and the multitude began to disperse.

Cade repented his acceptance of the pardon, again raised his flag, but found few men to join him. They retired to Rochester, where they commenced plundering, and then to quarrelling over the division of the booty. Their leader mounted his horse and fled towards Sussex. He was pursued by Alexander Iden, the new July 11. Sheriff of Kent, who slew him in a garden at Heathfield, and soon applied for the reward of 1,000 marks which had been offered for the traitor's head. The head was afterwards fixed on the gate-house with the face turned towards Kent. The body was quartered and sent to Blackheath and three towns, in different parts of the country.

There is a hamlet in Sussex called Cade Street, near Heathfield, on the Battle road, which is said to derive its name from this man. A pillar marks the supposed place where he was shot.

* Dr. Hook says that, although no longer Chancellor, he incurred the responsibility of attaching the seal, which was left in the Tower, though for doing so he might have been accused of treason.

It was probably about this time that King Henry received a present of the Golden Rose from Pope Nicholas V., who explained that it was annually consecrated by the reigning Pontiff on Mid-Lent, or Refreshment, Sunday, and bestowed only on such Kings as had great faith and devotion, who might be disposed to assist the Church in a war against the Turks. The King received the present with pleasure, and would gladly have assisted had his means allowed. But he was in a poverty-stricken condition, and Chancellor Kemp had to explain to the proper quarter in Rome that, in the present state of the country, it would not be possible to obtain any assistance towards the object indicated.

Without asking leave of absence, or permission of any kind, the Duke of YORK suddenly left Ireland, placing the government of the country in the hands of James Butler, Earl of Ormond, who is said to have been the originator of the deadly feud with the house of Kildare, which lasted for generations. York landed in Anglesey and soon gathered together an army of 4,000 men. With these he set off to London, proclaiming that the Duke of Somerset ought to be put on his trial, and that the King should have some competent person to assist him in the government, thereby, of course, meaning himself.

Sept. 1. He had an interview with Henry, whom he tried to bully into submission. On a promise being given him that a Parliament should be summoned, he retired to his castle of Fotheringhay.

The return of the Duke of SOMERSET was hailed with joy and thankfulness by both the King and Queen, and he soon occupied the position which had been held by Suffolk. Henry always regarded his Beaufort relatives with an eye of favour. In the present case he probably hoped to have some one sufficiently strong to effectually

Sept. 11. oppose the Duke of York. Somerset was appointed Constable of England, and in that capacity, accompanied by Cardinal Kemp, the Chancellor, attended upon King Henry when he rode to Rochester. An assize was held there for the trial of the men concerned in the late riots, and several were executed.

The people, generally, were enraged against Somerset, in consequence of his losses in France. They stigmatized him as a traitor, and declared he had surrendered Caen on account of a woman's fears. The story goes that, during the siege, a stone shot fell between the Duchess and her children, which so much frightened her that she besought her husband, with tears in her eyes, to leave the place. He had no option, for it could not have been defended without adequate forces. She did not come of a race likely to act a coward's part. She was Lady Eleanor Beauchamp, second daughter of Richard the 'good Earl' of Warwick, own sister to Margaret, Countess of Salisbury, and Elizabeth, wife of George Neville, Lord Latimer, third son of Ralph, Earl of Westmorland by his second marriage. She was also half-sister to Anne, Countess of Warwick, who had married Lord Latimer's nephew, Richard Neville, afterwards the well-known 'King-maker.' There is little doubt that Somerset, though inclined to justice, and gentle in manner, yet could be proud and haughty. He was rich, beyond the dreams of avarice, as one might suppose, and still he coveted more. As the nearest male relation of the King he may have cherished hopes of succeeding to the throne, should Henry die childless. Somerset was second-cousin, York only fourth-cousin, to the King. Hence the great dislike manifested for him by the Duke of York, and by York's friends and supporters, the populace.

Shakspere, in a poetical and dramatical scene in the Temple Gardens, which he places after the relief of Orleans by the 'Maid,' makes the Duke of York, or Richard Plantagenet as he is styled—he was actually the first to be called by that name—say :

> 'Let him that is a true-born gentleman
> From off this brier pluck a white rose with me,'

to which Somerset replies :

> 'Let him that is no coward, nor no flatterer,
> But dare maintain the party of the truth,
> Pluck a red rose from off this thorn with me.'

Suffolk then plucks a red and Warwick a white one. The Duke of Somerset at that time was John Beaufort, and he was a prisoner of war. Richard Plantagenet was then only seventeen, and the Earl of Warwick was Richard Beauchamp.

As a matter of fact, some years after the rose had been brought to England, it was adopted as a badge by the Houses of Lancaster and York respectively.

The Parliament met, in due course, at Westminster, and was opened by Cardinal Kemp as Chancellor. It was a stormy session, chiefly occupied by quarrels and disputes between the leaders of the two factions. _{Nov.}

It was proposed by Thomas Young, member for Bristol, that the King not having any child to succeed him, the Duke of York should be declared heir to the throne. The Government was, however, sufficiently strong to cause the mover's committal to the Tower.

The Commons adopted a Bill for the attainder of the late Duke of Suffolk, and the removal from court of the Duke of Somerset, the Duchess of Suffolk, Booth, Bishop of Coventry and Lichfield, and others who were attached friends of the King. Henry refused his consent to any attaint on Suffolk's memory. He saw no reason, he said, why he should dismiss the lords and others who had been about his person for many years, but the remainder he would send away for a year. The Duchess of Suffolk was afterwards put on trial at her own request, and triumphantly acquitted.

Somerset fared badly when he left the House. The populace pillaged his lodging at Blackfriars, and would most probably have killed him when he arrived in his barge, but for the timely intervention of Thomas Courtenay, Earl of Devon, who had married his sister, Lady Margaret Beaufort. _{Dec. 1.}

As a demonstration against such lawlessness, the King and his _{Dec. 3.}

Lords rode through the City in armour, the way on either side being kept by armed citizens. The Londoners, for the most part, had never seen a display so brilliant.*

Parliament was prorogued from time to time, and did not meet again for two years. York retired to his castle at Ludlow.

1451. Sept. 21. The court was at Greenwich when Somerset was released from his temporary arrest, appointed Captain of Calais and Controller of the King's Household.

Dec. 26. Amidst the disturbed feelings which at this time governed all men, friends and foes alike, Henry's contemplative mind, yearning for peace, sought refuge in prayer. Attended by the Duke of Somerset, the Earl of Shrewsbury and James Butler, Earl of Wiltshire, son of James, fourth Earl of Ormond, he made a pilgrimage to Canterbury. At the west door of the cathedral he was received by the Archbishops of Canterbury and York, Waynflete, Bishop of Winchester, and Thomas Bourchier, Bishop of Ely, together with the prior of the convent and members of the chapter. Soon he was seen prostrate before the shrine of St. Thomas, the once mighty prelate, who had made a stronger and more formidable Henry tremble. His devotions being ended, a Council was held. It was the last public appearance of the good Archbishop Stafford, who died on May 25 next following.

1452. Jan. 9. From his castle of Ludlow the Duke of York issued a manifesto of loyalty, and offered to make an oath on the sacrament to that effect, before the Bishop of Hereford and the Earl of Shrewsbury. About the same time he wrote to the burgesses of Shrewsbury that he intended marching against the Duke of Somerset, and prayed for their help.

Feb. 3. At the head of a large force he set off for the capital. The King, having received intimation of his movements, went forth at the head of an army to meet him.

Feb. 16. Being denied entrance to the City, York proceeded to Dartford, where he probably expected to be joined by many Kentish men.

March 1. The King followed in his steps, and encamped on Blackheath. Thus a royal, and apparently a rebel, army were only a few miles distant from each other. But neither made a move.

The Bishops of Winchester and Ely, together with the Earls of Salisbury and Warwick, friends and relatives of York, were sent to enquire the meaning of his appearance in arms. He declared he had no ill intentions towards the King, to whom he was perfectly loyal, and simply desired the removal and trial of certain persons, among whom Somerset was chief, who had misgoverned the people. The King weakly consented that Somerset, his greatest supporter, should be placed in custody until he answered such charges as York could bring against him, and that a new Council should be formed of which York himself should be one, in order to decide upon all matters in dispute. Satisfied so far, the Duke returned to camp, and disbanded his army. Then he went, unarmed, to visit the King in

* Introduction to Paston Letters.

his tent, and express his loyalty towards him. Much to his astonishment, he there found Somerset in attendance, Mutual recrimination followed between the rivals. York boldly charged Somerset with corruption, oppression, and other crimes. Somerset confidently rebutted such imputations. He turned the tables on York by accusing him of high treason, and a design to dethrone the King in his own favour. When York left the tent he was arrested and sent forward to London, but was only lodged in his own house.

The question was, how to dispose of him. Somerset advocated his being brought to trial and made to confess his sins. This would have led to his execution, and Henry had a horror of blood-shedding, especially in the case of a relative. Such a proceeding would have been full of danger, as Richard's eldest son, Edward, Earl of March, at that time not quite ten years of age, was reported to be advancing, at the head of 10,000 men, to the relief of his father. This alarmed the Council. The Duke was offered his liberty on condition that he would again swear fealty to the King. To this he consented.

> 'To his own good word
> The good and honourable man will act,
> Oaths will not curb the wicked.'

At the altar of St. Paul's, on the sacrament, Richard of York made oath to bear to King Henry faith and truth until his life's end, as a true and humble servant, and never attempt anything against his royal person. He was then allowed to retire to his castle at Wigmore. *March 10.*

The good and simple King, believing all danger to be now over, offered a general pardon to all who would apply for it. It showed the love of peace ruling the heart of a humane and gracious sovereign. Some thousands, among whom was Young, the member for Bristol, sought for and obtained these sealed pardons. *April 7.*

The King and court made a progress into the Midland and Western counties, going as far south as Exeter, and afterwards visited Cambridge, journeying from there to Peterborough. *July, Oct.*

A Parliament was summoned to meet at Reading, when liberal supplies of money and men were voted for the support of the Earl of Shrewsbury, the news of whose first successes had just been received. The King personally thanked the Commons for their great bounty. Henry took advantage of the occasion to ennoble his two half-brothers: Edmund of Hadham was created Earl of Richmond and Premier Earl of England; Jasper of Hatfield was created Earl of Pembroke. They were at that date respectively about twenty-three and twenty-two years of age. *1453. March 6.*

Parliament was summoned to meet again at Reading on November 12. But before that day arrived many unexpected things had happened. News had just come to hand of the loss of Guienne, and, at the same time, King Henry, while staying at the Palace of Clarendon, three miles from Salisbury, first showed symptoms of the malady which he had inherited from his grandfather, Charles VI. *Aug. 10.*

Oct. 13. France. By slow degrees he was brought back to Westminster There, at ten minutes before nine o'clock on Sunday, the feast of the Translation of St. Edward, was born the only child of Henry and Margaret, whom Speed quaintly but truly calls 'the child of sorrow and infelicity.'

Next day the boy was baptized EDWARD, after the Saxon Saint, by Waynflete, Bishop of Winchester. The sponsors were Cardinal Kemp, who had been translated from York to Canterbury, on the death of Archbishop Stafford; Edmund Beaufort, Duke of Somerset; and the Duchess of Buckingham, Lady Anne Neville, tenth daughter of the Earl of Westmorland. But the King was not present. He was for a time without the sense of feeling, and without memory. He had the power neither to walk properly, nor to raise himself up erect, nor was he well able to stir from the spot where he was sitting. In short, he was mentally and bodily a perfect wreck. The ceremony was consequently a very sad one.

Reports were spread by partisans of the Duke of York derogatory to the Queen's honour. As in a somewhat similar case 235 years afterwards, it was noised abroad that the child was a changeling, if not illegitimate. Some went so far as to name the Duke of Somerset as the father. The nation, as a whole, did not lend any countenance to such false statements, but received the news of the birth of an heir to the throne with joy, and looked forward to an undisputed succession.

Parliament had been called together for November 11, and, the King being ill, the Duke of York regained the ascendancy. One of his first acts was to commit his rival, the Duke of Somerset, to the Tower, on a demand made by John Mowbray, third Duke of Norfolk, that Somerset's conduct in France and England should be made subjects of enquiry by people learned in the laws in both countries. There for the present we must leave him.

SKETCH XXI.

UNITY, PEACE, AND CONCORD.

1454. THE New Year opened badly, to judge from a 'news-letter' in the Paston correspondence. Everybody appeared to be arming, in dread of some person or some event unknown. The attendants on the King asked for a garrison at Windsor. The Archbishop of Canterbury charged all his servants to be well and completely armed for the safeguarding of his person. The Duke of Buckingham caused to be made 2,000 'bandes with knottes'— scarves with the Stafford knot, his badge—for the use of his followers. The Earl of Wiltshire and Ormond, the Lords Bonville, Poynings, Clifford, and Beaumont were, each and all, gathering men together.

The last-named was sixth Baron and first Viscount, and married to Katherine Neville, widow of John Mowbray, second Duke of Norfolk. The writer of the letter then proceeds: 'The Duke of Exeter in his own person hath been at Tuxforth, near Doncaster, in the north countree, and there the Lord Egremont mette him, and they two be sworn together,' probably to gather troops and arrange matters with their friends. The Lord Egremont was Sir Thomas Percy, grandson of the well-remembered Hotspur.

In consequence of this report, it was deemed advisable that the Duke of York himself should go down into Yorkshire. His appearance sufficed to put an end to the disturbances. But Exeter, it would seem, left there, and later on we read of his being cited to appear before the Council on May 16. Probably he did not go, for, in another of the Paston Letters of June 8, the writer says: 'The Duke of Exeter is here covertly. God send him good counsel hereafter.'

The news-letter further says 'the Duke of Somerset's herbergeour' took up all the lodgings he could get in the neighbourhood of the Tower, and spies were sent by him into every lord's house, 'to report unto the said Duke all that they can see or hear respecting him.' The DUKE OF YORK and his son EDWARD were to come, each with his separate household and retainers. The Earl of Salisbury was to arrive about the same time, with some hundreds of followers. The Earl of Warwick was expected with 1,000 men. But the strangest part of the news is that the King's half-brothers, the newly-created Earls of Richmond and Pembroke, were to come with the Duke's party, each with a goodly following. The writer adds: 'The King's brethren ben like to be arrested if they come.'

About New Year's Day. when the royal family was at Windsor, Jan. 1. Humphrey, Duke of Buckingham, went on a visit of ceremony or condolence. While there he took the young Prince in his arms, and begged the King to give the child a father's blessing. No answer came. Once more he tried, but again he failed. Then Queen Margaret took the boy, and, kneeling down at her husband's feet, prayed him for a benison on their son. If the words reached the poor invalid's ears, they did not convey any meaning to his mind. For one moment his eyes seemed to rest on the babe, but they were lustreless and wavering, and he soon turned them away again.

The Parliament, which had been adjourned from Reading, met at Feb. 14. Westminster, and was opened by the Duke of York as Royal Commissioner. The Commons, however, had not a Speaker. Thomas Thorne, a Baron of the Exchequer as well as Speaker, had been thrown into prison by the Duke of York until he should pay the sum of £1,000, which had been awarded against him in an action for trespass. The Commons in vain petitioned for his release. They had to elect another Speaker.

The report of the death of Cardinal Kemp, Archbishop of Canter- March 22. bury and Chancellor, rendered it more than ever necessary that a

Council should be formed. A deputation of peers, headed by the Bishop of Winchester, was therefore appointed to wait on the King at Windsor, and receive his commands. They were ushered into the King's presence just after he had dined. The first question put was in regard to his health, and an assurance was given of their desire to hear of his recovery. Not a word came from Henry; not a sign did he give that he was even aware of their presence. They tried again, by telling him of their efforts to carry on the affairs of the State. Henry still continued mute. The Bishop of Winchester then told the King that, as the Lords had not dined, they would retire for that purpose, and wait on him again afterwards.

After dinner, accordingly, they went back. They found the King in precisely the same position. They tried him again; but to all their prayers they could get no answer. It was then proposed that he should be taken into another room. Two of his men were called in, who lifted him from his chair and led him to his chamber. Even that did not rouse him. One last attempt they made to get a reply by asking if his Highness wished them to remain any longer. Not a nod of approval, not a sign of dissent, was given. All was in vain, and with sorrowful hearts the peers returned to London.

March 27. On receipt of their report, which was made a record of Parliament, the lords spiritual and temporal elected and nominated RICHARD, DUKE OF YORK, to be 'PROTECTOR and defender of the realm and Church of England during the King's pleasure.' The actual date of the creation of the office was April 3.

The Protector's first act, the day before his own office was created, was to give the Great Seal to his brother-in-law, Richard, Earl of Salisbury, the only layman, as Dr. Hook observes, who was Chancellor in the reign of Henry VI.*

His next act was, at the request of the House of Commons, to nominate the Bishop of Ely to the Archbishopric of Canterbury. It no doubt gave him great pleasure to do so, as the prelate was a connection of his own by marriage.

THOMAS BOURCHIER, the Bishop in question, was a younger son of William, Earl of Eu, who had married ANNE, the daughter of Thomas of Woodstock, DUKE OF GLOUCESTER, and widow of Edmund Stafford, Earl of Stafford. HUMPHREY STAFFORD, Duke of Buckingham, her son, was therefore uterine brother of the Archbishop designate and of Henry Bourchier, Viscount Bourchier, his elder brother, who had married ISABEL OF YORK, sister of the Protector. There was a sister, Eleanor, married to John Mowbray, third Duke of Norfolk.

In a letter to his brother, on September 6, William Paston writes: 'My Lord of Canterbury hath received his cross, and I was with him in the King's chamber when he made his homage.'

Edward of Westminster, the son of King Henry, being Duke of Cornwall by birth, was created Prince of Wales and Earl of Chester.

* The first lay Chancellor was Sir Robert Bourchier, in 1340.

The guardianship of the sea was entrusted to five captains—the April 3.
Earl of Salisbury; John Talbot, second Earl of Shrewsbury, son of
the old hero; the Earl of Wiltshire; John Tiptoft, Earl of Worcester;
and Lord Stourton.

The captainship of the town and castle of Calais was taken from July 17.
the Duke of Somerset, and assumed by the Protector himself.

Towards the close of December, the King's health was so much
improved that on Christmas Day he received visitors. The first use Dec. 25.
he made of his recovered faculties was, on the next day but one, Dec. 27.
being St. John's Day, to send his almoner with an offering to Canterbury, and his secretary with a special gift to the shrine of St. Edward.

On the Monday, the Queen took the young Prince to him. Then Dec. 30.
he asked the boy's name, and, on being told it was Edward, he
thanked God therefor. And he said he never knew till that time
what had been said to him, nor where he had been while he was ill.
He asked who were the boy's godfathers, and was well pleased on
being told.

The Queen then told him that Cardinal Kemp was dead, and he
replied: 'Then one of the wisest lords of this land is dead.'

On the day after Twelfth Day, the Bishop of Winchester and the 1455.
Prior of St. John of Jerusalem were with him, and he spoke to them Jan. 7.
as well as ever he did; and when they came out they wept for joy.
'And he saith he is in charity with all the world, and so he would all
the lords were. And now he saith mattins of Our Lady, and even-
song, and heareth his Mass devoutly.'

With the King's recovery, the Protectorate of York of course Feb. 5.
ceased. Henry liberated the Duke of Somerset from the Tower,
who truly said he had been there confined without due cause, and
without being brought to trial, for a year and more than ten weeks.
In order to avoid any further dispute between York and Somerset, March 6.
Henry took the government of Calais into his own hands, and he
persuaded the two rivals to submit their other differences to the
arbitration of eight lords, who were to give in their decision by
June 20. Before that day arrived a verdict was rendered unnecessary
by the death of one of the principals.

The Great Seal was taken from the Earl of Salisbury and given to March 7.
Archbishop Bourchier, who, though a strong supporter of the Duke
of York and his party, was respected for his personal as well as his
official character. He received the seals at Greenwich and took the
oath of office before the King, who was with the Council.

The Duke of York was dissatisfied and retired to Ludlow. But it
is difficult to tell what position he intended to take up, and whether
he should be held as the friend or foe of his King. He was an able
man, and perhaps a moderate man. He was also an ambitious man.
But to a certain extent he was weak, irresolute, and easily swayed by
minds stronger than his own. Those he found in his brother-in-law,
the Earl of Salisbury, and his nephew, the Earl of Warwick. The
Nevilles of the second family of Earl Ralph, although he, as we have

seen, had been a firm supporter of Henry of Bolingbroke, and their mother was a Beaufort, were strongly, bitterly, opposed to the whole family, and while they drifted into rebellion, the Nevilles of the first marriage, the Earl of Westmorland and his brothers, remained staunch and true to King Henry. Both the Earl and Countess had now been many years dead.

Richard's visions of a crown were at first but shadowy. The birth of Prince Edward probably dispelled them for a time. He had had a taste of power, and appeared to view the loss of his office almost as an insult. He felt he had been mistrusted—

'Suspicion always haunts the guilty mind'—

and from that state of feeling, the transition to active disaffection was not difficult. Perhaps the most potent influence in eventually bringing him to a determination was that exercised by his wife, Cecily Neville, the sister of Salisbury, 'who was remarkable for her beauty, and still more so for her indomitable pride. She had a throne-room at Fotheringhay, where she gave receptions with the state of a Queen.'*

May.   Having taken counsel with his friends, Richard collected an army of three to five thousand Welshmen, and at their head marched
May 21. towards London. It was afterwards stated that from Ware he addressed a letter to the King, which was never delivered, protesting that he only appeared in arms to defend himself against his enemies, but was a liege-man and true, and simply desired an audience.

Hearing of York's muster, the King left London with a following of 3,000 men and remained the night at Watford. He had with him the Dukes of Buckingham and Somerset; the Earls of Pembroke, Dorset, Wiltshire, Stafford, Northumberland. Devonshire; Lords Clifford, Sudeley, Roos, with other knights and squires.

May 22.   Next day, being the Thursday before Whitsun Day, they marched to St. Albans. The royal standard was planted on a slight rise called Goselow, formerly Sandiford, in St. Peter's Street. The King ordered the barriers to be well and stoutly kept, as he had heard of York's arrival, indeed, might have seen the banners waving—now first raised in actual civil war.

The Duke's army was encamped in the Key field as early as seven o'clock. The Earls of Salisbury and Warwick, Lord Fauconberg and Sir Robert Clinton were in command. Richard sent, about ten o'clock, with the usual expressions of loyalty, to desire that such as he and his counsel should accuse might be dealt with according to their deserts. He then reminded Henry of former promises not kept, and said no such promise or security would now be of any avail, and there could be no satisfaction until the accused were dead, or they, the accusers, were dead.

Henry in reply charged York and his friends to avoid the field, and not offer resistance to him in his own kingdom. Rather than give up

---

* Miss Strickland's 'Life of Elizabeth Woodville.'

any of his lords to be dealt with by traitors, Henry declared he would fight, and, if necessary, die. 'I shall know what traitors dare rise up against me, whereby I am in great heaviness and distress. By the faith I owe to St. Edward and the Crown of England, I shall destroy them all.'*

Brave words these from peaceable Henry. He must have been extremely angered when he gave expression to them.

The struggle for power was now to be decided by blows, not words or votes. Between eleven and twelve it began.

The Royalists had the advantage in position, as the streets and lanes were narrow, and well barricaded. The inhabitants, it would appear, were neutral. York was three times repulsed at the barriers, which were defended by Thomas, Lord Clifford. Warwick, learning this, found a circuitous road, and broke through some gardens between the signs of the Key and the Chequers in Holywell Street. Then the trumpets blew, and there was a loud cry, 'A Warwick! a Warwick!' York and his forces soon followed. Sir Robert Ogle with 600 men took the market-place before anyone was aware of it, and thus contributed largely to the result of the day. There was a mighty fight between the contending parties. But it was short, sharp, and decisive. In half-an-hour all was over.

> 'The Lord Clifford o'er busie in werkyng,
> At the barres them met sore fighting,
> Was slain that day upon his own assaut,
> As eche man said it was his own defaute.'

Some writers claim for this Thomas, Lord Clifford the credit of suggesting the plan adopted by bold Talbot at the siege of Pontoise, an account of which you will find in a former sketch.

Sir Philip Wentworth, who bore the King's standard, threw it down and cowardly fled, for which, said the Duke of Norfolk, he ought to be hung.

> 'Th'erle of Wiltshire with five hundred men
> Fled fro the Kyng full fast that tyme awaye,'

and Thorpe, the late Speaker, followed his example.

Henry Percy, second Earl of Northumberland, son of Hotspur, who had married Eleanor Neville, sister of Salisbury, was among the slain.

Margery Jourdemain, the Witch of Eye, is credited with having told the Duke of Somerset that he would be defeated and slain at a castle; but that as long as he kept his forces out in the open field he would be sure of victory and safety.

Shakspere thus refers to it:

> ' Underneath an alehouse' paltry sign,
> The castle in St. Albans, Somerset
> Hath made the wizard famous in his death,'

an allusion to the prediction 'Let him shun castles' put into the mouth of one of the spirits called up by Bolingbroke.

* *Archæologia*, vol. xx.

Lord Clinton, Sir Bertram Entwyssle, Sir J. Wenlock, Knight, and many other knights and squires to the number of 41, were slain. The total number killed was at most 120. Of these, 48 were laid to rest with proper funeral rites in the Chapel of the Virgin, in the Abbey, and the remainder were buried in some less distinguished spot.

Several of the leaders were wounded—all by arrows: King Henry in the neck, the Duke of Buckingham in the face, and his son Humphrey, Earl of Stafford, in the hand. The Earl of Devonshire, Lord Sudeley, and the Marquis of Dorset, son of Somerset, were also among the sufferers. The last named was so badly wounded that he had to be taken home in a cart.

The majority of Henry's party was despoiled of horses and armour, and York's men began plundering the town. Fearing that they might attack his beloved Abbey, Abbot Whethamstede supplied them with food and drink, and thus saved it for a time.

York and his relatives found Henry all alone in the house of a tanner, to which he had fled for safety when wounded. Bending their knees, they, in cruel mockery, bade him rejoice that the traitor Somerset was slain. They besought grace and forgiveness for what they had done, and prayed to be taken as his liege-men, as they never intended any hurt to his person. The King took them to grace, subsequently acquitted them of all disloyal acts, and pronounced them good and faithful subjects.*

York then led his captive—such he actually was—with outward show and respect to the shrine of St. Alban, where Henry, at least, would doubtless be glad to offer up his prayers, and afterwards took him to the apartments allotted to him in the Abbey.

It is related that the Duke of Norfolk and the Earl of Oxford arrived the day after the struggle was over with 6,000 men. Also that the Earl of Shrewsbury, Lord Cromwell, and Sir Thomas Stanley were on the way with 10,000 more.

May 23. On the morrow, at six o'clock in the evening, the King and all the lords returned to London.

The excitement had been too much for Henry, and there were symptoms of a return of his malady, although he managed to bear up for a time. He was first lodged in the palace of the Bishop of London, but a week later he removed with the Queen and her boy to Hertford, where they remained some months.

July 9. The King was able to go up to Town and open Parliament in person. York and his party were acquitted of disloyal practices, and the whole blame for the late disastrous meeting was thrown on Somerset, as having suppressed the letters already mentioned. Little more was done than to renew vows of allegiance to King Henry and his son.

Henry, Viscount Bourchier was appointed Treasurer on May 9. Richard, Earl of Warwick, was appointed captain of Calais on August 4. Parliament was prorogued to November 12.

* *Archæologia*, vol. xx.

Before that day arrived Henry was again taken ill. York received Nov. 11. a commission to open the session as the King's Lieutenant. With well simulated humility he agreed to accept once more the office of 'Protector and Defender of the Realm and Church.' But he made it a condition that it should not be as before, revocable at the will of the King, but 'by the King in Parliament, with the advice and assent Nov. 19. of the lords spiritual and temporal.' The office was, however, to cease upon Prince Edward attaining to years of discretion.

Our constitutional historian, Hallam, remarks on this clause 'that whatever passed as to this second protectorate was altogether of a revolutionary complexion.'*

According to one of the Paston Letters, dated February 9, the 1456. Lords of York and Warwick went to Parliament with 300 men, in their leather coats and well armed, as the former expected to be discharged of his office. But no other lords put in an appearance. This same letter informs us that the King, who had by that time recovered, desired that York should be appointed Chief Counsellor and Lieutenant by patent, but with power not so great as that conferred on him by Parliament.

However true or not that may be, Henry went in person to the Feb. 25. House, and relieved York of his office of Protector. Parliament was thereupon dissolved.

The King retired to Shene, where he had the company of his half-brother, Jasper, Earl of Pembroke. The Queen and the young Prince made progresses in different parts of the country. We read of their being at Bristol, Tutbury, and Chester, where Margaret was always sure of a warm welcome. One strange piece of news is: 'My Lord of York is at Sandal still, and waiteth on the Queen, and she on him.' They were evidently watching each other's movements; but there is nothing to tell us with certainty what their object really was.

Both the King and Queen went to Coventry, a favourite place Oct. with them, where they were received with hearty demonstrations of welcome. Henry apparently travelled in a very leisurely manner. He set off from Windsor, where he was then staying, about the middle of August, and went through Wycombe, Kenilworth, Lichfield, Leicester, and then back to Coventry. There a Council was Oct. 7. called, to which the Duke of Buckingham and HENRY BEAUFORT, the new DUKE OF SOMERSET, then about twenty years of age, son of the Duke slain at St. Albans, were specially summoned. Two days Oct. 5. before the meeting, Viscount Bourchier was displaced from his office of Treasurer in favour of the Earl of Shrewsbury. Within a week Oct. 11. the Archbishop resigned the seals to Waynflete, Bishop of Winchester. It is said that the Duke of Buckingham was much offended at this removal of his half-brothers, the Chancellor and the Treasurer, and began to incline more to the side of the Duke of York, but it must have been a very temporary change, as he was a loyal man to

* Hallam's 'Middle Ages,' vol. iii., p. 287.

the last, and died fighting for his King four years later. Perhaps it was all owing to the circumstance that York discovered, or thought he had, a plot for his arrest, if not assassination, and that Buckingham then stood his friend and calmed him down.

Buckingham acted the part of peacemaker on another occasion. For some reason unknown, the Duke of Somerset's men and the watchmen of Coventry came to blows. The alarm-bell was rung, to the great disturbance of all the lords. The townsmen came to the help of the watch, and two or three of them were killed. Then Somerset himself was in jeopardy of being assaulted, but that, as said, Buckingham interposed and quieted the people.

1457. The state of the country was unsettled. Foreign cruisers infested
Aug. 20. the Channel. An attack was made by a French squadron, under the command of Pierre de Brézé, upon Sandwich, when they despoiled the town of much property, and carried away many prisoners. It may have been in consequence of this affray that the Earl of Warwick
Oct. 3. was appointed Captain to guard the sea. This annoyed the Duke of Exeter, who had held the office, and a few months later he received the sum of £1,000 as compensation.

At a Council held before the King at Westminster, the lords refused to proceed with any business until Reginald Pecock, Bishop of Chichester, had withdrawn. The Bishop was subsequently put on his trial for propagating false doctrine, and affirming the supremacy of the Pope over the Church and realm. Pecock was eventually degraded from his office and confined in Thorney Abbey, about seven miles north-east of Peterborough, where he died.

The opposing parties in the State were silently watching each
1458. other, and each making preparations. At length the King, urged on by the Archbishop of Canterbury, resolved to make an effort at reconciliation, and a Council was summoned to meet at Westminster.
Jan. First came the Duke of York, with his household only, 140 horse, and went to his fortified mansion, Baynard's Castle, which was burnt
Jan. 31. down in the Great Fire of 1666. The Duke of Somerset, with 200 horse, and the Duke of Exeter, arrived, and were lodged outside
Feb. 1. Temple Bar. The Earl of Salisbury came next, with 400 horse and 80 knights and squires, and took up his abode at his house in the City, called 'Le Erber.' Henry Percy, the third Earl of Northumberland, with his brother Thomas, Lord Egremont, and John, Lord Clifford (son of Thomas, slain at St. Albans), with 1,500 followers,
Feb. 13. were quartered at Charing Cross. The Earl of Warwick, having been kept back at Calais by contrary winds, came at last, with 500 men, all clothed in red jackets, with his badge, the ragged staff, embroidered on the front and back. He took up his quarters at the Grey Friars. Thus, all the Yorkists were within, and the Lancastrians outside, the walls.

The Mayor of London, fearing disturbances might arise, had 5,000 citizens fully armed, and he rode at their head during the day in all quarters, to make sure that the peace was being kept. At night,

3,000 men, under three aldermen, kept watch until seven o'clock in the morning.

The King, after opening the Council, retired with the Queen to Berkhamstead, and several of the judges were with them.

Archbishop Bourchier, with the Bishop of Winchester and others, stayed at his palace at Lambeth. They acted as intermediaries. The resolutions arrived at by the one party at the Black Friars were by them communicated to the other side at the White Friars in Fleet Street, and the result was daily carried to the King.

Ultimately it was decided, on the initiative of the Archbishop, to March 24. whom great credit is due, that a chantry should be founded by the Yorkist leaders, for the good of the souls of the Lancastrian lords slain at St. Albans; that York should pay 5,000 marks to the widowed Duchess of Somerset and her children, and Warwick 1,000 to Lord Clifford; that all the actors in the late affray, living and dead, should be esteemed loyal subjects; and that Salisbury should release Lord Egremont from damages obtained against him for assault, on Percy giving assurance to keep the peace for ten years.

Next day, the Annunciation of our Lady, a court was held in the March 25. palace of the Bishop of London. The King, sitting in a chair of state, had the crown solemnly placed on his head by the Archbishop, while all the nobles stood around, divested of their martial garb. The Archbishop then went in procession to St. Paul's. The royal procession followed. The Duke of Somerset walked hand-in-hand with the Earl of Salisbury. The Duke of Exeter and the Earl of Warwick followed in like manner. The King, crowned, and bearing his sceptre, walked alone. The Queen was led by the Duke of York, and when the people saw her lovely face lit up with smiles, as she talked affably with her cavalier, they shouted for joy and gladness. The other nobles followed. When the west door of the cathedral was reached, they found the Archbishop in his full robes and wearing his mitre, the Bishop of Rochester bearing his cross, and his suffragan bishops surrounding him. All now went silently up the nave, though the lips of most were observed to move as if in silent prayer. All were incensed on arriving at the east end. The King and Queen had a faldstool provided, at which they knelt. Behind them all the nobles, and as many as could gain admittance, were prostrate while Mass was sung. After Benediction by the Archbishop, a grand Te Deum was sung, in which many joined, and also the Thanksgiving for Reconciliation.

It was a function just in accordance with Henry's heart and mind, and it is related that his face was illuminated by a most lovely smile. He hoped that peace was now assured, and it was one of the happiest days of his life.

SKETCH XXII.

DEPOSED.

1458. June.
TIDINGS came from Calais of a great fight between a fleet of twenty-eight strange ships and five ships with seven small pinnaces, which were all that the Earl of WARWICK could muster wherewith to encounter them on the day after Trinity Sunday. Thus he was considerably overmatched. Nevertheless, after an engagement of six hours, he carried six of the ships into harbour. But, as one who took part in the fray says, it was after a loss of two hundred and eighty Englishmen, and two hundred and forty of the foreigners. He adds, 'Forsooth, we were well and truly beaten. Men say there was not so great a battle upon the sea these forty winters.'*

Complaints being received from the Hanse Towns, whose merchants were the owners of the above-named ships, and the merchandise contained therein, the Earl was summoned to London, to give an account of his proceedings to the Council.

Nov. It unfortunately happened that, one day as he left the court where the enquiry was being held, a quarrel arose between one of his retainers and one of the King's household, in which the latter was severely wounded. His fellow-servants seeing this, came to his assistance, and a general scrimmage ensued, in which the King's retinue fared the worst. Warwick declared afterwards that this was an attack made on himself, and that he had great difficulty in reaching his barge in safety.

'Coming events cast their shadows before.'

A turning-point was reached. The Earl suddenly left London, and went to consult his father, Salisbury, and his brother-in-law of York. Then he sailed to Calais, where he collected a large number of seasoned veterans who had served in the wars against France.

The 'dissimulated love-day,' as Fabyan styles it, was at an end.

Whatever schemes Salisbury and Warwick may have concocted at first, it is pretty evident that Richard of York soon became involved in them. Popular violence and general confusion were the results. Secret agents spread reports that the usurpation of the house of Lancaster had only been tolerated because the first two Kings were strong and able, but now, under a weak King, it was no good to sustain it for the sake of the 'foreign woman;' that the house of Mortimer had been unjustly deprived of its rights, and that the Duke of York, as lineal descendant of that house, ought now to be acknowledged as King.

To stigmatize Queen MARGARET as the 'foreign woman' was an absurdity, unless the slanderers had gone further and called our

* Paston Letters.

whole race of Kings, from the time of Henry II., also foreigners. Both sprang from the same county of Anjou. But Margaret's descent was nobler than that of Henry II., on his father's side, as she was a descendant in the direct line from Charles of Anjou, the brother of St. Louis, who traced his descent from Robert 'le fort' in the ninth century. Moreover, she had in her veins some of the same blood as her husband; Blanche of Castile, the grand-daughter of Henry II. of England, through her marriage with Louis VIII. of France, having been the mother of Louis IX. and his brother Charles.

Many of the Queens of England had, in truth, been 'foreign,' but it had never been brought against them as a stigma. Look only at the mother of Henry VI. If anyone was a foreigner, surely Katherine of Valois was one! And Katherine's sister, Isabel, the second wife of Richard II., whose first wife was Anne of Bohemia. Isabella of France, the curse of her husband, Edward II., and of the country; and another Isabella, she of Angoulême, who married that monster King John, were neither of them thought to be 'foreign.' Other instances will readily occur to anyone who reads these pages.

Margaret was one of the grandest and noblest, but at the same time one of the most unfortunate, of our Queens. Read what a French writer has said of her: 'England had never seen a Queen more worthy of a throne than Margaret; no woman surpassed her in beauty, and few men equalled her in courage: it seemed as if heaven had formed her in order to supply what was wanting in her husband to make him a great King.'

Margaret was forced by her husband's weakness to take the greater part of government on her own shoulders. That she should make many mistakes need not be a matter of surprise. Nor can one wonder that, in a cruel age, she should become assimilated to it.

'Doves will peck in safeguard of their brood.'

She had borne the taunts about her son's birth with patience, knowing how false they were. But when the time came that he was disinherited, then indeed she was roused. The lioness spirit within her awoke, and all England was amazed at her daring.

'What will not woman, gentle woman, dare,
When strong affection stirs her spirit up?'

The preparations of the discontented nobles were continued all through the winter.

KING HENRY retired to the Abbey of St. Alban to pass the Easter-tide, while his more energetic wife was travelling through the Midland counties and Cheshire with her boy, who distributed his badge of the white swan to all their well-wishers.

1459.

When Henry was leaving the Abbey, his total want of means prevented his acknowledging the hospitality he had experienced other than by ordering his best robe to be given to the abbot. The Treasurer, knowing that there was not such another robe in the royal wardrobe, and that he had not sufficient money to buy one, offered to the abbot fifty marks instead of the garment. Henry rather unwillingly consented to this arrangement, and only did so on the condition that the abbot should send some one up to London to receive the money, and that, when paid, it should be spent in vestments and altar frontals. The coins were subsequently counted out and handed over in the King's presence.

Meantime the EARL OF SALISBURY had been gathering an army around him. The King's friends were requested to assemble in arms at Leicester, and with money sufficient to last for two months.

At length it was known that Salisbury had set out from Middleham, about seventeen miles from Ripon, one of the great strongholds of the Nevilles, with a considerable force to join the Duke of York.

James Touchet, LORD AUDLEY, in obedience to the Queen's orders, gathered together an army of 10,000 men to oppose his progress.

Sept. 23. The two met, on St. Thekla's Day, which fell on a Sunday, at BLOREHEATH, in Staffordshire, and about one mile distant from Market Drayton, in Shropshire. The opposing forces were separated by a rivulet, which was an affluent of the river Tern. After one discharge of arrows on each side, the Yorkists received an order to retreat. It was a piece of generalship on the part of their leader that was crowned with success. Lord Audley, thinking the day was his own, ordered his men to cross the brook and pursue the flying enemy. The banks were steep, and rendered almost impossible to climb by the thousands of feet trampling them into mud. Before one half of the men had got across, and before they had time to re-form, Salisbury wheeled round upon them, and completely routed them. Lord Audley himself was slain, and with him 2,400 of the picked men of Cheshire.

Among the leaders who fell may be mentioned the following:

Sir John Egerton, of Egerton, a small village about three miles from Malpas. He was a grandson of Sir Urian de Egerton, who had fought for King Richard II. in the Scottish wars, and was progenitor of the present Sir Philip Henry Brian Egerton, of Oulton, near Tarporley.

Sir Hugh Venables, of Kinderton, now a suburb of Middlewich, the rise of whose family dated from the time of Hugh d'Avranches, Earl of Chester, 1070-1101.

Sir Thomas Dutton, of Dutton, five miles from Frodsham. At the survey for the Domesday Book the manor was vested in one Odard, but his descendants took the name of the place. The line continued until 1614, when an only daughter carried the estate to Lord Gerard.

Sir John Legh, of Booths, was of the same race as the Leghs of Lyme, a well-known Cheshire family. His father, Sir Robert Legh, is believed to have been one of the seven chief men who formed a bodyguard for the unfortunate Richard II. when in the hands of Bolingbroke at Chester, as told in Sketch VII.

Sir John Done, of Utkinton, near Tarporley, a family of hereditary chief foresters of Delamere from the time of King John, which continued until 1725. King James I., in 1617, honoured the then 'fair Lady Done' with his presence at a repast after he had enjoyed the sports of the forest.

Sir Richard Molyneux, of Sefton, in Lancashire, derived his descent from William de Molines, or Moleyns, who came in with the Conqueror. The name was changed to Molyneux in the reign of Richard II. by the then bearer of the title, Sir Richard. Adam, Bishop of Chichester, of whose murder you have read, was one of his sons. The Sir Richard slain in this battle was a grandson of the first Sir Richard Molyneux, and had married Elizabeth, eldest daughter of Thomas, Baron Stanley. He had stood very high in the estimation of King Henry.

Sir William Troutbeck, of Mobberley, Richard Done, and John Dutton, relatives of the knights above-named, were also slain, while Lord Dudley was wounded and taken prisoner.

Unfortunately, there was not unanimity among the men of Cheshire. Even families were divided.

> 'There Dutton Dutton kills; a Done doth kill a Done;
> A Booth a Booth; and Leigh by Leigh is overthrown;
> A Venables against a Venables doth stand,
> And Troutbeck fighteth with a Troutbeck hand to hand;
> There Molineux doth make a Molineux to die;
> And Egerton the strength of Egerton doth try.
> Oh Cheshire! wert thou mad? of thine own native gore
> So much until this day thou never shedd'st before!
> Above two thousand men upon the earth were thrown,
> Of whom the greater part were naturally thine own.'

The LORD STANLEY mentioned above had only been called to the House of Peers by the Duke of York during his first Protectorate. He died early in the year of which we are now treating, and was succeeded in the title by his eldest son, also named Thomas. This second Lord Stanley was a waverer, and even now, as in later life,

> 'Ever strong upon the stronger side.'

He had sent to Queen Margaret, who was at Eccleshall Castle, to assure her that he was coming to her assistance. Nevertheless, he stayed within six miles of Bloreheath while the battle was proceeding, and, after it was over, he wrote to the Earl of Salisbury, at Market Drayton, congratulating him upon his success, and expressing the hope that on some future occasion he might be of even greater service. His brother, Sir William Stanley, it would appear, actually went with some of his followers to the Earl's assistance. There is this much to be said for Lord Stanley's conduct, that he married Lady Eleanor Neville, Salisbury's daughter, but whether before or after this time cannot be determined.

Next morning Salisbury went with his forces to join the Duke of York at Ludlow, and the Earl of Warwick with his contingent soon arrived from Calais.

King Henry displayed a power and a vigour such as he had never previously manifested. At the time of the Battle of Bloreheath he had been very ill at Coleshill, in Warwickshire, and, when carried to the Queen at Eccleshall Castle, had only sufficient strength left to ask who had won the day. The emergency appeared to rouse him. He gathered 60,000 men under his standard, and soon commenced to march against the rebellious lords. As long as he was with the troops he shared all their discomforts. He never stopped two nights at the same place, except when Sunday came, as nothing was attempted on that day. Twice it is said that, in spite of rough, cold weather, he had to camp out, and did so without betraying any symptoms of inconvenience. The Earl of Salisbury, and some of the leaders at Bloreheath, could now only be looked upon as open enemies. But to the Duke of York, the Earl of Warwick, and the remainder of his opponents, Henry, when at Worcester, sent the Bishop of Salisbury with offers of full pardon, on condition of their submitting within six days. With arms in their hands against their King they again affirmed their loyalty, said their actions had been misconstrued, and in turn accused Henry of breaking his promises to them.

Oct. 10.

Oct. 13. The King's army came in sight of the Yorkists, who were strongly encamped, at Ludford in Herefordshire, separated from LUDLOW by the River Teme, and was received with a smart cannonade. Nothing more was attemped that night. To prevent any of his men going over to the royal side, a report was spread about that the King was dead, and York even went so far as to order a Mass to be chanted for the repose of his soul. Meantime the King's proclamation became known, and Sir Andrew Trollope, the leader of the veterans brought over by the Earl of Warwick from Calais, also learned, for the first time, the real intentions of the men under whom he was serving. Before midnight he took over almost the whole of the body of men under his command into the King's camp. The power of the insurgents was so much reduced thereby, that the leaders resolved at once to break up the encampment. The Duke of York, with his second son, Edmund, Earl of Rutland, fled to Ireland. The Earls of Salisbury and Warwick, with Edward, Earl of March, went down to Devonshire, and thence found their way to Calais. The Duchess of York and her younger children, including her sons, George and Richard, were captured next day in Ludlow Castle, and given into the tender keeping of Lady Anne Neville, Duchess of Buckingham, own sister to Duchess Cecily.

This was a bloodless victory, one after Henry's own heart. But old historians say that his followers plundered the town and castle.

Nov. A Parliament was convoked at Coventry, where an act of attainder was passed against the Duke and Duchess of York and their two eldest sons; the Earls of Salisbury and Warwick, Lord Powys; Sir John and Sir Thomas Neville, brothers of Warwick; Sir John Wenlock, who had gone to Calais; Sir Thomas Parre with other knights and squires. Henry was unwilling to go so far, and insisted upon the insertion of a clause enabling him to restore them at his pleasure.

From the Paston Letters it appears that about this time Sir John Fastolfe, an old acquaintance, died quietly on his estate in Norfolk.

The Duke of SOMERSET, Henry Beaufort, had been appointed captain of the town and castle of Calais in October in place of the Earl of Warwick, who was at the same time superseded in the command of the sea by Henry Holland, Duke of Exeter. But Warwick knew his own power. All the men in his service were devoted to him, and he set his two would-be supplanters at defiance. Somerset crossed over, but, instead of being admitted into the town, he was fired at by the batteries, although carrying the King's letters of appointment. He then landed at Guisnes, unfortunately for himself, as his ships were taken by the sailors to Calais and offered to the Earl of Warwick.

Richard WYDEVILLE, Lord Rivers, of whom we have not heard anything for a long time, appears to have collected some ships at Sandwich, with the intention probably of taking them to the relief of Somerset. Between four and five o'clock one morning, John Denham, who had come over secretly from the Earl of Warwick, surprised the noble lord and his son Anthony in bed, and took them and their ships back to Calais. *1460. Jan.*

Rivers was brought before the lords, with eight score torches burning. Salisbury rated him as a knave's son, asking how he could dare to call him and other lords traitors, when they were the King's true liege-men; and Warwick rated him as being only the son of a squire who had made his fortune by marriage; and the Earl of March rated him likewise; and Sir Anthony was rated by all three lords in like manner.

It would be interesting to know if my Lord of March remembered this incident when, four years later, he made the daughter of the rated Lord Rivers his wife.

Henry, Duke of Exeter, was scarcely much more fortunate than his namesake of Somerset. The Earl of Warwick had gone over to Ireland to arrange proceedings with the Duke of YORK. On St. Patrick's Day they made a public entry into Waterford, where they were received in grand state by the authorities. On his return to Calais, Warwick's fleet was observed by Exeter, who was cruising about in the Channel. But though superior in strength, he had doubts of the loyalty of his sailors, and the Earl was allowed to proceed unmolested on his way. *March 17.*

Some time during the season of Lent, which commenced on February 27, Easter Day being on April 13, King Henry, being inspired by feelings of devotion, and desirous at the same time to avoid the storm he saw impending, retired to Croyland Abbey in Lincolnshire, and presented his offerings at the shrine of the holy Father Guthlac. There he stayed, in the full enjoyment of tranquillity, three days and as many nights, taking the greatest pleasure in the observance of his religious duties, and most urgently praying that he might be admitted into the brotherhood of the monastery, a request which was accordingly complied with. Shortly after, being desirous to present the brethren with a due return, of his royal liberality he graciously granted and confirmed unto them the liberties of the whole vill of Croyland, to the end that its inhabitants might be rendered exempt from all demands on the part of the tax-gatherers of the King.*

Henry was soon to have a rude awakening from his dreams of piety and peace.

There was in England at this time Francesco Coppini, Bishop of Terni, who had been sent as legate by Pius II. to urge upon Henry the desirability of some concerted action against the Turks. This man, by some means, had been won over to the side of the enemies of the King. He did them the great service of bringing the Archbishop of Canterbury to regard their party with favour. Having failed in his mission, however, he set out on his return to Rome and soon arrived at Calais.

June. Now we come to the result of the meeting in Ireland. Salisbury, Warwick and Edward of York, having the Bishop of Terni in their company, crossed the Channel with 1,500 men and arrived early off Sandwich. So soon as the fleet was observed in the offing a large retinue of the Archbishop of Canterbury, all fully armed, marched down to the shore. When the debarkation took place, the Archbishop, in full pontificals, with the cross borne before him, went down to the landing-place. As each noble bent his knee and made the sign of the cross, the Archbishop gave his blessing, amid the deafening shouts of the people. He accompanied the army, which
July 2. was being continually augmented, until it arrived in London 25,000 strong.†

One Primate of all England, Arundel, as we have seen, had been principally instrumental in placing the house of Lancaster, in the person of Henry of Bolingbroke, on the throne. His action was probably induced by injuries he had borne himself. But now another sanctions, by his presence and support, the insurrectionary proceedings of men whose one object is the removal of the grandson of Henry IV. from his throne. What his reasons may have been in so acting it would be difficult to say. His family connection with York may have had something to do with it. He may have thought he was doing good service to the country. But, giving him all credit for good intentions, he brought upon her many years of misery and discord, and materially assisted in bringing about the downfall of the whole house of Plantagenet, of which he himself was a member.

July 3. The Primate convened a convocation at St. Paul's, which was opened with all due formality, in the presence of an immense congregation, but amid the clank of armour outside. The Earls of

* Peter of Blois' continuation of Ingulph's 'Chronicle,' where the form and tenor of grant may be read.
† Dr. Hook's 'Archbishops of Canterbury,' vol. v.

Salisbury and Warwick entered. Kneeling before the Archbishop, they made each a solemn oath of allegiance to King Henry VI., for whom they declared they had ever true faith. They added that they had only come to assert the rights of the people, and to vindicate their own honour.*

Attempts were made, but in vain, to open communications with the King, who was, with an army, at Coventry.

The rival forces met near NORTHAMPTON. The actual place of July 10. battle was Hardingstone Field, on the south side of the town, with the river Nene to the rear of the Royalists. Their position was strongly fortified with banks and deep entrenchments, and the leaders confidently looked for an easy victory. But there was a traitor in the camp. Edmund, Lord Grey de Ruthyn, put forward a claim to some lands belonging to Lord Fanhope, another of the Lancastrian lords, at Ampthill. He saw the Earl of March, and, on promise of taking over to his side the band of hardy Welshmen, obtained from Edward the assurance that, if he won the field, the lands at Ampthill should change owners. The battle commenced at seven o'clock in the morning, and there was a smart conflict for a couple of hours ; but, at the close, the royal army was completely routed. Lord Grey's treachery was the deciding feature. He turned against his King, showed the enemy where to enter, and allowed his men to assist them in passing the ditches. He obtained the lands he coveted, and was subsequently created Earl of Kent.

A heavy fall of rain, which lasted all the time, and, being in the faces of the Lancastrians, prevented them from keeping their powder dry, contributed materially to their defeat.

Humphrey, DUKE OF BUCKINGHAM ; John Talbot, second EARL OF SHREWSBURY, son of the old hero ; John Beaumont, VISCOUNT BEAUMONT; Thomas Percy, LORD EGREMONT, son of the second Earl of Northumberland, with 300 knights and gentlemen were killed, Warwick's policy being to spare the common men, but to strike down the nobles. Some writers, however, place the loss as high as 10,000 men, of whom a great part were drowned in crossing the Nene. The body of Buckingham was buried at the Grey Friars, in Northampton ; that of Shrewsbury at Worksop ; and many of the others in the Hospital of St. John, which still exists in Bridge Street, Northampton.

It is satisfactory to learn that the Bishop of Terni, who had intruded himself into English affairs in no way affecting him, and who had even presumed to set up the Papal banner at Northampton, was recalled by Pope Pius. He went, laden with bribes of plate and money, and was promptly sent to prison in the castle of St. Angelo. He was deprived of his bishopric, and became a Benedictine monk.

The Queen and the young Prince fled to Chester, being rifled on their way of their money and jewels by a follower of Lord Stanley, and thence to Harlech Castle, in Wales.

* Dr. Hook's 'Archbishops of Canterbury,' vol. v.

The King was found alone in his tent by the Earls of Warwick and March, who gave him every outward token of respect, and assured him they were his true friends. They afterwards took their prisoner —such he actually was—to London, which they entered in great state, Warwick riding before him bare-headed and carrying the sword of state, and, after a Te Deum had been sung at St. Paul's, then lodged him in the Bishop's palace.

It was all a piece of solemn mockery. Warwick knew, as well as did the EARL OF MARCH, the end which they intended to attain. Edward was at this time only eighteen years of age, but he had been brought forward early, and was now, to all intents and purposes, a man. A man, too, of most determined spirit, who was not likely to let any obstacles hinder him from reaching the goal of his ambition, utterly devoid of scruples, and with a conscience most elastic wherever his interests or pleasures were concerned. Thus, unlike his father in character, he was also dissimilar in appearance. He was tall, well made, a real Plantagenet in features and complexion, with the fair hair and blue eyes of his race; undoubtedly the handsomest man of the time.

July 25. 'To the victors the spoils!' In the place of Bishop Waynflete, George Neville, then Bishop of Exeter, a brother of Warwick, was appointed Chancellor, and Parliament was opened by him. The first act was to restore to their honours all those who had been
Oct. 7. attainted in the last Parliament at Coventry, and to repeal all Acts then passed.

The Duchess of York, with three of her children — George, Richard, and Margaret—was residing for the time in the house of Sir John Paston. On receiving the news of her husband's return from Dublin and arrival at Chester, and a summons to meet him at Hereford, she at once started on her journey, leaving the children to the care of their eldest brother, who went every day to see them.

Oct. 10. The DUKE OF YORK entered London like a conqueror, with a retinue of 500 armed and mounted men, trumpets blaring, and a sword of state carried before him. His approach to Westminster was heralded by a mob, which was so uproarious in its behaviour as to warrant the belief that friends of the Duke had been the inciters of it. Anyway, the turmoil alarmed the King and his attendants, who were assembled in the Queen's apartment.

On alighting from his horse, the Duke, instead of going to see the King, as was expected, went direct to the Chamber of Peers. Without deigning to address a word to anyone, he walked straight to the throne. He laid his hand upon it, as if waiting to be invited to seat himself thereon. But there was an ominous silence, and looks from many which were anything but friendly. He then turned, as if about to descend, and the movement was greeted with applause. At that instant Archbishop Bourchier, preceded by his cross-bearer, appeared on the scene. Courteously saluting the Duke, he asked, in a tone of reproof and surprise :

'Will not my Lord of York pay his respects to the King ?'

'I know no one in the realm,' York replied, 'who ought not rather to visit me,' and, so saying, he left the house. His clamorous reception by the people outside—the populace in London were always his partisans—may in some measure have made amends for the muteness of the peers, but he must have felt he had been premature. With only the mob for his friends, he could not expect just then to act the part of Henry of Bolingbroke. Without waiting upon Henry, however, he ordered the King's apartments to be prepared for his own use.

If York found he had been premature, the Primate must also have discovered that he had been utterly misled as to the intentions of the Yorkist leaders. A change of ministry, not a change of dynasty, was all which he desired.

The Duke of York, finding he had gone too far to recede, and spurred on by his son Edward, six days later delivered to the new Chancellor—his wife's nephew—a statement of his claim to the throne, as a descendant of Lionel, Duke of Clarence. Oct. 16.

The Lords declined to discuss such a matter without first laying it before the King. Henry's reply, when they came to him, was clear, definite, and really unanswerable : ' My father was King; his father was King. I have worn the crown forty years from my cradle; you have all sworn fealty to me as your sovereign, and your fathers did the same to mine. How, then, can my right be disputed?'

Philip de Commines, the eminent Minister of Louis XI., in his 'Memoirs,' declared 'that in the judgment of the world Henry VI. was the lawful King.'

Our great constitutional historian, Hallam, wrote : ' With us, who are to weigh these ancient factions in the balance of wisdom and justice, there should be no hesitation in deciding that the House of Lancaster were lawful sovereigns of England.'

Richard of York was, as he claimed, and as you have seen, descended from Lionel of Clarence. But it was through two females, —his mother, Lady Anne Mortimer, and her grandmother, Lady Philippa of Clarence; Edmund Mortimer, the last Earl of March of the name, had deliberately renounced his claim to the crown. By what right, then, could the son of his sister, Lady Anne, demand it ? Richard had taken oath upon oath of fealty to Henry, which, by some quibbling process, he declared formed no bar to his claim on the crown.

At length a compromise was agreed upon when not more than half the peers were present : that Henry should retain the crown as long as he lived, but that the Duke of York and his heirs should succeed to it. To this arrangement Henry weakly gave his assent. Richard, with his two sons, Edward and Edmund, then took another oath to maintain the King on his throne; and when Henry went to Oct. 24. Oct. 31.

St. Paul's in state to make his thanksgiving for another 'peace,' the Duke attended him as heir-apparent.

Henry's very virtues, his love of peace and justice, his hatred of strife and dissensions, were thus turned against him. He had, however, in thus disinheriting his son, forgotten to take into account the feelings of the Queen, who was thereby roused to a display of her energetic nature. Instead of returning to London, in obedience to a summons despatched in Henry's name, by order of the Duke of York, she went from Wales into Scotland, then back into the northern counties of England, where she raised a large army. She was soon joined by Henry Percy, third Earl of Northumberland; John, Lord Clifford; Lord Dacre, one of the famous Cumberland family; and Sir John Neville, brother of the Earl of Westmorland. Henry Beaufort, Duke of Somerset, and Thomas Courtenay, sixth Earl of Devonshire, also came with forces from their respective counties. Altogether, it has been computed that an army of 18,000 men was gathered together at York, and then marched on to WAKEFIELD.

Dec. The Duke of York and the Earl of Salisbury, on hearing of these movements, hastened to the spot, and arrived at Sandal Castle, about a mile from the last-named town, where they stayed over Christmas, the last Christmas which they were to spend on earth.

The Duke was desirous of going out at once to encounter his foes. His confidential servant, Sir David Hall, endeavoured to persuade him to await the arrival of the Earl of March with additional forces, seeing that they were then considerably overmatched. 'Ah, Davy, Davy!' said Richard, 'hast thou loved me so long, and wouldst have me dishonoured? Thou never sawest me keep fortress when in Normandy. Wouldst thou have me do it now for dread of a scolding woman, whose only weapons are her tongue and her nails?'

Dec. 30. He accordingly left his stronghold, and descended into the open plain, only to find himself not only with an army in front to contend against, but with two powerful companies, under the Earl of Wiltshire and Lord Clifford, in ambush on the right side and on the left, so that he was 'caught like a fish in a net, was slain manfully fighting, and his whole army discomfited within half an hour.' Two trees on the Barnsley road are said to mark the spot where the Duke fell. His head was cut off, and, after being adorned with a paper crown, was set up on the walls of York. When Edward IV. was on the throne, in 1464, he caused his father's head to be taken down, the remains of his body to be collected, and all buried with regal pomp in the chancel of the church at Fotheringhay. The EARL OF SALISBURY fled, but was pursued, captured, and beheaded next day at Pontefract, his head being put up to keep company with that of York. Upwards of two thousand of the Yorkists were slain, among whom William, Lord Bonville, and Harrington, who had married the Earl's daughter, Katherine, may be noticed; also Sir Thomas Neville, third son of Salisbury, Sir Hugh Hastings, Sir David Hall, and most of the leaders.

EDMUND, EARL OF RUTLAND, accompanied by his chaplain and tutor, Sir Robert Aspall, when flying for his life towards the town, was followed and captured by Lord Clifford before he could find shelter. In fear and trembling, without uttering a word, this son of York fell on his knees and raised his clasped hands as if entreating mercy.

'Save him,' said the priest, 'for he is a prince's son, and peradventure may do you good hereafter.'

'Then, as thy father slew mine,' exclaimed Clifford, 'so will I do thee and all thy kin.' So saying, he struck the young Earl with his dagger to the heart, and bade the chaplain carry the news to the youth's brother.

Many writers, following Hall, a confirmed Yorkist, speak of Edmund as a boy of twelve or thereabouts.

'Men ne'er spend their fury on a child;'

nor is it for a moment to be supposed that Clifford, a young man of five or six and twenty, would have done so. He would see before him a young man nearer eighteen than seventeen years of age, and would naturally expect him to defend himself. In an age when boys of fifteen or younger were knighted, it seems singular that Edmund should not have a sword, or not know how to use it, to defend himself, but must fall on his knees and cry for mercy. How he came to be wandering about the field at all there is nothing to show. Why he had a tutor with him, when his brother Edward, only one year older, was fighting battles, it is equally impossible to tell. It may have been that the youth was weak-minded, or that he was intended for the priesthood. In either case he had no business on a field of battle, and his tutor should be blamed for taking him there.

'Alas! it was a piteous deed!'

It was a cruel deed! But it was in accordance with the vindictive spirit of a merciless age. 'But who,' says an old writer, 'dare promise anything temperate of himself in the heat of martial fury?'

EDWARD, EARL OF MARCH, on hearing the disastrous news of Wakefield when he was at Gloucester, retired at once to his castle of 1461. Wigmore in Herefordshire, and rallied round him all the adherents of the House of York, to the number of 23,000, in order to interpose a barrier between the Lancastrian forces and the capital.

JASPER TUDOR, Earl of Pembroke, with a force considerably Feb. 1. inferior, consisting partly of Welshmen and partly of Irishmen, thought to intercept him. They met at Mortimer's Cross, a hamlet on the river Lugg, about four miles from Wigmore, where a stone pillar at four cross roads marks the site of the engagement. The battle lasted from early morn until dewy eve, and great was the slaughter, but ended in a complete victory for the Yorkists, leaving 4,000 of their opponents dead on the field. Pembroke got away to Brittany, and carried with him his young nephew, Henry of Richmond, then about four years old. His father, Owen Tudor, the

Feb. 2. husband of Queen Katherine, was taken prisoner, and, with eight other leaders, carried to Hereford, where they were all beheaded. This was in revenge for the executions at Wakefield, and is an early instance of Edward's fierce temper. Owen Tudor was buried in the church of the Black Friars.

On the morning of the battle the Earl of March saw what seemed to him three suns, which suddenly joined together. Accepting this as a sign of good fortune, he adopted the sun with rays as his badge,* in addition to the white rose.

Meanwhile Queen MARGARET, with her army, was on her way to London, and Warwick, having the King with him, advanced to meet her at the head of a large body of the trained bands of London citizens and men of Kent. The two opposing forces of Lancaster and York again met near ST. ALBANS on Shrove Tuesday, February 17.

Feb. 17. The Royalists took up a position at Bernard's Heath to the north of the town. The Yorkists encamped on a range of low hills on the south side.

The rival forces met in the market-place and a fierce fight ensued, in which eventually the Yorkists, by incessant storms of arrows, drove their opponents back. Nothing daunted by this mishap, the Queen, who was really Commander-in-Chief, forced her way through some narrow streets and lanes out of the town, and, with her fierce Northern followers, obliged Warwick to fall back towards Barnet. On the common between that town and St. Albans he made his last stand. The combat was prolonged till nightfall, when Warwick and all his men fled, leaving the King behind in a tent under the care of his chamberlain, John Neville, Lord Montague, a brother of Warwick's, and two or three attendants. The Yorkists had lost about two thousand men, and next day Lord BONVILLE and Sir THOMAS KYRIEL, whom you may remember as commander at the unfortunate affair at Fourmigni, who had been made prisoners, were executed, in retaliation for the beheadings at Hereford. Thus after every encounter party vengeance went on increasing.

Margaret did not know that her husband was so near her, until his faithful attendant Howe brought her the news. She at once went to him, taking young Edward with her. The King was overjoyed at seeing them again, and bestowed the honour of knighthood on his seven-year-old boy, and several of his adherents who had distinguished themselves during the day. Among these was Sir JOHN GREY of Groby, the heir of Lord Ferrers, a zealous Lancastrian, who had married Elizabeth Wydeville, the eldest daughter of Lord Rivers and Jaquetta, Duchess of Bedford. He had been severely wounded and was lying in great danger at the village of Colney,

* Nearly 190 years afterwards—to be exact, on February 25, 1649, a month after the martyred King's head had been struck off—a somewhat similar incident is recorded in Reilly's 'History of Manchester.' Three mock suns, or parhelia, appeared in that town about ten o'clock in the morning, to the great dismay of many of the inhabitants, but one by one they vanished, and an hour later none were visible.

whither the King went to see him. He was quite a young man, of great promise, but succumbed to his wounds on the 28th of the month.

The royal family and the lords of the army went immediately to the Abbey. They were met at the door by Abbot Whethamstede and his monks, who chanted hymns of triumph and thanksgiving for the safety of the King. The whole party then went to the high altar, and afterwards to the shrine of St. Alban, where thanks were offered for the late victory. Then the King, Queen, and Prince were shown to their apartments in the Abbey, where they remained three or four days.

This fight of St. Albans proved the downfall of the House of Lancaster.

The royal army was composed in great measure of marauders from the Scottish borders and Northern counties, who even on the march southward had committed all manner of wild excesses against towns and churches. Now they destroyed all the advantage which had been gained through their prowess by plundering and demolishing the town of St. Albans. Even the Abbey would have been sacked and burned if Henry had not interfered. As it was, they did so much damage that Whethamstede from that time became a Yorkist instead of a firm Lancastrian as heretofore.

The news having reached London, along with intelligence that Margaret had given her troops license to plunder up to the gates, the citizens stopped some carts at Cripplegate in which the mayor was sending some provisions which had been requisitioned by the Queen. After an interview with the Lord Mayor, who represented that he was almost the only one left in London who was faithful to the Red Rose, the Queen decided upon returning to the North.

Before doing so, HENRY issued a proclamation, stating that his assent to the late award had been extorted by violence, and ordering the arrest of Edward, late Earl of March, son of the late Duke of York. *Feb. 22.*

But EDWARD'S forces were by this time united with those of Warwick, and greatly exceeded those of the Royalists. He entered London with all the pomp and display of a conquering hero. The charms of his appearance and manner, the late victory at Mortimer's Cross, the cruel fate of his father and brother, the ravages of the Royalists, all worked together for his good in the eyes of the people. *Feb. 25.*

There was a great gathering of Londoners in St. George's Fields, when William Neville, Lord Fauconberg, reviewed 4,000 troops. George Neville, Bishop of Exeter, in a spirited harangue, spoke of the unfounded claim of Henry to the throne, his known incapacity, and then placed in contrast the splendid abilities of Edward. The House of Neville was coming decidedly to the front. Both the above-named were brothers of Richard Neville, Earl of Warwick, whose badge of the bear and ragged staff was everywhere visible on the red coats of his followers. Loud and long continued were *March 2.*

the acclamations of the people at the close of the Bishop's address. His cause appeared to be won. Then arose the cry, 'King Edward! KING EDWARD!' repeated again and again.

March 3. Next day a meeting of peers spiritual and temporal then in London, who, from the position of affairs, must have all been of one party, was held at Baynard's Castle, York's house. There it was resolved that Henry, by joining the Queen's forces, had violated the award and forfeited the crown to Edward, the heir of Richard, late Duke of York.

What a mockery of justice! The Yorkist leaders had deserted Henry, left him behind them when they fled, perhaps—who knows?—hoping that someone might put an end to his existence. What choice had he but to join the Queen? It could not be expected of him that he would voluntarily leave her and his son and place himself again in the hands of men who had 'broken oath on oath, committed wrong on wrong.'

> 'Oaths will not curb the wicked.'

Shakspere tersely puts into the mouth of Edward of York the principle which guided him and many others:

> 'For a kingdom any oath may be broken:
> I would break a thousand oaths to reign one year.'

When the resolution which had been arrived at was announced, Edward rode in procession to Westminster Hall, and there publicly explained his right. He then went to the Abbey and repeated his speech, which was frequently interrupted by the plaudits of the crowd, and loud cries of 'King Edward!'

March 4. In the city he was immediately proclaimed in various parts, and his reign dates from that day, although he was not crowned until June 29 following. Edward at the time was two months short of being nineteen years of age. He was born April 28, 1442.

Thus was the House of Lancaster 'thrust from the crown' by the descendants of the very people who had raised it to that proud pre-eminence.

Henry suffered from comparison with his father:

> 'Childer ofte been
> Unlike her worthy eldris hem bifore;
> Bounté cometh al of God, nought of the streen
> Of which they ben engendrid and i-bore.'

The treatment he received was very different to that meted out to his grandfather, Charles VI. of France, by all his subjects, more particularly the lower orders, who revered him for his very weakness. It does not speak well for the English people of that day. But then, as now, a glib tongue and an unctuous manner carried away men's reason and made them blind partisans.

Henry's very virtues were made to tell against him because they were not in accordance with the times. His talents were not those suitable for his station. He was clear-sighted, candid, just, peace-loving, but he was unable to carry his thoughts and ideas into practice. He was vacillating from his hatred of all strife, and though we have seen him lead an army, threats of armed men generally quenched any show of courage he might make. Thus it was that he agreed to a compromise, and admitted York's claim to the crown at the expense of his own son.

Hardynge writes that Henry was

> 'Of suche symplenesse and disposicion
> As menne maye se by his discrecion;'

and goes on to say that his deposition was foretold:

> 'For when Henry the Fourth first was crouned,
> Many a wyseman sayd then full commenly,
> The third heyre shuld not ioyse, but be uncrouned,
> And deposed of all regalitee.
> To this reason they dyd their wittes applye,
> Of evill gotten good the third should not enioyse,
> Of long agone it hath bene a commen voyse.'

SKETCH XXIII.

IMPRISONED.

THOUGH EDWARD OF YORK had been acknowledged as King, 1461. it was only by the citizens of London, and a few of the nobles who had been always supporters of the claims of his father.

Dr. Whitaker, in his vindication of Mary Queen of Scots, wrote: 'London was always ready to lend its ears to the clamours of sedition, and to give its hand to the operations of rebellion.'

Miss Strickland, in her 'Life of Margaret of Anjou,' writes: 'In three great political struggles the suffrages of the city of London turned the balance. The Empress Maud, Margaret of Anjou, and Charles I. lost all with the good-will of the Londoners.'

However, London was not all England. The greater part of the midland counties and all the northern ones were Lancastrian heart and soul. The crown had, therefore, still to be contended for by force of arms.

An army of 60,000 men was collected near York under Henry Beaufort, Duke of Somerset, while King Henry, with his Queen and son, remained in the city.

The Earl of Warwick, at the head of his well-tried men, marched March 27. to meet them, and King Edward had to hurry after him to defend his ill-gotten throne. Their united forces amounted to 50,000 men by the time they reached Pontefract. A detachment, under Lord Fitzwalter, was sent on in advance, and secured the passage over the river Aire at Ferrybridge, about three miles from Knottingley. But

March 28. JOHN, LORD CLIFFORD, surprised it in the early dawn, and the leader was slain. Clifford, in turn, was defeated by William Neville, Lord Fauconberg—of whom you have read as uncle to the Earl of Warwick—and killed by an arrow hitting him in the neck. FAUCONBERG was rewarded for his timely arrival by being created Earl of Kent on June 30 following.

Lord Clifford had left two sons, Henry, about seven years of age, and Richard. Edward of York both hated and dreaded the very name of Clifford, and was anxious to get them into his power. They were hunted for, and there can be but little doubt that they would have been slain without scruple if the avengers of blood could only have found them. But their loving mother had taken care to remove her boys out of the tyrant's way. Richard was taken to the Netherlands, where he died not long afterwards. Henry was placed in the charge of a former nurse of his, who had married a shepherd in Yorkshire, and with them he remained seven or eight years, passing as their son, and attending to such duties as would fall to the lot of a boy in that position. At the end of that time, it being told Lady Clifford—or Lady Threlkeld, as she had meanwhile married Sir Lancelot Threlkeld—that her son's present residence was known at Court, she caused him and his foster-parents to be removed to a farm in Cumberland. Here fifteen years more of his life were passed, without any communication with the busy world, except at rare intervals with his mother. At length the battle of Bosworth put an end to all danger. On the accession of Henry VII. to the throne, Henry, Baron Clifford, was restored to his title and estates, and summoned to take his place in Parliament. It can well be imagined that he would feel out of place in London. He therefore soon returned to the country, where he employed his time in learning to read and write, in prosecuting his study of astronomy, the love of which had been one of the solaces of his lonely life as a shepherd, and in repairing or rebuilding his many castles. Among other places he built or enlarged was Barden Tower, near Bolton Abbey, which became his favourite place of residence. He was known in after years as the shepherd-lord :

> ' In him the savage virtue of the race,
> Revenge and all ferocious thoughts were dead :
> Nor did he change ; but kept in lofty place
> The wisdom which adversity had bred.
> Glad were the vales, and every cottage hearth ;
> The shepherd-lord was honoured more and more ;
> And ages after he was laid in earth
> " The good Lord Clifford " was the name he bore.'

Although he had not received the training of a warrior, Lord Clifford proved that the military genius of his family was not extinct. He took a numerous retinue to Flodden Field, September 9, 1513, and showed himself an able commander. He died April 23, 1523, when about seventy years of age, at Barden Tower.

Lord Clifford's son, another Henry, was created Earl of Cumberland in 1525 by King Henry VIII.

At the same time as Lord Clifford, there was also slain Sir John Neville, brother of Ralph, the second Earl of Westmorland, who had married Anne Holland, the widow of his nephew, John Neville, slain at St. Albans in 1455, and daughter of John Holland, Duke of Exeter. Their son Ralph succeeded his uncle as third Earl in 1484.

The fighting began about four o'clock in the afternoon, and was continued far into the night. Warwick evidently anticipated a fierce struggle. He said to his men: 'Whoever chooses to return home may do so; but I shall live or die with those who remain.' He then drew his sword, and, after kissing the cross on the handle, killed his horse, as an earnest of his intention never to flee, whatever the issue might be. His policy had always been to spare the people and only strike down the nobles, and he did not now intend to alter it. But Edward, with his cruel, vindictive nature, and a tigerish thirst for blood, issued general orders that no quarter was to be given, but that all were to be killed, regardless of age or rank.

In remembrance of the above-mentioned action of Warwick's, perhaps in emulation of the famous White Horse in Berkshire, the large, rough figure of a red horse was cut on the side of a hill in a Warwickshire village, about ten miles from Stratford-on-Avon. For many years this figure was regularly scoured out on each succeeding Palm Sunday, and possibly the process may be still continued.

Palm Sunday dawned, but thick clouds obscured the sky. Ere March 29. long the clouds emptied themselves in the form of heavy snow, which was driven by a high wind full in the faces of the Lancastrians, so that the very elements were against them. Lord Fauconberg took advantage of this circumstance to order his men to send against them a shower of what are called flight-arrows, and then retire several paces.* The Lancastrians, thinking the enemy had come to close quarters, sent volley after volley of their arrows, until they had nearly emptied their quivers, which fell harmless. These same arrows were, however, afterwards gathered from the ground, and shot against their original owners when the Yorkists, in turn, had used up their own supply. Still, there was no sign of wavering on either side. But at this juncture John Mowbray, third Duke of Norfolk, came with fresh forces to the assistance of Edward and Warwick. His arrival really decided the day.

Somerset, Northumberland, and Sir Andrew Trollope urged on their men. Bows, now being useless, were cast aside. A hand-to-hand fight with sword, spear, and battle-axe was begun. 'Conquer or die!' was the word, and right gallantly they bore themselves.

The actual field of battle was between the villages of Saxton and Towton, about two miles from Tadcaster. The fight was thickest in what is called the 'Bloody Meadow,' about a mile south of Towton.

About three o'clock in the afternoon the Lancastrian ranks were broken, and they began to give way. They retreated in good order until reaching the small Cock Beck, an effluent of the Wharfe, near

* You will remember a similar stratagem at Bloreheath in 1459.

Tadcaster, when a sudden panic seized them. The way was steep and narrow, horsemen and footmen were jammed together, and hundreds of the latter were probably either trampled to death by their fellow-soldiers or drowned in the beck. The same scene occurred in crossing the bridge at Tadcaster, while the Yorkists, pressing on them from the rear, gave no quarter, but cut them down just like so many sheep. The slaughter was tremendous, as many as 38,000 men—nearly three-fourths being Lancastrians—having fallen in the fight, in addition to those drowned or otherwise killed in flight. Corpses strewed the ground almost up to the gates of York, a distance of ten miles. For days afterwards the melted snow, crimsoned with the blood of the slain, might be seen running in the furrows and ditches for two or three miles. It was the bloodiest battle ever fought between fellow countrymen.

> 'Cressy was to this but sport,
> Poictiers but a pageant vain,
> And the work of Agincourt
> Only like a tournament.'

Among the slain were HENRY PERCY, third Earl of Northumberland; RANULPH, LORD DACRE, of Gilsland; LYON WELLES, LORD WELLES; HENRY, LORD STAFFORD, son of the Duke of Buckingham; SIR ANDREW TROLLOPE; LORD SCALES; LORD WILLOUGHBY; and others. THOMAS COURTENAY, sixth EARL OF DEVONSHIRE; and JAMES BUTLER, EARL OF WILTSHIRE AND ORMOND, were taken prisoners, and carried to York. When Edward entered the city next morning, not satisfied with the immense slaughter, he ordered their heads to be struck off, and substituted for those of his father and uncle, placed on the walls after the Battle of Wakefield. WILLIAM TAILBOIS, LORD KYME, styled Earl of Kyme, was beheaded in the following month of May.

The above-named Ranulph Dacre was succeeded by his brother Humphrey, who ultimately recovered the estates of the family, and his descendants were the well-known Lords Dacre of the North. Humphrey died in 1485, leaving a large family by his wife, Mabel Parr, a daughter of Sir Thomas Parr, slain at Barnet in 1471, the great-uncle of Queen Katherine Parr, the last wife of Henry VIII.

Edward doubtless hoped to get the rival King into his power; but in that he was disappointed, as Henry, with his Queen and son, the Dukes of Somerset and Exeter, Lords Roos and Hungerford, and a few more, had fled into Scotland. There was some delay before they could cross the Border, which led to their being besieged by 20,000 men, sent by Edward under Sir Robert Ogle and Sir John Conyers, in the castle of Wark, on the Tweed. 'Certaine esquires of the Earl of Northumberland gathered together 5,000 or 6,000 Lancastrians, and effected their rescue after 3,000 north-countrymen had fallen in the bicker.'* The royal fugitives then continued their way to Scotland. They were well received by the Queen-

* C. J. Bates's 'History of Northumberland.'

mother, Mary of Gueldres, widow of King James II., who had been unfortunately killed about eight months previously by the accidental bursting of a gun. But they could not obtain any assurance of help until the surrender of Berwick was made, and Prince Edward was betrothed to Mary, the eldest sister of the young King James III. The services of the Earl of Angus were secured by the promise of an English dukedom.

As soon as EDWARD had sent off LORD MONTAGUE to the relief of June 1. Carlisle, which was besieged by the Scots, he hastened back to London, and went direct to his favourite palace at Shene. There he remained until three days before his coronation at Westminster, on June 29. St. Peter's Day, which was also a Sunday. He then, or shortly afterwards, created his brothers GEORGE and RICHARD, DUKES OF CLARENCE and GLOUCESTER.

> ' Let me be Duke of Clarence ; George of Gloster ;
> For Gloster's dukedom is too ominous.'

says Richard in Shakspere's 'Henry VI.' They had been sent for safety to Utrecht, with their sister Margaret, soon after the Battle of Wakefield, and had but recently returned. George was at that time not quite twelve years of age, and Richard was three years younger.

HENRY BOURCHIER, elder brother of the Archbishop of Canter- June 30. bury, was created EARL OF ESSEX the day after the coronation. He was uncle to Edward, having married Isabel, the sister of Richard, Duke of York.

In the first Parliament of King Edward IV., which was attended Nov. by only one duke, four earls, and twenty-nine barons, the reigns of the last three Kings were declared to have been tyrannical usurpations. The grants made by them were annulled as of no value. Even all gold and silver coins were changed, in order to obliterate their names. King Henry, Queen Margaret, and their son Prince Edward were attainted, together with dukes, earls, knights, priests and esquires, to the number of 140, or thereabouts. The double effect was nearly to annihilate the Lancastrian party, and to fill the coffers of the new King, so as to enable him to reward his supporters.

The first to suffer for their loyalty to a losing cause were JOHN DE 1462. VERE, twelfth EARL OF OXFORD, and his eldest son AUBREY, who Feb. 26. were beheaded, without any trial, because it was said they were in correspondence with Queen Margaret.

One of the first acts of Edward, in order to counteract the efforts March. of Queen Margaret in Scotland, was to make an alliance with the Earl of Ross, and offer his own hand to the widowed Queen Mary. The effect intended was obtained in diminishing the interest felt for the banished family, but of the projected marriage nothing more was heard. It was simply one of Edward's usual acts of duplicity, but it answered its purpose. The Queen-Dowager died two years later.

KING HENRY appears to have taken refuge in Harlech Castle, Merionethshire, which was held by the loyal chieftain Dafydd ap

Jevon ap Einon, who had given shelter to the heroic Queen Margaret after the disastrous overthrow at Northampton.

April 16. MARGARET still supported the apparently desperate cause of the Red Rose. She left Kirkcudbright with four Scottish ships, landed at Ecluse in Brittany, and received from Duke François II. a present of 12,000 crowns. She next proceeded to Chinon to see her cousin, the new King of France, Louis XI., who had succeeded his father Charles VII. on July 22 in the previous year. Louis received his relative with kindness, but he was not the man to give away anything without a *quid pro quo*. He turned pawnbroker. On condition of her pledging Calais as a security he lent her 20,000 crowns, and, in accordance with a secret treaty that the Channel Islands should be made over to Pierre de Brezé, he permitted that baron to raise and conduct a force of 2,000 men on her behalf.

Oct. With this small number of followers Margaret returned. Bamburgh, Alnwick and Dunstanburgh Castles surrendered to her, and were committed to the charge of Lancastrians. Warwick's arrival caused the dispersion of her French forces to their fleet. The winds and waves, which ever seemed adverse to her fortunes, now rose in their might against her. The Queen, indeed, escaped to Berwick, but of her followers many were killed, more drowned, and all her treasures were lost.

The Earl of WARWICK, at the head of 20,000 men, marched northwards as the King's Lieutenant, and fixed his headquarters at Warkworth, about three miles from Alnwick. Edward had set out at the same time, but only got as far as Newcastle, being utterly incapacitated for any exertion by immoderate indulgences and disease.

Dec. 10. The three castles were all invested at the same time, and Warwick rode round every day to superintend the operations.

When Bamburgh surrendered to the Queen Margaret's forces it was held by Sir RALPH PERCY, a brother of the third Earl of Northumberland, who, contrary to the tradition of his family, had mounted the White Rose. Now it was defended by him and Henry Beaufort, Duke of SOMERSET, with some 200 men for the Red Rose against John Tiptoft, Earl of WORCESTER, and Sir RALPH GREY. The garrison being reduced to eating their horses, the leaders agreed to capitulate, if all lives were spared, and the men allowed to march out to Scotland or elsewhere. Somerset and Percy were restored to their estates and honours on condition of swearing fealty to King Edward, which they did. Nevertheless both went back to their old allegiance and both suffered for so doing. PERCY was slain at Hedgeley Moor, near Wooler, April 25, 1464, with the well-known words on his lips, 'I have saved the bird in my bosom.' As he had twice deserted the Red Rose, this can only mean that he had at last returned to his original faith, and therefore did not feel that he had anything with which to reproach himself. These words cannot be, therefore, taken as an expression of unsullied honour, which they often are.

Dunstanburgh held out for three days longer, under the charge of Sir RICHARD TUNSTAL, Sir Philip Wentworth, and Dr. John Morton, the well-known 'Parson of Blokesworth,' who, many years later, became Archbishop of Canterbury. Morton, after the surrender, went abroad, and was one of the small court of Margaret of Anjou. He was included in the general Act of attainder and convicted of high treason.*

Alnwick was still unsubdued, but, like the others, was suffering for want of provisions. Lord Hungerford and young Brezé, with the assistance of the Earl of Augus, cut their way out with the greater part of the garrison, and the remainder then capitulated. The castle was given in charge to Sir John Astley, much to the disgust of Sir Ralph Grey, a grandson of Sir Thomas, executed for participation in the Earl of Cambridge's conspiracy, who considered that he had a better claim to it. He was thereby converted into a staunch Lancastrian. Sir Ralph's grandmother was Alice Neville, a daughter of the Earl of Westmorland by his first wife. 1463. Jan. 6.

Authorities differ so much about dates that it is a doubtful matter what Queen MARGARET was doing. She must have had a very hard winter somewhere.

At the head of some Scots and Frenchmen the Queen appears to have pushed forward to near Hexham, to attack a strong position held by the Yorkists at Ryal, on the right bank of the Devilswater. A panic, however, seized her Scottish allies. They deserted the braver Frenchmen, and a hopeless rout ensued. Margaret mounted a horse ridden by an esquire, and placing her little boy in front, they rode off into the recesses of Dipton Wood.† April 3.

There she was beset by a band of robbers, who despoiled her of her money and all articles of value, and even menaced her life. The ruffians commencing to quarrel over a divison of the booty, she plunged with her boy into a thicker part of the wood. Another robber there confronted them. Margaret, with her usual resolution, though probably not without some misgivings, went boldly up to him, leading young Edward by the hand. 'Friend,' she said, 'to your loyalty I entrust the son of your King.' The man was much moved at this exhibition of confidence in him. He knelt down and explained that he was a ruined Lancastrian who would do all he could for her and her son. He conducted them to a cave, where they received shelter for three days. They then rejoined their friends, and sailed from Bamburgh for Sluys in Flanders, and thence to her father's duchy of Bar, in Lorraine. July 30.

It is possible, as some writers have suggested, that the man who thus assisted the Queen was Robert Hillyard, the leader of the Rising in the North in 1469.

The place where the heroic Queen found refuge still goes by the name of 'Queen Margaret's Cave.' It is situated on the south bank

* Dr. Hook's 'Archbishops of Canterbury,' vol. v., p. 391.
† C. J. Bates's 'History of Northumberland.'

of a little stream at the foot of Black Hill, about two miles from Hexham.

The Lancastrians had not given up the struggle for mastery. Sir RALPH GREY delivered Sir John Astley, the Governor of Alnwick, to the care of Sir Ralph Percy, and again admitted Robert, Lord Hungerford, and some Frenchmen into the castle. Bamburgh and Dunstanburgh were at the same time seized by a party of Scots and French with the passive connivance of Sir Ralph Percy, the Governor.*

About Christmas the Duke of Somerset left his own county secretly. His purpose is supposed to have been to deliver up Newcastle, which was garrisoned by his retainers, to the Lancastrians, but John Neville, Lord MONTAGUE, was too quick for him.

1464. A Parliament had been summoned to meet at York on May 5. As an Embassy was expected from Scotland, a strong escort was required to enable it to pass safely through Northumberland. Montague, with 4,000 men, set out for that purpose towards Norham, which had been occupied by the Lancastrians.†

In the meantime Somerset and Percy had again raised the banner of the Red Rose, and had brought the ex-King HENRY from his retreat in Wales to put himself, nominally, at the head of the small mixed force they had collected together. On St. Mark's Day they

April 25. barred Montague's way at Hedgeley Moor. Percy, as already told, was slain, the remainder took to flight.

The Scottish commissioners reached York in safety. A peace was concluded for fifteen years, one condition being that the King of Scotland should not give any assistance to Henry calling himself King of England, to Margaret his wife, to Edward his son, or to any of his friends and supporters.

Montague did not deem it necessary to accompany the Scots on their return. He reached Newcastle in time to defend it from a sudden attack made upon it by Sir Ralph Grey, and then marched westward to Hexham. There he found his passage over the Devils-

May 15. water opposed by Somerset, who had two strong castles of Langley and Bywell in the neighbourhood.‡ But the Duke had only a few hundred men, quite insufficient to cope with a force of eight times the strength. Grey fairly ran away, and many followed his example. SOMERSET and a few faithful ones made a last stand on a hill about a mile out of Hexham. He was taken and beheaded, and was buried in the Augustine Priory. Lord HUNGERFORD and THOMAS LORD ROOS were found hiding in a wood hard by. They were carried to Newcastle and beheaded on the Sandhill near that town. Many more executions, to the number as some say of thirty, followed, there and at York.

The castles of Hexham above named did not long resist Montague's forces. In one of them were found King Henry's helmet, cap of state, and sword, also the trappings of his horse.§

* C. J. Bates's 'History of Northumberland.' † *Ibid.* ‡ *Ibid.* § *Ibid.*

Lord MONTAGUE for his great services was created Earl of   May 27.
NORTHUMBERLAND, and received a grant of a great portion of the
Percy estates.

Grey, with many of those who had fled from Hexham, took refuge
in Bamburgh. The three strong castles had to be recaptured. For
that purpose the Earl of Warwick came up to the assistance of his
brother. The first to fall was Dunstanburgh. The captain was
taken to York and there beheaded. Alnwick at once surrendered June 23.
when the royal forces appeared before it. The day after St. John
Baptist's Day the siege of Bamburgh was commenced. Warwick had June 25.
brought with him two great guns of iron, besides three or four other
smaller ones of brass. The heralds called upon the garrison to
surrender, when all but the leaders would receive a pardon. Sir
RALPH GREY decidedly refused, saying he meant to hold the castle
till he died. The bombardment then began. One of the brass guns
'smote through Sir Ralph's chamber oftentimes.' A portion of the
wall fell and knocked him down, breaking his leg. The garrison,
thinking he was dead or dying, agreed to surrender. He was carefully
nursed that he might die the death of a traitor, and taken to Edward,
who was at Doncaster, suffering as usual under his excesses.
Tiptoft, Earl of Worcester, Constable of England, sentenced him to
be degraded from his knighthood; to have his coat-of-arms torn off
his back, and another coat, with arms reversed, put in its place; to
walk bare-foot to the town, and then to be laid on a hurdle and
drawn to the scaffold, where his head was to be struck off.

Among those who fled from Hexham, King HENRY, according to
Hall, 'was the best horseman of his company that day, for he fled so
fast that no one could overtake him. Three of his bodyguard,
trapped in blue velvet, were taken, one of them wearing the King's
cap of state.' Henry and his followers must have suffered great
privations, as we read of them being reduced to live in caves at
times. At length they found refuge with one John Machell, at
Crakenthorpe in Westmorland. How long they remained there
history telleth not. Anon we hear of Henry at Bolton by Bowland,
in the West Riding of Yorkshire. Bolton Hall, about three and a
half miles west of Gisburn, and six miles north of Clitheroe, was at
that time owned by Sir Ralph Pudsey, who came of a family noted
for their loyalty, benevolence, and hospitality. Sir Ralph had married
a daughter of Sir Richard Tunstal, of Thurland Castle*—demolished
by the Roundheads in 1643—in the parish of Tunstal, Lancashire.
Now Thomas Tunstal, a son of Sir Richard, was one of King
Henry's esquires, and it was probably at his instigation that Bolton,
as being a safer place than Thurland, was chosen. Bolton Hall is still
in existence, but it does not seem probable to a gentleman who lived
there forty years ago that the present structure could have existed in
the time of Henry VI., though there is an apartment there still called
King Henry's room. A well, which was dug by the King's desire,

* Some writers say she was a daughter of Thomas, the King's squire.

also goes by his name. Knowing Henry's religious feelings, it is a pleasure to think that he may have visited the Cistercian Abbey of Whalley, not far from Clitheroe, and perhaps, further afield, the famous Augustinian Abbey of Bolton and Embsay Priory.

Whether Henry got tired of the solitude of the place, or feared to trespass too long on his host, or began to dread discovery if he remained in the same spot, cannot be said, but after he had been there many months he decided to make a change. He may have intended going only for a visit and then coming back to his kind entertainers. A boot, a glove, and a spoon were long preserved in the family as having belonged to the King. These articles, it is understood, are now in the Liverpool museum. The boot and glove are no larger than could be worn by a middle-sized woman, which will show that Henry must have been of small proportions.

Henry repaired to Waddington Hall in the parish of Mitton Magna, in the mountainous, thinly-inhabited district of the north-eastern part of Lancashire, about five miles from Bolton Hall and three miles from Clitheroe. The hall itself is really in Yorkshire, and at that time belonged to Sir John Tempest of Bracewell, whose family had intermarried with the Talbots. It was strongly built of stone, and consisted of a centre part, with two projecting gables. It was in existence fifty years ago, and may be so still, but was even then in a very dilapidated condition, and used as a farmhouse. King Henry's room was the upper one in one of the gables, and had a strong oak floor. It still keeps his name.*

It is singular that one of the very class of men whom Henry delighted to honour should be his betrayer. He was seen sitting at dinner by a Black, or Benedictine, monk of Abingdon named 1465. Cantlow, who carried the news to Sir James Harrington of Brierley, June 29. who, with his associates—Thomas Talbot, son of Sir Edmund Talbot, of Bashal, and his cousin, John Talbot, of Coleby—effected his capture.

This Thomas Talbot married Florence Pudsey, a daughter of Sir Ralph, of Bolton. Thomas died in 1497, and his widow became the second wife of Henry Clifford, the 'shepherd-lord' of whom you have read.

Henry was not going to be taken without a run for it. He went down one staircase while his pursuers went up another. He finally got out of a window at the back of the house and fled for his life. But his enemies were too many to let him escape altogether. He reached the Brungerley Hyppingstones, a ford for crossing the Ribble. He even contrived to get into the Cletherwoode on the other side the river, but there he was made prisoner. Being placed on horseback, his legs were tied to the stirrups, and he was led to London.

The Talbots received, as a reward for their treachery, or, as the grant says, 'in consideration of their good and faithful services in

* 'Pictorial History of the County of Lancaster.'

the capture of our great adversary,' the sum of twenty marks a year from Kings Edward and Richard. Naturally it ceased when Henry of Richmond came to the throne. Sir John Tempest and Sir James Harrington also were rewarded with the spoils of the faithful Lancastrians.

When the poor dethroned King reached London he was met by the Earl of Warwick, who, to his shame be it said, ordered his gilt spurs to be taken off, and called out, ' Behold the traitor !' No one saluted him or did him the least honour, it having been strictly forbidden. He was then led three times round a tree in the manner of a pillory, which stood in front of the Tower, and afterwards confined in the hall tower of the outer ward. He was treated with humanity in prison, and allowed to see such persons as were supposed to have become loyal to King Edward and the House of York. To a man of his monastic tastes a seclusion from the troubles of the world might not be so difficult to bear as it would have been to one of a more energetic spirit.

The apartments in which he was confined would naturally be well furnished, and not have the comfortless appearance they now exhibit. He had his oratory, properly supplied with a cross, relics, and massbooks. He had, besides, other books, birds, and a dog as means of amusement and recreation. Henry had always been fond of field sports, and this dog may have been one of his old companions in the chase. It seems very possible that, thus left in quietude and in peace, Henry was happier than in the grandeur of State, surrounded as he always had been by the discords of contending factions.

SKETCH XXIV.

' MARRYING AND GIVING IN MARRIAGE.'

THERE were now two Kings in London, a deposed one and a reigning one, both of them living in the Tower. which was large enough to contain a palace as well as a prison.

Let us for a moment compare the characters of the two, and see which of them was likely to be the happier.

' Fam'd for mildness, peace, and prayer,'

Henry may have been weak and credulous. He pardoned men who had broken the strongest oaths that could be taken, and then accepted their simple word, though contrary to his own interests.

Edward, with all his bravery and brilliant exterior, was, even at this early date, a slave to voluptuous pleasures, selfish, arbitrary, and treacherous. In the first days of his reign, on March 12, 1461, he had caused a poor tradesman named Walter Walker, a haberdasher or a grocer, to be hung for simply saying 'he would make his son *heir to the Crown*,' meaning thereby the sign which hung over his shop-door. He was just the man we can imagine might exclaim with Satan :—

> ' Better to reign in hell than serve in heaven !'

On the other hand, Henry's feelings are expressed in Shakspere's words :—

> ' My crown is call'd content ;
> A crown it is that seldom kings enjoy.'

So far as human judgment can go, Henry's seemingly hard fate should be preferred to the promising one of his rival. But until the day when the secrets of all hearts are laid bare, nothing can be surely known.

1464. EDWARD had often been urged to marry, and more than one lady of princely extraction had been named as likely, but, though twenty-two years of age, he did not appear inclined to tie himself down to one partner for life.

It, however, happened that one day, when he was following the chase in Whittlebury Forest, on the borders of Northamptonshire, not far from Stoney Stratford, in Buckinghamshire, he met a fair lady, clad in the deepest mourning, who asked to be informed where she could meet the King, to whom she had a petition to present. Edward, of course, had to acknowledge that he himself was the King. The lady then immediately knelt down ; she said she was the widow of Sir John Grey, of Groby in Leicestershire, who had been slain at the second battle of St. Albans, fighting for the cause of King Henry, that her husband's lands had been confiscated in consequence, and she was left destitute with two young children. She therefore prayed that her husband's property might be restored to her and her bereaved boys.

Edward, at all times susceptible, was particularly impressed by the modest, downcast look of the beautiful fair face in its melancholy, shrouded in long pale-yellow hair. Needless to say, the lady gained her suit, and at the same time the King's affection, or what he called such. But his suit was not founded on honour, and the lady could only reply :—

> ' I know I am too mean to be your queen ;
> And yet too good to be your concubine.'

Edward was baffled, but not dismayed. Other meetings followed at the home of the lady's parents, but that this was the first tradition in the neighbourhood maintains ; and the hollow trunk of the oak, called the ' Queen's Oak,' on the spot where it took place, not far from Grafton Manor, Towcester, and Stoney Stratford, was not many years ago, and may be is still, pointed out.

The lady was ELIZABETH, eldest daughter of Jaquetta, Duchess of Bedford, and her second husband Richard WYDEVILLE,* Baron

---

* Probably no name in English history has been spelt in a greater variety of ways. The only letters never changed are the first, third, fifth and sixth, W, D, V, and I.—Doyle's ' Official Baronage ' has been followed.

Rivers, and was probably born in 1436. Historians generally write of her as ten years older than Edward. Even Miss Strickland allows that she may have been born in 1431. As John Duke of Bedford only died September 14, 1435, Elizabeth, if born in 1431, can but have been Wydeville's daughter by a former marriage, and no such marriage is named in Doyle's 'Baronage,' or else an illegitimate child. The Duchess always treated Elizabeth as her own daughter, which she would scarcely have done had there been any doubt as to her parentage. Marriages were made at a very early age in those days, and there is no reason to doubt that Elizabeth's elder son, Thomas, afterwards Marquis of Dorset, might have been born when she was only fifteen years old. At about the same age, if not younger, Margaret Beaufort, Countess of Richmond, gave birth to her only child Henry, who succeeded Richard III. on the throne.

Finding his passion only increase the more he saw of the object of his choice, Edward formally proposed marriage, and was accepted. The nuptials were, however, to be strictly private. Setting out early, from Stoney Stratford, he rode to Grafton. There, in the presence only of the Duchess and two female attendants, with an assistant for the priest at Mass, Edward and Elizabeth were made man and wife. After a protracted visit he returned to Stoney Stratford and allowed it to be understood that he was fatigued with his day's hunting. *May 1.*

This was the one good act of Edward's life, and yet one that, in a great measure, was the cause of succeeding troubles.

A few days later, Edward went on a visit to Grafton, but, during the time he was there, Duchess Jaquetta took the precaution of sending all the household to rest before the married pair came together alone. At the end of four days he returned to London.

Rumours had been spread abroad that the King was actually married, and as, by the battles of Hexham and Hedgeley Moor, the struggle for the crown appeared to be ended, he thought it desirable to acknowledge it publicly, more especially as the names of foreign princesses were being mentioned as suitable consorts for the King of England. Among others, Isabella of Castile has been named by some writers. But Prescott, in his life of Ferdinand and Isabella, says he 'finds nothing in the Spanish accounts of that period to throw any light on the subject.' He also writes: 'Among the suitors for her hand was a brother of Edward IV., not improbably Richard, Duke of Gloucester.' This was adverted to by Isabella, in a letter to her brother, dated October 12, 1469, a week before she was married to Ferdinand of Aragon. *May 10.*

The public announcement was made in one of the finest and richest abbeys of the kingdom, that of Reading in Berkshire. Elizabeth entered in full bridal array, escorted by the Duke of Clarence and the Earl of Warwick. The remainder of the lords there assembled, in the presence of the King, saluted her most respectfully, and acknowledged her as Queen. At a subsequent *Sept. 29.*

council in Westminster an income of 4,000 marks a year was settled upon her.

There was considerable outcry and alarm among the remnant of the old baronage at the raising, for the first time, of an English-born lady, of comparatively humble birth, to the proud position of England's Queen. On the father's side there was not much rank of which to boast. He was simply the son of a private gentleman, and was not created even a baron until some years after his marriage. The earldom was only created two years after his daughter became Queen. But her mother was of princely rank, a daughter of Pierre de Luxemburg, Count of St. Pol, who claimed descent from Henry VII., Emperor of Germany. According to Burke's 'Noble Families,' Jaquetta was a lineal descendant also of Simon de Montfort and Eleanor, daughter of Henry II. of England, so that she was doubly endowed with royal blood.

The King's mother, Duchess Cecily, was strongly, almost bitterly, opposed to this marriage. She regarded it not only as impolitic, and contrary to his own interests, but as an act of bigamy, Edward having been contracted, some say married, to Lady Elizabeth Butler of Sudeley, and name Robert Stillington, Dean of St. Martin's, afterwards Bishop of Bath and Wells, as the priest who performed the ceremony. This lady is said to have been one of Edward's numerous mistresses. The Duchess kept steadily aloof from Court. Her son Clarence shared her views, but, as we have seen, took a prominent part in welcoming the Queen. The Earl of Warwick had hoped for a higher alliance to strengthen the throne of his cousin, but hid his feelings for a time.

1465. The coronation of Elizabeth took place with great pomp on May 26. Whitsun Day at Westminster Abbey. On the previous day Edward had created thirty-six Knights of the Bath, Cook, the Mayor of London, and four citizens being of the number. Feasts and tournaments followed. To satisfy those who had grumbled at the low rank of the Queen Consort, her uncle, Sir Jaques de St. Pol, Count of Luxemburg, was invited to grace the ceremony with his presence. He came, accompanied by more than a hundred knights and gentlemen, whose presence gave great satisfaction. When about to return home the King presented to Sir Jaques three hundred nobles, and to each knight and gentleman fifty nobles, besides most handsome entertainment. This appears to prove that their presence was bought and paid for.

Elizabeth's first care was to find husbands for her six unmarried sisters. All had more or less of the Queen's beauty, with cultivated minds, which, in their retired life hitherto, had not been fully appreciated by the owners of birth and strong limbs.

MARGARET in October, 1464, married Thomas FitzAlan, Lord Maltravers, subsequently twelfth Earl of Arundel. He was a son of Joan Neville, a sister of the Earl of Warwick, and consequently a second-cousin of the King. KATHERINE married Henry Stafford,

Duke of Buckingham, in February, 1466, when he was about twelve years of age. He also had Neville blood in his veins, being a grandson of Lady Anne, the sister of Duchess Cecily, and was thus also second-cousin to King Edward. JAQUETTA married John, Lord Strange, of Knockyn. Their daughter, Jane, became the wife of George, son and heir of Thomas Stanley, first Earl of Derby. As George died in 1407, before his father, his eldest son, Thomas, succeeded as second Earl of Derby. ANNE married William, Viscount Bourchier, son of Henry, Earl of Essex, and nephew of Richard, Duke of York, the King's father. Their son, William Henry, was second and last Earl of Essex of the name. JANE married Sir Richard Haute, and MARY in 1466 married William Herbert, second Earl of Pembroke, a boy only five years of age, who was subsequently created Earl of Huntingdon in exchange.

Elizabeth had five brothers. JOHN received for his bride the Lady Catherine Neville, sister of Duchess Cecily, and widow of John Mowbray, second Duke of Norfolk, who had died thirty-two years previously. She must have been a blooming old lady of over seventy years of age, while he was not much over twenty, at the most twenty-four. But the pill was well gilded and so he swallowed it. He thus became uncle to his brother-in-law. ANTHONY had already married an heiress, Elizabeth, only daughter of the Lord Scales, slain at Towton, and in her right became Baron Scales. LIONEL became Bishop of Salisbury. RICHARD succeeded his brother Anthony in the earldom, but with him it ended. EDWARD appears to have been a kind of free lance fighting abroad. He does not figure in English history.

THOMAS GREY, the Queen's elder son by her first marriage, succeeded his father as ninth Lord Ferrers of Groby. He married Lady ANNE HOLLAND, only child of HENRY, Duke of EXETER, in 1466, and five years later was created Earl of Huntingdon. Countess Anne died without leaving any children; and in 1475 the Earl took for his second wife, Cicely, daughter and heir of William, Lord Bonville and Harrington—who was slain at Wakefield—and he was created Marquis of Dorset in exchange for the earldom. By his second marriage he had seven sons and eight daughters. His grandson, Henry Grey, married Lady Frances Brandon, second daughter of Charles Brandon, Duke of Suffolk, and Mary Tudor, the sister of King Henry VIII. Their daughter was the celebrated, but unfortunate, Lady Jane Grey, who on the death of Edward VI. was proclaimed Queen. Both father and daughter had to pay the penalty by losing their heads. The Earls of Stamford and Warrington are also descended from this same Thomas Grey.

The Duke of Exeter had been very unfortunate in the choice of a wife, as in other matters. He had married King Edward's eldest sister Anne, an infamous woman, who left him and went to live with Sir Thomas St. Leger. As a lineal descendant of John of Ghent, the Duke was naturally a strong partisan of the House of Lancaster.

He was attainted in 1461, and all his estates bestowed on his wife. He was afterwards seen running barefoot in Flanders begging for bread, and received assistance from Duke Philippe of Burgundy. A divorce was not obtained until 1472.

Another Anne, the sole daughter of Anne Plantagenet and Sir Thomas St. Leger, married Sir George Manners, Lord Roos of Hamlake, and died April 22, 1526. Their son, Thomas, was created Earl of Rutland, and from him the present Duke, the seventh in the family, is descended.

The above-mentioned first marriage of Thomas Grey caused considerable annoyance to the one man in all England who had done the most to place Edward on the throne—Richard, the mighty Earl of Warwick, whose wealth, power, and influence almost overshadowed the King's. The Earl had solicited the hand of the little Lady Anne Holland for his own nephew, George, son of John, Earl of Northumberland, and he could not tamely submit to such a rebuff. It was 'the little rift within the lute,' which ere long was to widen and entail serious consequences.

By way of contrast to all this 'marrying and giving in marriage,' compare the actions of other ladies, as recorded in the continuation of the Croyland Chronicles. The Lady Margaret, relict of John Beaufort, Duke of Somerset, one who had always proved gracious and well disposed to the monastery, was desirous of sharing in the prayers, and was therefore admitted to be a sister of the chapter. She also induced her daughter, the Lady Margaret, Countess of Richmond, who had been married to Henry Stafford—younger son of Humphrey, Duke of Buckingham, and Lady Anne Neville, sister of Duchess Cecily—to become a sister along with her.

The Countess Margaret was one of the most virtuous and learned ladies of the time, and spent a pious and devout life. She was liberal to the poor and sick, tender-hearted to those in misery, courteous and gentle to everyone. She remembered all acts of kindness to herself, and was ever ready to forgive all injuries. Her aim was to 'do good unto all men.' At the same time—perhaps in consequence of all these virtues—she was a strong-minded woman, and did not scruple to attend the Court of King Edward, and that of his brother Richard afterwards.

1466. The Wydeville family having been provided with husbands, the King thought it advisable to find one for his beautiful youngest sister, MARGARET, then twenty-one years of age. The Earl of Warwick was strongly in favour of an alliance with France, in order to put an end to any help which Margaret of Anjou might hope to receive in that quarter. He therefore proposed Charles, Duke of Berri and Guienne, twenty years of age, the only brother of Louis XI. The Wydeville faction, on the other hand, urged that it would be wiser to give her in marriage to CHARLES, COUNT OF CHAROLOIS, the only legitimate son of Philippe le Bon, Duke of Burgundy, a Lancastrian by birth, who might thus be converted into a friend of the opposite party. To this Warwick would not agree, as he 'pursued that man with a most deadly hatred,' says one of the continuators of the Chronicles of Croyland.

The Wydevilles, as you have seen, had themselves been Lancastrians up to the time of Elizabeth's marriage. They thought the Duke would do as they had done, and when Charles became Duke he proved that they were right.

The Queen and all her family disliked Warwick, and undermined 1467. his credit with the King, whom they encouraged to break the ties which bound him to his powerful subject. Edward therefore determined to diminish the Earl's power, and rule according to his own will. With that end in view, he sent him over to France on a fool's errand.

WARWICK landed at Harfleur, and went by boat up the river Seine May 7. to the village of La Bouillé, about five miles from Rouen. There he found dinner prepared for himself and his retinue. King Louis met him there, and, after the repast was finished, both went to Rouen, the King by land and the Earl by water. On arrival, the Earl was met and welcomed by a great concourse of the inhabitants, headed by priests in their copes, with crosses borne before them, and banners waving everywhere. They conducted him first to the cathedral, where he made his offering, and then to the Jacobins, where a lodging had been prepared for him and his suite. There he remained for twelve days, being daily visited by King Louis, from whom he received many rich presents, amongst the rest a piece of gold plate and a large gold cup set with precious stones; as he did also from the Duke de Bourbon a fine diamond and other valuables. On leaving, he found that all expenses of himself and his attendants had been defrayed by the King.

At the time of the Queen's coronation, her best and bravest brother, ANTHONY, LORD SCALES, who was an especial favourite with all the ladies at Court, received a letter from them, in which he was requested to send a challenge to some foreign noble to attend a feat-of-arms. He accordingly wrote to the most redoubted knight of the period, ANTHONY, COUNT DE LA ROCHE, better known as the Bastard of Burgundy, he being an illegitimate son of the Duke Philippe, and prayed him to accept the challenge, which he did in due course. He had been expected at the same time as Sir Jaques de Luxemburg, and there was great disappointment at his non-appearance.

Now, however, he came over with a large following, all magnifi- June. cently equipped. as befitted the favourite son of the most powerful ruler of the time. By the King and Queen no expense was spared to do honour to the occasion.

The lists, 120 yards long by 80 yards wide, were erected in June 11. Smithfield. Galleries were carried all round, wherein the whole Court in their richest array assembled, together with lords, knights, and ladies of England as well as foreign countries. On the first day they encountered with spears, in which they were equally matched.

On the second day they were on horseback, when the Count got the worst of it. In one of the tourneys a steel spike which was attached to the chaffron of Lord Scales' horse was thrust into the nostril of the one ridden by the Bastard. The poor beast, maddened with pain, reared and fell, carrying its master down at the same time. Lord Scales rode about him brandishing his sword, until the King called upon the Earl Marshal, John Mowbray, fourth Duke of Norfolk, to render assistance to the Count, who said : ' I cannot hold me by the clouds ; for though my horse fail me, I will not fail my companion.' On the third day the antagonists fought on foot with poleaxes. Both were valiant, and the tug-of-war was exciting. But at last the point of the Englishman's weapon entered the Burgundian's helm at the eye-hole, and he might have been blinded or dragged about had not Edward at that moment cast his warder down. The Bastard asked that he might complete his enterprise, and Lord Scales did not refuse. But the King, having called the Earl Marshal and the Constable of England, John Tiptoft, Earl of Worcester, to counsel, it was declared that, if the combat was to go on, it must be continued, according to the law of arms, in the same position as when it was stopped by the King. That would, of course, have entailed the replacing English Anthony's poleaxe in the Burgundian Anthony's vizor, to which the latter demurred. The friendly contest, therefore, was ended,* but Lord Scales carried away the prize, much to the satisfaction of his countrymen, and especially of the ladies. You may read a more stirring account of this memorable tournament in Lord Lytton's ' Last of the Barons.'

This opportune arrival of the Count de la Roche may have had some effect on the betrothment of Lady Margaret to the Count de Charolois, though it is possible that the contract had been previously June 16. decided upon. But DUKE PHILIPPE died, aged seventy one years, less two weeks, and the Count had at once to return home.

The Earl of Warwick, on coming back to England, and finding out the state of affairs, complained bitterly of the manner in which he had been treated, and retired in high dudgeon to his castle of Middleham in Yorkshire. Of this ancient and once magnificent stronghold there still remain a tower and keep, with some ruins of more modern buildings.

The French ambassadors who had accompanied the Earl were treated with scant courtesy. The King did not even grant them an interview, but dismissed them with some paltry presents. such as hunting-horns and leathern bottles, for King Louis. This treatment humiliated Warwick, as it was probably intended that it should do, and now another blow was dealt him. His brother George, who was Chancellor, being unable through sickness to attend the opening of Parliament, Edward went to his house with armed men, forced him to deliver up the seals, and afterwards took from him two manors which had been granted him by the crown. Warwick felt his

* Dr. Henry's ' History of Great Britain.'

ascendancy in the Council was gone, his policy thwarted. Though, by means of the Archbishop of York and Earl Rivers, a nominal reconciliation was effected at Coventry between him and the ungrateful King, there was no real forgiveness, but only dissembling for a time. The Archbishop recovered his two manors as a reward for his services.

Meantime, the negotiations for the marriage of MARGARET OF YORK with Charles, Duke of Burgundy, had been completed. The King and Queen escorted her to Margate, where she embarked. It may be noted, as a token of reconciliation between Edward and his mightiest subject, that the Earl of Warwick rode before her on her horse.

MARGARET OF 1468.

It June.

Margaret was accompanied by her youngest brother, Richard, and Anthony, Lord Scales. In her retinue she had a number of fair damsels.

The landing took place at Sluys, where the Duchess Isabel came with her grand-daughter, Marie, to meet the bride. Charles, though only in his thirty-fifth year—he was born November 10, 1433— had been twice married, but had only this one daughter, and it is probable that he only took a third wife in the hope of leaving a male heir to all his vast possessions.

July 1.

On Sunday the Duke and Lady Margaret were married at Damme, at five o'clock in the morning, and the whole party went afterwards to Bruges, a distance of only three miles. There the bride was welcomed with the usual processions of ladies and gentlemen, and many well-devised pageants—'the best that ever I sye,' writes John Paston—were produced for her pleasure and edification.

July 3.*

The Bastard of Burgundy, at the head of twenty-three knights, challenged other twenty-four to a tournament on the following day. All were richly dressed in cloth of gold and velvet, with goldsmiths' work upon them. The whole were resplendent with gold and pearls and precious stones. 'Never saw I such great plenty.' Anthony, Lord Scales, was present, but did not joust with his namesake, as they had agreed in London never again to meet one another in arms. The Lord Scales jousted with a gentleman of the country, and the Count de la Roche accompanied him to the field. Unfortunately someone's horse struck the Count, and hurt him so seriously that there was great doubt whether he would be able to fulfil his engagements, which 'is gret pete,' continues the writer, 'for by my trowthe never was a mor worchepfull knight.' He goes on to say that he never heard of any Court like it except that of King Arthur.†

Another piece of information to be gathered is that the Duke of Somerset was at Bruges, but left the day before the bridal, as it was supposed, to meet Queen Margaret.

It was soon after Duke Charles's marriage that, in order, if possible, to avert a war between France and Burgundy, the wily

* Sandford gives Sunday, July 9, as the date of the marriage.
† Paston Letters.

King Louis went to pay him a visit at Peronne. This visit forms one of the main incidents in Sir Walter Scott's novel of 'Quentin Durward.' It was in consequence of this visit also that the famous Philippe de Commines forsook his natural master, Charles, for the more congenial service of Louis.

Margaret, Duchess of Burgundy, resembled her brother Edward in general appearance. Her beauty, haughtiness, and passion were derived from her mother, 'Proud Cis' of Raby. She led a happy though childless life with her husband, Charles *the Rash*, for over eight years, until he was defeated warring against the Swiss on the field of Morat, June 22, 1476, and slain at Nancy, in Lorraine, January 5, 1477.

She outlived all of her own family, and was a determined opponent of Henry VII. At her court all insurgents against that King could find an asylum. She countenanced Lambert Simnel's imposture, and was a principal supporter of Perkin Warbeck. The latter, she may have had reason to believe, was really a son of her brother King Edward, whom he remarkably resembled. But whether she thought him to be the Richard Duke of York presumably murdered in the Tower is open to doubt.

Margaret died in 1503.

SKETCH XXV.

'COMING EVENTS CAST THEIR SHADOWS BEFORE.'

1467. THE chronicler of Croyland tells of many strange occurrences in this year, which distressed the people generally. There was such continued rain for a month as had never been seen before. The consequence was an overflow of the rivers Nene and Welland, whereby an inundation was caused that threw down houses, and the embankments in the low-lying lands were in serious danger. Fires, caused sometimes by lightning, but oftener by carelessness, raged in various districts of the country, and the strong winds which blew continuously fanned the flames, so that many buildings were destroyed. An infectious disease spread over the land and carried off many thousands of people. These evils were regarded as punishments for the grievous transgressions and general unrighteousness of the whole land. In addition to all these disasters, there were showers of blood, which came down like rain; three suns and other marvellous sights in the heavens, which disquieted the dwellers alike in town and country. All these signs were supposed to foretell the disasters which happened within a few years.

1468. Some new characters must now be introduced, and their pedigree can be traced in Collins. They are Welshmen. Thomas ap Gwyllem ap Jenkin married Maud, daughter and heir of Sir John Morley, Knight, the owner of Raglan Castle, Monmouthshire, now one of the most beautiful ruins in the country. Their son, Sir William ap Thomas, married Gwladys, a daughter of Sir David Gam, who was slain at Azincour. They had three sons, William, Richard, and Thomas, whose patronymic would properly be ap William ap Thomas. But, by royal command, they took the name of HERBERT after a remote ancestor. William, the eldest son, was created Baron Herbert in 1461, Knight of the Garter in 1462, and EARL of PEMBROKE, September 8, 1468, in place of Jasper of Hatfield, who had been attainted. It was his son William who, as shown in the last sketch, married Lady Mary Wydeville. But it was from an illegitimate son of the first Earl, Sir Richard Herbert of Ewyas, that the third and succeeding Earls descended.

The strong Castle of Harlech, which had given shelter to King Henry and Queen Margaret, and had been held in the Lancastrian interest for many years by the loyal Welshman, DAFYDD AP JEVON AP EINON, was about this time besieged by a large force under the command of the Earl's brother, Sir Richard Herbert. When called upon to surrender, the Welsh hero made answer: 'I held a castle in France till all the old women in Wales heard of it, and will now hold this castle in Wales till all the old women in France hear of it.' Famine, however, is a sore enemy, and he was at last compelled to agree to a surrender on condition of all lives being spared. King Edward, with his usual faithlessness and brutality, refused to ratify the terms. 'Then,' said Sir Richard, 'I will put Dafydd and his garrison back into Harlech, and you may search for some one else to turn them out. If you want a life, take mine, not his.' Edward had to give way.

The disagreement between the King and the lord of Middleham increased in proportion to the continual favours, rich presents, and lucrative offices showered upon the Wydevilles. It became a struggle for power between the *old* and the *new* men. Warwick's popularity with the commonalty was unbounded, for, as an old chronicler writes, ' wherever he was, he kept open house.' Every tavern also dispensed hospitality at his cost, and anyone having acquaintance there could take away as much sodden meat as he could carry on a dagger. He had been cementing his relations with the remaining few of the ancient nobility, and he had the King's brother on his side. George of Clarence was a restless, undecided young man about twenty years of age. He bore no goodwill, as we have seen, to the Queen's kindred, and did not pay due deference to the King, unlike his younger brother Richard ; Edward therefore distrusted him. When the Earl sided with him in his complaints, his heart was won ; the more readily that he was in love with Warwick's elder daughter, Isabel. There had been some project of the King's two brothers marrying the Earl's two daughters. But though this eventually was

1469.

1469. the case, Edward now refused his consent to George's marriage. At this Warwick naturally took offence, and perhaps hastened his proceedings more than he otherwise would have done. On Clarence taking an oath to remain true to his prospective father-in-law, he and the Earl crossed over to Calais, where the Countess and her two daughters were at that time in residence.

July 11. There, at the Church of St. Nicholas, by the hands of the Archbishop of York, the bride's uncle, GEORGE PLANTAGENET, Duke of CLARENCE, and ISABEL NEVILLE, daughter of the Earl of Warwick, were joined together in holy matrimony. It has been conjectured by some writers that Warwick at this time entertained the idea of deposing King Edward, and putting his own son-in-law, Clarence, in his place.

During the Earl's absence there was an insurrection in Yorkshire.

There was in the city of York an old rich hospital of St. Leonard, originally founded by the great Alfred's grandson, Athelstan, 960 years ago, the ruins of which still remain, where the poor, the halt, and the blind were received and comforted. The house was maintained by the first-fruits of corn and other produce, contributed by the husbandmen of the country round about. A certain number of these men, at the instigation, so it is said, of Warwick, refused to give their share, on the ground that it did not go to the poor and sick, but into the coffers of the rulers of the house. The proctors, maintaining their absolute right to the claim, attempted to enforce it. The men, to the number of 10,000 or more, banded themselves together under the leadership of one ROBERT HILYARD, or ROBIN OF REDESDALF, as he was styled, and marched towards York. The citizens, in great tribulation, called upon Warwick's brother, John Neville, Earl of Northumberland, but better known as Baron Montague, for help. He complied, met the insurgents, routed them, and cut off their leader's head. Montague thus appeared still to hold to King Edward, though it may possibly have been done in order to hide ulterior designs. He certainly did not offer any more opposition to the rebels. Hilyard's place was, however, filled by Sir JOHN CONYERS, with Montague's cousin, Sir HENRY NEVILLE, son of George, Lord Latimer, and his nephew, Lord FITZHUGH, son of Henry Lord Fitzhugh and Alice Neville, Montague's sister. It should be noted that the Latimers, being descendants of Earl Ralph's first marriage, had always been Lancastrians, and there was no good feeling between the two branches of Earl Ralph's family.

King Edward was alarmed at hearing rumours of these risings in the North. To a certain extent he was an outwardly religious man, in so far that he strictly observed all the offices of the Church. Yet that did not prevent him from immediately afterwards pursuing his own sinful pleasures, or remorselessly cutting down his people. He went on a pilgrimage to the shrine of St. Edmund the Martyr, in Suffolk, and thence to Norwich, where he appears to have been on the

21st of June. From there he made another pilgrimage to the far-famed priory of Our Lady of Walsingham, one of the most splendid in the kingdom at that time, but ruthlessly destroyed, only a few years later, by order of the tyrant Henry VIII. On June 26 Edward was at Lynn, and passed through Wisbeach to Croyland. He stayed a night in the Abbey, and, according to the chronicler, expressed himself delighted with his visit, but we do not hear of any gifts, such as the pious Henry would have made, being bestowed, or of any expression of a wish to share the prayers of the confraternity. Next morning he continued his journey by water, up the River Nene, to his castle of Fotheringhay in Northamptonshire, and there he remained while levies of troops were being made. With all he could gather together there he went to Newark in Nottinghamshire. Hearing that the rebels numbered three to his one, and finding that the people did not flock to his banner as he expected, he hastened to Nottingham, there to wait the arrival of the Earl of Pembroke, whom he had summoned, with all the forces he could collect, to his assistance. There Edward first heard that his brother Clarence was with Warwick and Archbishop Neville at Calais. He accordingly wrote to them, on July 9, to come to him, adding to all three, 'ye shalbe to us right welcome.'[*] The Queen at this same date went to Norwich.

The Earl of Pembroke and his brother Sir Richard Herbert were on their way, at the head of 10,000[†] followers, principally Welshmen, to meet the disaffected. SIR HUMPHREY STAFFORD, Baron Stafford of Southwick, who had been created EARL OF DEVONSHIRE in the previous May, in place of Henry Courtenay, the seventh Earl, deprived and beheaded, was also on his way with 6,000 archers.

The Northerners were overtaken not far from BANBURY on their way to Northampton. A detachment under Stafford and Sir Richard Herbert came up in time only to set upon the rearward. But the men of the North faced about, and gave the Welsh more than they bargained for, as few were left to tell the tale. The insurgents, however, had to bewail the loss of one of their leaders, Sir Henry Neville, who, with overweening courage, venturing too far, was taken prisoner, and, though he had yielded himself, was cruelly slain that St. James's July 25. Day.

On entering the town of Banbury, in Oxfordshire, Stafford took up his quarters at a certain inn where there was a damsel with whose charms he was much smitten. Pembroke, arriving soon afterwards at the same house, required him to leave it and find lodgings elsewhere, contrary to an agreement they had made not to interfere with each other's private arrangements. Stafford naturally felt much aggrieved, but he carried it too far. He left, but he took all his men with him, thus deserting his colours in face of the enemy. Less than a month afterwards he was captured at Brentmarsh, and by order of the King deservedly beheaded at Bridgewater in Somersetshire on

---

[*] Paston Letters.   [†] 18,000 by some accounts.

August 17, having only enjoyed his dignity of Earl for the short space of three months.

July 26. The rival forces met on the DANES MOOR, near the town of EDGECOTE, three miles from Banbury, on the borders of Northamptonshire and Oxfordshire. There are three little hills, east, west and south, which mark the spot where the battle was fought. It began soon after daybreak. The Northern men encamped on the south hill. The Welshmen got the west hill, and tried hard for the east hill. Had they gained it the result of the day's action might have been different. The cruel and unwarrantable execution of their leader, young Neville, had exasperated the Northerners to such a pitch that they launched themselves with full force against the Welsh and drove them from their point of advantage. Sir Richard Herbert, a mighty man of valour, with his pole-axe twice made his way, singly, through the ranks of the enemy, and back again unscathed. His brother, the Earl, also fought valiantly, and at one time it was thought their party had the advantage. But, in the very nick of time, John Clapham, a retainer of the Lord of Middleham, stood on an eminence, and displaying the well-known badge of the white bear, called out with a loud voice, 'A Warwick! a Warwick!' The cry was taken up by the rebels, and the Welsh, believing that the Earl was nigh at hand, turned away and fled, leaving 4,000 men dead on the field. The leaders, being thus deserted, were captured and beheaded next

July 27. day at Banbury, along with ten others, to avenge the death of Sir Henry Neville.

By order of the King the Earl's body was interred in Tinterne Abbey, although in his will he had specially directed that it should be buried in the priory church of Abergavenny, the resting-place of his mother, who died in 1454, and of former Earls of Pembroke of the Hastings family.

The Welsh had undertaken the expedition in accordance with a prophecy made in the time of King Cadwallader, that, on expelling the English, the ancient Britons should once more obtain the sovereignty of the land.

Edward's troops all deserted him. Not a man remained to show fight for his King. Even his favourites, the Wydevilles, sought safety in flight. EARL RIVERS and his son SIR JOHN were captured in their own house at Grafton, or, as some write, in hiding in the forest of Dean, carried to Northampton, and there, without any pretence at trial, beheaded on August 12.

Where, meanwhile, were Clarence and Warwick? They had arrived in England towards the middle of the month, but before going to the King they had a meeting at Canterbury with the partisans of the Northern insurgents. These complained of the Wydeville family as being the authors of all oppression, whose removal from the Council they desired; of the coins being debased by Earl Rivers in his office as Treasurer, whereby they suffered great loss; of forced loans being made and heavy fines being imposed to the still further impoverishment of the needy to enrich the newly-created nobility; and other matters of a similar nature.

The original cause of the rising was thus entirely swept away. Warwick undertook to place their views before the King, and promised strict enquiry into all grievances. With his son-in-law and the Archbishop of York he therefore set out.

They found Edward at Olney,* in the north of Buckinghamshire, almost entirely deserted, and in great distress at the result of the Battle of Edgecote. After Warwick, with one word, had dismissed the insurgents, they approached the King with outward respect; but he soon discovered that he was in reality their prisoner. He was first taken to Warwick, but soon removed to Middleham Castle, where the Archbishop had him in charge.

England had thus the novel spectacle of two Kings in prison at the Aug. same time—Henry in the Tower, Edward in the stronghold of the mightiest subject in the realm.

If Warwick entertained the idea at this time of replacing Edward by George, his plans were suddenly thwarted.

There was a rising in the North of England and the borders of Scotland of the remnant of the Lancastrian party. The leader chosen by them was SIR HUMPHREY NEVILLE, a cousin of the third Earl of Westmorland, who had lain hidden for five years in a cave on the banks of the Derwent after the Battle of Hexham, in 1464. The Earl of Warwick, in the King's name, summoned the lieges to oppose them, but apparently he was not obeyed, owing to the uncertainty existing as to Edward's fate. However, he raised a force sufficient to march against the rebels. Once more, and for the last time, he utterly routed the forces of the Red Rose, and took the Aug. 17. leader prisoner. Sir Humphrey was handed over to King Edward, by whose orders he was executed at York. Presumably as a reward for this service, the Earl received no less than six appointments—as Chief Justice, Constable, and steward of various castles and places in South Wales.

In the meantime, how fared it with King Edward? It is difficult to tell. It would appear that he remained at Middleham the whole of the month of August. But the Earl discovered it would be a mistake to detain him any longer, and it seems very probable that Warwick was cognizant of, even if he did not suggest, the next move. Edward contrived to bribe some of the servants in the castle, who connived at his escape. One day, when out hunting, he met Sir John Howard, Sir William Parr, Sir Thomas Borough, and others, in whose company he rode to York, where he stayed a few days. Thence he went into Lancashire, and, in company of William, Lord Hastings, proceeded to London.

On nearing the capital, Edward was met and welcomed by his Oct. 13.

---

* Charles Knight, in his history, says Honiley, near Warwick. County guides say Wolvey, between Hinckley and Shilton. Hall writes Wolney, four miles from Warwick.

brother Richard, Duke of Gloucester; his brother-in-law, John de la Pole, Duke of Suffolk; William FitzAlan, eleventh Earl of Arundel, who had married the King's cousin, Lady Joan Neville; Lords Dacre, Mountjoy, and many other knights and squires. The City authorities received him in great state. The Mayor and twenty-two Aldermen appeared in their scarlet robes of office, and the craftsmen, to the number of 200, in robes of blue. Thus escorted, the King rode through Chepe, in order to avoid being seen. Why he should have done this we are not told. The same writer of the Paston Letters adds: 'The King himself hath good language of the Lords of Clarence, of Warwick, and of my Lords of York and Oxford, saying they be his best friends. But,' he significantly adds, 'his household men have other language.'

The Archbishop of York and the Earl of Oxford came with the King part of the way, but remained at the seat of the former, the Moor, in Hertfordshire.

A nominal peace was patched up between Edward and his mightiest subjects, and all grievances on either side were to be forgotten. But there was no sincerity with any of them. Edward, with his usual habit of simulation—he was a past-master in the art—called them his friends, the better to hide his purposes.

'I can smile, and murther whiles I smile'

are words put by Shakspere into the mouth of Richard of Gloucester. They would just as well suit his elder brother, the King.

Warwick, on the other hand, had received an affront which he never forgave, and which at once and for ever put an end to his loyalty to the House of York.

Edward was the most lascivious monarch who had sat on the throne of England since the days of John Lackland. But, whereas John had principally confined his attentions to the families of the nobility, Edward divided his attentions between them and the wives and daughters of the citizens of London. His reign, indeed, is generally best remembered as the time of his favourite mistress, JANE SHORE, whom he induced to desert her husband, a prosperous young goldsmith in the City.

'Lightly from fair to fair he flew,
And loved to plead, lament and sue,—
Suit lightly won, and short-lived pain,
For monarchs seldom sigh in vain.'

Edward attempted the honour of some lady in the Earl of Warwick's house—whether a daughter or niece was not generally known—says Grafton, and other chroniclers tell the same tale. Shakspere, following Holinshed, in the last scene of act iv. of 'King Henry VI.,' makes Warwick observe to Louis XI.:

'Did I let pass the abuse done to my niece?'

Edward, we may feel sure, would never publish the wrong he had endeavoured to commit. The Earl would be equally desirous of preventing any breath of scandal from touching his relative. But it was an insult never to be forgotten or condoned.

In order to cement the good understanding arrived at with the Nevilles, Edward proposed giving his eldest daughter Elizabeth in marriage to George Neville, then thirteen years of age, the only son of John, Earl of Northumberland—in fact, the only male heir in the family of the late Earl of Salisbury. The King's choice being approved, the boy was created Duke of Bedford. _{1470. Jan. 5.}

It is very possible that this alliance may have been intended by the crafty Edward to arouse jealousy in the minds of the remaining nobility against Warwick, who would thus be doubly connected with the royal house, and might be disposed to think there was a good chance for someone of his blood eventually to come to the throne. The marriage never took place. George Neville was degraded from all his honours six years after the Battle of Barnet, and died, without issue, in 1483, and was buried at Sheriff Hutton, one of the many seats of the Nevilles, about ten miles from York, but now in ruins. There is an effigy in the church of the young Duke.*

Two months later, March 25, 1470, the boy's father was created MARQUIS OF MONTAGUE, in exchange for the earldom he held, and he did not appreciate the advancement in rank. He grumbled that 'the King had only given him a pie's nest to maintain his estate with.' It was probably a principal reason for his desertion, later on, of the King's party.

The fact is, that Henry Percy, son of the third Earl of Northumberland, killed at Towton, had lately been released from the Tower on making his submission. Edward restored the earldom to him, giving him the custody of the estates and the wardenry of the East and Middle Marches.

George Neville, Archbishop of York, gave a grand entertainment at his place in Hertfordshire before the commencement of Lent, to which he invited the King, the Duke of Clarence, and the Earl of Warwick. While washing his hands, previous to sitting down to table, Edward received the whispered advice of an attendant to be very careful, as there were many parties of armed men about who had evil intentions towards him. Taking the hint at once, Edward slipped out, mounted his horse, and rode off in all haste to Windsor. _{Feb.}

Another reconciliation took place through the good offices of Duchess Cecily, but it did not last even so long a time as the previous one.

In consequence of the extortions of a purveyor of the royal household, the inhabitants of Lincolnshire were provoked to insurrection. Under the leadership of SIR ROBERT WELLES, they chased the man away, burnt his house, and destroyed all his property. The King ordered Clarence and Warwick to levy troops and put down the rising. At the same time he summoned RICHARD, LORD WELLES, the father of Sir Robert, to appear before him. He arrived, in due _{March.} _{March 7.}

* Dr. Swallow's 'De Nova Villa.'

course of time, along with his brother-in-law, SIR THOMAS DYMOCK, the champion. But they went immediately into sanctuary on hearing that the King was much angered against them. Edward promised, on his faith, that if they would come to him he would not harm them; and they foolishly believed his word. He bade Lord Welles warn his son to dismiss his troops; but, at the instigation of Warwick, the latter resolved to persevere.

The King went with his forces towards Stamford. When about two days' journey off that place, Edward learnt that the troops had not been dismissed, which so angered him that, in violation of his oath, he caused the heads of the two hostages to be struck off. A broken promise, more or less, was a matter of no moment to Edward.

> 'To his own good word
> The good and honourable man will act,
> Oaths will not curb the wicked.'

The King again sent a summons to Sir Robert Welles to yield. He most naturally replied that he would never trust the man who had murdered his father, regardless of all promises of safety.

March 12. A battle ensued at ERPINGHAM in Rutlandshire, in which the insurgents were defeated with great slaughter. Some thousands fell; the rest fled, flinging away their outer coats so as not to impede their movements. Hence the action is known as the battle of *Lose Coat Field*.

Thursday, March 18. According to one of the series of Paston Letters, the King went to Grantham in Lincolnshire, where he remained a day. During his stay Sir THOMAS DELALAUNDE, one of the leaders in the late rising, was captured and executed. He next proceeded to Doncaster, where Sir Robert Welles and another of the captains forfeited their lives.

Monday, March 22.

From their confessions it appeared that, but for their premature rising, Clarence and Warwick would have joined them, the object of the whole being to put Clarence on the throne. Hearing that those two nobles were only twenty-five miles distant, at Chesterfield in Derbyshire, he sent to summon them to appear before him and answer for their misdeeds.

Tuesday, March 23. The King took the field at nine o'clock in the morning, and mustered his people. It was said that never before had so many goodly men, so well arrayed, been seen in a field in England.

The Duke and Earl, however, instead of obeying the summons, went to Manchester, in the hope of securing the assistance of Thomas LORD STANLEY, who had married the Earl's sister, Lady Eleanor Neville. But from him they received little encouragement, and therefore marched to the South.

Thursday, March 25. King Edward went to York and thence to Nottingham, but he did not succeed in overtaking the fugitives, who had been proclaimed traitors. By the time he reached Exeter, they had taken ship at Dartmouth, along with the Countess of Warwick and her two daughters.

April 15.

On arriving at Calais, they were dismayed to find the cannon of the place turned upon them. Warwick had been captain of the town and castle for nine years, and the man now in charge had been so placed by him as his deputy. To be now told that if he entered the place he was a lost man must have been galling to the proud Earl. How the man had obtained the news of the state of matters we are not told, but he sent word to Edward of what he had done, and was rewarded by being appointed sole governor.

Hearing of the sore plight of the Duchess of Clarence, the deputy, LORD WENLOCK, sent for her benefit two flagons of good wine, but before reaching land her first child was born.

This child grew up to be known as MARGARET, COUNTESS OF SALISBURY, and an attached friend of Queen Katharine Parr. In consequence of some proceedings of her son, Cardinal Pole, about the time of the Pilgrimage of Grace, she and her other sons were cast into the Tower. Under a despotic Act of Attainder, without previous trial or confession, which Thomas Cromwell had caused to be passed, and by which he himself suffered, the Tudor tyrant, Henry VIII., condemned his second-cousin to death. On May 27, 1541, the very last legitimate Plantagenet in a direct line, one of the best, noblest, most pious women of the time, a martyr, as her son Reginald called her, was murdered at the age of seventy-one.

Sail was made for Harfleur, where they safely arrived, having added to their fleet several Flemish ships captured *en route*. There they found the Admiral of France, who received them all with the greatest respect. The ladies and their attendant suites were subsequently taken to Valognes, where fine apartments had been provided for their use. The gentlemen of the party, including John de Vere, thirteenth Earl of Oxford, meanwhile remained chiefly at Honfleur, where some of their vessels were in harbour, during the months of May and June. They had many conferences, at Amboise, Tours, and other places, with King Louis as to the state of public affairs in England, and the result will appear in the next sketch.

SKETCH XXVI.

CHANGING SIDES.

LOUIS XI., King of France, had no great love for the House of Lancaster; but he had still less for the House of York, particularly since his aspiring neighbour, Charles, Duke of Burgundy, had become Edward's brother-in-law. Edward, moreover, had been talking of an invasion of France. Louis, therefore, for purposes of his own, thought it advisable to bring about a reconciliation between Queen Margaret and the man who had hurled her

1470.

husband from the throne. It was a serious undertaking, but one entirely suited to the crafty politician.

He first sounded Warwick, and made it clear that assistance could not be got from him for the purpose of replacing Edward by George, but only for restoring King Henry. Much as the mighty Earl might seek for revenge on Edward, he did not see his way to disappointing his own son-in-law, who was looking forward to a crown. When Clarence at last—we may well believe very reluctantly—gave his consent, it only remained for Louis to see QUEEN MARGARET.

He accordingly invited her to go to him at Amboise and take her son and her father, King René, with her. He then broached the matter of a reconciliation with Warwick; but he found Margaret very difficult to deal with. She was as resolute, as hot and impetuous, in resisting all his efforts as though she still sat on the throne of England. She reminded Louis that it was Warwick, more than anyone else, who had deprived her husband of a crown, and had afterwards wantonly and maliciously treated him with insult and contempt, and who had also in every possible way traduced her own character. For fifteen days she persisted in her refusal to have any dealings with the Earl.

June 30. On Saturday morning early was born the only son of King Louis who lived to grow to manhood. He was baptized Charles by the Archbishop of Lyons, who was one godfather, the other being Edward, Prince of Wales, son of King Henry. His godmother was King Louis' sister Jeanne, Duchess of Bourbon. Great were the rejoicings at this event, which was celebrated by *Te Deums* in most of the churches.

July 15. At length Queen Margaret consented to have an interview with her great enemy, on condition that the Earl should acknowledge all his misdoings towards her and hers. Accordingly they met in the presence of King Louis, the Queen being accompanied by her son, and WARWICK by JOHN DE VERE, thirteenth Earl of Oxford, who had married his sister, Lady Margaret Neville.

It must have been a trying interview for everyone. True to his undertaking, Warwick avowed all the wrongs he had committed, but added that he had been driven to it, and that no nobleman had ever been so outraged and *despaired*. Finally the proud man humbled himself to kneel and pray for pardon, which Margaret, after some little hesitation, granted.

The Earl of Oxford also sued for grace. 'That,' said the Queen, 'is easily accorded, for you did but yield to necessity.'

When, however, as a further means of cementing the peace, it was proposed that Prince Edward should marry Warwick's second daughter Anne, the Queen refused her consent, saying that she had a letter, in which the hand of King Edward's daughter Elizabeth had been offered to her son. When, however, that idolized son added his entreaties to those of others, she gave way.

In the whole transaction no one acted with such nobleness and honesty as Queen Margaret She was the grandest figure there. Louis, the wily, thought only how, in the cheapest and easiest manner, to injure Edward. He would very possibly have preferred assisting Warwick, whom he greatly admired, to the throne, if the Earl had desired it, which he did not. Warwick looked only for revenge on the man whom he had raised to power, and who, after many studied insults, had wounded him in a very tender point. Margaret thought only of her husband and her son. She meditated deeply; she hesitated, but at length she forgave the man who, according to her views, had wronged her more than any other man in England, and accepted all propositions without reserve.

The whole of the company then went to Angers. There the July 30. marriage-contract between PRINCE EDWARD and LADY ANNE NEVILLE was signed at the church of St. Mary, in the presence of King Louis and his brother Charles, Duke of Guienne, as well as other relatives of both parties. It has been doubted whether any *actual marriage* ever took place, and there is not any record of the fact; but, whether it was so or not, in those days, as also in these in many places abroad, a betrothment entered into with full and free consent on both sides was as binding as a marriage solemnized in church.

The Earl of Warwick had thus two strings to his bow, and might reasonably think that one of his daughters would become Queen.

Before the Cross on the high altar of the church, the Earl of Warwick swore 'faithfully to hold to the party of King Henry without change; and to serve him, the Queen, and Prince as a true and loyal subject.' The King of France and his brother, the Duke, clad in canvas robes, swore 'they would help and sustain the Earl of Warwick in the quarrel of King Henry.' Finally Queen Margaret swore 'to treat the said Earl as true and faithful to King Henry and the Prince, and never more to reproach him for the past.'

There were two persons very much discontented with these arrangements. The Duke and Duchess of Clarence felt wounded to the quick at their prospect of succeeding to the crown being made dependent on the death of Prince Edward without heirs. Unfortunately, at this juncture, one of the ladies in attendance on the Duchess, who had been left behind in England, came over and brought with her a letter from the King to the Duke. Edward reproached his brother for taking part with the Earl of Warwick in his meditated treachery, which meant ruin to the House of York. The unstable Clarence, whether of his own free will or convinced by female blandishments none can positively say, wrote to his brother that, at a fitting time, he would prove himself true to those of his own blood.

It is very possible that the lady above mentioned may also have been the bearer of the letter which Queen Margaret had received, as before narrated.

Warwick had also had letters, not by the same hand, telling him that foreign help was not needed, as so many were ready to espouse his cause so soon as he should put foot on English soil. However, King Louis had provided money, men, and ships, and King René had also contributed to the extent of his ability. The Duke of Burgundy, on the other hand, who was himself at Boulogne, had sent a fleet to blockade the mouth of the Seine and prevent egress. But a storm arose, which scattered it far and wide, and destroyed many of the ships. The English squadron, as soon as the weather Sept. 13. cleared, set sail, and landed, some at Plymouth, others at Dartmouth, the very port whence the Earl and his friends had embarked five months before.

As soon as it was known that the mighty Earl was again in England, crowds of people flocked to his banner. Proclamation was made, in the name of King Henry, that all of lawful age should assemble to fight against Edward, Duke of York, who now held the crown against all right and reason. With a large force thus collected, the march to London was commenced.

Meantime, KING EDWARD had been attending to his hunting and other less innocent recreations. He laughed to scorn the idea of the Duke of Burgundy trying to prevent Warwick from sailing, saying he should know how to deal with the Earl if he landed. Even when his brother-in law sent him word of Warwick's intended place of landing, he did not take any steps towards putting the kingdom in a state of defence. With what troops he had he marched north against Henry Lord Fitzhugh, who, in the interests of his brother-in-law, the Earl of Warwick, had there raised a pretence of rebellion, but retreated still further north as Edward advanced. The King had reached Doncaster ere he came to a halt.

There, while either resting himself in bed, or feasting at table, he had two pieces of unwelcome news communicated to him. Firstly, that all the men under the command of Warwick's brother, Viscount Montague, who had hitherto been perfectly loyal, were throwing up their caps and shouting, 'God bless King Henry!' Secondly, that Warwick himself, at the head of an enormous army, was on the march against him. Now was the time for Edward to show how he would 'deal with the man' who was in actual rebellion. The greater part of his forces left him. With his few friends remaining he mounted and rode as fast as he could to Lynn Regis, or, as it was called in those days, Lynn Episcopi, in Norfolk, a distance, as the crow flies, of ninety miles. There he found two Dutch vessels and another small ship. On board these he embarked, in company with his brother of Gloucester, his brother-in-law, Earl Rivers, William Lord Hastings, William Lord Say de Sele, and some few hundred men, not one of the party having any money in his pocket, or any Oct. 3. other clothes than those on his back, and sailed away for Holland.

'It was very surprising to see this poor King—for so he might justly be called—run away in this manner, and be pursued by his own servants. He had indulged himself in ease and pleasures for twelve or thirteen years together, and enjoyed a larger share of them than any prince of his time. His thoughts were wholly employed upon the ladies, and far more than was reasonable, hunting and adorning his person. In his summer hunting his custom was to have several tents set up for the ladies, where he treated them after a magnificent manner; and, indeed, his person was as well turned for love intrigues as any man I ever saw in my life, for he was young and the most handsome man of his time, but afterwards he grew very corpulent.'*

In London Dr. Godard preached a sermon at St. Paul's Cross, advocating the rights of the House of Lancaster. The Kentish men had taken up arms to defend their cause, and Warwick, deeming the capital secure, did not enter it at that time, but marched in pursuit of Edward with an army which kept continually increasing. On hearing of the flight from Lynn, he retraced his steps, and entered London in triumph, accompanied by the Lord Mayor and Aldermen, Oct. 6. who, deeming the better part of valour to be discretion, had gone out to meet him. The common people received him with great demonstrations of joy, as they had always loved him.

His first act was to release from the Tower the captive King, whom, five years previously, he had conveyed there with the words, 'Behold the traitor!'

HENRY may have been informed of the fact of his having been again proclaimed King. It is possible that he may have heard the shouts in the streets of 'Long live King Henry.' Nevertheless, he must have been surprised when he saw Warwick enter the apartment. At first sight of the

'Proud setter up and plucker down of kings,'

he would probably be startled, but bodily fear was unknown to him. He had found

'Imprisonment a pleasure,
Ay, such a pleasure as incaged birds
Conceive, when, after many moody thoughts,
At last, by notes of household harmony,
They quite forget their loss of liberty.'

We have no positive record of the meeting, but it is very possible that, when the Earl humbly bent his knee in homage, and begged Henry again to accept the crown, he would be answered by the following lines, said to have been composed by the captive monarch:

'Kingdoms are but cares,
State is devoid of stay;
Riches are ready snares,
And hasten to decay.'

The King was at first conducted to the Bishop's palace. A week Oct. 13. later, on the feast of the Translation of St. Edward the Confessor, he walked in grand state procession to St. Paul's with the crown on his head.

The ex-Queen Elizabeth, who had left her residence in the Tower,

* 'Memoirs of Philippe de Commines.'

fled with her mother and her three young daughters to the Sanctuary at Westminster. As many as two thousand Yorkists followed her example, and took to sanctuary in different religious houses. Let it be specially noted that, by the Lancastrians, the right and inviolability of sanctuary had ever been respected, and was so now.

The only one who suffered under this new revolution was JOHN TIPTOFT, EARL OF WORCESTER. He was perhaps the most learned man of the time in the country. But he had earned from the people the name of 'The Butcher,' from the following circumstance. At the time of Warwick's flight some twenty prisoners had been captured in one of his vessels. These men had been handed over to Worcester as Constable of England. By him they were condemned to be hanged, drawn, quartered, and afterwards impaled in a manner which inspired horror and disgust in all beholders, as it was believed that some of the victims were still sensible of pain. This man, who was found hid in a tree at Weybridge, was now condemned and
Oct. 18. beheaded, but his remains were handed over to his friends, and were interred with all due solemnity at the Black Friars.

According to the Chronicle of Jean de Troyes, and Monstrelet, the Earl of Warwick released all the French prisoners that were in England and sent them home without ransom, but seized all the effects belonging to the subjects of the Duke of Burgundy.

Nov. 26. In the Parliament at Westminster Edward of York was declared a usurper. Henry was recognised as lawful King, and his son Edward as Prince of Wales and heir to the crown. During the minority of the latter, the Earl of Warwick and the Duke of Clarence were appointed Protectors of the Kingdom, and, failing issue to Prince Edward, Clarence, who was acknowledged as Duke of York, in place of Edward attainted, was declared to be the successor to the throne.

He was also appointed Lieutenant of Ireland, but, unfortunately as it turned out, did not go to his seat of government. All the partisans of the Yorkists were attainted; and the attainders of the Lancastrians, the Dukes of Somerset and Exeter, the Earls of Richmond, Pembroke (Jasper Tudor) and Oxford were reversed.

JASPER, EARL OF PEMBROKE, received various appointments in Wales. On one of his visits he found in the care of the widow of William Herbert, Earl of Pembroke, his own nephew HENRY, EARL OF RICHMOND, at that time about twelve years of age. He brought the boy up to London, and presented him to King Henry, who observed to the nobles in attendance: 'This is he to whom both we and our adversaries shall have to give place.' Or as Shakspere has it:

'England's hope.
This pretty lad will prove our country's bliss.'

The King of France was highly pleased at the result of this peaceful revolution. He gave instructions for the free admission, with or without passports, of all adherents of Henry VI., whether coming on private affairs or for mercantile transactions; but the exclusion of all belonging to the party of the late King Edward IV. He also ordered grand processions to be held in Paris and other principal towns, for the space of three days, as a special thanksgiving for the victory obtained over the Earl of March, and for the happy peace now subsisting between the two countries. On the occasion of a visit to Paris by Queen Margaret, her son and his bride, the Countess of Warwick, and other ladies, King Louis commissioned the Counts d'Eu, de Vendôme, de Dunois, the Lord de Châtillon, and other noblemen to attend upon and escort them. By his express commands, the Court of Parliament, the University, the provosts, and all the principal inhabitants in gala array went to meet them and accompany the party, through streets adorned with tapestry, to the palace, which had been sumptuously prepared for their reception. Nothing was left undone to testify the joy and satisfaction felt in France, and a treaty of peace between the two countries was soon afterwards concluded.

We must now see how the fugitives prospered. Their three ships were chased by seven or eight belonging to the Easterlings, or merchants of the Hanse Towns, whose pursuits were not always of a peaceful nature, but fortunately escaped capture, and arrived safely Oct. 11. at Alkmaar, on the coast of what is now termed North Holland, though they could not enter the harbour, as the tide was out. The Duke of Burgundy's governor of Holland, Louis de Bruges, Lord of Gruthuyse, hearing of the sad condition of the exiled King, charged the Easterlings to keep quiet, and invited Edward and his party to land. But the master of the ship had to be paid, and there was no money. Edward therefore gave him a cloak lined with marten skins, promising to do more when he had the opportunity. The Lord of Gruthuyse bore all the expenses of the poor company until he could learn the wishes of the Duke of Burgundy, who was much surprised at the news, and would have been better pleased to hear of his brother-in-law's death, as his affection was greater for the House of Lancaster, from which he was descended, than for that of York.

It may be noted that Edward did not forget the civilities he had received from the Lord of Gruthuyse, whom, a year later, he created Earl of Winchester.

CHARLES OF BURGUNDY had no desire for a visit from his brother-in-law, as he did not wish to add to his present embroilments with the King of France. The Dukes of Somerset and Exeter, who were then at his Court, vigorously supported him in his leaning towards Henry's cause. His Duchess, however, warmly pleaded the cause of her brother.

When EDWARD arrived at St. Pol, he pressed the Duke hard for supplies to enable him to recover his kingdom, where, he declared, he had still great influence, and begged Charles not to abandon him.

The Duke was embarrassed by conflicting claims, and knew not which side to favour. In the end he adopted an equivocal policy.

He declared publicly that he could not give any assistance to King Edward, and issued a proclamation forbidding any of his subjects to do so. Privately he sent to Edward 50,000 florins, ordered three or four ships to be equipped for him at La Vere—now called Ter Veer—in the Isle of Walcheren, and caused fourteen Easterling ships, well manned and armed, to be secretly provided for his service.

1471. March 2. Thus reinforced, Edward set sail from Ter Veer.
John de Vere, Earl of Oxford, had evidently received intimation of some of these proceedings, for we read of him and his brother Thomas collecting troops in the Eastern counties. But it was not until some days after Edward's arrival that the people were called upon to meet at Lynn and march to Newark to meet the rebels. At the same time it was reported that Lord Howard had proclaimed King Edward in Suffolk.

The fugitive King's return was hindered by great storms and tempests. He sent two of his officers on shore at Cromer in Norfolk, who reported that it would not be wise to attempt a landing there.

March 14. The ships were driven apart. It was not until after twelve days that Edward, with 500 men, landed at Ravenspur, like Henry of Bolingbroke seventy-two years before. The Duke of Gloucester landed about four miles from there, and Earl Rivers still ten miles further away. Their united forces amounted to 900 English and 300 foreigners.

In order to pass without opposition through divers places not well affected to him, where the people had gathered together in arms, Edward openly announced that he only claimed his own inheritance and his title as Duke of York. He even ordered his followers to cry 'Long live King Henry!' as they marched through the towns and villages, and placed in his bonnet an ostrich feather, the badge of the Prince of Wales.

March 17. When approaching York he was met by two of the aldermen, who admonished him to go no nearer. But, with lowly words and gentle entreating, Edward assured them he came not to demand the realm of England, but only his own duchy. The whole day was consumed in doubtful communings and dispute. At length it was determined that, if Edward would swear to entertain the citizens of York after a gentle fashion, and be hereafter obedient to all King Henry's commands, they would receive him into the city and furnish him with money.

March 18. Next morning, at the gate of the city, a priest being there ready to say Mass, Edward received the blessed Body of our Saviour, solemnly swearing to keep and observe the two articles above mentioned. Again, following the example set by Bolingbroke, he repeated a similar oath before the high altar of the cathedral.* 'So that oftentimes we see noble men, as well as lay people, through ambition and filthy coveteousness, forgetting God and all godliness, do swear great oaths in promising things, intending before they make

* Hall-Fabyan.

their oath to break it shortly after. Yet such persons ofttimes have their reward of God at one or other time, as this Edward had in his progeny.'*

The march was then commenced southwards. As they passed on, a letter, purporting to be from Henry, Earl of Northumberland, was exhibited, which, although the signature was a forgery, did good service in bringing recruits to the invading force.

Pontefract, which was occupied by Warwick's brother Montague, was passed about four miles to the left, and no attempt was made thence to bar their progress. Clarence, the Unstable, had commenced his promised change of sides by sending word to the Marquis 'not to fight till he came.'† Thus, in the opinion of many, Montague seemed to be in favour of Edward. The march was continued by Wakefield, Doncaster, Nottingham, to Leicester, fresh recruits constantly joining their ranks, which encouraged Edward to reassume his title of King; and as such he issued a proclamation, summoning all loyal people to his banner.

The Duke of Exeter and the Earl of Oxford, instead of coming out of Newark to endeavour to stem the advance, appear to have withdrawn their forces, possibly thinking they were overmatched in number.

The Earl of WARWICK, on hearing of Edward's advance past Pontefract, had hastened back from Coventry, where he left Clarence in command, to London, in order to put the capital into a proper state of defence, and to place King Henry in the care of his brother, the Archbishop of York. That done, he returned in all haste. But he received a blow which staggered even his stout heart. During his short absence his son-in-law, the Duke of CLARENCE, had gone over to Edward's side, and taken with him four or five thousand men, who had been raised in the name, and for the service, of King Henry. The Duke had even the effrontery to offer himself as a mediator between his father-in-law and his brother. 'Tell your March 29. master,' said the outraged Earl, who had returned to Coventry, to the messenger, 'that I would rather be myself than a false and perjured Duke, and that I leave not the war until I have lost my life, or have put down my foes.'

Having failed in inducing Warwick to fight, King Edward, who had occupied the town of Warwick, proceeded to Northampton, thus getting between the Earl and the capital, and soon after arrived at St. Albans.

The Earl of Warwick sent letters to his brother George, the April 9. Archbishop of York, to hold the city but for two days and he would come to his help. In order, therefore, to keep up the spirit of loyalty to the House of Lancaster, he conducted the King in grand state procession to St. Paul's. It may have been well intended, but it was a mistake. Henry was at the time in one of his weak moods.

* Grafton.
† Stow's 'Chronicle,' quoted by Lord Lytton in the 'Last of the Barons.'

He looked so meek, so helpless, that, though some pitied, more were inclined to scoff at him.

Edward had also written to assure the Archbishop of his affection, and to beg him to keep King Henry out of sanctuary. The poor man was puzzled what to do. But 'he who hesitates is lost.' George Neville hesitated, and at last gave a blow to his brother as hard as that of Clarence had been. 'He ordered the recorder Urswick to admit Edward by a postern in the walls,'* thus securing a pardon for himself, but ruining both his brothers. But, as the learned Cambridge Doctor writes, 'suche goodes as were gaderide with synne, were loste with sorwe.' He was subsequently despoiled of all his possessions, by order of Edward, and imprisoned until a few months before his death in 1476.

April 11. It was Maundy Thursday, and the Archbishop of Canterbury, Thomas Bourchier, in full pontificals, was seen in St. Paul's Cathedral, attended by the Dean and Chapter and a numerous body of clergy. Shouting was heard outside in the distance. It came nearer and nearer. Amid a dense mob of people, with banners flying, and trumpets sounding, rode the handsomest man in England. Soon was the proud King seen on bended knee, lowering his head beneath the hand of the Archbishop, who now, for the second time, gave him a solemn benediction; and through that benediction he was regarded as reinstated in his kingdom.†

Edward then went to the Sanctuary at Westminster, to embrace his Queen and daughters, and the young son who had been born on November 1 during his absence.

Edward soon returned to the City, and took up his abode at the Bishop's palace, whence King Henry was sent back to his lodgment in the Tower. It was Holy Week, but the fast, even on Good Friday, was converted into a festival.

Commines gives three reasons for Edward's reception into London: The number of persons in sanctuary, and the birth there of a young prince; the great debts which he owed in the town, which obliged all his creditors to appear for him; thirdly, that the ladies of quality, and rich citizens' wives, with whom he had formerly intrigued, forced their husbands and relations to declare themselves on his side.

April 13. Edward stayed but two days in town, and on Easter Eve, taking the captive King Henry with him, he marched out, reinforced by 2,000 men out of sanctuary under the Earl of Essex, to encounter the Earl of Warwick, who was in pursuit of him, and, after tarrying awhile at St. Albans to rest his men and himself from the fatigue of their forced marches, had taken up a strong position on Gladmore Heath, a rising ground to the north of Monken Hadley, which itself is north of CHIPPING BARNET.

When Edward arrived in the vale below it was already dark, and he could not clearly make out the ground. Fortunately for him, as it turned out, he marched too far to the west, so that his right wing

* Lingard.   † Dr. Hook's 'Archbishops of Canterbury,' vol. v.

and centre were opposite the enemy's centre and right wing, while his left wing, towards Hadley, was unopposed. During the night a cannonade was kept up from the one great bombard on the Lancastrian left, where Warwick and Exeter were posted, which consequently proved harmless, while the Earl expected it was having deadly effect. When daylight allowed it, a fresh disposition of the forces on either side was made. Edward is reported to have slept that night at Barnet.

Easter Day dawned raw and cold, with a dense mist which was April 14. attributed to the arts magical of the famous Friar Bungay, but between four and five o'clock, Edward, whose forces now far outnumbered his opponents, commenced the attack, and for five or six hours the battle raged with varying success. The Lancastrian right, under Montague and Oxford, made a terrific onslaught on the Yorkist wing under Hastings, whose men were put to flight, and spread the news that Edward had been defeated. This action was ultimately the cause of the rout of Warwick's forces. On returning from pursuit of the fugitives, the silver star of the Veres (for origin see Sketch IV.) was mistaken by their friends for the sun of York, and the returning company was received by showers of arrows from the Lancastrian centre under Somerset. The cry of 'treason' resounded on each side, and Oxford withdrew his men in confusion. For a short time the bloody battle continued with great obstinacy on both sides till Montague was slain. Edward and Warwick, pupil and teacher, were at length opposed to each other for the first and last time. The Earl fought as only such a man could fight, with the courage of despair, against overwhelming odds. But the last and mightiest of the barons being at length slain, the battle was won and the power of the feudal nobility was destroyed for ever.

The finest, most stirring account of this battle of Barnet can be read, by those who wish a good description, in Lord Lytton's 'Last of the Barons.'

On the side of the victors there were slain 1,500 men, including Humphrey Bourchier, Lord Cromwell, *jure uxoris*, third son of Henry Earl of Essex; his nephew, another Humphrey Bourchier, son of Lord Berners; William Fiennes, second Lord Say de Sele, with several knights and squires. The vanquished, in addition to the two leaders, Warwick and Montague, lost Sir William Tyrrell, Sir Lewis Johns, and, according to general accounts, 3,000 men. Among the wounded were Sir John Paston and his brother, from whose letters so much interesting news of the time may be gathered. Sir John wrote to his mother on April 18, that he 'was in good case and in no joparte of his lyffe' and that his brother John, who was hurt with an arrow beneath the elbow 'farethe well and in no perell off dethe.'

HENRY HOLLAND, Duke of EXETER was wounded early in the action and lay untended for hours. Late in the afternoon he was discovered by one of his servants, who took him and nursed him, provided a surgeon for him, and when well enough to be moved carried him to the Sanctuary at Westminster. Thence he found the means of going abroad. But in 1473 the last of a family descended from Edward I., at times the most powerful of subjects, but from first to last the most unfortunate of men, was found floating in the sea near Dover, having apparently been murdered.

The Duke of SOMERSET fled into Wales to join Jasper, Earl of Pembroke. We shall hear of him again.

JOHN DE VERE, thirteenth Earl of OXFORD, escaped abroad. He had an adventurous career for a year or two. With a band of men in the guise of pilgrims he arrived in September at Mount St. Michael, off Marazion in Cornwall, at that time both a fortress and monastery. Having once obtained admission, they overpowered the garrison, and held the place for some time against the forces of King Edward. They were at length, about the middle of February, induced to surrender, on a promise being given that all lives should be spared. Promises we know were not held sacred by Edward, and his officers were not much better. Imprisonment to active men is even worse than death, and that was what Oxford had to endure for eleven or twelve years in the castle of Hamme, in Picardie. His Countess, Lady Margaret Neville, had to support herself by needle-work, as her husband was attainted and all his possessions confiscated. They never met again, as she died in 1482, before his release. The Earl escaped, with the connivance of the governor of the castle, Sir Walter Blount, joined Henry, Earl of Richmond, May, 1485, and did him great service at the Battle of Bosworth. Under the name of Philipson this Earl is one of the principal characters in Sir Walter Scott's interesting romance 'Anne of Geierstein.'

A stone obelisk was erected near the village of Hadley, about a hundred and fifty years ago, to mark the spot where the Battle of Barnet took place.

The bodies of the 'King-maker' and his brother Montague were, by order of King Edward, carried to London and exposed in St. Paul's Church, naked from the waist upwards, for three days, so that all men might see how they had died, and that no excuse might exist for further rebellion on their behalf. They were afterwards taken to Bisham Priory, in Berkshire, and there, among their ancestors on the mother's side, they were laid to rest.

Immediately on his return to London after his victory, the King went straight to St. Paul's, where all the Yorkist lords, spiritual and temporal, the knights and the City authorities, assisted at a grand *Te Deum*.

He also, with his Queen and Court, made a pilgrimage to Canterbury on the occasion of the jubilee of St. Thomas, which was very fully attended. The jubilee should have been held in the previous year, but so many had been prevented from attending that the Archbishop extended the indulgence over the year 1471.*

Ever since she had heard of her husband's restoration, QUEEN

* Dr. Hook's 'Archbishops of Canterbury.'

MARGARET had been making great exertions to return to England. She had, indeed, made two or three attempts, but the winds and waves were always against her, and she had been driven back. She made a final start from Harfleur on March 24, but it was only after three weeks' tossing about that she landed at Weymouth, in Dorsetshire, on the very day that the fatal Battle of Barnet had been fought. She went at once, with her son and his bride, to Cerne Abbey, distant about twenty miles, to recover from the effects of their sea journey. Of this once magnificent abbey, founded upwards of a thousand years ago, the only remains now are a gatehouse and a barn.

While staying there the Queen received the news of the battle, and immediately hastened to Beaulieu Abbey, in Hampshire, where the Countess of Warwick, who had disembarked at Portsmouth the day before the Queen and her party landed, had found refuge.

Beaulieu Abbey had been founded by that eminently pious man, King John, in expiation of some of his many vile misdeeds. There are a few remains of the cloisters, and a gateway, but the church has been swept away. What now serves as the church of the village was, in older times, the refectory, and one of the few remaining old stone pulpits, entered from outside the wall, may there be seen.

Queen Margaret was utterly overcome, and desired now only to give up the contest and return to France. But EDMUND BEAUFORT, Duke of Somerset, the second son of her old friend, his brother, JOHN BEAUFORT, JOHN COURTENAY, Earl of DEVONSHIRE, with other Lancastrian leaders, tried to persuade her that the cause was not yet lost, and when Prince Edward added that he would wish to strike one blow for his father's crown she agreed to continue the struggle.

A considerable number of troops were gathered together in addition to the few French whom Margaret had brought over, and they marched on to Bath. Margaret's wish appears to have been to go into Wales and join Jasper, Earl of Pembroke. But, hearing that King Edward was in pursuit, the leaders did not agree with her. From Bath they went to Bristol with the intention of crossing the Severn at Gloucester, and thence making their way to Cheshire and Lancashire, where they hoped to gather men skilled in archery, as those counties had the reputation of being still in favour of the Red Rose. They were disappointed at Gloucester, as the governor, Lord Beauchamp, refused to open the gates to them, and consequently they had to proceed to TEWKESBURY, where they arrived utterly worn out with hunger and fatigue.

Learning that Edward was close upon them, and knowing it would May 3. be dangerous to attempt the passage of the Severn, they encamped in what was considered a safe position, and hard to be assailed, with their back to the abbey, and to their front cumbersome lanes, deep ditches and many hedges. Somerset appears to have further added to the defences by trenching round the camp.

KING EDWARD and his forces, who had been close on their track, May 4.

arrived next morning. The Duke of Gloucester led the van, the King himself the centre, and Lord Hastings the rear guard.

On the Lancastrian side Somerset, with his brother John, led the van, Prince Edward, with Sir John Longstrother, Prior of St. John's, and Lord Wenlock the centre, and the Earl of Devonshire the rear.

The attack was commenced by Edward, who had the advantage in the number of his guns and archers, with a heavy cannonade, which was returned with spirit.* Gloucester assaulted the trenches, which were vigorously defended by Somerset. But the wily Richard got the better of his opponent. He feigned a retreat, and Somerset, with more courage than circumspection. gave chase, expecting the centre to follow him. But they came not, and Gloucester, turning round upon his pursuers, utterly discomfited them. He was soon within the entrenchments, the King followed, and in a short space of time the victory was won. Somerset, seeing Lord WENLOCK standing still, reviled him as a traitor, and smote out his brains with stroke of axe.

Of the Queen's party three thousand were slain, including the Earl of Devonshire, the third Earl of the family who had lost his life in defence of the Red Rose, Lord John Beaufort, Sir John Seymour, Sir William Fielding, and many other knights and gentlemen; Somerset and many more fled for safety to the monastery, others were taken prisoners.

King Edward issued a proclamation, offering £100 a year for life to the captor of EDWARD, called Prince, and the Prince's life to be spared. The young Prince, then seventeen years of age—a year younger than Richard of Gloucester—was a goodly well-featured young gentleman, of almost feminine beauty, with brilliant eyes and light flaxen hair, like his mother. In figure he resembled his paternal grandfather, being tall and spare. Sir Richard Crofts, *nothing mistrusting* the King's promise, brought forth his prisoner,† who had surrendered to him.

Edward was true to his word as usual. The captor did *not* receive his reward, and the Prince's life was *not* spared.

On being asked by the King how he dared to invade his realm, the young Prince boldly made answer: ' To recover the kingdom — the heritage to me from my forefathers.' Edward brutally struck him on the mouth with his gauntletted hand, and some of those standing by despatched him with their daggers.‡

The generally received version of the tragedy is that portrayed by Skakspere, following Holinshed and Hall, who makes Clarence and Gloucester the murderers. Out of regard for the character of Lady Anne Neville the milder version is here given, as it is scarcely conceivable that she would have accepted for her second husband the man who had willingly slain her first one.

The body of the young Prince was thrown, with many others, into one common grave in the church. But a slab under the tower of

* Lingard. † Hall. ‡ Stow.

Tewkesbury Abbey bears a brass plate to the memory of the last Prince of the legitimate line of Lancaster.

Edward's insatiable desire for blood was only stimulated by this murder. With his drawn sword in his hand, he attempted to enter the church where many had taken refuge. A priest, bearing the Host in his hands, met him at the door, and obtained from him a solemn promise to spare the lives of all who had there taken sanctuary. The King then went to the high altar, and a prayer of thanksgiving was offered up for the victory.*

As already told, Queen Elizabeth and many more were indebted for their lives to the respect with which the Lancastrians regarded the right of sanctuary. Now let us see how Edward requited their forbearance. To him

> 'Oaths were but words, and words but wind,
> Too feeble instruments to bind.'

Trusting to the royal promise, all these men remained in the church from the Saturday, the day of battle, until the Monday; on that day Edward sent armed men, who dragged all, from the very altar, and took them before the Dukes of Gloucester and Norfolk—the former as Constable, the latter as Marshal of England—by whose orders they were beheaded. Among those who suffered were EDMUND, fourth and last Beaufort Duke of SOMERSET, the Prior of St. John's, Sir Jervis Clifton, Sir HUMPHREY AUDELEY, Sir HUGH COURTENAY, and thirteen other knights and gentlemen.

May 16.

Queen Margaret and her daughter-in-law, being found in a religious house in the neighbourhood, were carried as captives in the King's triumphal march to London, and thrown into the Tower. Lady Anne was soon afterwards placed under the care of her uncle, the Archbishop of York, and there we will leave her. Queen Margaret, although in the Tower, never saw her husband again. She was subsequently removed for a short time to Windsor, and finally placed under the care of her old friend Alice Chaucer, Duchess Dowager of Suffolk, at Wallingford, in Berkshire. There she received from King Edward the munificent! allowance of five marks weekly for the support of herself and her attendants. After being in captivity for five years, she was ransomed by her cousin, King Louis, for fifty thousand crowns of gold, when she retired into France. There she dragged on a weary existence, despoiled of everything, until she died at the Château of Dampierre, near Saumur, on August 25, 1482,† a few months before her great enemy, King Edward.

One more attempt was made for the liberation of KING HENRY. WILLIAM NEVILLE, Lord FAUCONBERG, who had been created Earl of Kent after the great battle of Towton, had left a natural son, called Thomas, generally known as the BASTARD OF FAUCONBERG. This Thomas had been Warwick's Admiral, and being disaffected to the

* Lingard.   † Miss Strickland's 'Queens of England.'

May 17. government of Edward, came up the Thames and made a violent assault on the City, both by his ships and land forces. He burnt Bishopsgate and captured Aldgate, but was at length driven back by an unexpected sally of Anthony, Earl Rivers. He summoned his Kentish followers to Blackheath, when another assault was arranged, but Edward's approach warned him to withdraw. 'It is probable that this bold, but unsuccessful, attempt, sealed the doom of the unfortunate captive.'*

May 21. On Tuesday afternoon, KING EDWARD entered London in state. That same night KING HENRY was found dead in the Tower. 'May God spare and grant time for repentance to the person, whoever he was, who thus dared to lay sacrilegious hands upon the Lord's anointed. Hence it is that he who perpetrated this has justly earned for himself the title of tyrant, while he who thus suffered has gained that of a glorious martyr.' Thus wrote the continuator of the 'Chronicles of Croyland,' who must have alluded to one of the two brothers, Edward or Richard. It may be that neither of them actually committed the deed as depicted by Shakspere in the last scene but one of 'King Henry VI.' But it is pretty evident that it was done by orders from one of them, and therefore at his door must lie the guilt. Considering the positions of the two, their characters, so far as had been shown, and their ages, it seems very possible that Edward was the guilty one, and if so, on his shoulders should rest the blame. Richard had not as yet given any signs of the murderous disposition which he afterwards developed. But the mystery has never been cleared up.

'How great Henry's deserts were, by reason of his innocence of life, his love of God and of the Church, his patience in adversity, and his other remarkable virtues, is abundantly testified by the miracles which God has wrought in favour of those who have with devout hearts implored his intercession.'†

May 22. Again following the example of Henry IV., in his treatment of the remains of Richard II., the corpse of the late King was, by Edward's orders, carried with bills and glaives to St. Paul's, and there allowed
May 23. to rest the whole day. 'In his lying he bled on the pavement there.'‡ Next morning it was taken by boat to the Benedictine Abbey of Chertsey in Surrey, without priest or clerk, torch or taper, singing or saying.§ Pilgrims swarmed to the tomb of 'Holy Henry,' and many miracles were reported as being worked there. When the Duke of Gloucester became King as Richard III., he ordered the remains to be removed to Windsor, but he was unable to stop either the pilgrims or the miracles. Thus ended the legitimate line of Lancaster.

'The sins of the fathers shall be visited upon the children.'

Henry of Bolingbroke obtained the crown by an act of rebellion,

---

* Lingard. † Croyland Chronicle.
‡ Warkworth, Sandford's History. § Holinshed.

and secured it by murder. His innocent grandson had to pay the penalty.

Richard, Duke of York, rose in arms against his King. His son, Edward, 'waded through slaughter to a throne.' Edward's sons were eventually killed by order of their uncle, who, as King Richard III., was slain on Bosworth Field, fourteen years later than the time of which we are now treating, and the mighty race of Plantagenet Kings came to an end.

It is somewhat singular that there was an interval of ten years between Henry's birth, December 6, 1421, and his coronation at Paris, December 16, 1431, as also between his deposition, March 4, 1461, and his murder, May 21, 1471. It will also be noticed that each event happened in the first year of the decade.

THE END.

NOTES.

VARIOUS ACCOUNTS OF THE DEATH OF HENRY VI.

Polydore Vergil.—The continuall report is that the Duke of Gloucester killed him with a sword.

Hall.—Henry was spoiled of his life and all worldly felicity by Richard of Gloucester as the constant fame ran.

Fabyan.—Divers tales were told, but the most common fame went that he was stykked with a dagger by the hands of the Duke of Gloucester.

Grafton.—The Duke of Gloucester was suspected to have done the deed, which sticked him with a dagger.

Holinshed.—He was spoiled of his life by the Duke of Gloucester as the constant fame ran, who murdered him with a dagger.

Warkworth Chronicle.—He was put to death on Tuesday night, between eleven and twelve, the Duke of Gloucester being at the time in the Tower, and many others.

Leland's Collectanea repeats almost word for word the Warkworth account.

Stow.—He was murdered in the Tower.

Rous Roll.—Richard killed by other, or, as many say, by his own hands that most holy man.

Commines.—If what was told me be true, the Duke of Gloucester killed Henry with his own hands, or caused him to be killed while he stood by.

Historie of the Arrivall.—He died of pure displeasure and melancholy on the 23rd.*

Sandford.—Was cruelly murdered, while at his devotions, by Richard, Duke of Gloucester.

Hume.—He expired in confinement, but whether he died a natural death or a violent one is uncertain.

The most curiously circumstantial account, whencesoever it may have been derived, is given in Timbs's 'Castles and Abbeys,' under the heading of 'The Tower.' 'Henry was murdered by the Duke of Gloucester, who crossed the Thames for that purpose in a small boat at two o'clock in the afternoon of Tuesday, the 21st May, 1471; the weapon was a knife, and the wound was in the ribs.'

---

* All other accounts give the twenty-first. It may be asked, Whence then came the bleeding of the body?

BATTLES OF THE ROSES.

		Victors.
1455.	May 22, St. Albans	Y
1459.	Sept. 23 (Sunday), Blore Heath	Y
	Oct. 13, Ludlow	L
1460.	July 10, Northampton	Y
	Dec. 29, Wakefield	L
1461.	Feb. 2, Mortimer's Cross	Y
	Feb. 17 (Shrove Tuesday), St. Albans	L
	March 28, Ferrybridge	L
	March 29 (Palm Sunday), Towton	Y
1464.	April 25,* Hedgeley Moor	Y
	May 15, Hexham	Y
1469.	July 25, Banbury	L
	July 26, Edgecote	L
1470.	March 12, Erpyngham	Y
1471.	April 14 (Easter Day), Barnet	Y
	May 4, Tewkesbury	Y

Three of these battles, it will be seen, were fought on the Sunday. The elements seemed to be against the Lancastrians. There was snow at Towton, heavy rain at Northampton and a dense mist at Barnet. At Blore Heath, Northampton and Towton, rivers contributed to their overthrow.†

---

* Variously stated as April 20 and 24.
† Dr. Swallow's 'De Nova Villa.'

www.ingramcontent.com/pod-product-compliance
Lightning Source LLC
Chambersburg PA
CBHW021203230426
43667CB00006B/540